The Lease Manual

A Practical Guide to Negotiating Office, Retail, and Industrial Leases

April F. Condon
with Rodney J. Dillman

SECOND EDITION

AMERICAN BAR ASSOCIATION
Real Property Trust and Estate Law Section

Cover design by Andrew Alcala/ABA Design

Printed in the United States of America.

26 25 24 23 22 5 4 3 2 1

A catalog record for this book is available from the Library of Congress.

Dedication

To

David E. Condon

Preface

The first edition of *The Lease Manual* broke new ground by providing Landlords, Tenants, Lenders, Attorneys, Brokers, and other Leasing Professionals insights into the world of commercial real estate leasing. It looked at the commercial Lease from the point of view of the key participants: Landlord, Tenant, and Lender. *The Lease Manual* then dissected typical commercial Lease Paragraphs found in Office, Retail, and Industrial Leases and provided Compromises and Alternatives that would be useful in Lease negotiations.

The feedback we received from the First Edition was excellent, but our readers wanted more: updated Lease Paragraphs, more Compromises and Alternatives, and more Analysis of each party's negotiating position.

The second edition provides all that and much, much more. More content, more Alternatives, more Compromises, and more Analysis, along with new Lease negotiation strategies.

The second edition has a new lead author, April F. Condon, and her expertise takes *The Lease Manual* to the next level. April has updated the Lease Paragraphs to those used in more contemporary Leases and has provided a fresh analysis of those Paragraphs along with additional Compromises and Alternatives. April has lived through the challenges Landlords and Tenants have faced with the COVID-19 pandemic and has provided insights and alternatives on COVID-19 leasing issues. April, together with Richard P. Levine of CBRE, Inc., have also provided a new Broker's Perspective in the second edition, and has indicated those Lease provisions that should be captured by the Broker in the Letter of Intent.

Energy-efficient buildings have come to the forefront of new office building construction and April has provided best in practice Lease requirements for Tenants that desire a lease in a "green building."

For larger Tenants that have a need for expansion capabilities, the second edition provides Right of First Refusal and Right of First Offer alternatives to lease additional space in an office building, along with a Unilateral Option to Lease Additional Space.

Telecommunication needs of Tenants continue to expand exponentially and the second edition of *The Lease Manual* provides Lease Alternatives to meet those needs, including telecommunication equipment installations that may be located exterior to the leased premises.

The scope and timing of the completion of Landlord's Work and Tenant's Work continues to be of prime importance in getting the Tenant up and running. The second edition provides several Alternatives to fit individual Tenant needs.

Without the new lead author, April F. Condon, the second edition of *The Lease Manual* would not have been possible. As a former partner of the law firm known today as Day Pitney, LLP, collaborating with April, who is a present Partner at Day Pitney LLP, seemed like a natural choice for the lead author of the second edition. Day Pitney Associates provided support to me as I authored the first edition, and a new group of Day Pitney Associates and Partners assisted with the preparation of the second edition. Day Pitney LLP's consistent support of *The Lease Manual* over both editions is much appreciated, and it reflects their values and commitment to developing new leaders.

We hope the next generation of Real Estate Lease Professionals will be inspired by this second edition of *The Lease Manual* and find their own real estate expertise enhanced by it.

Rodney J. Dillman

Acknowledgements

I would like to express my appreciation to the following people who assisted in the preparation of this Second Edition of *The Lease Manual*:

Foremost, to Rodney J. Dillman for entrusting me with his best-selling first edition of *The Lease Manual*, for allowing me the freedom to build on it in every way I wished to express my passion for the subject matter.

To Richard P. Levine of CBRE, Inc. who contributed much of the "Broker's Perspective" to this second edition. Without his generosity of time and talents, the "Broker's Perspective" could not have come into being in this second edition.

To Josh Crowfoot of Daspin & Aument, LLP, a member of the American Bar Association Real Property Media/Books Products Committee, for his assistance in peer reviewing and editing Part 3 of this second edition of *The Lease Manual.*

To my colleagues at Day Pitney LLP and particularly to Michael P. Byrne, for their ardent support of this project.

To the following lawyers (from several law firms) who also generously contributed to the preparation of this second edition of *The Lease Manual*:

Taylor C. Amato
Marie Caroline Bertrand
Gemma R. Cashman
Steven L. Elbaum
Lauren Grillo
Brooke Luxenberg Kaplan
Amanda M. Kronemeyer
Nicole M. Magdziak
Charles F. Martin
Dennis A. Massimi
Ashely Membrino
Luke S. Pontier
Jared P. Ross
Alan Ruiz

I also wish to acknowledge that many present and former colleagues (and even opposing counsel) have inspired my love of leasing and have helped to shape my voice that fills the pages that follow. In particular, I wish to acknowledge Jonathan B. Mills who, in the earliest years of my career, helped me to develop my craft by the thoughtful stroke of his red-inked pen on nearly my every lease provision, which revealed the important nuances of each lease provision and helped me to sharpen both my critical thinking and the intention of my written words.

Lastly, but with special emphasis, I wish to extend a very special thank you to Richard M. Frome (Acquisitions Editor of the American Bar Association Real Property Media/Books Products Committee) for his mighty contributions of both time and leasing expertise to both the First Edition and the Second Edition of *The Lease Manual* as a peer reviewer and editor of both Editions, and to Jeffrey Salyards (Executive Editor, Book Publishing of the American Bar Association) for his steadfast support of this Second Edition.

April F. Condon

Introduction

PARTS AND PERSPECTIVES

This second edition of *The Lease Manual* is divided into four parts. The first three parts are a description and analysis of typical (1) office lease paragraphs, (2) retail lease paragraphs, and (3) industrial/warehouse lease paragraphs, respectively. Finally, Part 4 is a collection of commonly used forms that are ancillary to a lease transaction.

In each of the first three parts of *The Lease Manual*, there is an analysis of the lease paragraphs and a critical review of the landlord's, tenant's, lender's and broker's perspectives with respect to each lease paragraph. This second edition of *The Lease Manual* includes, for the first time, the broker's perspective in recognition of the fact that brokers are integral to the process of successfully procuring, negotiating, and finalizing most leases. Brokers are, of course, at the forefront of each leasing transaction, and are critical to the proper development of any letter of intent prepared in anticipation of a lease. Therefore, brokers and attorneys should consider themselves as partners working together, collaboratively, in the best interest of their mutual client. Brokers are relied upon and expect to play a vast array of roles in any given lease transaction (including that of chief business term negotiator, market intelligence agent, and design and construction team liaison). Brokers also act as a both "watch dog" and "trouble shooter" in the interest of their clients (especially when representing tenants with little leasing experience). For these reasons, the "Broker's Perspective" was added in this second edition of *The Lease Manual* with the hope that both leasing brokers and leasing attorneys would be well served by a real estate treatise that analyzes the perspective of each member of the "team." As it takes the entire team working consistently together for a lease to get executed and delivered in a form that appropriately and fairly reflects the needs of the landlord, tenant, and lender (and, sometimes, even tenant's lender and/or franchisor, as may be applicable).

Finally, please note that all lease paragraph cross-references within each "Part" of *The Lease Manual* refer only to the paragraphs contained in the "part" in which the cross-reference occurs unless expressly noted otherwise.

RISK RATINGS

The lease paragraphs analyzed in *The Lease Manual* are comprehensive lease provisions that are moderate in their approach, but generally favor the landlord. Accordingly, the "risk rating" was developed from an institutional-landlord point of view. If the user of *The Lease Manual* is a tenant or lender, consider assigning other risk ratings and criteria that are apropos to the user's leasing program. The following criteria were used in determining the risk ratings:

Risk Rating 1 *Giveaway.* Items rated 1 are not critical and may be negotiated.

Risk Rating 2 *Negotiable.* Care should be taken to consider the overall picture, but items rated 2 may be negotiated.

Risk Rating 3 *Very Important.* Items rated 3 are very important to the lease transaction and may have legal or business implications. These paragraphs may be the subject of negotiation, but should only be changed if a change is necessary to conclude the transaction. If the lease negotiator is not a lawyer, the negotiator may want to consult a supervisor and/or legal counsel to determine compromises and alternatives that are not readily apparent.

Risk Rating 4 *Critical.* Any item rated 4 should not be modified without the advice of legal counsel and no legal counsel should negotiate these provisions without the input and guidance of his or her client.

Risk Rating 5 *Nonnegotiable.* The substance of these items is not subject to change. It is recommended that only nonsubstantive language changes be made with the advice of legal counsel and, from legal counsel's perspective, the active input of his or her client.

COMPROMISES AND ALTERNATIVES

Each lease paragraph may or may not have acceptable compromises or alternatives depending on the risk rating assigned to that paragraph and the relative leverage of the parties to the lease. A risk rating of 4 or 5 for a landlord indicates that the landlord's counsel will be involved in any negotiation and may have limited ability to compromise the terms of the paragraph. A risk rating of 4 or 5 for a tenant, however, means those paragraphs likely are to be the ones the tenant would most like to change. The size of the leased premises, the length of the term of the lease, the creditworthiness of the tenant, and market conditions will be important factors in determining whether to negotiate the terms of each lease paragraph. Brokers can assist in understanding the market conditions and what leverage a tenant may or may not have in any particular lease. The landlord is more likely to compromise its position, and the tenant more likely to demand concessions if the tenant is an investment-grade credit tenant leasing a significant amount of space for a long term. Another significant factor is the legal and business costs and expenses involved in protracted lease negotiations. Any changes that might impact a sale of the property or landlord's ability to control the asset will be scrutinized by the landlord. The parties should also consider any operational implications that may result from granting certain rights to tenants, including rights of first refusal, options, and rights of first offer.

COMMENTARY

Each lease paragraph may or may not have specific comments. Commentary is provided to address certain business and legal issues and to reiterate very important concepts contained in the lease paragraph or the analysis of the perspectives of the landlord, tenant, or lender.

FORMS

Form of Letter of Intent. Many lease transactions begin with a letter of intent negotiated by a broker or representative of the principals to the transaction. The form provided should be adapted to reflect the specifics any particular contemplated lease transaction. The "Broker's Perspective" contained throughout Parts 1, 2, and 3 of *The Lease Manual* provides important guidance as to how the form letter of intent provided should be adapted for any particular contemplated lease.

Form of Lease Commencement Date Agreement. Many leases require that a Commencement Date Agreement be executed after lease execution if a date certain for commencement of the lease term is not specified in the lease. This generally arises where either the landlord or the tenant will be performing substantial tenant improvement work at the premises, and it is the parties' intent that the commencement date and the payment of rent not begin until such work is completed. By executing a Commencement Date Agreement, the parties to the lease are able to establish and the lender is able to confirm the commencement and expiration of the lease term.

Form of Subordination, Nondisturbance, and Attornment Agreement. Both a landlord/lender form SNDA and a tenant mark-up thereof are provided.

Forms of Tenant Estoppel Certificates. Both a landlord/lender form Tenant Estoppel Certificate and a tenant mark-up thereof are provided.

Form of Landlord's Waiver of Lien Rights. Both a lender form Waiver of Lien form (to be signed by a landlord in favor of a lender requiring a first-priority lien on certain of a tenant's personal property in the premises) and a landlord mark-up thereof are provided.

Form Notice of Lease and Form Release of Notice of Lease. Many states have statutory requirements listing the information that must be contained in a recordable form of "Notice of Lease," "Memorandum of Lease," or "Short Form Lease." A form of

Notice of Lease that should be adapted to the statutory requirements of the appropriate state is provided. A form Release of Notice of Lease is also provided as, oftentimes, landlords will not provide a Notice of Lease without simultaneously obtaining from tenant a Release of Notice of Lease to be held by landlord in escrow until the lease expires or is earlier terminated.

Overall, *The Lease Manual* is intended to outline the actions and facilitate the decisions required for lease negotiations and approvals. *The Lease Manual* is not static but will continue to be updated periodically as new developments occur in leasing, and current information is needed to adequately respond to requests for changes to lease forms.

DEFINITIONS OF MOST NEGOTIATED AND LEAST UNDERSTOOD LEASE TERMS

The following definitions are the most commonly accepted usage of these terms. However, variations do exist, and it is therefore recommended that when using any of these terms in a lease, term sheet, or letter of intent, that these terms be specifically defined.

Types of Rent and Additional Rent

Net Rent—Net rent, or triple net rent as it is sometimes known and is at times abbreviated as NNN, does not include in the quoted base rent any allocation for maintenance and operating expenses, real estate taxes, or insurance costs. Thus, the tenant is responsible for the payment of all maintenance and operating expenses, real estate taxes, and insurance costs. Beginning on the rent commencement date, tenant pays, in addition to base rent, as "additional rent," tenant's proportionate share of all maintenance and operating expenses, real estate taxes, and insurance costs for the property.

Gross Rent—The opposite of net rent is gross rent. A lease that is quoted as fully gross includes in the base rent all maintenance and operating expenses, real estate taxes, and insurance costs for the entire term of the Lease. The tenant has no obligation to pay any rent other than the base rent. Gross rent is unusual today because rent is fixed for the entire term of the lease, and the landlord assumes the risk of inflationary and other increases in maintenance and operating expenses, real estate taxes, and insurance costs.

Base Year Rent—Base year rent, though often quoted as "gross rent," is really a modified gross rent. The quoted base year rent includes net rent, maintenance and operating expenses, real estate taxes, and insurance costs through the end of the base year. For each year subsequent to the base year, tenant agrees to pay as "additional rent" tenant's proportionate share of increases in maintenance and operating expenses, real estate taxes, and insurance costs over those maintenance and operating expenses, real estate taxes, and insurance costs incurred during the base year. Thus, the base year acts as a comparison year. Base year variations include tenant paying its own electricity charges or tenant paying all real estate taxes in addition to tenant's payment of tenant's proportionate share of the remaining maintenance and operating expenses and insurance costs.

Additional Rent—As indicated above, additional rent generally occurs in a lease containing provisions for net rent or base year rent, and refers to all amounts payable to landlord that are in addition to base rent. For example, in a lease having base year rent, additional rent would generally mean tenant's proportionate share of increases in maintenance and operating expenses, real estate taxes, and insurance costs over those maintenance and operating expenses, real estate taxes, and insurance costs incurred during the base year. Many leases also contain a "catch-all" clause that states that all amounts payable to landlord under the lease shall be deemed to be "rent" or "additional rent." This type of clause would permit landlord to invoke the remedies under the lease not only for nonpayment of base year rent or the additional rent referred to above, but would also permit landlord to invoke remedies for nonpayment of charges relating to replacement of lightbulbs or other reimbursable charges due landlord under the lease. Landlord's remedies for such nonpayment of rent or additional rent would generally include the right to terminate the lease and evict tenant from the premises. See Part 1, Paragraph 7 for a full discussion of additional rent.

Percentage Rent—Percentage rent generally occurs in retail leases and most often requires that tenant pay to landlord a specified percentage of "gross sales" in excess of a specified "minimum gross sales" break point. For example, a retail shoe store lease at a regional mall may require that tenant pay to landlord, as percentage rent, 1% of all gross sales in excess of minimum gross sales of $1 million. Thus, in any year where tenant's gross sales exceed $1 million, percentage rent will be due to landlord. See Part 2, Paragraph 4 for a full discussion of percentage rent.

Real Estate Taxes

Real estate taxes are determined by the municipal and/or county taxing authority where the property is located. The taxing authority first determines the "assessment," or valuation, of the property based on specific statutory criteria. In some jurisdictions this assessment occurs annually, and in others on some other periodic basis, such as every five or ten years. In some jurisdictions reassessment can also occur upon a sale or refinancing of the property, or upon the occurrence of improvements to the property. The assessment is then multiplied by the "mill rate" to determine the amount of real estate taxes due on the property. The mill rate is usually expressed as an amount per $100 or $1,000 of the assessed value.

The time for payment of real estate taxes varies from jurisdiction to jurisdiction, sometimes even within the same state. In some jurisdictions real estate taxes are paid annually, in others quarterly or semiannually. In some jurisdictions taxes are paid in arrears; in others they are paid in advance. In some jurisdictions taxes are paid and assessed on a calendar-year basis, and in other jurisdictions a special tax year is created. In every jurisdiction the vagaries of real estate taxes must be examined to determine the calculation, frequency of payment, and due date of real estate taxes.

Subordination, Nondisturbance, and Attornment

While the words "subordination," "nondisturbance," and "attornment" are often linked together in leases, they each have distinct meanings.

Subordination—Subordination relates to the priority that the lease and tenant's rights under the lease have relative to other matters affecting title to the property that have been recorded on the land records where the property is located or of which tenant has knowledge at the time of the execution of the lease. Examples of parties holding an interest in the property prior to tenant's (and therefore meaning that tenant's interest is subordinate) include: fee mortgages, ground leases, leasehold mortgages, air space leases, deeds of trust, utility easements, rights of way, and operating and reciprocal easement agreements. Subordination can also occur by agreement among parties having an interest in the property. Thus, by agreement contained within the lease document, the tenant generally agrees to subordinate the lease to any mortgage or ground lease that may come into existence after the execution of the lease. This agreement among the parties may also be restated in a Subordination, Nondisturbance, and Attornment Agreement (SNDA).

Nondisturbance—While the existence and recording of mortgages and ground leases are generally beyond the control of tenant, tenant does have means of protecting itself. The key word for a tenant is "nondisturbance." The lease and an SNDA with nondisturbance protection will generally provide that in the event of a foreclosure of a mortgage or the termination of a ground lease, lender or ground lessor agrees not to disturb tenant's possession of the premises, provided tenant is not then in default under its lease. Without nondisturbance, if the lease is subordinate to a mortgage, and if lender forecloses, lender can elect to name the tenant as party in the foreclosure action and terminate the lease. Tenant does not want to risk being left on the street if landlord defaults on its mortgage loan payments and thus tries to negotiate nondisturbance being added to the Lease or the SNDA. Lender, on the other hand, prefers to retain the option to disturb tenant's occupancy of the premises, because if tenant is paying rent below the current market, lender can terminate the lease and obtain a new tenant who will pay a market rent.

Attornment—While nondisturbance is key to tenant, attornment is crucial to lender. The attornment part of the lease and the SNDA states that upon foreclosure or deed in lieu of foreclosure, tenant will attorn to, or recognize, the new landlord (who either used to be the lender or is a third-party purchaser at a foreclosure sale) as the current landlord under the lease. Tenant further agrees to be bound by all provisions of the lease. Since in some jurisdictions, foreclosures can be beneficial to tenant, allowing tenant the opportunity to walk away from a lease to which tenant no longer wants to be bound, lender wants to make sure that this will not happen and that tenant will continue to pay rent. Attornment waives tenant's right to walk away and reaffirms the lease.

PART 1

Description and Analysis of Office Lease Paragraphs

PARAGRAPH 1

The Parties and the Effective Date

RISK RATING: 4

A. DESCRIPTION AND SCOPE

This Paragraph is typically the first introductory paragraph of the Lease and sets forth the names, addresses, and types of entities of each party to the Lease. It also serves to identify the effective date of the Lease.

B. ANALYSIS

1. Landlord's Perspective

Landlord wants to ensure that the Lease lists the proper name, type of legal entity as Tenant, and Tenant's state of organization in the event Landlord must sue Tenant to collect rent, enforce Tenant's obligations under the Lease, or evict Tenant.

Landlord wants to ensure that Tenant is bound to the Lease on the date the Lease is executed (i.e., the "Effective Date") even if the Term of the Lease is not expected to "commence" until a later date. This is because Landlord may be expending a substantial sum of money between the Effective Date and commencement of the Term (especially if Landlord is performing initial improvements to the Premises in preparation of Tenant's initial occupancy thereof) and wants to be sure that Tenant is bound to its obligations under the Lease before expending any such sums. The Lease Term and issues surrounding the commencement date of the Lease are discussed in Paragraph 5.

2. Tenant's Perspective

Tenant wants to ensure that the Lease lists the proper legal entity as Landlord and Landlord's state of organization in the event Tenant must sue Landlord to enforce Landlord's obligations under the Lease.

Similarly to Landlord, Tenant wants to ensure that Landlord is bound to the Lease on the Effective Date whether or not the Lease Term commences simultaneously with the Effective Date or not.

3. Lender's Perspective

Lender wants to make sure that the Landlord described in the Lease and Lender's borrower are the same entity. A Lender is also interested in the name and state of organization of the Tenant obligor under the Lease for purposes of underwriting the credit of that particular Tenant. Additionally, Lender may request that the Lease be assigned to the Lender as additional collateral for the mortgage loan. An "Assignment of Leases and Rents" may be recorded on the land records and Tenant may be asked to acknowledge the existence of this document. Lender's interest in the Lease being effective upon execution is aligned with Landlord's interest in this regard.

4. Broker's Perspective

Both a Landlord and Tenant Broker will want to pay careful attention that there is either (i) consistency of the named Tenant entity across any Request for Proposal, Lease Proposal, Term Sheet or Letter of Intent (each hereinafter referred to, for efficiency, as the "LOI"), Tenant delivered financial statements and the Lease, or (ii) an understandable reason for any inconsistency in the named Tenant entity.

A Broker representing Tenant will want to be sure that the Tenant entity named in any LOI is the actual entity the client wants to be named in the Lease as Tenant. If the Tenant entity is not yet selected by Tenant at the LOI stage, then it should be clarified when the Tenant financial statements are submitted for Landlord's review since Landlord will be making a decision on any necessary security deposit (and/or or guaranty) to secure Tenant's performance of its obligations under the Lease based upon the financial statements it receives. Landlord will expect that the Tenant entity named under the Lease will match the entity associated with the financial statements. Landlord Broker will want to focus on this detail as well.

If there is a disconnect between the proposed Tenant entity and the entity associated with the financial statements provided, it is important that the Tenant Broker asks its client to explain the relationship between the proposed Tenant entity and the entity associated with the financial statements so that Tenant Broker is in a position to explain the reasons therefor to the Landlord Broker. Landlord will naturally push for the most credit-worthy entity to sign the Lease and/or guaranty the Lease. Broker should confirm that the Tenant entity stated in the initial draft Lease document issued by the Landlord is consistent with what Tenant proposed and intended.

If Tenant does not currently have an office location in the state where the leased premises are located, Broker may wish to inquire whether Tenant is registered to conduct business in that state and, if not, encourage that process to begin.

With respect to the Effective Date of the Lease, both Landlord and Tenant Broker will want to make sure the Effective Date is clear as such date is typically the date that triggers the Broker's right to a commission with respect to the Lease even if the commission is not due and payable until a later date (such as upon the satisfaction of any conditions to the effectiveness of the Lease). It is prudent for any Tenant Broker to have a written and executed commission agreement in place with Landlord (or, if applicable, a written agreement between Tenant's Broker and Landlord's Broker if the commission payment is being handled that way) prior to the Effective Date (usually the execution date of the Lease).

C. COMPROMISES AND ALTERNATIVES

Tenant may want to create or has already created a judgment-proof subsidiary of a rated corporate parent to execute the Lease. Consideration should thus be given as to whether a full or partial guaranty of the Lease by the corporate parent will be required. This should be of particular concern if substantial tenant improvement dollars are being spent by the Landlord in connection with the Lease, and Tenant is an unrated subsidiary of a corporate parent that is not providing credit support via a lease guaranty. Corporate parents may wish to avoid such a guaranty and, thus, Tenant may endeavor to negotiate the posting of a cash security deposit or letter of credit as security for Tenant's fulfillment of its obligations under the lease.

D. COMMENTS

Landlord and Tenant entity information should be verified as accurate and complete.

It is important to specify the type of entity and state of organization for both Landlord and Tenant so that appropriate service of process and credit information can be obtained.

From the Landlord's perspective, it is good practice to also confirm and require, where required by applicable state law, that the Tenant is registered to do business in the state where the leased premises is located as it is often different from Tenant's state of organization. State laws vary with respect to what businesses (not formed under the laws of the State where the leased premises is located) need to register. Landlords should be aware of the local law requirements and, when applicable, confirm that Tenant is compliant to such law prior to lease execution. Nearly every State in the United States maintains a readily accessible online database (generally associated with the applicable State's Office of the Secretary of State) of registered businesses, which makes confirming Tenant's registration status easy.

From a Tenant's perspective, Tenant leasing property to operate its business outside of its state of organization should also review the local law requirements of the State where the leased premises is located to confirm whether foreign entity registration is legally required, failing which Tenant may risk violating local law.

In addition, it is also prudent for Tenant to confirm that Landlord is the fee title owner or lessee (typically through a ground lease) of the property to be leased. Tenant typically can confirm that the named Landlord owns or leases the property in question by reviewing online records available through the applicable tax assessor's office for the leased property or obtaining a title search from a title insurance company.

With respect to the Effective Date of the Lease, it should not be confused with the commencement date of the Lease Term. The Effective Date is the date Landlord and

Tenant agree to be bound by the terms and conditions of the Lease. The time period for which Tenant will be leasing the leased premises is one of those terms and conditions and that time period properly commences on the commencement date of the Lease Term, as is further discussed in Paragraph 5.

E. TYPICAL PARAGRAPH

1. **THIS AGREEMENT OF LEASE (the "Lease"), is made as of the [DAY] day of [MONTH], [YEAR] (the "Effective Date"), between [LANDLORD NAME] ("Landlord"), a [ENTITY TYPE AND STATE OF FORMATION], having an office at [ADDRESS], and [TENANT NAME] ("Tenant"), a [ENTITY TYPE AND STATE OF FORMATION], having an office at [ADDRESS].**

____

____

____

____

PARAGRAPH 2

Building, Premises, Land, Property, and Common Areas

RISK RATING: 3

A. DESCRIPTION AND SCOPE

This Paragraph defines and describes the location of the Building, the Premises, the Land, and the Common Areas and defines the term Property as all of the foregoing. This Paragraph also sets forth the rentable area of the Premises and often the rentable area of the Building. Note that a definition of the Land is not always included in an office lease where Tenant is only leasing just a portion of the interior office space of the Building.

The Premises and the Building are stated in "rentable square feet" rather than "usable square feet." Usable square feet represent the actual square footage of a space. The rentable square feet of a Premises is determined by taking the usable square feet of the Premises and adding Tenant's Pro Rata Share of the Common Areas (commonly called the Building's "load factor"). By attributing the Common Areas to the tenantable portions of the Building, Landlord is able to collect a rental stream on the entirety of the Building.

Subparagraph 2(c), pertaining to Premises and Building measurement, requires that the "BOMA" method be used to calculate the rentable area of the Premises and requires a remeasurement of the Premises upon completion of any initial improvements to the Premises in preparation of Tenant's initial occupancy thereof. This provision may be in the Lease but not always in space leased with existing demising walls where typically parties stipulate to the rentable area of the Premises and the Building within the Lease at Lease execution. This provision is more typically included in a "built to suit" Lease or when the Premises are not yet separately demised but will be separately demised after Lease execution. If there is a remeasurement of the Premises, any increase or decrease in the rentable area of the Premises will result in equitable adjustment of the Annual Base Rent, Tenant's Pro Rata Share of Operating Expenses and Real Estate Taxes (if applicable), and any other Tenant rights or obligations tied to the size of the Premises. The required adjustments are self-operative under the Paragraph; however, the parties may agree, for their mutual convenience, to execute a lease amendment within 30 days documenting the adjustments.

B. ANALYSIS

1. Landlord's Perspective

This Paragraph, which provides a description of the Premises and the Building (and the Land, when needed), is important because a clear and understandable description of the Premises is required for the enforceability of the Lease.

With respect to the definition of Common Areas in Subparagraph 2(b), Landlord wants an expansive definition so that the most Annual Base Rent and Pro Rata Share for Tenant can be achieved.

Subparagraph 2(c), pertaining to Premises and Building measurement, protects Landlord against inaccurate calculation of the rentable area of the Premises and disputes over rent adjustments brought about by changes in rentable area. In certain geographic locations, it may be more appropriate to use a measurement standard other than the BOMA standard, or a specific additional percentage common area factor may be used in the calculation of the rentable area of the Premises.

2. Tenant's Perspective

From this Paragraph, Tenant needs an accurate definition of the Premises for space planning purposes and for estimating tenant improvement costs. Tenant also wants a precise method of calculating the rentable area of the Premises in order to accurately budget the amount of Annual Base Rent and Additional Rent.

It is important that the Lease state the rentable square footage of the Building as of the Effective Date so Tenant's Pro Rata Share can be confirmed as accurate at Lease execution. The rentable square footage of the Building can also be used for calculating any changes to Tenant's Pro Rata Share in the event the size of the Premises changes during the Lease Term due to expansions or contractions of the Premises.

Tenant will want to make sure the definition of Common Areas in Subparagraph 2(b) contains all of those areas of the Property that Tenant is expecting to use.

Subparagraph 2(c) protects Tenant against inaccurate calculation of rentable area of the Premises and against disputes arising from a rent adjustment based upon a change in the rentable area. Tenant may wish to not permit remeasuring of the Building unless the Building actually physically changes size during the Lease Term, otherwise it risks escalating Rent liability. If the Lease does not permit remeasuring of the Premises after Lease execution, Tenant should consider having the Premises professionally measured prior to Lease execution and, if able, on a confidential basis, in the event Tenant should discover that the Premises is under-measured.

3. Lender's Perspective

With respect to this Paragraph, a correct description of the Building and the Premises (and the Land, when included) is important to Lender, as it assures Lender that the Lease is enforceable. Lender desires certainty in the definition of Building and Premises so that cash flow available for debt service can be accurately predicted.

4. Broker's Perspective

Landlord Broker and Tenant Broker should focus on the actual size of the proposed Premises at the inception of trading LOIs. The initial proposals should clearly state the method by which Landlord proposes to measure the difference between actual useable area within the Premises and what will be the "rentable square foot measurement" of the Premises in the Lease. Landlord Broker should have a clear understanding of Landlord's Building-standard measurement process.

It is best that any Broker rely upon an architect or space planner familiar with the methods of measurement to confirm that the Premises measurement provided is fair and accurate. As measurement standards vary from market to market, it's important that Tenant Broker be aware of the applicable market practice prior to preparation of a space survey or options list for the Tenant.

With respect to the Building measurement and the delineation of the common areas, both Landlord Broker and Tenant Broker will want to particularly understand how common areas that may be considered Tenant amenities (such as gyms, cafes, etc.) figure into the Building measurement. Tenant Broker will want to understand whether Tenant's use of such amenities will be separately charged or included in operating expenses so as to appropriately advise Tenant.

Upon receipt of the Lease draft, Broker will want to confirm that the Premises measurement included reflects the size agreed to in any preceding LOI. Broker will also want to confirm that the Lease includes the rentable area of the Building and that such rentable area meets expectations.

C. COMPROMISES AND ALTERNATIVES

With respect to Subparagraph 2(a), if the Building is under construction and the exact address of the Property is unknown at the time of execution of the Lease, the following language should be inserted:

> *The address of the Building shall be determined by the appropriate governmental authorities and, when determined, this Lease shall be amended to reflect the appropriate address.*

With respect to Subparagraph 2(c), office Leases typically now stipulate the size of the Premises and Building at Lease execution as set forth in Subparagraph 2(a) and do not permit remeasuring after Premises fit-out. Measurement of the Premises and the Building thus is important prior to Lease execution. An exception to this is if the Building is being "built to suit" for the Tenant and does not exist at Lease signing, or if the Premises are not yet separately demised but will be separately demised after Lease execution. This is more common under an industrial lease than an office Lease.

D. COMMENTS

A diagram of the Premises should be attached as Exhibit A to the Lease. The legal description of the Land where the Building is located may also be attached as an Exhibit, but including such a legal description and/or survey is rare in the case of office and retail leases for spaces within multi-tenanted buildings where, more typically, the mailing address is considered sufficient to identify the Building and the Property. An Exhibit to the Lease providing the legal description of the Land is more routinely attached in leases for single-tenant buildings in the office, retail, and industrial sectors. The Common Areas include parking facilities. See Paragraph 38 (Parking) for a more complete discussion of Parking.

In addition to the BOMA method of measuring space it should be noted that depending upon the geographic area where the Property is located, either a modified BOMA or some other measurement standard may be used, or in most cases the parties may simply agree upon the rentable square feet of the Premises without any standard or measurement.

E. TYPICAL PARAGRAPH

2. Building, Premises and Common Areas.

Premises. Landlord, for and in consideration of the rents herein reserved and of the covenants and agreements herein contained on the part of Tenant to be performed, hereby leases to Tenant and Tenant accepts and leases from Landlord, certain space (the "Premises") shown on Exhibit A attached hereto and made a part hereof, containing approximately [AMOUNT] rentable square feet in area located on the [NUMBER] floor of the building located at [ADDRESS] which building contains approximately [NUMBER] rentable square feet (the "Building"). The Premises, Building, the "Common Areas" (defined below) and the land upon which the same are located (the "Land"), together with all other improvements thereon and thereunder are collectively referred to as the "Property."

Common Areas. Landlord hereby grants to Tenant during the term of this Lease, a license to use, in common with the others entitled to such use, the Common Areas as they from time to time exist, subject to the rights, powers, and privileges herein reserved to Landlord. The term "Common Areas" as used herein will include all areas and facilities outside the Premises that are provided and designated by Landlord for general nonexclusive use and convenience of Tenant and other tenants of the Building. Common Areas include but are not limited to the [fitness center], [cafeteria], [hallways], [lobbies], [stairways], [elevators], [pedestrian sidewalks], [landscaped areas], [loading areas], [roadways], [parking areas], and [recreational areas], if any.

Premises and Building Measurement; BOMA. For purposes of this Lease, the Premises and the Building shall be measured in accordance with the Building Owners and Managers Association International Standard Methods of Measurement, ANSI/BOMA Z65.1-2017, and its accompanying guidelines ("BOMA"). All references to rentable area or rentable square feet as used in this Lease shall refer to rentable area calculations derived by the application of BOMA. Landlord shall provide, upon Tenant's request, the calculations showing how the total rentable area of the Building and rentable area of the Premises were derived. IF APPLICABLE, ADD THE FOLLOWING: Upon completion of the Premises, the rentable square footage of the Premises and the Building, if applicable, shall be measured by authorized representatives of Landlord and Tenant in accordance with BOMA. If the rentable square footage of the Premises is increased or decreased, the Annual Base Rent, Additional Rent (if any), monthly rent installment, and Tenant's Pro Rata Share shall be equitably adjusted. The adjustment to Annual Base Rent, Additional Rent (if any), monthly rent installment, and Tenant's Pro Rata Share shall be self-operative, and no additional agreement between Landlord and Tenant will be necessary to effectuate such adjustment; provided, however, Landlord and Tenant shall, for their mutual convenience, execute an amendment to this Lease within thirty (30) days following Tenant's occupancy, stating the Commencement Date, the Rent Commencement Date, the rentable square footage of the Premises, the Annual Base Rent, the Additional Rent (if any), the monthly rent installment, and Tenant's Pro Rata Share (as hereinafter defined) developed through the operation of this Paragraph 2(c). The failure of either party to execute and deliver such an amendment shall not affect the aforesaid adjustment of the Annual Base Rent and Additional Rent.

PARAGRAPH 3

Leasing Clause

RISK RATING: 3

A. DESCRIPTION AND SCOPE

This Paragraph sets out the basic agreement of Landlord to lease the Premises to Tenant and the agreement of Tenant to lease the Premises from Landlord, including any and all appurtenant rights thereto.

B. ANALYSIS

1. Landlord's Perspective

From Landlord's perspective, this Paragraph is the operative Paragraph that binds Tenant to the Lease and all the covenants and conditions of Tenant set forth throughout the Lease. In addition, this Paragraph protects Landlord against a claim that the Lease creates some legal relationship other than a leasehold interest, for example, a sale of the Premises by Landlord to Tenant, a license, or some other arrangement whereby Tenant would become an occupant of the Premises.

2. Tenant's Perspective

From Tenant's perspective, this Paragraph is the operative Paragraph that binds Landlord to the Lease and, more specifically, the paragraph that indicates that Landlord is "leasing" the Premises to Tenant (versus licensing) and, hence, granting Tenant a "leasehold interest" in the Premises. With a leasehold interest in the Premises, Tenant has certain statutory protections relating to termination and enforcement of the Lease. Tenant wants an expansive definition of Appurtenant Rights so that it will be able to use all Building facilities outside of the Premises that Tenant will need in order to satisfy the needs of Tenant's employees. Tenant should get a general representation from Landlord in the Lease that it is the fee owner of the property, has the authority to lease the property pursuant to the terms of the Lease and that the property is not subject to a ground lease. This is because if the Property is subject to a ground lease, Tenant will want to confirm that the term of the ground lease extends beyond the term of Tenant's Lease. Tenant may also desire to obtain a nondisturbance agreement from any ground lessor, as further discussed in Paragraph 25.

3. Lender's Perspective

Lender wants assurance that both Landlord and Tenant are bound to the Lease. This Paragraph is the operative paragraph that binds Landlord and Tenant to the Lease and all of Landlord's and Tenant's respective covenants set forth throughout the Lease.

4. Broker's Perspective

Tenant Broker should review this Paragraph to ensure that Tenant's rights extend to areas of the Building and surrounding property needed by Tenant for the operation of Tenant's business and the use and enjoyment of Tenant's employees, visitors and guests, and whether the Common Areas are granted to Tenant for exclusive or nonexclusive use by Tenant.

C. COMPROMISES AND ALTERNATIVES

Tenant may request that Landlord make certain warranties and representations regarding Landlord's ownership of the Property and Landlord's right to enter into the Lease. The following may be an acceptable addition to the Lease:

> *Landlord is the owner of the Property and warrants and represents to Tenant that Landlord has full right and authority to make this Lease. Landlord further warrants and represents that, to the best of Landlord's actual knowledge, the provisions of this Lease do not conflict with or violate the provisions of existing agreements between Landlord and third parties.*

If the Property is fairly uncomplicated (i.e., a single, multi-tenanted building with minimal amenities and common areas), the Lease can forego the detail contained in Subparagraph 3(b) and the concept of appurtenances can be added to the general leasing clause in Subparagraph 3(a) as follows (underscored language to indicate revised language):

> *Landlord, for and in consideration of the rents and other charges and payments payable by Tenant and of the covenants, agreements, terms, provisions, and conditions to be kept and performed hereunder by Tenant, does hereby demise and lease to Tenant, and Tenant does hereby hire and lease from Landlord the Premises <u>and any and all appurtenances related thereto necessary for Tenant's access, use and enjoyment of the Premises</u>. Said demise is and shall be upon and subject to the covenants, agreements, terms, provisions, and conditions of this Lease.*

D. COMMENTS

In lieu of the Landlord warranties and representations recommended in Section C above, Landlord may suggest that Tenant purchase leasehold title insurance if Tenant is concerned about the status of Landlord's title to Property. If a Tenant is investing its own funds to prepare the leased space for its tenancy, it is advisable for Tenant to purchase leasehold title insurance. Note purchasing leasehold title insurance is not at all typical in leases where the Tenant is leasing a portion of a multi-tenant office building or even retail space in a multi-tenant retail complex, but it becomes important, is more common and should be considered for single tenant properties where significant improvements are being made by or paid for by Tenant (such as "built to suit" leases) in the office, retail and, most typical, industrial sector.

E. TYPICAL PARAGRAPH

3. Leasing Clause and Appurtenant Rights

(a) <u>Leasing Clause</u>. Landlord, for and in consideration of the rents and other charges and payments payable by Tenant and of the covenants, agreements, terms, provisions, and conditions to be kept and performed hereunder by Tenant, does hereby demise and lease to Tenant, and Tenant does hereby hire and lease from Landlord the Premises. Said demise is and shall be upon and subject to the covenants, agreements, terms, provisions, and conditions of this Lease.

(b) <u>Appurtenant Rights</u>. Appurtenant to the Premises (subject to the rules and regulations of Landlord promulgated from time to time) are the following rights, privileges, and licenses (the "Appurtenant Rights") of Tenant and its invitees:

(i) the nonexclusive right to use, in common with Landlord and other tenants and invitees of Landlord, the loading docks, the freight elevators, and all areas and passageways reasonably necessary for the use of such loading docks and freight elevators; and

(ii) the nonexclusive right to use, in common with Landlord and other tenants and the invitees of Landlord and such other tenants, and the general public, the parking facilities of the Building; the nonexclusive right to use, in common with Landlord and other tenants and invitees of Landlord and such other tenants, the Common Areas for all purposes for which the Common Areas are customarily used, including full, uninterrupted access to and from the Premises.

The Appurtenant Rights are not and are not intended to be construed to be included in the definition of the word "Premises" for any purposes whatsoever under this Lease.

PARAGRAPH 4

Use of Premises

RISK RATING: 2

A. DESCRIPTION AND SCOPE

This Paragraph states the permitted uses of the Premises: executive and general offices and related uses. Of course, for retail and industrial leases this would be revised to reflect either retail uses or some combination of manufacturing, product assembly, warehousing, research, laboratory and testing, distribution, and associated office use (as applicable), respectively.

B. ANALYSIS

1. Landlord's Perspective

If Landlord has intended that the Building be used exclusively for office purposes, even if zoning laws and other laws permit the Building to be used for retail or residential purposes, this Paragraph protects Landlord against use of the Premises by Tenant for purposes other than office purposes. This Paragraph also ensures a successor Landlord that the use of the Building and the Premises may not be changed without its consent.

Landlords sometime take the position that they will not represent that the Premises may be lawfully used for the permitted use, shifting the risk to Tenant as further mentioned below.

2. Tenant's Perspective

Tenant wants the broadest possible use of the Premises, not only for Tenant's own operations but also in the event that Tenant assigns the Lease or sublets the Premises to a third party. Therefore, Tenant may ask for a clause that permits Tenant to use the Premises for "any other purpose permitted by law." Tenant may also request that Landlord permit "all lawful related or incidental use of the Premises for other purposes." Tenant should avoid any language that provides "use for the operation of [TYPE] business." This might be seen as limiting language should Tenant endeavor to later sublease or assign the Lease to an entity that needs an office (or retail and industrial use, as the case may be) but operates a different business than the original Tenant. Tenant desires for clarity that the Premises may be used lawfully for the permitted use and may ask for Landlord's representation that the Property may be lawfully used for the stated permitted use. Note that we will get to compliance with law more broadly later. Tenant may object to Landlord's limiting this representation to the best of Landlord's knowledge.

If Landlord does not represent that the Premises may be used for the stated permitted use, Tenant bears the risk in which case Tenant may wish to ask for or otherwise obtain a copy of the Certificate of Occupancy for the Building or otherwise perform a review of local zoning laws. This is particularly true if the Building is new and has not been historically used as an office building. This is also important if Tenant is intending to use the Premises for a specialized office use like "medical" office use. This is because certain localities treat/zone certain uses differently including, without limitation, requiring different parking ratios.

Tenant also wants to ensure that it can use the Premises twenty-four (24) hours per day, seven (7) days per week during the Term. Proposed language to be inserted is provided in Section C below.

3. Lender's Perspective

Lender desires to preserve the cash flow generated by the Lease as well as by the cash flow generated by leases to other tenants on the Property. Lender therefore desires that Tenant not use the Premises for purposes that are harmful or offensive to other tenants or prospective tenants on the Property and, thus, Lender may require that the Lease include a list of uses that are expressly prohibited. Also, because violations of legal requirements may impair the value of the Property and therefore Lender's security, Lender desires assurance that the Property be used in compliance with the permitted use under applicable zoning laws.

4. Broker's Perspective

It behooves both Landlord Broker and Tenant Broker to understand and agree upon Tenant's proposed use of the Premises during the LOI stage to avoid problems arising during the Lease negotiation of this Paragraph.

Tenant Broker should confirm during the up-front needs assessment phase of its assignment how its client/tenant intends to use the proposed leased space. This can be trickier than it seems. For example, if Tenant is contemplating an office use Broker should inquire (i) what Tenant's normal density needs are (and whether same are expected to change over the Term); (ii) whether Tenant has any need for occasional large gatherings within the space for either company training, client event purposes or otherwise; (iii) whether Tenant has any need for consistent use of the Premises outside of typical Building hours (i.e., after 6:00 p.m. and on weekends or holidays); and (iv) whether Tenant has any special cooking or other entertaining needs, as some of these activities may require specific zoning approvals and/or construction permits.

Thus, all special Tenant use needs should be investigated at the onset of discussions with any potential Landlord as all parties should confirm (prior to the first draft of a Lease) that any such special use can be accommodated, including that the Building's certificate of occupancy permits same and the Building systems and services are available to accommodate any such special use.

Additionally, Tenant Broker will always want Tenant's permitted use provided in this Paragraph to be drafted broadly as possible, because (i) Tenant's needs and activities may change during the Term and (ii) a broadly drafted permitted use Paragraph broadens the pool of prospective subtenants should the space need to be subleased by Tenant during the Term.

C. COMPROMISES AND ALTERNATIVES

As a compromise to Tenant's request that Tenant be permitted to use the Premises for "any use permitted by law," Tenant should request and Landlord should be able to give the following as a matter of standard course:

> *Tenant may not use and occupy the Premises other than for executive and general office purposes and other uses related thereto incidental to such purposes and permitted by law.*

Additionally, Tenant should include the following concept in the use clause of the Lease:

> *Tenant shall have access and use of the Premises twenty-four (24) hours per day, seven (7) days per week, at no extra charge, except to the extent Tenant requests any additional Building services requiring additional fees under the Lease.*

To protect against Tenant (or any potential subtenant) using the Premises in a manner which might be harmful or offensive to other tenants or prospective tenants on the Property, Landlord may wish to include a list of particular uses that are specifically prohibited. The list is generally compromised of users who might be nuisances, impact the character or reputation of the Building, or might result in higher density or intensity of occupancy of the Premises or Building. An example of such a provision is as follows:

> *Tenant shall not use the Premises or any part thereof, or permit the Premises or any part thereof to be used (i) for the business of photographic, multilith, or multigraph reproductions, except to the extent incidental to Tenant's own business being conducted in the Premises; (ii) for any enterprise which conducts business in the Premises with the general public on an off-the-street retail basis; (iii) by any Governmental Authority or any other Person having sovereign or diplomatic immunity; (iv) as an employment agency, executive search firm, or similar enterprise, labor union, school, or vocational training center (except for the training of employees of Tenant to be employed at the Premises); (v) as a television or radio studio; (vi) in a manner which may cause unusually high levels of employee density or visitors or a nuisance to others at the Building or which may otherwise interfere with the Building Systems, parking, or operation of the Property; or (vii) as a kitchen, cafeteria, or restaurant, except that Tenant may install a customary office pantry unit in the Premises to warm food and prepare light meals solely for Tenant's officers, employees, and guests.*

D. COMMENTS

If the Premises are to be used for purposes other than general offices (such as commodity, bond, or stock trading for asset managers), the additional uses desired should be specified.

E. TYPICAL PARAGRAPH

4. **Use of Premises. Tenant may use and occupy the Premises for executive and general office purposes only (the "Permitted Use"), and no other use of the Premises shall be permitted without the express written consent of Landlord.**

PARAGRAPH 5

Term; Commencement Date (and Delivery Delays)

RISK RATING: 4

A. DESCRIPTION AND SCOPE

This Paragraph specifies the date on which the Lease term shall begin (the "Commencement Date"), the date on which it ends (the "Expiration Date"), and the duration of the Lease between the Commencement Date and the Expiration Date (the "Term").

While it seems that the Paragraph stating the Term of any Lease should be simple as the length of any time period is indeed simple to state (i.e. five (5) years from the Commencement Date (or Rent Commencement Date, as the case may be)), the circumstances that give rise to the triggering of the Commencement Date can vary widely and, thus, lease provisions surrounding the Commencement Date can be among the trickiest provisions of the Lease, are often incorrectly drafted and are often hotly negotiated. We will review this in detail below.

For the purposes of Paragraph 5, we will analyze the two (2) most common alternative ways a Commencement Date is defined or triggered with two (2) alternatives of Paragraph 5 below. Factual circumstances determine which Alternative Paragraph is best to use, and the relevant factual circumstances are as follows:

Alternative 1: When (i) Landlord is not required to make any initial improvements to the Premises for Tenant's initial occupancy thereof and Tenant is taking the Premises in its then "as-is" condition, (ii) the Premises are vacant on the Effective Date (reminder this is the date the parties signed the Lease), and (iii) Landlord otherwise stands ready to deliver the Premises on a date certain, the Alternative 1 Paragraph is most appropriate because the parties are able to stipulate as of the Effective Date a calendar date for the Commencement Date, the Rent Commencement, and the Expiration Date without much risk to either party.

Alternative 2: When either (i) Landlord is performing initial alterations to the Premises in order to prepare the Premises for Tenant's initial occupancy thereof (for either Tenant to immediately operate its business therein or for Tenant to commence its initial build-out of the Premises), and/or (ii) the Premises is occupied by an existing tenant on the Effective Date of this Lease, the Alternative 2 Paragraph is most appropriate because there is risk associated with respect to what calendar date Landlord will be able to deliver the Premises to Tenant in the condition required.

The differing issues surrounding the two (2) Alternative Paragraphs will be described in detail below but the ***common element*** with respect to the Commencement Date in each of Alternative Paragraphs is that the Commencement Date should occur on the date that Landlord delivers to Tenant exclusive possession of the Premises in the condition required under the Lease and certainly not before. This is critical because liability for the Premises (including who is responsible for any personal injury that occurs within the Premises, which is allocated in the Lease's indemnification provision) should be with the party who is in possession or control of the Premises.

B. ANALYSIS

Alternative 1:

1. Landlord's Perspective

The Alternative 1 Paragraph allows Landlord to specify, on the Effective Date, the exact time period of Tenant's leasing of the Premises. With the Commencement Date as a fixed calendar date, the Rent Commencement Date (if applicable) and the Expiration Date can also be drafted as fixed calendar dates. This allows for simple Lease administration for Landlord.

Note with Alternative 1, Landlord is committing to deliver to Tenant the Premises on a date certain so Landlord should only use this Alternative Paragraph if there is little-to-no risk of Landlord delivering the Premises to Tenant late as any such delay would be a Landlord default under the Lease.

Some Landlords have been pre-building vacant tenant space in recent years as a marketing tactic to attract tenants who want new, freshly updated and already fit-out space for near immediate occupancy. The Alternative 1 Paragraph is perfect for vacant "pre-built" space that is ready for delivery to Tenant.

2. Tenant's Perspective

If the factual circumstances permit the Alternative 1 Paragraph, the Paragraph is advantageous to Tenant because it allows Tenant to plan for its move into the Premises with precision on the Effective Date.

Tenant should be careful that the Lease includes an express provision obligating Landlord to deliver to Tenant exclusive possession of the Premises in the condition required under the Lease on the Commencement Date. This sentence is often missing from a first draft Lease when Alternative 1 is used but, with Tenant's inclusion of the express provision, Tenant has a clear and actionable claim if Landlord fails to deliver the Premises on the Commencement Date.

3. Lender's Perspective

In general, Lenders need to know the Term of the Lease to verify that borrower will have funds available to repay the loan amount for a defined period of time based on the length of the Lease Term. The Alternative 1 Paragraph enables Lender to underwrite the Lease rollover risk in connection with the loan with specificity not afforded by the Alternative 2 Paragraph.

4. Broker's Perspective

Landlord Broker and Tenant Broker will be most interested in obtaining the best Term length to meet the needs of their respective clients (together with any Term flexibility options desired such as early termination and renewal options) and less concerned about the legal considerations around the Lease properly documenting the Term in this Alternative 1 which has little risk. Both Brokers will rightly be more concerned in Alternative 2.

That said in both, Alternative 1 and Alternative 2, each Broker will, at the onset of its assignment, during the up-front needs assessment phase, want to define the length of Term to reflect their respective clients' needs and preferences. It is critical to have the discussion as prospective Landlords may have timing constraints impacting available space to meet certain requirements of other tenants of the Building resulting in Landlord requiring a shorter or longer Term than the Tenant is willing to consider. Thus, the Term should always be agreed upon prior to initial Lease preparation.

In addition, with Alternative 1 and Alternative 2, Broker should review any draft agreement or letter establishing the occurrence of the Commencement Date and, along with legal counsel, confirm that all conditions precedent to establishment of the Commencement Date have been met prior to Landlord or Tenant executing the Commencement Date letter.

Alternative 2:

1. Landlord's Perspective

The Alternative 2 Paragraph allows Landlord some timing flexibility in meeting its Premises delivery requirement on the Commencement Date. Alternative 2 Paragraph is not tied to a calendar date but to Landlord's actions. This flexibility is helpful because Landlord may be delayed in Premises delivery because of an existing tenant holding-over in the Premises and/or because Landlord needs to complete certain improvements to the Premises prior to delivery. The Alternative 2 Paragraph is used universally when Landlord is performing an extensive "build out" of the Premises to meet Tenant's specifications. With the use of the Alternative 2 Paragraph, the Commencement Date, on the Effective Date, is uncertain. Likewise, because the Rent Commencement Date and the Expiration Date are typically defined as time periods from the Commencement Date, they too are uncertain on the Effective Date. However, because the Lease is binding upon the parties on the Effective Date, Landlord has reasonable comfort that a rent stream from the Tenant is forthcoming despite the fact that commencement of that rent stream is unclear on the Effective Date.

2. Tenant's Perspective

The Alternative 2 Paragraph ensures that Tenant's obligations under the Lease with respect to the Premises shall not commence until Landlord delivers to Tenant exclusive possession of the Premises in the condition required under the Lease. This is helpful but brings some risks. With the Commencement Date being an uncertain and even an arguably "floating date," it can be difficult for Tenant to manage the timing of a move from existing space to the Premises without paying double rent or being forced to hold over in its existing space or being without any space at all for a period of time. Compromises that help to mitigate these risks are discussed in Subsections C and D.

3. Lender's Perspective

The Alternative 2 Paragraph, like the Alternative 1 Paragraph, allows Lender to know the Term of the Lease to verify that borrower will have funds available to repay the loan amount for a defined period of time based on the length of the Lease Term, but, of course, the timing of the funds is uncertain on the Effective Date. If Tenant successfully negotiates specified automatic penalties for delays in the Commencement Date, as discussed in Subsection C below, the Alternative 2 Paragraph elevates Lender's underwriting risk.

4. Broker's Perspective

In this Alternative 2, Tenant's Broker may wish to negotiate, at the LOI stage, (i) that the Commencement Date cannot occur prior to a date certain to meet the needs of the Tenant, as may be applicable, and/or (ii) the expected Tenant remedies in the event the Commencement Date occurs later than expected/desired by Tenant (i.e., additional free rent and/or a Tenant termination right, as further discussed below).

If the Premises is occupied by an existing tenant when the LOI is being negotiated, it would helpful for the Tenant Broker to learn when the existing lease is expiring, when existing tenant is expected to surrender the Premises and, to the extent possible, the status of the existing tenant's new lease negotiations and the status of the build out of any new space for existing tenant. Such information will help assess the risk of the existing tenant holding over and causing a delay of the Commencement Date for the Lease being negotiated.

C. COMPROMISES AND ALTERNATIVES

Alternative 1:

The Alternative 1 Paragraph typically requires little negotiation between the parties if the factual circumstances reveal that there is no impediment to Landlord delivering the Premises to Tenant when promised. The only caveat to this is if the Lease goes on to say, *and it often does*, that Landlord shall bear no liability to Tenant if Landlord fails to deliver the Premises on the stated Commencement Date (calendar date) and the only result is that the Commencement Date shall be delayed until the date that Landlord delivers to Tenant exclusive possession of the Premises. Any such provision is arguably an unfair and unrestricted shift of the timing risk associated with the Commencement

Date from Landlord to Tenant. Tenant should strike from the Lease any such provision or some version of the Tenant (and Landlord) protections for late delivery described with respect to the Alternative 2 Paragraph should be considered for inclusion into the Lease to more fairly allocate the timing risk of the Commencement Date between Landlord and Tenant.

Alternative 2:

The Alternative 2 Paragraph, as drafted below, is drafted as Landlord's strongest position. It arguably shifts all Commencement Date timing risk to Tenant as Premises delivery could happen at any time without any consequence to Landlord. Landlords can and do argue against any express Tenant remedies for late delivery stating that Landlord has every interest in delivering the Premises as soon as possible to start the rental stream so they have a natural incentive to avoid delays and so Tenant does not need express rights protecting them from such delays. This is usually not a winning argument for Landlord when negotiating against a sophisticated Tenant.

With the Alternative 2 Paragraph, Tenant should evaluate whether Tenant might be negatively impacted if (i) the Commencement Date occurs *prior to* a particular calendar date, and (ii) if the Commencement Date occurs *after* a particular calendar date.

If Tenant is locked into a lease for existing space and is paying rent thereon until the end of the term of that lease, Tenant may wish to avoid or minimize any period that Tenant is paying rent on both its existing space and its new Premises by limiting how soon the Commencement Date can occur. To mitigate that risk Tenant may wish to revise Paragraph 5(b) as follows (underscored words to indicate the proposed revisions to Paragraph 5(b) as originally drafted):

> *(b) As used herein, "Commencement Date" shall mean the date which is the later of (i) the date Landlord delivers to Tenant exclusive possession of the Premises with "Landlord's Work" Substantially Completed and otherwise in the condition required under the Lease, or (ii) [CALENDAR DATE].*

Conversely, if Tenant needs to exit any existing space by a date certain or be subject to holdover rent and penalties, Tenant may wish to mitigate that risk by revising Paragraph 5(b) further to include automatic and escalating express Tenant remedies in the event Landlord delays delivery beyond an expected Commencement Date. To mitigate that risk Tenant may wish to further revise Paragraph 5(b) as follows (underscored words to indicate the proposed revisions to Paragraph 5(b) as originally drafted):

> *(b) As used herein, "Commencement Date" shall mean the date which is the later of (i) the date Landlord delivers to Tenant exclusive possession of the Premises with "Landlord's Work" Substantially Completed and otherwise in the condition required under the Lease, or (ii) [CALENDAR DATE]. Notwithstanding the foregoing, if the Commencement Dates does not occur for any reason not caused by Tenant (including, without limitation, any reasons due to "Force Majeure" conditions) by [CALENDAR DATE] (the "Rent Abatement Date"), then, in addition to any initial abatement of Base Rent provided under the Lease, Tenant shall receive an additional day of Base Rent abatement for each day the Commencement Date occurs for any reason not caused by Tenant (including, without limitation, any reasons due to "Force Majeure" conditions) beyond the Rent Abatement Date. In addition, if the Commencement Dates does not occur for any reason not caused*

> *by Tenant (including, without limitation, any reasons due to "Force Majeure" conditions) by [CALENDAR DATE] (the "Conditional Termination Date"), Tenant shall have the right to cancel the Lease, without liability, by written notice to Landlord, in which case the Lease shall be deemed terminated on the Conditional Termination Date and Landlord shall immediately return to Tenant any prepaid Rent and Security Deposit.*

Note: The use of the word "penalty" in leases should be avoided since there exists some case law relating to damages that voids penalties but upholds reasonable damages.

Landlords, however, should look to mitigate their risks resulting from any express Tenant remedies for delays in the Commencement Date. They can do this by (i) making sure the Rent Abatement Date contains a reasonable buffer of time beyond any expected Commencement Date, (ii) making sure the Conditional Termination Date is well beyond the "worst case" scenario for delays to the Commencement Date, and (iii) expressly providing that both dates can be extended for "Force Majeure" conditions (which should now expressly include pandemic related conditions). From our COVID-19 experience, parties encountered all sorts of unexpected delays, including government mandated construction stop work orders, building department closures or delays and/or construction material delivery delays. To mitigate against those risks, Landlords may wish to revise the immediately above version of Paragraph 5(b) as follows (underscored and stricken words to indicate the proposed revisions to the Paragraph 5(b) immediately above):

> *(b) As used herein, "Commencement Date" shall mean the date which is the later of (i) the date Landlord delivers to Tenant exclusive possession of the Premises with "Landlord's Work" Substantially Completed and otherwise in the condition required under the Lease, or (ii) [CALENDAR DATE]. However , if the Commencement Dates does not occur for any reason not caused by Tenant ~~(including, without limitation, any reasons due to "Force Majeure" conditions)~~ by [CALENDAR DATE] (the "Rent Abatement Date"), then, in addition to any initial abatement of Base Rent provided under the Lease, Tenant shall receive an additional day of Base Rent abatement for each day the Commencement Date occurs for any reason not caused by Tenant ~~(including, without limitation, any reasons due to "Force Majeure" conditions)~~ beyond the Rent Abatement Date. In addition, if the Commencement Dates does not occur for any reason not caused by Tenant ~~(including, without limitation, any reasons due to "Force Majeure" conditions)~~ by [CALENDAR DATE] (the "Conditional Termination Date"), Tenant shall have the right to cancel the Lease, without liability, by written notice to Landlord, in which case the Lease shall be deemed terminated and Landlord shall immediately return to Tenant any prepaid Rent and Security Deposit. Notwithstanding the foregoing, the parties agree that the Rent Abatement Date and the Conditional Termination Date each shall be extended one day for each day the Commencement Date is delayed due to a delay caused by Tenant or a "Force Majeure" condition.*

As you can imagine, the foregoing "push back" proposed by Landlords often becomes highly negotiated, and even more so in this post-COVID-19 environment. What is at stake here is the allocation of risk for unforeseen delays beyond anyone's control. That risk includes an existing Tenant who holds over in the Premises because of a construction delay due to pandemic related event, or otherwise. **The very pressing question is who should fairly bear that risk?**

There is no consensus on who should bear that risk but often the risk is shared between the parties as follows: either (i) by allowing the Rent Abatement Date to be extended for "Force Majeure" conditions (including pandemic related delays), but not allowing the Conditional Termination Date to be extended for "Force Majeure" conditions (because the Conditional Termination Date should already be so far beyond the expected Commencement Date that it accounts for the "worst case" scenario), and/or (ii) limiting the extent by which Rent Abatement Date and/or the Conditional Termination Date can be delayed due to "Force Majeure" conditions. Either scenario looks for Landlord and Tenant to equitably share in the risk. Below are two examples of how the immediately above revised Paragraph 5(b) can be further revised to reflect the two compromises described in this Paragraph (underscored and stricken words to indicate the proposed revisions to the updated Paragraph 5(b) immediately above):

> *(b) As used herein, "Commencement Date" shall mean the date which is the later of (i) Landlord delivers to Tenant exclusive possession of the Premises with "Landlord's Work" Substantially Completed and otherwise in the condition required under the Lease, or (ii) [CALENDAR DATE]. Notwithstanding the foregoing, if the Commencement Date does not occur for any reason not caused by Tenant by [CALENDAR DATE] (the "Rent Abatement Date"), then, in addition to any initial abatement of Base Rent provided under the Lease, Tenant shall receive an additional day of Base Rent abatement for each day the Commencement Date occurs for any reason not caused by Tenant beyond the Rent Abatement Date. In addition, if the Commencement Date does not occur for any reason not caused by Tenant by [CALENDAR DATE] (the "Conditional Termination Date"), Tenant shall have the right to cancel the Lease, without liability, by written notice to Landlord, in which case the Lease shall be deemed terminated and Landlord shall immediately return to Tenant any prepaid Rent and Security Deposit. Notwithstanding the foregoing, the parties agree that the Rent Abatement Date ~~and~~ but not the Conditional Termination Date shall be extended one day for each day the Commencement Date is delayed due to a delay caused by Tenant or a "Force Majeure" condition.*

Or

> *(b) As used herein, "Commencement Date" shall mean the date which is the later of (i) Landlord delivers to Tenant exclusive possession of the Premises with "Landlord's Work" Substantially Completed and otherwise in the condition required under the Lease, or (ii) [CALENDAR DATE]. Notwithstanding the foregoing, if the Commencement Date does not occur for any reason not caused by Tenant by [CALENDAR DATE] (the "Rent Abatement Date"), then, in addition to any initial abatement of Base Rent provided under the Lease, Tenant shall receive an additional day of Base Rent abatement for each day the Commencement Date occurs for any reason not caused by Tenant beyond the Rent Abatement Date. In addition, if the Commencement Date does not occur for any reason not caused by Tenant by [CALENDAR DATE] (the "Conditional Termination Date"), Tenant shall have the right to cancel the Lease, without liability, by written notice to Landlord, in which case the Lease shall be deemed terminated and Landlord shall immediately return to Tenant any prepaid Rent and Security Deposit. Notwithstanding the foregoing, the parties agree that the Rent Abatement Date and the Conditional Termination Date shall be extended one day for each day the Commencement Date is delayed due to a delay caused by Tenant, or a "Force Majeure" condition; provided, however, in no event shall*

the Rent Abatement Date or the Conditional Termination Date be extended due to "Force Majeure" conditions for more than [NUMBER OF DAYS] (time being of the essence) despite any "Force Majeure" condition extending beyond such date.

Of course, any combination of the two compromises suggested immediately above can be used by the parties to allocate this risk and resolve this often highly negotiated issue.

D. COMMENTS

With respect to Alternative 2, leases are often incorrectly drafted to provide that the Commencement Date shall occur on the Substantial Completion of Landlord's Work. While the occurrence of that event is certainly a required precondition of the Commencement Date, it is not the operative event from a Tenant's perspective. The operative event is Landlord delivering to Tenant exclusive possession of the Premises with Landlord's Work Substantially Completed and/or otherwise in the condition required under the Lease. Tenant may even wish to stipulate that the Commencement Date shall not occur without a certain amount of advance notice so that Tenant may prepare to move into the Premises and/or obtain early entry for installation of communication systems and furnishings.

Beyond the complexities of the Commencement Date described above, a few additional factors regarding the Term should attended to any Lease.

The definition of Term should include the concept, as it does in Paragraph 5(a) below in both Alternates, that the Term shall expire on the defined Expiration Date "unless: (i) sooner terminated in accordance with the terms and conditions contained in this Lease; or (ii) extended pursuant to the provisions of this Lease." This protects Landlord and Tenant from any confusion as to whether their respective obligations under the Lease shall terminate early or be extended in the event either Landlord or Tenant exercises an express right under the Lease to terminate the Lease early or to extend the Term for a renewal term.

In addition, with respect to Alternative 2, if the Expiration Date is defined in a manner that is tied to the occurrence of the Commencement Date (or Rent Commencement Date, as applicable), and the Commencement Date (or the Rent Commencement Date, as applicable) does not occur on the first calendar day of a month, the parties may wish to extend the Term so that the Term expires on the last day of a calendar month. Such a provision may look like the following (underscored words to indicate the proposed revisions to Paragraph 5(a) of Alternative 2 below):

(a) The term of this Lease ("Term") shall begin on Commencement Date (as hereinafter defined) and expire on the day immediately prior to occurrence of the [[X] anniversary of the [Rent] Commencement Date] (the "Expiration Date"), unless: (i) sooner terminated in accordance with the terms and conditions contained in this Lease; or (ii) extended pursuant to the provisions of this Lease; but, provided, in the event the [Rent] Commencement Date does not occur on the first calendar day of a month, the parties hereto agree that the Term shall be extended as required to expire on the last calendar day of the month in which the [X] anniversary of the [Rent] Commencement Date occurs.

Lastly, it is very important that if Alternative 2 is used, Subparagraph 5(c) is included and acted upon. Upon the occurrence of the Commencement Date, Landlord should promptly prepare and circulate a written statement accurately fixing the Commencement Date, Rent Commencement Date and Expiration Date and such statement should be countersigned and delivered by Tenant. Not only does this help avoid confusion later for Landlord and Tenant, it brings precision of these dates to the current Lender, any future lender and/or any prospective successor Landlord. For these reasons, Landlord should make it standard routine to affix these dates by written statements executed by Tenant.

E. TYPICAL PARAGRAPH

Alternative 1:

5. Term. The term of this Lease ("Term") shall begin on [CALENDAR DATE] (the "Commencement Date") and expire on [CALENDAR DATE] (the "Expiration Date"), unless: (i) sooner terminated in accordance with the terms and conditions contained in this Lease; or (ii) extended pursuant to the provisions of this Lease.

Alternative 2:

5. Term.

(a) The term of this Lease ("Term") shall begin on Commencement Date (as hereinafter defined) and expire on the day immediately prior to occurrence of the [[X] anniversary of the [Rent] Commencement Date] (the "Expiration Date"), unless: (i) sooner terminated in accordance with the terms and conditions contained in this Lease; or (ii) extended pursuant to the provisions of this Lease.

(b) As used herein, "Commencement Date" shall mean the date Landlord delivers to Tenant exclusive possession of the Premises with "Landlord's Work" Substantially Completed and otherwise in the condition required under the Lease.

(c) At Landlord's request, Tenant shall promptly execute and deliver a reasonable statement prepared by Landlord in the form of Exhibit [X] hereto accurately fixing the Commencement Date, Rent Commencement Date, and Expiration Date in accordance with this Lease, but any failure to prepare, execute, or deliver such statement shall not affect such dates, respectively.

PARAGRAPH 6

Condition of Premises

RISK RATING: 4

A. DESCRIPTION AND SCOPE

Landlord makes no representations or promises with respect to the condition of the Building or Premises other than those specifically set forth in the Lease. Tenant agrees to accept the Premises in an otherwise "as-is" condition.

B. ANALYSIS

1. Landlord's Perspective

Landlord wants Tenant to acknowledge that Tenant has accepted the Premises in their "AS-IS" condition, subject only to the completion of Landlord's Work, if any, and only the express Landlord representations and warranties contained in the Lease.

2. Tenant's Perspective

Tenant wants to be satisfied that the condition of the Premises is sufficient to permit Tenant to use and occupy the Premises in accordance with the permitted use of the Premises and its needs.

3. Lender's Perspective

Lender's perspective is aligned with Landlord's perspective in this Paragraph.

4. Broker's Perspective

Landlord Broker will be well acquainted with the condition of the Premises. Tenant Broker should inspect the Premises prior to negotiation of a Lease Proposal and make note of any conditions that it believes Landlord should address prior to delivery of the Premises, and ask an architect and/or engineer representing the Tenant to review and edit the list based upon its own inspection. The items identified and accepted by Landlord will appear in the "Landlord's Work" section of the Lease.

C. COMPROMISES AND ALTERNATIVES

In every circumstance, Tenant should endeavor to get Paragraph 6 modified to include as much of the following provision as the facts warrant and the market will bear:

> *Notwithstanding the foregoing, Landlord hereby warrants and represents that, as of the Commencement Date (a) the Premises shall be vacant, broom-clean and ready for Tenant's exclusive occupancy; (b) Landlord's Work, if any, shall be substantially completed such that a final and unconditional certificate of occupancy permitting lawful occupancy of the Premises has been duly issued, and such that Tenant may reasonably commence its business operations; (c) all mechanical equipment and utility systems serving the Premises shall be in good working order and repair; (d) the Premises shall be structurally sound and "water-tight"; (e) Tenant's access to the Premises shall be reasonably secure and unimpeded; and (f) the Premises and the Property shall be in compliance with all applicable laws, codes, statutes, ordinances, guidelines, rules, and regulations. Landlord's warranties and representations under this Paragraph shall survive the commencement of the Term. Any provisions in the Lease purporting to require Tenant to accept the Premises "as is" shall be subject to Landlord's covenants, warranties and representations in the Lease, and shall be further subject to any preexisting conditions not created by Tenant, including, without limitation, any latent defects.*

If Tenant is unable to obtain reasonable Landlord representations and warranties in the Lease with respect to the condition of the Premises on the Commencement Date, then prior to signing the Lease, Tenant should inspect the structural aspects of the space plus the Building systems serving the Premises to confirm that they are in satisfactory condition and meet the needs of the Tenant (i.e., the available electricity load and HVAC are sufficient for Tenant's needs). Tenant's counsel would be prudent to advise Tenant to perform this due diligence and perhaps measure the floor area of the Premises.

D. COMMENTS

The [bracketed] language regarding the completion of Landlord's Work, should be removed if Landlord is not obligated to perform any Landlord' Work.

E. TYPICAL PARAGRAPH

6. **<u>Condition of Premises</u>. Landlord and Landlord's agents and representatives have made no representations or promises with respect to the Building, the Property or the Premises except as herein expressly set forth, and no rights, easements or licenses are acquired by Tenant by implication or otherwise except as expressly set forth herein. [Except for the completion of Landlord's Work,] Tenant hereby accepts the Premises in their "as-is" condition existing as of the date hereof.**

PARAGRAPH 7

Base Rent (with Fixed Escalations) and Additional Rent

RISK RATING: 3

A. DESCRIPTION AND SCOPE

This Paragraph sets forth the Annual Base Rent, which is calculated by multiplying the rentable square footage of the Premises by the cost per rentable square foot, and specifies that such rent is to be paid in equal installments beginning on the Rent Commencement Date and on the first day of each month thereafter throughout the Term. The Paragraph also includes the terms and conditions upon which Annual Base Rent and Additional will be paid and, if applicable, the terms upon which Annual Base Rent may be initially abated.

The Commencement Date and the Rent Commencement Date may be the same date but such an occurrence is usually limited to the circumstance of when the Premises, on the Commencement Date, is in a condition permitting Tenant to immediately commence its business operations therein. This might occur if the Premises was "pre-built" on the Effective Date and/or Landlord is responsible for completing any improvements to the Premises necessary for Tenant's initial occupancy thereof for the operation of its business.

Most often, however, the Commencement Date and the Rent Commencement Date differ (with the Rent Commencement Date occurring at some defined period after the Commencement Date) to provide Tenant with a free rent "ramp up" period, a "move-in" period, and/or a period during which Tenant may construct initial Tenant improvements required for Tenant's initial occupancy of the Premises. Note that free rent periods attributable to Tenant just "ramping up" or "moving in" are typically much shorter than free rent periods provided for Tenants to improve the Premises for its particular needs for the operation of its business in the Premises.

B. ANALYSIS

1. Landlord's Perspective

Landlord is concerned with making a clear and accurate statement of the Annual Base Rent. Landlord also wants to state exactly when each installment of Annual Base Rent is due, and that each installment is due without any demand by Landlord. If any free rent period is given, Landlord may want to limit such free rent period to the Annual Base Rent so that Tenant is paying at least its applicable share of Operating Expenses and Real Estate Taxes during the free rent period. If the Tenant's credit or business prospects are not certain, Landlord may want to layer in the free rent period over several months or years. In addition, should Tenant default under the Lease, Landlord may want the right to recapture the free rent. The Typical Paragraph requires that the first month's rent be paid at the time of the execution of the Lease, rather than on the Rent Commencement Date. This requirement may be waived for Tenants with a credit rating satisfactory to Landlord.

2. Tenant's Perspective

Tenant is similarly concerned with making a clear and accurate statement of the Annual Base Rent; however, Tenant is also concerned with any provisions within the Lease which may limit Tenant's free rent period prior to the Rent Commencement Date.

3. Lender's Perspective

Lender's primary concern is to confirm Tenant's obligation to pay Annual Base Rent in the stated amount and to determine whether Tenant is entitled to any free rent period or reduced rent period so that Lender can properly underwrite the cash flow from the Property and project a satisfactory debt service coverage ratio. Lender will want to make sure the Lease contains a provision similar to Paragraph 6(a) so as to ensure that Tenant has no rights of offset or deduction against Annual Base Rent and thus no diminution in the net income available for debt service.

4. Broker's Perspective

The Annual Base Rent Paragraph under the Lease may be the most noticed business term of the Lease and it requires an understanding of market conditions and rent rates for comparable buildings. The Broker's perspective on this issue is grounded in the concept that Base Rent and Additional Rent, as agreed to for any given transaction, should reflect the amount Tenant is willing to pay in exchange for the leasing of the Premises. Landlord Broker should be well versed in understanding (and Tenant Broker must inquire to understand) the "all in" cost for leasing the Premises.

Brokers should be aware that Annual Base Rent amounts tend to vary depending upon the extent of other Tenant inducements and the length of the Term. Such inducements include, the inclusion of any "free rent period" (and whether any such "free rent period" is applicable to just Annual Base Rent or whether it extends to operating expenses and utility costs too), renovation allowances provided to Tenant and/or renovations to be performed by Landlord. All such business terms have the ability to impact the ultimately agreed to Annual Base Rent. Annual Base Rent can also vary depending upon the extent to which it includes the cost of utilities used at the Premises.

Tenant Broker's job is to get as much value as possible in return for an agreed upon Annual Base Rent and then to be sure that all value bargained for is explicitly and accurately stated in the Lease.

It is also very important that Tenant Broker prepare financial projections (for all Lease transactions being considered) that show Tenant the sum of Annual Base Rent, escalations, utilities, and any other Additional Rent so that the anticipated financial impact over the entire Term of the Lease is understood by Tenant before a Lease draft is even requested.

Once the Lease draft is issued, each Broker should review this Paragraph closely to confirm that it conforms with what was negotiated and stated in the Lease Proposal.

C. COMPROMISES AND ALTERNATIVES

When a Tenant is contemplating significant initial improvements to the Premises and/or entirely building out the Premises following the Commencement Date from raw space, Tenant will want to get expert construction advice on the time period expected to substantially complete their build out and make sure the free rent period at least covers the expected build-out period. Otherwise, Tenant is bearing the entire timing risk associated with the completion of the initial improvements to the Premises. Tenant can endeavor to shift all or a portion of the timing risk to Landlord by modifying the definition of the Rent Commencement Date. Two samples of such modified definitions are as follows (underscored and stricken words to indicate the proposed revisions to the definition of the Rent Commencement Date contained in Paragraph 7(b) below):

> *As used herein, "<u>Rent Commencement Date</u>" shall mean the date which is the ~~early~~ <u>later</u> of (i) [NUMBER] days from the Commencement Date, or (ii) the date Tenant first occupies the Premises for the operation of its business therein.*

Or

> *As used herein, "<u>Rent Commencement Date</u>" shall mean the date which is the later of (i) [NUMBER] days from the Commencement Date, or (ii) the date Tenant first occupies the Premises for the operation of its business therein; <u>provided that the Rent Commencement Date shall be delayed one (1) day for each day Tenant is delayed in completing the initial Tenant improvements to the Premises due to "Force Majeure" conditions or Landlord Delays. As used herein, "Landlord Delays" mean any delays to the substantial completion of the Initial Improvements to the Premises caused by the actions or omissions of Landlord and/or its employee's, contractors or agents.</u>*

Landlords, of course, should resist as much shifting of the timing risk from Tenant to Landlord as the market will bear since Tenant is generally in control of the timing of its construction work. Compromises between the various Rent Commencement Date definitions proposed immediately above should be considered including, but not limited to, (i) limiting the amount of days of delay attributable to "Force Majeure" conditions, and (ii) tightening up the definition of "Landlord Delays" by including a Landlord notice and cure period prior to any Landlord act or omission being deemed a Landlord delay to the extent such delay is not attributable to Landlord missing an express time deadline provided in the Lease. It should be noted, however, that during the height of the COVID-19 pandemic, in order to get Leases executed, some Landlords were forced to expressly permit delays of the Rent Commencement Date to the extent such delays were caused by pandemic-related conditions.

With respect to the impact of a Default during the Base Rent Abatement Period on the Abated Base Rent, it is arguably unfair for Landlord to terminate Tenant's right to all Abated Base Rent in the event Tenant cures its Default and the Lease continues. If Tenant cures the Default, Tenant should arguably have its right to abated Base Rent reinstated from the date of the cure through the remainder of the Base Rent Abatement Period (subject, of course, to suspension again for any later periods of time Tenant is in default under the Lease again). Also, if Landlord has the right to immediately collect all Abated Base Rent upon a Default but Landlord elects *not* to terminate the Lease due to the Default, Landlord may be unjustly enriched by an immaterial Default. Tenant should argue (and Landlord should agree) that if any Tenant Default occurred but was not serious enough for Landlord to terminate the Lease over it, Landlord should not have the right to collect all of the Abated Base Rent as the Abated Base Rent was likely a material inducement for Tenant entering into the Lease. Such a Landlord right to collect all Abated Base Rent might be unjustly punitive to Tenant as Landlord may have not have suffered any damages at all from the Default or damages amounting to much less than the aggregate amount of all Abated Base Rent. Below is a proposed compromise of the Abated Base Rent provision under the Base Rent Table for consideration (with stricken and underscored words indicating the changes made to the applicable provision in Paragraph 7 below):

> **Notwithstanding anything to the contrary contained herein, as long as Tenant is not in Default, Tenant shall be entitled to an abatement of Base Rent in the amount of [AMOUNT] for each of the first [NUMBER] calendar months of the Term from the Commencement Date through the day prior to the Rent Commencement Date (the "Base Rent Abatement Period"). The total amount of Base Rent abated during the Base Rent Abatement Period shall equal $[AGGREGATE AMOUNT] (the "Abated Base Rent"). In the event Tenant Defaults at any time during the Base Rent Abatement Period, ~~all~~ Abated Base Rent shall be suspended from the date of such Default until such Default is cured and the Abated Base Rent attributable to such period shall become due and payable within five (5) days~~, and all future Base Rent that would have otherwise been abated but for such Default shall be due and payable as and when Base Rent is payable hereunder~~. In the event of a Default during the Base Rent Abatement Period resulting in Landlord terminating the Lease under Paragraph 29 hereof, all Abated Base Rent shall become immediately due and payable by Tenant to Landlord. The payment by Tenant of the Abated Base Rent in the*

event of a Default shall not limit or affect any of Landlord's other rights, pursuant to this Lease or at law or in equity as a result of a Default. In addition, if Landlord terminates the Lease due to a Default at any time during the Term, all Abated Base Rent shall be included in Landlord's damages under Paragraph 29. During the Base Rent Abatement Period, only Base Rent shall be abated, and all Additional Rent (defined below) and other costs and charges specified in the Lease shall remain as due and payable pursuant to the provisions of this Lease.

D. COMMENTS

Many Tenants try to remove the requirement to pay the first installment of Monthly Base Rent on lease execution but Landlord should resist this unless it has an exceptionally credit-worthy Tenant.

The definition of Lease Year and, specifically, whether Annual Base Rent escalates on the anniversary of the Commencement Date or the Rent Commencement Date is often a negotiated business term. If there is a substantial gap in time between the Commencement Date and the Rent Commencement Date, Tenant will want the right to pay Base Rent at the lowest rate for an entire year before Base Rent escalates. Of course, Landlord wants the opposite with Base Rent escalating on the earlier of the dates. This issue is typically resolved in favor of the Tenant (with Base Rent escalating on the Rent Commencement) and especially if the Expiration Date is tied to the Rent Commencement Date (versus the Commencement Date).

Any Base Rent schedule should be careful to show Base Rent attributable to any time period between the Commencement Date and the Rent Commencement Date, if applicable, even though the Base Rent is subject to abatement. That way, Landlord has a clear measure of damages for such period in the event the Lease is terminated due to a Tenant default.

E. TYPICAL PARAGRAPH

7. Base Rent.

(a) Base Rent. The annual net base rental for the Premises (the "Annual Base Rent") shall be payable at the rates and upon the schedule set forth below, which Annual Base Rent Tenant shall pay in equal monthly installments ("Monthly Base Rent") in advance, on the first (1st) day of each calendar month during the Term commencing on the Commencement Date, without any set-off, offset, abatement or deduction whatsoever (except to the extent otherwise expressly provided herein). Notwithstanding the foregoing, the first month's Monthly Base Rent payment shall be due upon Tenant's execution of this Lease. As used herein, "Rent Commencement Date" shall mean the date which is the earlier of (i) [NUMBER] days from the Commencement Date, or (ii) the date Tenant first occupies the Premises for the operation of its business therein.

Time Period	Annual Base Rent Rate Per SF of Premises	Square Footage of the Premises	Annual Base Rent	Monthly Base Rent
Commencement Date until Rent Commencement Date*				
Lease Year 1**				
Lease Year 2				
Lease Year 3				
Lease Year 4				
Lease Year 5				

*Notwithstanding anything to the contrary contained herein, as long as Tenant is not in Default, Tenant shall be entitled to an abatement of Base Rent in the amount of [AMOUNT] for each of the first [NUMBER] calendar months of the Term from the Commencement Date through the day prior to the Rent Commencement Date (the "Base Rent Abatement Period"). The total amount of Base Rent abated during the Base Rent Abatement Period shall equal $[AGGREGATE AMOUNT] (the "Abated Base Rent"). In the event Tenant Defaults at any time during the Base Rent Abatement Period, all Abated Base Rent shall become due and payable within five (5) days, and all future Base Rent that would have otherwise been abated but for such Default shall be due and payable as and when Base Rent is payable hereunder. The payment by Tenant of the Abated Base Rent in the event of a Default shall not limit or affect any of Landlord's other rights, pursuant to this Lease or at law or in equity as a result of a Default. In addition, if Landlord terminates the Lease due to a Default at any time during the Term, all Abated Base Rent shall be included in Landlord's damages under Paragraph 29. During the Base Rent Abatement Period, only Base Rent shall be abated, and all Additional Rent (defined below) and other costs and charges specified in the Lease shall remain as due and payable pursuant to the provisions of this Lease.

**"Lease Year" shall mean, with respect to the first Lease Year, the time period commencing on the [Rent] Commencement Date and ending on the day immediately preceding the first anniversary thereof (provided that if the [Rent] Commencement Date does not occur on the first day of a calendar month, the first Lease Year shall include the balance of the calendar month in which the first anniversary of the [Rent] Commencement Date occurs), and each subsequent Lease Year shall mean the ensuing twelve (12) month period during the Term, with the last Lease Year ending on the last day of the Term.

(b) Partial Months. If the Rent Commencement Date occurs on a day which is not the first day of a calendar month, or if the Expiration Date occurs on a day which is not the last day of a calendar month, then the Monthly Base Rent payable under this Lease for such month shall be appropriately adjusted so that Tenant pays Base Rent only for the portion of such calendar month occurring on or after the Rent Commencement Date and within the Term.

(c) Additional Rent. Any sums payable by Tenant under this Lease other than Base Rent shall be deemed "Additional Rent" under this Lease, and shall, except as otherwise provided in this Lease, be paid to Landlord within ten (10) days after Landlord gives notice or demand for payment therefor. Landlord shall have the same rights and remedies for Tenant's breach of its Additional Rent obligations as for a breach of Tenant's Base Rent obligations. As used herein, "Rent" shall mean Base Rent, all Additional Rent and any other sums payable by Tenant hereunder.

(d) Rent Payments. All Rent payments due hereunder shall initially be payable and deliverable as follows (Landlord reserving, however, the right to modify Rent payment instructions): [INSERT INSTRUCTIONS]. ______________________________.

PARAGRAPH 8 (ALTERNATIVE 1)

Operating Expenses and Real Estate Taxes (the Base-Year Model)

RISK RATING: 4

BACKGROUND ON LEASE STRUCTURES AND THE APPLICABILITY OF PARAGRAPH 8

Some leases are "gross leases" wherein all of the costs and expenses incurred by Landlord in operating the Property are included within the Base Rent payable by Tenant. Such leases are less common and gross lease forms are usually used only for short term leases as Landlords do not wish to take the risk of operational costs of the Property rising above the projected amount built into the Base Rent of gross leases. *No Paragraph 8 will be included in such gross leases.*

Tenant's responsibility for the payment of Operating Expenses and Real Estate Taxes are typically structured in one of three (3) Alternative ways as follows:

Alternative 1 (herein, for convenience, called the "Base-Year Model") is sometimes referred to as a "modified gross lease" because the Base Rent for an initial period of time negotiated by the parties (the "Base Year") includes all of the costs and expenses of Landlord operating the Property for that year. Following the Base Year, a Tenant then pays Base Rent plus Tenant's proportionate share of increases in Landlord's operational costs for the Property above those operational costs incurred by Landlord in the Base Year.

Alternative 2 (herein, for convenience, called the "Direct Pass-Through Model") is similar to Alternative 1 except that Tenant is required to pay Base Rent and Tenant's proportionate share of Landlord's operational costs for the Property attributable to the Term directly as a "pass-through" expense and not subject to a Base Year. This type of Lease is sometimes referred to as a "net lease" to reflect that Tenant is paying for Base Rent and operational expenses but it can be argued that the Direct Pass-Through Model in a multi-tenanted office, retail or even industrial Building is not a classic "net lease" because Landlord is still responsible for operating the Building and many operational costs remain with Landlord and are not passed through to Tenant (including capital repair or improvement costs and casualty restoration, etc., as further explored below).

Alternative 3 (herein, for convenience, called the "Triple Net Model") differs from the Base-Year Model and the Direct Pass-Through Model because, generally, in the Triple Net Model, Tenant pays Base Rent to Landlord but then often Tenant (versus Landlord) is the party responsible for operating the Property and often pays all (or substantially all) of the operational costs for the Property not to Landlord but to the governmental authorities (with respect to Real Estate Taxes) and to the contractors and vendors who help Tenant operate the Property (such as landscapers, cleaning contractors, refuse and snow removal contractors, repair and maintenance personnel, and insurance companies, etc.). Alternative 3 is typically only used in an office Lease (or a retail Lease) when the Tenant is leasing all of the available rentable space in a Building and will be the sole tenant thereof for an extended period of time. An office lease for a Tenant's national "headquarters" location or a retail lease for a stand-alone retail establishment may use the Triple Net Model. However, Alternative 3 is much more often used for industrial leases and, for that reason, a discussion of net leases can be found in Part 3, Paragraph 1 and a discussion of the Triple Net Model with respect to Operating Expenses and Real Estate Taxes can be found in Part 3, Paragraph 3. The provisions of those Paragraphs are not being repeated here for the rare net office or retail leases that might follow such a model for efficiency and sustainability considerations only.

A. DESCRIPTION AND SCOPE (THE BASE-YEAR MODEL)

This Paragraph requires Tenant to make monthly payments for Operating Expenses and Real Estate Taxes equal to 1/12th of Landlord's reasonable estimate of increases in Operating Expenses and Real Estate Taxes for the current year over the Base Year. This Paragraph (i) establishes the Lease as a "Base Year" lease; (ii) sets forth Tenant's Pro Rata Share of any increases in Real Estate Taxes and Operating Expenses over the Real Estate Taxes and Operating Expenses for the Base Year; (iii) bifurcates which items are included and excluded from Real Estate Taxes and Operating Expenses; (iv) requires Tenant to pay monthly Additional Rent equal to 1/12th of Landlord's reasonable estimate of any increases in Operating Expenses and Real Estate Taxes for the current year in excess of the Base Year; (v) provides for a reconciliation mechanism following the end of each Comparison Year after the Base Year whereby Landlord reconciles the amounts paid by Tenant against the actual costs incurred by Landlord and Tenant receives a credit toward future Additional Rent for any excess (or in the event that the Term has expired, receives a refund of any such excess payment), or Tenant makes a payment to Landlord for any deficiency in Tenant's payments of Additional Rent; and (vi) provides Tenant with the right to verify and, if necessary, dispute Landlord's reconciliation statement of Real Estate Taxes and Operating Expenses for up to ninety (90) days following Tenant's receipt of same, with any unresolved dispute being subject to resolution by an independent accounting firm.

Additional Rent is calculated by multiplying Tenant's Pro Rata Share by any increases in Operating Expenses and Real Estate Taxes over the Operating Expenses and Real Estate Taxes for the applicable Base Year.

This Paragraph provides that certain Operating Expenses that vary with occupancy are subject to being "grossed up" to reflect the Building being at least 95% leased and occupied (even if the Building is not actually 95% leased, this assumption is used). Because the "grossing up" of Operating Expenses is a complex topic, it is separately and more substantively explored in Paragraph 9.

B. ANALYSIS (THE BASE-YEAR MODEL)

1. Landlord's Perspective

Generally, this Paragraph protects Landlord from having to absorb any increases attributable to the Premises in the costs of Real Estate Taxes and any increases in Operating Expenses following the Base Year because increases are passed through to Tenant based on Tenant's Pro Rata Share.

Landlord will typically want to designate the Base Year as the year in which the Lease is executed since that is the year for which Landlord should have the most reliable and recent information in order to estimate the Real Estate Taxes and Operating Expenses. Annual Base Rent for the Premises for the Base Year presumably includes Landlord's estimate of Real Estate Taxes and Operating Expenses payable during the Base Year.

With respect to calculating Tenant's Pro Rata Share, Landlord may require that the denominator of the ratio be the "leased" area of the Building rather than the "rentable" area of the Building. Tenant should object to this manner of calculating Tenant's Pro Rata Share because such a change shifts the fixed costs of vacant space in the Building such as Real Estate Taxes from Landlord to the tenants of the Building. Landlord may also require that in mixed-use buildings, the denominator exclude the retail portion of the Building. This is because certain Operating Expenses that are solely applicable to office uses may warrant exclusion of the retail portion in calculating Tenant's Pro Rata Share, but, in such event, Tenant should be cautious and revise the Lease, as needed, to provide that (i) any such exclusion of the retail portion of the Building in the denominator not apply to the calculation of Tenant's Pro Rata Share of Real Estate Taxes, and (ii) the definition of Operating Expenses expresses exclude operational costs associated with the retail portions of the Building. Landlord will want to make sure that Tenant's Pro Rata Share can be recalculated in the event that Tenant exercises any applicable options to lease additional space in the Building.

2. Tenant's Perspective

For Tenant to comfortably agree to the Base-Year Model (and the Direct Pass-Through Model), Tenant should request and review the last three (3) years of Landlord's Operating Expenses and Real Estate Taxes for the Property to understand what Additional Rent it can expect to pay Landlord over the Term above the Base Rent.

Like nearly all Paragraphs of the Lease, Tenant should expect that any Operating Expense and Real Estate Paragraph of the first draft lease prepared by Landlord will lean toward being Landlord-favorable in differing degrees depending upon the style of the Landlord. Some Landlords like to lead the Lease negotiations with a Landlord-aggressive form and some Landlords prefer a more balanced approach to minimize negotiation. Paragraph 8 below is arguably somewhere in the middle and offers some opportunities to explore, in the Compromises and Alternatives section below, the kind of protections Tenant should seek in any Operating Expense and Real Estate Tax section of a Lease.

3. Lender's Perspective

Lender's primary concern is that Tenant be obligated to pay its share of increases in Operating Expenses and Real Estate Taxes so that cash flow designated for debt service will not be burdened with any lack of payment of increases in Operating Expenses and Real Estate Taxes, and that any dispute between Landlord and Tenant relating to that obligation (i) can be resolved quickly, and (ii) will not in any case result in Tenant having the right to withhold payments of Additional Rent.

Lender wants to be able to determine a net effective rent during the term of its loan so that it can calculate the net cash flow available for debt service. Lender may also object to any rights of offset for any overpayments of Additional Rent. Rather such overpayment should be credited against the next due installment of Additional Rent.

4. Broker's Perspective

The Brokers can expect that Landlord and Tenant's counsel will largely be responsible for negotiating this Paragraph but, in the event that Operating Expenses include any Property management fees, Tenant Broker should expect that Tenant will inquire from Tenant Broker what the market rate is on Property management fees in the geographical area of the Building. In anticipation of being asked, Landlord Broker should stay updated on the current Property management fees being charged at the Building.

That said, Broker's role on this topic is critical prior to the Lease Paragraph being drafted. Both the Landlord Broker and the Tenant Broker will have negotiated the general outlines of the Operating Expenses and Real Estate Taxes provisions of the Lease (including, any "gross up" of Operating Expenses (discussed later) and any Tenant audit rights) in the LOI. When negotiating the LOI, Tenant Broker should always request from Landlord Broker (i) a history of Operating Expenses and Real Estate Taxes for the Building for at minimum the immediately preceding two (2) full calendar years, (ii) the estimated amounts being charged to Building occupants during the current year, and (iii) any projections that have been established for subsequent years. While Operating Expenses are typically not a matter of public record, Real Estate

Taxes are and Tenant Broker should verify that the information provided by Landlord is consistent with the published values and methods of Real Estate Taxes calculation. Landlord Broker should know and Tenant Broker should inquire as to whether there are any existing or anticipated abatements of Real Estate Taxes in effect for the Building, and, if so, the terms and conditions of such abatement programs to determine how they may impact Tenant's liability under the Lease for Real Estate Taxes.

C. COMPROMISES AND ALTERNATIVES (THE BASE-YEAR MODEL)

Landlord Compromises and Alternatives:

Landlord's form Lease should contain all protections needed for Landlord. Note that in Subparagraph 8(a)(v)(11) a new capital expense not traditionally passed through to Tenant previously has emerged in response to the COVID-19 pandemic. It is defined as "Safety Improvements" and it is meant to capture the capital improvements Landlords may make in response to COVID-19 or future pandemics in order to make their Buildings healthier and safer for their tenants. As an example, some Landlords are installing air filtration systems within their Buildings in response to the COVID-19 pandemic. Whether this new express capital expense inclusion will become widely accepted has yet to be determined.

Landlord can expect that most of the negotiation of Paragraph 8 shall be centered around Landlord responding to any Tenant requested changes to the Paragraph. That said, here are a few issues that Landlord will want to be careful to protect against:

(i) With respect to Tenant's right to audit Landlord's books and records relating to Operating Expenses and Real Estate Taxes, as a result of Tenants' increased use of auditors specializing solely in these types of audits who are compensated on a contingent fee based on a percentage of any refund due Tenant or reduction in Additional Rent that results from such audit, many Landlords prohibit Tenant's use of such contingent fee auditors.

(ii) Tenant will often want to limit the time period within which Landlord may charge Real Estate Taxes or Operating Expenses from the time they were first incurred by Landlord to one (1) year after they were first incurred by Landlord. Landlord should resist this or extend it to several years in the event of the discovery of an accounting error later.

In addition, on occasion, in order for Landlord to attract a Tenant to the Building, Landlord may agree to a "cap" on annual increases in Operating Expenses or, more often, to "cap" annual increases on just those Operating Expenses that are deemed to be Controllable Operating Expenses. Of course, in such case, Landlord wants to define Controllable Operating Expenses as narrowly as possible. Here is a sample paragraph capturing the concept in a Landlord-friendly manner:

Notwithstanding anything to the contrary contained in this Paragraph 8, it is agreed that Tenant's Pro Share of "Controllable Operating Expenses" (as hereinafter defined) for each Comparison Year shall not increase, in the aggregate on a compounding cumulative basis, by more than [five percent (5%)] over Tenant's Pro Rata Share of Controllable Operating Expenses over the Base Year (for the first Comparison Year) and, thereafter, over the immediately preceding Comparison Year(s), as applicable. As used herein, the term "Controllable Operating Expenses" shall mean Operating Expenses over which Landlord has direct control and which are not (i) determined by a third party, or (ii) subject to collective bargaining requirements or union contracts. The term "Controllable Operating Expenses" shall exclude, without limitation, utilities, permits and licenses, repairs and replacements, mandated minimum wages and personnel tax rates or assessments, security, insurance and snow and ice removal and costs.

Tenant Compromises and Alternatives:

Depending upon Tenant leverage, Tenant will typically highly negotiate the Operating Expense and Real Estate Taxes provision of any Lease. Tenant will begin by focusing on what Landlord expenses should be ***expressly included*** and ***expressly excluded*** from the definitions of Operating Expenses and Real Estate Taxes but a Tenant should also carefully review and modify the operational aspects of Landlord charging Tenant for Operating Expenses and Real Estate Taxes and Tenant's audit and dispute rights with respect thereto.

The following is a summary of compromises and alternative language that Tenant may wish to consider and request in response to a first draft of a Lease prepared by Landlord, and Tenant reasonably has the leverage to request them given the particular deal and market constraints:

(i) Exclusions from Operating Expenses: To the extent not already excluded from the definition of Operating Expenses, Tenant may wish to add the following express exclusions from Operating Expenses: Landlord's debt service (principal and interest) of any kind; any insurance expenses other than insurance premiums (including insurance deductibles); any environmental compliance or remediation or legal compliance costs of any kind; any operating or maintenance costs allocable to non-office portions of the Property (including, without limitation, any residential and/or retail portions thereof); any costs, fees or expenses not expressly referred to in the Lease, or any costs required to be paid by Landlord alone hereunder, or otherwise provided to be paid by parties other than Tenant; wages, salaries, fees and fringe benefits paid to administrative or executive personnel or officers or partners of Landlord who are not directly involved in the daily management and operations of the Property; all costs, fees and disbursements relating to activities for the solicitation and execution of leases for space in the Property or other marketing of the Property (including, without limitation, legal fees and brokerage costs); the cost of correcting defects in the construction of the Property or in the building equipment and mechanical systems thereof (other than conditions which result from ordinary wear and tear); the cost of any repair made by Landlord because of the total or partial destruction of the Property or the condemnation of a portion of the Property; the cost of any items for which Landlord is reimbursed by insurance or other parties; **the cost of any additions or capital improvements to the Property and the cost of any repairs, alterations, additions,**

replacements, and other items which under generally accepted accounting principles are properly classified as capital expenditures and any capital expenditures, other than those capital items expressly referenced in [subparagraph [X]] above; the cost of any work or service performed for, or facilities furnished to, any tenant of the Property to a greater extent or in a manner more favorable to such tenant than the work or services regularly performed for or generally furnished to other tenants of the Property; the cost of alterations to, or the decorating or redecorating of space in the Property leased to other tenants; the cost of overtime or other expense to Landlord in curing its defaults under the Lease or performing work expressly provided in the Lease to be borne at Landlord's sole expense; the cost of any electric current or HVAC costs furnished to rentable areas in the Property not comprising Common Areas; any costs representing an amount paid to a corporation, entity or person related to Landlord which is in excess of the amount which would be paid in the absence of such relationship; any late charges, interest, fines or penalties due to Landlord's failure to fulfill its obligations; any costs incurred by Landlord due to the violation by Landlord of any terms and conditions of any leases or mortgages affecting the Property; any costs of selling, syndicating, financing, mortgaging or transferring any of Landlord's interest(s) in the Property; any costs of Landlord's general corporate overhead and general administrative expenses to the extent not directly attributable to the management, operation, maintenance or repair of the Property; any costs or expenses for sculpture, paintings or other works of art; any bad debt loss or rent loss; **any reserves of any kind; Property management fees in excess of [PERCENT] of [Operating Expenses or Base Rent for the Building, as may be applicable] for the applicable Base Year or Comparison Year**, and any costs or expenses not considered building operating expenses under generally accepted accounting principles.

All of the exclusions above are important but three (3) are **bolded** to underscore their particular importance as herein further described. **Capital Items**: Any and all costs attributable to capital expenditures and capital improvements should be excluded from Operating Expenses except for the few that are traditionally acceptable (in Paragraph 8 they can be found in Subparagraph 8(a)(v)(11)) and even those should only be included on an amortized basis. Note that the Safety Improvements included in those expressly included capital items, is new in response to the COVID-19 pandemic and is meant to capture and even encourage Landlords to install new technology to make Buildings safer for all tenants. Whether this capital expense becomes widely accepted is not yet determined. **Property Management Fees:** Operating Expenses often contain the salary and benefits or a Property Manager so additional Property management fees should only be included to the extent the Property is managed by a third-party manager and even those fees should be capped at marked rates. **Reserves**: Reserves should never be included as an Operating Expense as reserves are not an operating expense at all but a cash pool Landlord is collecting for future needs.

(ii) <u>Real Estate Taxes</u>: The definition of Real Estate Taxes should exclude any fines, interest or penalties arising due to Landlord's late payment or nonpayment of same as well as all franchise, income, profit, sales, conveyance, death, inheritance, succession, transfer or other non-real estate taxes, as well as any Real Estate Taxes not fairly allocable to any relevant base period and/or the Term. In the event Landlord receives any refunds or abatements of Real Estate Taxes during any periods for which Tenant has made Additional Rent payments therefor, Landlord should promptly so notify Tenant and Tenant should promptly receive Tenant's Pro Rata Share of such refunds or abatements in the form of reimbursement(s) or Additional Rent credit(s). If Tenant is the only tenant of the Property or even a very significant tenant of Property, Tenant may wish to have the right, by appropriate proceedings conducted diligently and in good faith, to contest the amount(s) or validity of any Real Estate Taxes, and Landlord should agree to reasonably cooperate with Tenant in such proceedings.

(iii) Operating Expense and Tax Statements. Any statements delivered to Tenant containing estimated or actual representations of Operating Expenses or Real Estate Taxes (or calculations thereof), should contain reasonably itemized breakdowns thereof so Tenant can appropriately evaluate them and determine if an audit is necessary. Any such statements containing estimates should be based on reasonable, good faith projections of the immediately preceding year's operating budget. Landlord should commit to a "no later date" for delivering to Tenant an annual Operating Expense and Tax reconciliation statement.

(iv) Audit Rights; Expenses. Tenant should obligate Landlord to make available, upon two (2) business days' notice, its statements, books and records relating to Operating Expenses and Real Estate Taxes for audit, inspection and copying by Tenant and/or Tenant's accountant. Landlord should be obligated to maintain its statements, books and records at the Property or within a reasonable distance therefrom. To the extent that the audit indicates an overstatement of actual Real Estate Taxes or Operating Expenses in excess of 5%, Landlord should be liable for the cost of Tenant's audit as well as any dispute resolution required.

(v) Dispute Resolution. Tenant should have a reasonable time to dispute any annual Operating Expense and Real Estate Taxes reconciliation statement provided by Landlord. In the event Tenant disputes any of Landlord's Additional Rent charges under the Lease, the parties should have thirty (30) days following Tenant's notice of such dispute to resolve same by written agreement, failing which, Tenant should have the right to refer such dispute to a reputable, independent, certified public accountant for prompt determination. Said determination should be issued in written form and should be final and binding on the parties. Tenant should pay the costs of said accountant, unless Landlord is proven to have overcharged Tenant, in which case Landlord should pay for said costs.

(vi) Refunds of Excess Payments. Landlords typically agree to credit Tenant against the next Rent coming due for any excess Operating Expenses or Real Estate Taxes paid by Tenant, but Landlord should also have the obligation to reimburse Tenant for such excess if no future Rent is due.

(vii) No Prejudice. Any payment for Operating Expenses or Real Estate Taxes made by Tenant pending any dispute(s) should be without prejudice to Tenant's position.

(vii) Gross-Up Clause: If not already included in the Lease, Tenant should negotiate that any "gross up" of Operating Expenses include the Base Year. If Real Estate Taxes are assessed in a manner that incorporates the rental stream of the Building, Tenant may also wish to have Real Estate Taxes "grossed up" for the Base Year if the Building had significant vacancy during the Base Year.

(viii) Limitation on Time Period to Charge Tenant: Leases often include provisions indicating that Landlord will "endeavor" to provide Tenant with statements for Operating Expenses and Real Estate Taxes within a reasonable time following the expiration of a Comparison year but then go on to say that any failure of Landlord to invoice Tenant by such date will not extinguish Tenant's liability to pay invoices delivered beyond the time period specified. Any such Landlord right to invoice Tenant late should be restricted to a reasonable time period or Tenant runs the risk of a disorganized Landlord forgetting or failing to invoice Tenant for several years and then delivering Tenant with several years' worth of Operating Expenses or Real Estate Taxes that need to be paid within the short time period permitted for the payment of Additional Rent. This should be avoided by limiting Landlord from invoicing Tenant for any Operating Expenses or Real Estate Taxes beyond one (1) or two (2) years from the expiration date of the Comparison Year in which the Operating Expense or Real Estate Tax was incurred by Landlord.

(ix) Caps of Operating Expenses or Controllable Operating Expenses: If Tenant has negotiated an annual "cap" on the increases of all Operating Expenses or on Controllable Operating Expenses, Tenant may wish to modify any provision to expand the definition of Controllable Operating Expenses to the extent possible and to otherwise modify the provision as follows (with the underscored and stricken language below being the most favorable to Tenant):

> *Notwithstanding anything to the contrary contained in this Paragraph 8, it is agreed that Tenant's Pro Share of "Controllable Operating Expenses" (as hereinafter defined) for each Comparison Year shall not increase, in the aggregate on a compounding cumulative basis, by more than [five percent (5%)] over Tenant's Pro Rata Share of Controllable Operating Expenses over the Base Year (for the first Comparison Year) and, thereafter, over the immediately preceding Comparison Year(s), as applicable. As used herein, the term "Controllable Operating Expenses" shall mean Operating Expenses over which Landlord has direct control ~~and which are not (i) determined by a third party, or (ii) subject to collective bargaining requirements or union contracts. The term "Controllable Operating Expenses" shall exclude, without limitation, utilities, permits and licenses, repairs and replacements, mandated minimum wages and personnel tax rates or assessments, security, insurance and snow and ice removal and costs~~. In the event Controllable Operating Expenses for any Comparison Year exceeds [five percent (5%)] of the Controllable Operating Expenses from the preceding Base Year or Comparison Year(s), as applicable (such amount in excess of [five percent (5%)] being referred to as the "Excess Controllable Expense Amount"), such Excess Controllable Expense Amount shall be included in the next succeeding Comparative Expense Year(s) to the extent to which the Controllable Operating Expenses increases are less than five percent (5%) over the preceding Comparative Expense Year(s).*

D. COMMENTS (THE BASE-YEAR MODEL)

The method of calculating and determining Real Estate Taxes and Operating Expenses is likely to be one of the most negotiated provisions of the Lease. A clear understanding of the ramifications of any changes is imperative.

Subparagraph 8(d) allows for the "grossing up" of certain Operating Expenses. Because the "grossing up" of Operating Expenses is a complex topic, it is separately and more substantively explored in Paragraph 9 even though most leases will imbed the concept within the Operating Expense and Real Estate Taxes section of the Lease like Paragraph 8 below.

If the Property is part of a multi-building development ("Complex"), those Operating Expenses and Real Estate Taxes attributable to such Complex as a whole (and not attributable solely to any individual building therein) should be allocated to the Property/Building and to the other buildings within the Complex development on an equitable basis which is typically on a proportionate basis calculated by the rentable square feet of the Building being divided by the rentable square feet of all of the buildings within the Complex. Subparagraph 8(f) below is [bracketed] as optional to address this issue.

E. TYPICAL PARAGRAPH

8. Additional Rent (Base-Year Model).

(a) Definitions:

(i) "Base Year" with respect to Operating Expenses shall mean the calendar year [CALENDAR YEAR), and "Base Year" with respect to Real Estate Taxes shall mean the [tax fiscal year [or calendar year] [APPLICABLE YEAR].

(ii) "Operating Expense Base" shall mean the Operating Expenses incurred during the Base Year for Operating Expenses.

(iii) "Tax Base" shall mean Real Estate Taxes incurred during the Base Year for Real Estate Taxes.

(iv) "Tenant's Pro Rata Share" shall be determined and adjusted by Landlord from time to time, and is expressed as a percentage, by dividing the rentable area of the Premises by the then rentable area of the Building and multiplying the resulting quotient, by one hundred (100). Tenant's Pro Rate Share, as of the Commencement Date shall be [PERCENTAGE%].

(v) "Operating Expenses" shall mean all operating expenses of any kind or nature which are necessary, ordinary or customarily incurred in connection with the operation, maintenance, ownership or repair of the Property as determined by Landlord.

Operating Expenses shall include, but not be limited to:

(1) costs of supplies, including, but not limited to, the cost of relamping all Building standard lighting outside of leased areas in the Building as the same may be required from time to time;

(2) costs incurred in connection with obtaining and providing all utilities to the Property, including but not limited to, energy for the Property, including, but not limited to, costs of propane, butane, natural gas, steam, electricity, solar energy and fuel oils, coal or any other energy sources, including any taxes thereon;
(3) costs of water and sanitary and storm drainage services;
(4) costs of janitorial, sanitation and security services;
(5) costs of general maintenance and repairs, including costs incurred under HVAC, the intrabuilding network cable and other mechanical maintenance contracts and maintenance, repairs and replacement of equipment and tools used in connection with operating the Property and the parking facilities;
(6) costs of maintenance and replacement of landscaping;
(7) insurance premiums, including fire and special causes of loss coverage, together with loss of rent endorsements, the part of any claim required to be paid under the deductible portion of any insurance policies carried by Landlord in connection with the Property, commercial general liability insurance and any other insurance carried by Landlord on the Property, or any component parts thereof (all such insurance shall be in such amounts as may be required by any holder of a Mortgage or as Landlord may reasonably determine);
(8) labor costs, including wages and other payments, costs to Landlord of worker's compensation and disability insurance, payroll taxes, employment taxes, general welfare benefits, pension payments, medical and surgical benefits, fringe benefits of employees up to the level of Property manager, and all legal fees and other costs or expenses incurred in resolving any labor dispute;
(9) professional building management fees required for management of the Property;
(10) legal, accounting, inspection, and other consultation fees (including, without limitation, fees charged by consultants retained by Landlord for services that are designed to produce a reduction in Operating Expenses or to reasonably improve the operation, maintenance or state of repair of the Property) incurred in the ordinary course of operating the Property or in connection with making the computations required hereunder or in any audit of operations of the Property;
(11) the costs of capital improvements and structural repairs and replacements made in or to the Property (i) in order to conform to changes, subsequent to the date of this Lease, in any applicable Laws, ordinances, rules, regulations or orders of any governmental or quasi-governmental authority having jurisdiction over the Property (herein "<u>Required Capital Improvements</u>"),

(ii) to install a new or replacement capital item for the purpose of reducing Operating Expenses (herein "Cost Savings Improvements"), (iii) in the ordinary, prudent operation and maintenance of the Property (herein "Replacement Improvements"), and (iv) for the purpose of reducing any risk to the health or safety of the occupants of the Property, provided that the capital improvement involved is recommended by a governmental authority or recognized industry group as a means of reducing a specified health or safety risk (herein "Safety Improvements"). The expenditures for Required Capital Improvements, Cost Savings Improvements, Replacement Improvements, and Safety Improvements) shall be amortized over the useful life of such capital improvement or structural repair or replacement (as determined by Landlord) and only included in Operating Expenses to the extent amortized in any year plus interest. All costs so amortized shall bear interest on the amortized balance at the rate of twelve percent (12%) per annum or such higher rate as may have been paid by Landlord on funds borrowed for the purpose of accomplishing these capital improvements.

In making any computations contemplated hereby, Landlord shall also be permitted to make such adjustments and modifications to the provisions of this Subparagraph 8(a)(v) and Subparagraph 8(b) as shall be reasonable and necessary to achieve the intention of the parties hereto.

Excluded from Operating Expenses shall be the following: (a) interest on and amortization of debts; (b) brokerage commissions (whether for sale, leasing or financing), and advertising expenses for procuring new tenants of the Property; (c) financing and refinancing costs; (d) Real Estate Taxes; (e) leasehold improvements made exclusively for one or more particular tenant(s) of the Property (which do not benefit or are not made available to the Tenant); (f) the cost of any item included in Operating Expenses Subparagraph 8(a)(v) to the extent that such cost is reimbursed by a warranty, guaranty, service contract, an insurance company, a condemnor, or a tenant (except as a reimbursement of Operating Expenses) or any other party, but if at the time Operating Expenses are determined for a particular year such reimbursement has not been made, such expenses may be included in Operating Expenses and an adjustment shall be made when and if such reimbursement is actually received; (g) ground rent, or any other rent payments under any superior lease of the Property; (h) expenses incurred in the sale, transfer, or other disposition of any of the Property, or any interest therein; (i) legal fees and court costs relating to acquisition, financing, refinancing and sale of the Property, or any interest therein, or related to disputes with other tenants or other occupants of the Property, or associated with the preparation, negotiation or enforcement of any leases; (j) administrative salaries, benefits and other compensation of Landlord's or its agents' employees above the grade of Property manager; (k) costs of additional or extra services furnished to other tenants for which Landlord is separately reimbursed; (l) depreciation and amortization of Landlord's acquisition cost of the Property; and (m) the cost of any work performed or service provided to the extent the fees charged or other compensation received would result in a duplicative recovery by the Landlord.

(vi) "Real Estate Tax" or "Real Estate Taxes" shall mean all real property taxes and assessments levied against the Property by any governmental or quasi-governmental authority. The foregoing shall include all federal, state, county, or local governmental, special district, improvement district, municipal or other political subdivision taxes, fees, levies, assessments, charges or other impositions of every kind and nature, whether general, special, ordinary or extraordinary, respecting the Property, including without limitation, real estate taxes, general and special assessments, interest on any special assessments paid in installments, transit taxes, water and sewer rents, taxes based upon the receipt of rent, personal property taxes imposed upon the fixtures, machinery, equipment, apparatus, appurtenances, furniture and other personal property used in connection with the Property which Landlord shall pay during any calendar year, any portion of which occurs during the Term (without regard to any different fiscal year used by such government or municipal authority except as provided below). Provided, however, any taxes which shall be levied on the rentals of the Property shall be determined as if the Property were Landlord's only property, and provided further that in no event shall the term "taxes or assessment," as used herein, include any net federal or state income taxes levied or assessed on Landlord, unless such taxes are a specific substitute for real property taxes. Such term shall, however, include gross taxes on rentals. Expenses incurred by Landlord for tax consultants and in contesting the amount or validity of any such taxes or assessments shall be included in such computations.

Real Estate Taxes shall also include all "assessments," including so-called special assessments, license tax, business license fee, business license tax, levy, charge, penalty or tax imposed by any authority having the direct power to tax, including any city, county, state or federal government, or any school, agricultural, lighting, water, drainage, or other improvement or special district thereof, against the Premises of the Property or any legal or equitable interest of

Landlord therein. For the purposes of this Lease, any special assessments shall be deemed payable in such number of installments as is permitted by law, whether or not actually so paid and only included in any year to the extent of such minimum installment due. If as of the Commencement Date the Building or Property has not been fully assessed as a completed project, for the purpose of computing the Real Estate Taxes for any adjustment required herein or under Paragraph 8, the Real Estate Taxes shall be adjusted by Landlord, as of the date on which the adjustment is to be made, to reflect full completion of the Building and other improvements to the Premises including all standard Tenant finish work. If the method of taxation of real estate prevailing at the time of execution hereof shall be, or has been altered, so as to cause the whole or any part of the taxes now, hereafter or theretofore levied, assessed or imposed on real estate to be levied, assessed or imposed on Landlord, wholly or partially, as a capital levy or otherwise, or on or measured by the rents received therefrom, then such new or altered taxes attributable to the Property shall be included within the term real estate taxes, except that the same shall not include any enhancement of said tax attributable to other income of Landlord. If there shall be any retroactive assessments or retroactive changes to original assessments, then Tenant shall be responsible for any increase and to any credit in the Base Year in Real Estate Taxes resulting therefrom, provided that any such assessment and resulting increase in Real Estate Taxes relates to a period occurring within the Term of this Lease or during the Base Year.

(b) Payment of Real Estate Taxes and Operating Expenses. Commencing upon the expiration of the applicable Base Year and for each year, or portion thereof, thereafter during the Term (each a "Comparison Year"), Tenant shall pay Landlord (i) an amount equal to Tenant's Pro Rata Share of increases in Operating Expenses over the Operating Expenses Base and (ii) an amount equal to Tenant's Pro Rata Share of increases in Real Estate Taxes over the Tax Base (the "Escalation Increases"). Landlord shall have the right to change the Comparison Year from a calendar year to a fiscal year from time to time (or vice versa), provided that equitable adjustment is made so that Tenant shall not be charged more than once for the same period. Commencing with the first (1st) month of the first (1st) Comparison Year and on the first (1st) day of each month thereafter during the original Term or any extension thereof, Tenant shall pay Escalation Increases to Landlord, as Additional Rent due concurrently with Monthly Base Rent, in installments equal to one-twelfth (1/12) of Landlord's estimate (as determined by Landlord in its sole discretion) of any projected Escalation Increases for the particular Comparison Year (the "Estimated Escalation Increases"). A final adjustment

("Escalation Reconciliation") shall be made by Landlord and Tenant as soon as practicable following the end of each Comparison Year as further provided in the following Subparagraph (c). In computing the Estimated Escalation Increases for any particular Comparison Year, Landlord shall take into account any prior increases in Tenant's Pro Rata Share of Real Estate Taxes and Operating Expenses, respectively. If any Estimated Escalation Increases are less than the Estimated Escalation Increases for the immediately preceding Comparison Year, the payments to be paid by Tenant for the new Comparison Year attributable to said Estimated Escalation Increases shall be decreased accordingly; provided, however, in no event will the Rent paid by Tenant hereunder ever be less than the Monthly Base Rent.

(c) Escalation Reconciliation. As soon as practicable following the end of each Comparison Year, with good faith efforts to provide such statement within one hundred twenty (120) days after the last day of such Comparison Year, Landlord shall submit to Tenant a statement setting forth the actual Escalation Increases for the Comparison Year which was just completed and the Estimated Escalation Increases for the current Comparison Year (the "Escalation Statement"). To the extent that the actual Escalation Increases exceed the Estimated Escalation Increases paid by Tenant for the Comparison Year just completed, Tenant shall pay Landlord the difference, in cash within thirty (30) days following receipt by Tenant from Landlord of the Escalation Statement. If the actual Escalation Increases for the Comparison Year just completed is less than the Estimated Escalation Increases paid by Tenant for such year, then Tenant shall receive a credit on future Rent owing under this Lease (or cash, if there is no future Rent owing hereunder). Until Tenant receives the Escalation Statement, Tenant's Estimated Escalation Increases for the new Comparison Year shall continue to be paid at the rate being paid for the particular Comparison Year just completed. Tenant shall commence payment to Landlord of the Estimated Escalation Increases for the then current Comparison Year, beginning on the first (1st) day of the month following the month in which Tenant receives the applicable Escalation Statement.

(d) Changes in Escalations During the Lease Year; Gross-up. In addition to the above, if, during any particular Comparison Year, there is a change in the information upon which the then current Estimated Escalation Increases are based, Landlord shall be permitted to revise such Estimated Escalation Increases by notifying Tenant, and such adjustment shall be made in the payment of Estimated Escalation Increases, commencing on the first (1st) day of the month following the delivery of such notice to Tenant. When the Escalation Statement for the Comparison Year in which this Lease terminates is delivered to the Tenant, Tenant shall pay to Landlord within ten (10) days after Landlord's delivery

of the same, any additional amounts due as calculated pursuant to this Paragraph 8. Landlord's and Tenant's responsibilities with respect to Escalation Increases shall survive the expiration or early termination of this Lease.

If the Building is less than ninety-five percent (95%) occupied during the Base Year or any particular Comparison Year, Landlord may adjust those Operating Expenses which are affected by Building occupancy for the Base Year or the particular Comparison Year, or portion thereof, as the case may be, to reflect an occupancy of not less than ninety-five percent (95%) of all such rentable area of the Building. In addition, if during the Base Year or any Comparison Year any utilities or services for any occupied space in the Building are directly billed to, or paid by, the occupant thereof, Landlord may adjust those components of Operating Expenses for the Base Year or the particular Comparison Year to the amount they would have been if the utilities or services in question had not been directly billed to or paid by the applicable tenant.

(e) **Disputes Over Real Estate Taxes or Operating Expenses. If Tenant disputes the amount of an Estimated Escalation Increase or an actual Escalation Increase, Tenant shall give Landlord written notice of such dispute within ninety (90) days after Landlord delivers the applicable Escalation Statement. Tenant's failure to give such notice shall waive its right to audit the amounts so determined. Tenant shall not be entitled to audit the foregoing amounts if Tenant is then in default hereunder. Said audit will be conducted at Tenant's expense by a certified public accountant paid on an hourly basis unrelated to actual savings identified. Tenant shall only be permitted to conduct such a review during regular business hours at Landlord's office or, at Landlord's option, its management office, after Tenant gives Landlord twenty (20) business days prior written notice, and no more than once in any twelve (12) month period. Any audit of the Base Year must take place simultaneously with Tenant's first audit of a Comparison Year. Any such audit shall be completed within thirty (30) days following Tenant's receipt of the necessary information or documentation from Landlord relative to the calendar year in question. If such review discloses that the charges actually incurred by Landlord are less than those used by Landlord in calculating Escalation Increases, then Landlord shall reimburse Tenant for the amount Tenant paid in excess of Tenant's actual Escalation Increases. If any such review discloses that the charges for Operating Expenses or Real Estate Taxes for the Building used by Landlord in calculating the Escalation Increases exceeds the actual charges for Operating Expenses and Real Estate Taxes for the Building (the "Actual Expenses") by five percent (5%) or more of the Actual Expenses for such Comparison Year, then Landlord shall pay the reasonable out-of-pocket costs of such review. If Tenant does not review Landlord's records within one hundred eighty (180) days after**

receipt of the Escalation Statement, Tenant shall have no further right to review Landlord's records for the applicable period. No subtenant shall have the right to conduct an audit and no assignee shall conduct an audit for any period during which such assignee was not in possession of the Premises. Tenant shall keep the existence and results of any audit confidential and shall not disclose the same to anyone other than its attorneys and accountants.

In the event Tenant elects to exercise its audit rights hereunder, Tenant shall nevertheless timely pay Landlord the amount of the prior year's Escalation Reconciliation and continue to pay Estimated Escalation Increases as set forth in the then applicable Escalation Statement until the parties have agreed as to the appropriate adjustment. Landlord's delay in submitting any Escalation Statement for any Comparison Year shall not affect the provisions of this Paragraph 8, nor constitute a waiver of Landlord's rights as set forth herein for said Comparison Year or any subsequent Comparison Year during the Term or any extension thereof.

[(f) **Building as Part of Multi-Building Development. If the Property is a part of a multi-building development (the "Complex"), those Operating Expenses and Real Estate Taxes attributable to the Complex as a whole (and not attributable solely to any individual building therein) shall be allocated to the Property and to the other buildings within such Complex on an equitable basis, with the Property being responsible for [PERCENTAGE%] of those Operating Expenses and Real Estate Taxes attributable to the Complex.]**

PARAGRAPH 8 (ALTERNATIVE 2)

Operating Expenses and Real Estate Taxes (Direct Pass-Through Model)

RISK RATING: 4

A. DESCRIPTION AND SCOPE

The primary difference between this Paragraph and Typical Paragraph 8 (Alternative 1, Base-Year Model) is that this Paragraph (Alternative 2, Direct Pass-Through Model) incorporates the concept whereby Tenant pays, as a direct pass-through, its proportionate share of all Real Estate Taxes and Operating Expenses incurred by Landlord attributable to the Term, rather than using the "Base-Year" concept whereby tenant pays only its proportionate share of any increases in Real Estate Taxes and Operating Expenses over said expenses for a Base Year.

Paragraph 8 below looks similar to language in Alternative 1 but indeed it is revised to reflect the Direct Pass-Through Model.

This Paragraph provides that certain Operating Expenses that vary with occupancy are subject to being "grossed up" to reflect the Building being at least 95% leased and occupied. Because the "grossing up" of Operating Expenses is a complex topic, it is separately and more substantively explored in Paragraph 9.

B. ANALYSIS (THE DIRECT PASS-THROUGH MODEL)

1. Landlord's Perspective

Generally, this Paragraph protects Landlord from having to absorb any of the costs of Real Estate Taxes or of the maintenance and operation of the Building and the Premises, which costs are passed through to Tenant on a prorated basis.

With respect to payments of Tenant's Pro Rata Share of Operating Expenses, Landlord may desire that any free rent period not be applicable to such Additional Rent payments and therefore may require that Tenant begin paying such installments on the Commencement Date rather than on the Rent Commencement Date.

Other than above, nearly all of the considerations added in Paragraph 8 (Alternative 1) should be reviewed as they are not being repeated here for efficiency and sustainability considerations.

2. Tenant's Perspective

Tenant's Perspective as provided in Paragraph 8 (Alternative 1) should be reviewed as nearly all concepts contained therein are applicable to Alternative 2 and are not being repeated here for efficiency and sustainability considerations.

3. Lender's Perspective

Lender's primary concern is that Tenant be obligated to pay its share of Real Estate Taxes and Operating Expenses so that cash flow designated for debt service will not be burdened by any lack of payment of Real Estate Taxes and Operating Expenses, and that any dispute between Landlord and Tenant relating to that obligation (i) can be resolved quickly, and (ii) will not in any case result in Tenant having the right to withhold payments of Additional Rent.

Lender wants to be able to determine a net effective rent during the term of its loan so that it can calculate the net cash flow available for debt service. Lender may also object to any rights of offset for any overpayments of Additional Rent. Rather such overpayment should be credited against the next due installment of Additional Rent.

4. Broker's Perspective

Broker's perspective to this Direct Pass-Through Model is consistent with Broker's perspective to the Base-Year Model discussed previously and should be reviewed accordingly.

C. COMPROMISES AND ALTERNATIVES (THE DIRECT PASS-THROUGH MODEL)

Section C of Paragraph 8 (Alternative 1) should be reviewed as nearly all concepts contained therein are applicable to Alternative 2 and are not being repeated here for efficiency and sustainability considerations.

Landlord and Tenant should negotiate this Paragraph 8 (Alternative 2) as provided in Section C of Paragraph 8 (Alternative 1) because all of the concepts are nearly identical.

D. COMMENTS (THE DIRECT PASS-THROUGH MODEL)

The method of calculating and determining Real Estate Taxes and Operating Expenses is likely to be one of the most negotiated provisions of this Lease. A clear understanding of the ramifications of any changes is imperative.

If Tenant is the sole tenant of the Property, then, arguably, Alternative 2 is the not the most advantageous for Tenant because it contemplates Landlord operating (or controlling the operation of the Property) and Tenant is subjected to whatever costs Landlord incurs. In that case, if Tenant has an interest and the necessary expertise to operate the Property, Tenant may wish to consider forcing Landlord into Alternative 3 (Triple Net Model) which allows Tenant to operate the Property and potentially control costs by bidding out contractors and vendors. In such as case, Alternative 3 should be reviewed in Part 3, Paragraph 3.

E. TYPICAL PARAGRAPH

8. Additional Rent (Direct Pass-Through Model).

(a) Definitions:

(i) "Tenant's Pro Rata Share" shall be determined and adjusted by Landlord from time to time, by dividing the rentable area of the Premises by the then rentable area of the Building and multiplying the resulting quotient, by one hundred (100). Tenant's Pro Rate Share, as of the Commencement Date shall be [AMOUNT%].

(ii) "<u>Operating Expenses</u>" shall mean all operating expenses of any kind or nature which are necessary, ordinary or customarily incurred in connection with the operation, maintenance, ownership or repair of the Property as determined by Landlord.

Operating Expenses shall include, but not be limited to:

(1) costs of supplies, including, but not limited to, the cost of relamping all Building standard lighting as the same may be required from time to time;

(2) costs incurred in connection with obtaining and providing all utilities to the Property, including but not limited to, energy for the Property, including, but not limited to, costs of propane, butane, natural gas, steam, electricity, solar energy and fuel oils, coal or any other energy sources, including any taxes thereon;

(3) costs of water and sanitary and storm drainage services;

(4) costs of janitorial, sanitation and security services;

(5) costs of general maintenance and repairs, including costs under HVAC, the intrabuilding network cable and other mechanical maintenance contracts and maintenance, repairs and replacement of equipment and tools used in connection with operating the Property and the parking facilities;

(6) costs of maintenance and replacement of landscaping;

(7) insurance premiums, including fire and all-risk coverage, together with loss of rent endorsements, the part of any claim required to be paid under the deductible portion of any insurance policies carried by Landlord in connection with the Property, commercial general liability insurance and any other insurance carried by Landlord on the Property, or any component parts thereof (all such insurance shall be in such amounts as may be required by any holder of a Mortgage or as Landlord may reasonably determine);

(8) labor costs, including wages and other payments, costs to Landlord of worker's compensation and disability insurance, payroll taxes, employment taxes, general welfare benefits, pension payments, medical and surgical benefits, fringe benefits up to the level of Property manager, and all legal fees and other costs or expenses incurred in resolving any labor dispute;

(9) professional building management fees required for management of the Property;

(10) legal, accounting, inspection, and other consultation fees (including, without limitation, fees charged by consultants retained by Landlord for services that are designed to produce a reduction in Operating Expenses or to reasonably improve the operation, maintenance or state of repair of the Property) incurred in the ordinary course of operating the Property or in connection with making the computations required hereunder or in any audit of operations of the Property;

(11) the costs of capital improvements or structural repairs or replacements made in or to the Property (i) in order to conform to changes, subsequent to the date of this Lease, in any applicable Laws, ordinances, rules, regulations or orders of any governmental or quasi-governmental authority having jurisdiction over the Property (herein "<u>Required Capital Improvements</u>"), (ii) to install a new or replacement capital item for the purpose of reducing Operating Expenses (herein "<u>Cost Savings Improvements</u>"), (iii) in the ordinary, prudent operation and maintenance of the Property (herein "<u>Replacement Improvements</u>"), and (iv) for the purpose of reducing any risk to the health or safety of the occupants of the Property, provided that the capital improvement involved is recommended by a governmental authority or recognized industry group as a means of reducing a specified health or safety risk (herein "<u>Safety Improvements</u>"). The expenditures for Required Capital Improvements, Cost Savings Improvements, Replacement Improvements and Safety Improvements) shall be amortized over the useful life of such capital improvement or structural

repair or replacement (as determined by Landlord). All costs so amortized shall bear interest on the amortized balance at the rate of twelve percent (12%) per annum or such higher rate as may have been paid by Landlord on funds borrowed for the purpose of constructing these capital improvements.

In making any computations contemplated hereby, Landlord shall also be permitted to make such adjustments and modifications to the provisions of this Subparagraph 8(a)(ii) and Subparagraph 8(b) as shall be reasonable and necessary to achieve the intention of the parties hereto.

Excluded from Operating Expenses shall be the following: (a) interest on and amortization of debts; (b) brokerage commissions (whether for sale, leasing or financing), and advertising expenses for procuring new tenants of the Property; (c) financing and refinancing costs; (d) Real Estate Taxes; (e) leasehold improvements made exclusively for one or more particular tenant(s) of the Property (which do not benefit or are not made available to the Tenant); (f) the cost of any item included in Operating Expenses Subparagraph 8(a)(ii) above to the extent that such cost is reimbursed by a warranty, guaranty, service contract, an insurance company, a condemnor, or a tenant (except as a reimbursement of Operating Expenses) or any other party, but if at the time Operating Expenses are determined for a particular year such reimbursement has not been made, such expenses may be included in Operating Expenses and an adjustment shall be made when and if such reimbursement is actually received; (g) ground rent, or any other rent payments under any superior lease of the Property; (h) expenses incurred in the sale, transfer, or other disposition of any of the Property, or any interest therein; (i) legal fees and court costs relating to acquisition, financing, refinancing and sale of the Property, or any interest therein, or related to disputes with other tenants or other occupants of the Property, or associated with the preparation, negotiation or enforcement of any leases; (j) administrative salaries, benefits and other compensation of Landlord's or its agents' employees above the grade of Property manager; (k) costs of additional or extra services furnished to other tenants for which Landlord is separately reimbursed; (l) depreciation and amortization of Landlord's acquisition cost of the Property; and (m) the cost of any work performed or service provided to the extent the fees charged or other compensation received would result in a duplicative recovery by the Landlord.

(iii) "Real Estate Tax" or "Real Estate Taxes" shall mean all real property taxes and assessments levied against the Property by any governmental or quasi-governmental authority. The foregoing shall include all federal,

state, county, or local governmental, special district, improvement district, municipal or other political subdivision taxes, fees, levies, assessments, charges or other impositions of every kind and nature, whether general, special, ordinary or extraordinary, respecting the Property, including without limitation, real estate taxes, general and special assessments, interest on any special assessments paid in installments, transit taxes, water and sewer rents, taxes based upon the receipt of rent, personal property taxes imposed upon the fixtures, machinery, equipment, apparatus, appurtenances, furniture and other personal property used in connection with the Property which Landlord shall pay during any calendar year, any portion of which occurs during the Term (without regard to any different fiscal year used by such government or municipal authority except as provided below). Provided, however, any taxes which shall be levied on the rentals of the Property shall be determined as if the Property were Landlord's only property, and provided further that in no event shall the term "taxes or assessment," as used herein, include any net federal or state income taxes levied or assessed on Landlord, unless such taxes are a specific substitute for real property taxes. Such term shall, however, include gross taxes on rentals. Expenses incurred by Landlord for tax consultants and in contesting the amount or validity of any such taxes or assessments shall be included in such computations.

Real Estate Taxes shall also include all "assessments," including so-called special assessments, license tax, business license fee, business license tax, levy, charge, penalty or tax imposed by any authority having the direct power to tax, including any city, county, state or federal government, or any school, agricultural, lighting, water, drainage, or other improvement or special district thereof, against the Premises of the Property or any legal or equitable interest of Landlord therein. For the purposes of this Lease, any special assessments shall be deemed payable in such number of installments as is permitted by law, whether or not actually so paid. If as of the Commencement Date the Building or Property has not been fully assessed as a completed project, for the purpose of computing the Real Estate Taxes for any adjustment required herein or under Paragraph 8, the Real Estate Taxes shall be adjusted by Landlord, as of the date on which the adjustment is to be made, to reflect full completion of the Building and other improvements to the Premises including all standard Tenant finish work. If the method of taxation of real estate prevailing to the time of execution hereof shall be, or has been altered, so as to cause the whole or any part of the taxes now, hereafter or theretofore levied, assessed or imposed on real estate to be levied, assessed or imposed on Landlord, wholly or partially, as a capital levy or otherwise, or on or measured by the rents received therefrom, then such new or altered taxes attributable to the Property shall be included within the term real estate taxes, except that the same shall not include

any enhancement of said tax attributable to other income of Landlord. If there shall be any retroactive assessments or retroactive changes to original assessments, then Tenant shall be responsible for any increase in Real Estate Taxes resulting therefrom, provided that any such assessment and resulting increase in Real Estate Taxes relates to a period occurring within the Term of this Lease.

(b) Payment of Real Estate Taxes and Operating Expenses. Commencing upon the Commencement Date, Tenant shall pay Landlord (i) an amount equal to Tenant's Pro Rata Share of Operating Expenses ("Operating Payment"), and (ii) an amount equal to Tenant's Pro Rata Share of Real Estate Taxes (the "Tax Payment"). Commencing with the Commencement Date and on the first (1st) day of each month thereafter during the original Term or any extension thereof, Tenant shall pay the Operating Payment and the Tax Payment to Landlord, as Additional Rent due concurrently with Monthly Base Rent, in installments equal to one-twelfth (1/12) of Landlord's estimate (as determined by Landlord in its sole discretion) of any projected Operating Payment and Tax Payment (the "Estimated Payments"). Landlord shall inform Tenant of the Estimated Payments prior to the Commencement Date for the first Lease Year. In preparing the Estimated Payments, Landlord shall take into account the actual Operating Expenses and Real Estate Taxes incurred in the immediately preceding year, respectively.

(c) Payment Reconciliation. As soon as practicable following the end of each Lease Year, with good faith efforts to provide such statement within one hundred twenty (120) days after the last day of such Lease Year, Landlord shall submit to Tenant a statement setting forth the actual Operating Expenses and Real Estate Taxes incurred during the Lease Year which was just completed and the Estimated Payments for the current Lease Year (the "Actual Expense Statement"). To the extent that the actual Operating Expenses and Real Estate Taxes exceed the Estimated Payments paid by Tenant for the Lease Year just completed, Tenant shall pay Landlord the difference, in cash within thirty (30) days following receipt by Tenant from Landlord of the Actual Expense Statement. If the actual Operating Expenses and Real Estate Taxes for the Lease Year just completed is less than the Estimated Payments paid by Tenant for such year, then Tenant shall receive a credit on future Rent owing under this Lease (or cash, if there is no future Rent owing hereunder). Until Tenant receives the Actual Expense Statement, Tenant's Estimated Payments for the new Lease Year shall continue to be paid at the rate being paid for the particular Lease Year just completed. Tenant shall commence payment to Landlord of the Estimated Payments for the then current Lease Year, beginning on the first (1st) day of the month following the month in which Tenant receives the applicable Actual Expense Statement.

(d) **Changes in Escalations During the Lease Year; Gross-Up. In addition to the above, if, during any particular Lease Year, there is a change in the information upon which the then current Estimated Payments are based, Landlord shall be permitted to revise such Estimated Payments by notifying Tenant, and such adjustment shall be made in the payment of Estimated Payments, commencing on the first (1st) day of the month following the delivery of such notice to Tenant. When the Actual Expense Statement for the Lease Year in which this Lease terminates is delivered to the Tenant, Tenant shall pay to Landlord within ten (10) days after Landlord's delivery of the same, any additional amounts due as calculated pursuant to this Paragraph 8. Landlord's and Tenant's responsibilities with respect to Operating Payments and Tax Payments shall survive the expiration or early termination of this Lease.**

If the Building is less than ninety-five percent (95%) occupied during the Base Year or any particular Lease Year, Landlord may adjust those Operating Expenses which are affected by Building occupancy for the particular Lease Year, or portion thereof, as the case may be, to reflect an occupancy of not less than ninety-five percent (95%) of all such rentable area of the Building. In addition, if during any Lease Year any utilities or services for any occupied space in the Building are directly billed to, or paid by, the occupant thereof, Landlord may adjust those components of Operating Expenses for the Base Year or the particular Lease Year to the amount they would have been if the utilities or services in question had not been directly billed to or paid by the applicable tenant.

(e) **Disputes Over Real Estate Taxes or Operating Expenses. If Tenant disputes the amount Operating Expenses or Real Estate Taxes, Tenant shall give Landlord written notice of such dispute within ninety (90) days after Landlord delivers the applicable Actual Expense Statement. Tenant's failure to give such notice shall waive its right to audit the amounts so determined. Tenant shall not be entitled to audit the foregoing amounts if Tenant is then in default hereunder. Said audit will be conducted at Tenant's expense by a certified public accountant paid on an hourly basis unrelated to actual savings identified. Tenant shall only be permitted to conduct such a review during regular business hours at Landlord's office or, at Landlord's option, its management office, after Tenant gives Landlord twenty (20) business days prior written notice, and no more than once in any twelve (12) month period. Any audit of the Base Year must take place simultaneously with Tenant's first audit of a Lease Year. Any such audit shall be completed within thirty (30) days following Tenant's receipt of the necessary information or documentation from Landlord relative to the calendar year in question. If such review discloses that the charges actually incurred by Landlord are less than those used by Landlord in calculating the Operating Payment and Tax Payment, then Landlord shall reimburse Tenant for the**

amount Tenant paid in excess of the actual Operating Expenses and Real Estate Taxes. If any such review discloses that the charges for Operating Expenses or Real Estate Taxes for the Building used by Landlord in calculating the Operating Payment and Tax Payment exceeds the actual charges for Operating Expenses and Real Estate Taxes for the Building (the "Actual Expenses") by five percent (5%) or more, then Landlord shall pay the reasonable out-of-pocket costs of such review. If Tenant does not review Landlord's records within one hundred eighty (180) days after receipt of the Actual Expense Statement, Tenant shall have no further right to review Landlord's records for the applicable period. No subtenant shall have the right to conduct an audit and no assignee shall conduct an audit for any period during which such assignee was not in possession of the Premises. Tenant shall keep the existence and results of any audit confidential and shall not disclose the same to anyone other than its attorneys and accountants.

In the event Tenant elects to exercise its audit rights hereunder, Tenant shall nevertheless timely pay Landlord the amount of the prior year's Operating Payment and Tax Payment then due and continue to pay Estimated Payments as set forth in the then applicable Actual Expense Statement until the parties have agreed as to the appropriate adjustment. Landlord's delay in submitting any Actual Expense Statement for any Lease Year shall not affect the provisions of this Paragraph 8, nor constitute a waiver of Landlord's rights as set forth herein for said Lease Year or any subsequent Lease Year during the Term or any extension thereof.

[(f) Building as Part of Multi-Building Development. If the Property is a part of a multi-building development (the "Complex"), those Operating Expenses and Real Estate Taxes attributable to the Complex as a whole (and not attributable solely to any individual building therein) shall be allocated to the Property and to the other buildings within such Complex on an equitable basis, with the Property being responsible for [PERCENTAGE%] of those Operating Expenses and Real Estate Taxes attributable to the Complex.]

PARAGRAPH 9

Gross-Up of Operating Expenses

RISK RATING: 3

A. DESCRIPTION AND SCOPE

As mentioned in the commentary to Paragraph 8, the provision of Paragraph 8 concerning the "gross up" of Operating Expenses is being restated in this Paragraph 9 (for both the Base-Year Model and the Direct Pass-Through Model) for the purpose of deeper analysis, as Operating Expenses are typically subject to "gross up" in both models, but the issue is arguably more complex in the Base-Year Model.

Let's first explore why the Paragraph is necessary. Without the express gross-up provision for Operating Expenses, Landlord risks that for any year the Building is less than 100% leased and occupied, Landlord will not be able to collect from Building tenants the full amount of variable Operating Expenses actually incurred by Landlord in any given year. Variable Operating Expenses are those Operating Expenses that increase as occupancy of the Building increases. A good example of this is janitorial expenses because Landlord generally only pays the janitorial contractor for cleaning those rentable areas of the Building actually occupied by tenants (as vacant space does not need to be cleaned) and for the Common Areas. For example purposes only, let's assume the rentable area of the Building is only 60% leased and occupied for a year and Landlord's annual cost for janitorial services for that year is $100,000. Without a gross-up clause, the aggregate tenants of the Building (with their aggregate Pro Rata Share totaling 60%) will only be required to pay 60% of the $100,000 or $60,000 and Landlord will not have the ability to recoup the remaining $40,000 that Landlord actually incurred for the janitorial services provided. So, Landlord would lose $40,000 and the tenants would not be responsible for paying for the full cost of the janitorial service provided to and enjoyed by them. That is an inequitable result.

Thus, to avoid the inequitable result, the Lease should include a gross-up provision so, to follow our example, the janitorial expenses for that year can be grossed up to

$166,667, resulting in the tenants paying 60% of that amount (their aggregate Pro Rata Share) resulting in Landlord collecting $100,000, which is Landlord's actual cost.

The vacancy rate to which variable Operating Expenses are grossed up is a point of negotiation. It is typically agreed to that Landlord should solely absorb the losses related to the last 5% to 10% of vacancy. Thus, grossing up to 90% to 100% vacancy is generally the negotiating range for Landlord and Tenant.

B. ANALYSIS

1. Landlord's Perspective

From Landlord's Perspective, gross-up provisions are necessary to avoid the inequitable result in our example above. Gross-up provisions in the Direct Pass-Through Model are not overly complicated or nuanced because the gross up applies to every Lease Year during the Term without negatively impacting one party over another.

In the Base-Year Model, because grossing up Operating Expenses in only the Base Year benefits Tenant and grossing up in only Comparison Years benefits Landlord during the Comparison Years, some initial drafts of Leases prepared by Landlord will not include the Base-Year gross-up provisions of this Paragraph.

2. Tenant's Perspective

From Tenant's Perspective, gross-up provisions in the Direct Pass-Through Model are not overly complicated or nuanced because the gross up applies to every Lease Year during the Term without negatively impacting one party over another.

For any Lease drafted with the Base-Year Model, Tenant will want to ensure that any gross-up provision expressly requires variable Operating Expenses to be grossed up in the Base Year as well as succeeding Comparison Years.

Most Tenants will negotiate for the highest possible Base-Year gross-up percentage.

3. Lender's Perspective

Lender's primary concern is that Landlord not risk being in a position where it cannot collect from tenants the actual amount of Operating Expenses incurred. Thus, Lenders look favorably at gross-up provisions.

4. Broker's Perspective

Brokers typically stipulate in the LOI that variable Operating Expenses shall be subject to grossing up and Brokers also typically include the agreed to gross-up percentage. This helps to avoid disagreement on the issue during Lease negotiations.

C. COMPROMISES AND ALTERNATIVES

Because vacancy may vary during any Lease Year (in the Direct Pass-Through Model) or the Base Year or any Comparison Year (in the Base-Year Model) for just a portion of the Year and not the entire year, a Landlord may experience a "windfall" if Landlord

grosses up the variable Operating Expenses for an entire year based upon the lowest (temporary) occupancy during the year. To protect against this, Tenant may request the following sentence as protection immediately following any gross-up provision:
In no event shall the gross up of any Operating Expense result in Landlord collecting any amount of money in excess of the actual cost of the Operating Expense being grossed up.

Note that the foregoing protection is applicable and helpful in both the Base-Year Model and the Direct Pass-Through Model.

D. COMMENTS

In smaller buildings with smaller tenants, Landlord may be able to use a form Lease that does not provide for grossing-up Operating Expenses for the Base Year. In larger Leases, this Paragraph is likely to be one of the most heavily negotiated sections of the Lease.

One issue for Tenant to be sensitive to is that some initial drafts of Leases may provide for a gross-up of all Operating Expenses rather than just variable Operating Expenses. Fixed Operating Expenses such as landscaping, snow removal, roof repairs and building systems maintenance will not vary based on tenant occupancy of a Building and therefore should not be included in any gross-up calculation.

Another issue both parties should be sensitive to is that Tenant sometimes tries to "gross-up" Real Estate Taxes for the Base Year, too, since Real Estate Taxes on commercial buildings may be assessed and calculated not just on the value of the land and improvements but also on the revenue stream from the property (i.e., tenant occupancy). Tenants entering into newly built buildings or substantially vacant buildings are especially sensitive to this. Landlord, of course, should endeavor to resist this but relent when the market or the factual circumstances require it.

E. TYPICAL PARAGRAPH

Alternative 1: For the Base-Year Model

9. Gross Up of Operating Expenses. If the Building is not at least [95%] leased and occupied during the Base Year or any Comparison Year during the Term, those Operating Expenses that vary with occupancy shall, for the Base Year and any applicable Comparison Year, be equitably adjusted to reflect that Building being [95%] leased and occupied.

Alternative 2: For the Direct Pass-Through Model

9. Gross Up of Operating Expenses. If the Building is not at least [95%] leased and occupied during any Lease Year during the Term, those Operating Expenses that vary with occupancy shall, for the applicable Lease Year, be equitably adjusted to reflect that Building being [95%] leased and occupied.

PARAGRAPH 10

Late Payments

RISK RATING: 3

A. DESCRIPTION AND SCOPE

This Paragraph permits Landlord to (i) impose a late charge on Tenant in the event Tenant fails to pay any installment of Annual Base Rent or Additional Rent ("Late Fee"), and (ii) impose an interest rate ("Default Interest") on any late Annual Base Rent or Additional Rent until it is paid.

The Late Fee is generally meant to go towards the immediate cost of Landlord having an attorney draft a default notice and the Default Interest is applied to late Rent because Landlord will be required to cover its debt service, if applicable, even if Tenant does not pay Rent.

B. ANALYSIS

1. Landlord's Perspective

This Paragraph will encourage Tenant to make timely payments of any monies due Landlord under the Lease. Even if Tenant fails to make timely Rent payments, Landlord will be required to make any mortgage payment on time. Therefore, Landlord wants a strong disincentive in the Lease for Tenant not paying the Rent in a timely manner.

2. Tenant's Perspective

Tenant should expect consequences for any late Rent but Tenant will want to minimize those consequences to the extent possible and, at least, protect against the occasional unintentionally late payment. It is unlikely that any Tenant will be able to remove this Paragraph from the Lease but Tenant has several options for softening the Paragraph as provided in Compromises and Alternatives below.

3. Lender's Perspective

Lender, which may have its loan affected by Tenant's late payments to Landlord, will want to be sure Tenant is timely paying any monies due Landlord, and that Landlord is protected from the additional costs associated with late payments to Lender. Landlord's promissory note with Lender will also likely contain a provision for late fees or default interest if Landlord fails to make a loan payment on time. Also, if Lender must assume ownership of the Premises, Lender will want to have the late charge available to Lender as a remedy for any late payment by Tenant.

4. Broker's Perspective

Each Broker will want to consult with their respective client to determine any sensitivity to or any particular client need relating to this Paragraph that should be covered in the LOI. If none exist, this Paragraph can be handled by the attorneys in Lease negotiations.

C. COMPROMISES AND ALTERNATIVES

Tenant's negotiating options for this Paragraph include the following:

(1) Revise the Paragraph so Rent is not deemed "late" until five (5) days beyond its due date so that Landlord cannot impose any Late Fee or Default Interest until the expiration of the five (5) day period.
(2) Revise the Paragraph by lowering the Late Fee by either lowering the percentage rate charged against the Rent due or revise the Late Fee to be a fixed dollar amount such as $500.00. Moving to a fixed dollar amount Late Fee is preferable for Tenants who are paying high monthly Base Rent installments because any percentage of that amount may be well in excess of Landlord's actual cost for preparing a Default notice and, thus, unnecessarily punitive.
(3) Revise the Paragraph to include that Tenant shall not be subject to a Late Fee or Default Interest for any first late Rent payment in any 12-month period if Tenant pays such late Rent within any applicable notice and cure period.
(4) Revise the Paragraph to lower the Default Interest rate.
(5) Revise the Paragraph so that Default Interest is not computed from the first day Rent is late but from either five (5) days thereafter or, better yet, the expiration of any notice and cure period.

Different percentage amounts for the Late Fee may be agreed to by Landlord and Tenant. As a guiding principle, the charge should be reasonably related to the costs that may be incurred by Landlord in dealing with a late rental payment. For example, Landlord may need to engage counsel to prepare a default notice and other documents relating to any subsequent litigation. Most leases provide for 4% or 5%, but leases do exist with late charges ranging from 1% to 10%. If the Tenant is leasing a large space and thus paying a high monthly rent, Tenant may attempt to lower the percentage amount for the late fee, or cap the late fee at a fixed maximum dollar amount (i.e., $2,500.00 or a similar amount).

Landlord may insist that the Default Interest be tied to any default interest for which Landlord may be liable for under its mortgage loan. Landlord may request that Tenant pay Default Interest from three to six percentage points above Landlord's mortgage interest rate.

Tenant should consult with its accountant or banker to determine what steps can be taken to assure Landlord's timely receipt of the rent payment following an initial Late Fee being incurred. Landlords are increasingly permitting Tenants to make Rent payments by wire or ACH payment allowing Tenants to set up automatic monthly payments for scheduled Rent.

D. COMMENTS

Tenant's failure to make Rent payments to Landlord on time can result in significant adverse financial consequences to both Tenant and Landlord.

E. TYPICAL PARAGRAPH

10. <u>Late Payments</u>. Tenant acknowledges that the late payment to Landlord of Annual Base Rent, Additional Rent, or any other sum due hereunder will cause Landlord to incur costs not contemplated under this Lease. Tenant further acknowledges that the exact amount of such costs is and will be extremely difficult to ascertain. Accordingly, if any Annual Base Rent, Additional Rent, or such other sum is not received by Landlord when due and payable, then Tenant shall pay to Landlord an amount equal to (i) a late fee equal to five percent (5%) of such overdue amount (the "<u>Late Fee</u>"), plus (ii) interest on such overdue amount at two (2) percentage points above the "prime rate" as published in The Wall Street Journal per annum or at the highest rate permitted by law, whichever is less, from its due date until paid (the "<u>Default Interest Charge</u>"). Landlord and Tenant agree that the Late Fee and the Default Interest Charge represents a fair and reasonable estimate of the costs Landlord will incur as the result of Tenant's late payment of any such amount. Landlord's acceptance of any Late Fee and Default Interest Charge shall not constitute Landlord's waiver of Tenant's default with respect to such overdue amount or estop Landlord from exercising any of its rights or remedies under this Lease.

PARAGRAPH 11

Utilities and Services

RISK RATING: 3

A. DESCRIPTION AND SCOPE

This Paragraph provides a summary of those certain utilities and services that Landlord has agreed to provide Tenant, including HVAC, elevators, janitorial, security, water, and electricity. This Paragraph also requires Tenant to pay for any excess usage of such services.

B. ANALYSIS

1. Landlord's Perspective

Landlord must be careful about covenanting to provide Tenant with heat, air conditioning, hot water, elevators, cleaning or other services with specifications in excess of capacity or availability. Landlord may wish to endeavor to enter into a lease without service specifications if at all possible but a savvy Tenant will typically push on this point. In addition, Landlord will want to be sure to incorporate a "breakdown" or "diminution-of-services" clause in the Lease and same is provided in Paragraph 12.

2. Tenant's Perspective

To assure Tenant the right to such services, the list of services to be provided by Landlord should be comprehensive and detailed in its scope and specifications, especially with respect to electricity, HVAC and janitorial specifications. As further discussed in Paragraph 12, Tenant may ask for a rent abatement or termination right if such cessation of utilities or services makes the Premises unusable for more than a specified number of days. If the Building has broadband internet access or fiber optic cable service, Tenant may wish to specify these services as required services.

3. Lender's Perspective

Lender wants to ensure that the Landlord offers services consistent with those found in a first-class office building. Lender will be less interested in this Paragraph dealing with the specifics of what utilities and services are being provided by Landlord and how Tenant is paying for them than the consequences to Landlord in the event of a diminution of services, which is discussed in Paragraph 12.

4. Broker's Perspective

Landlord Broker should be well versed in what utilities and services Landlord will provide to Tenant and how they will be charged and Tenant Broker should inquire about same during the LOI stage. It is prudent that the LOI capture all relevant details about how utilities are to be measured and paid for, including, any specific charges (e.g., electricity meter reading fees, if applicable) and the cost of any utilities or services needed outside of normal Building business hours. If any utility meters need to be installed, an allocation of installation cost responsibility should be included in the LOI.

Tenant Broker would be prudent to inquire with Tenant if Tenant's proposed use is especially dependent upon any particular utility or service. If so, Tenant Broker should work with Tenant's engineer or facilities person to confirm such utility or service is captured in the LOI with any required specificity to meet Tenant's needs. Both Brokers should confirm that this Lease Paragraph matches what was agreed to by the parties in the LOI.

C. COMPROMISES AND ALTERNATIVES

The Typical Paragraph 11 provided below assumes that Tenant is paying for its electrical consumption on a fixed fee per rentable square feet of the Premises. Alternatives to this are that (i) the Premises are submetered and Tenant pays Landlord, as Additional Rent, for the cost of the electricity consumed by Tenant as measured on the submeter, or (ii) the Premises are separately metered and Tenant pays the utility company directly for the cost of the electricity consumed by Tenant as measured on the meter. If Tenant is paying Landlord by submeter, Tenant should try to eliminate any Landlord profit and/or reasonably limit any Landlord administration or "meter reading" fee.

Tenant generally wants performance specifications for electricity, HVAC and janitorial services and should push for same. Here is a sample HVAC paragraph that would be favorable for Tenant to include in the Lease:

Landlord hereby warrants and represents that the HVAC system serving the Premises shall be in good working order and condition on the Commencement Date, and shall, throughout the Term, provide levels of ventilation, humidity, heating and cooling which are appropriate for executive office occupancies in a first-class building and, at all times, in accordance with the following performance specifications: [ADD PERFORMANCE SPECIFICATIONS HERE]. Except for damage caused by Tenant's negligence or misuse, Landlord shall be responsible for maintenance, repairs, replacements and additions to said HVAC system during the Term, said maintenance to include periodic testing and cleaning of the duct work as is reasonably necessary to avoid unsafe or unhealthy interior air conditions. Any overtime charges for Tenant's HVAC usage shall be proportionately reduced to reflect any simultaneous usage by other tenants. In addition, the rates for such overtime usage shall not exceed the normal and customary rates charged at comparable first-class office buildings in the area of the Building.

D. COMMENTS

This Paragraph should be extended to other services a Landlord may be providing in any particular building including: security, Wi-Fi and transportation services.

Subparagraph 11(f) exculpating Landlord from liability for interruption of services is likely to be negotiated. Paragraph 12 discusses this further. Whether or not Tenant is permitted to abate rent or terminate the Lease in connection with an interruption in services will generally depend on the relative leverage of Landlord and Tenant in the Lease transaction.

Tenant should be on the lookout for the rare but occasional Landlord lease forms that inappropriately only include provisions relating to Tenant's obligation to pay for utilities and services but conveniently omit the Landlord obligation to provide them for the duration of the Term.

E. TYPICAL PARAGRAPH

11. Services and Utilities.

(a) Electricity:

(i) Subject to the provisions of this Subparagraph 11(a), Landlord shall provide to the electrical closet on the floor of the Building where the Premises are located [X] of electrical capacity (for lighting and power) per rentable square foot of the Premises (the "<u>Maximum Capacity</u>"). Tenant shall not use any electrical equipment in the Premises (or otherwise permit any use therein) which causes Tenant's demand for electricity to exceed the Maximum Capacity. Landlord shall not be liable in any way to Tenant for any failure or defect in the supply or character of electric service furnished to the Premises (except to the extent such failure or defect results from Landlord's negligence or willful misconduct).

(ii) Tenant shall pay to Landlord, as Additional Rent for the electricity being furnished to the Premises and the Building during the Term, an amount (the "<u>Electricity Additional Rent</u>") equal to $[AMOUNT] per rentable square foot of the Premise per year payable in equal monthly payments due in advance on the first day of each calendar month during the Term. Said Electricity Additional Rent shall be subject to increase, from time to time, during the Term, to the extent Landlord's costs for providing electricity to the Building (including all applicable surcharges, demand charges,

time-of-day charges, energy charges, fuel adjustment charges, rate adjustment charges, taxes, use charges and other amounts payable in respect thereof and net of any rebates or credits actually received by Landlord in respect of such electricity supplied to the Premises), are increased.

(iii) Without the consent of Landlord, Tenant's use of electrical service shall not exceed the Maximum Capacity. Landlord's electrical consultant may from time to time conduct surveys in the Premises (which surveys shall be the only acceptable method of measuring Tenant's electrical consumption within the Premises) covering the electrical equipment and fixtures and use of current therein. If it is determined, based only upon such surveys, that Tenant is using excess electricity, Tenant shall pay Landlord Additional Rent for the cost of such excess electrical usage and for the cost of performing such survey(s) and Landlord may adjust the Electricity Additional Rent by the amount of such excess, effective as of the earlier of (i) the date of such survey or (ii) the date on which increases in the connected power load or changes in electric consumption occurred (as determined by Landlord's electric consultant). Electrical service to the Premises may be furnished by one or more companies providing electrical generation, transmission and distribution services, and the cost of electricity may consist of several different components or separate charges for such services, such as generation, distribution and standard cost charges. Landlord shall have the exclusive right to select any company providing electrical service to the Premises, to aggregate the electrical service for the Property and Premises with other buildings, to purchase electricity through a broker and/or buyers group and to change the providers and manner of purchasing electricity. In addition to the Electricity Additional Rent, in the event Tenant installs any supplemental HVAC, Tenant shall, at Tenant's sole cost and expense, install separate electricity meters to measure the usage for such supplemental HVAC and pay when due all electricity charges reflected on such meters.

(iv) If Landlord is required by any applicable law to discontinue furnishing electricity to Tenant, then this Lease shall continue in full force and effect and shall be unaffected thereby, except that from and after the effective date of such discontinuance, Landlord shall not be obligated to furnish electricity to Tenant and Tenant shall not be obligated to pay the Electricity Additional Rent. If Landlord so discontinues furnishing electricity to Tenant, then Tenant shall use diligent efforts to obtain electric energy directly from the public utility furnishing electric service to the Building. The costs of such service shall be paid by Tenant directly to such public utility. Such electricity may be furnished to Tenant by means of the existing electrical facilities serving the Premises, at no charge, to the extent the same are available, suitable and safe for such purposes in each case as reasonably determined by Landlord. Landlord, to the extent permitted by applicable law, shall not discontinue furnishing electricity to the Premises until Tenant is able to obtain electricity directly from the public utility.

(b) Elevator Service: If the Building is equipped with elevators, Landlord shall furnish elevator service during normal business hours to be used by Tenant in common with others. At least one elevator shall remain in service during all other hours. Landlord may designate a specific elevator for use as a service elevator.

(c) HVAC. Landlord, at Landlord's expense (but subject to expense recovery through Operating Expenses), shall furnish heating, ventilation and air conditioning ("HVAC") to the Premises through the HVAC System, when required for the comfortable occupancy of the Premises on a year round basis from 8:00 a.m. to 6:00 p.m. on Business Days. Tenant shall keep all draperies or blinds for the windows of the Premises closed at all times. If Landlord furnishes HVAC to the Premises at the request of Tenant at times other than 8:00 a.m. to 6:00 p.m. on Business Days, (any such times other than during such hours on Business Days being referred to herein as "Overtime Periods"), then Tenant shall pay to Landlord Additional Rent for such services at a commercially reasonable rate to be determined by Landlord (which rate shall be subject to commercially reasonable increase from time to time). Any amount of money collected for such Overtime Periods that exceeds the actual cost of providing HVAC during said periods will be applied to reduce the Building's common area electricity charges included in Operating Expenses. Landlord shall not be required to furnish any such services during any Overtime Periods unless Landlord has received advance notice from Tenant requesting HVAC services prior to 2:00 p.m. of the day upon which such services are requested or by 2:00 p.m. of the last preceding Business Day if such Overtime Periods are to occur on a day other than a Business Day.

(d) Janitorial Services: Provided Tenant shall keep the Premises in order, Landlord, at Landlord's expense (but subject to recovery through Operating Expenses), shall cause the Premises, excluding any portions thereof used for the storage, preparation, service or consumption of food or beverages to be cleaned, substantially in accordance with the standards set forth in Exhibit "[X]" attached hereto and made a part hereof. Tenant shall pay to Landlord, promptly after Landlord's request, the cost of removal of refuse and rubbish from the Premises to the extent that such refuse and rubbish exceeds the amount thereof usually attendant to the use of the Premises as offices. Tenant, at Tenant's sole cost and expense, shall cause all portions of the Premises used for the storage, preparation, service or consumption of food or beverages to be cleaned daily in a manner reasonably satisfactory to Landlord, and to be exterminated

against infestation by vermin, rodents or roaches regularly in a manner reasonably satisfactory to Landlord, and by Persons reasonably approved by Landlord. If Tenant performs any cleaning services in addition to the services provided by Landlord as aforesaid, then Tenant shall employ the cleaning contractor providing cleaning services to the Building on behalf of Landlord, provided that such cleaning contractor's rates are commercially reasonable. Tenant shall comply with any recycling program and/or refuse disposal program (including, without limitation, any program related to the recycling, separation or other disposal of paper, glass, or metals) which Landlord imposes or which is required pursuant to any applicable laws.

(e) **Water: Landlord, at Landlord's expense (but subject to recovery through Operating Expenses), shall furnish hot and cold potable water to the Premises for ordinary cleaning and lavatory use only. If Landlord reasonably determines that Tenant is using water in excessive quantities, Landlord may install, at Tenant's expense, separate meters for the Premises to register Tenant's consumption of water and charge Tenant therefor as Additional Rent.**

PARAGRAPH 12

Diminution of Services

RISK RATING: 3

A. DESCRIPTION AND SCOPE

This Paragraph provides that Landlord is not liable to Tenant if Landlord fails to provide any service for certain reasons beyond its control or during repairs and that the Annual Base Rent and Additional Rent shall continue notwithstanding any interruption of services.

B. ANALYSIS

1. Landlord's Perspective

This Paragraph is intended to protect Landlord from liability and rent abatements for interruptions in services Landlord is obligated to provide. Such a clause excuses Landlord from liability for damages in case of interruption of these services due to a necessity for repair, inspection, or causes beyond a Landlord's reasonable control. This clause usually does not provide for rent abatement during a period of such interruption but, again, a savvy Tenant with some leverage will endeavor to get rent abatement during an extended period of interruption.

2. Tenant's Perspective

Tenant will want to abate rent if essential services are interrupted for a specified period of time. Tenant may also want the bargaining mechanism of termination in order to get the services restored as soon as possible. These arguments have some merit because any service failure will cause a disruption in the Tenant's operations at the site, and a service disruption could cause substantial harm to the Tenant's business. A negotiation is likely over the period of time and the materiality of a failure of service in order to qualify for an abatement of rent. Landlord will argue that Tenant can obtain business interruption insurance to cover this risk but business interruption insurance is "add on" coverage to Tenant's property insurance policy and coverage only kicks in if Tenant has a property damage claim. Tenant will counter that Tenant is already paying its pro rata share of Landlord's rent loss insurance as part of the operating expense load, and therefore Landlord should permit a rent abatement if services are not restored. If Landlord concedes the point, Landlord may require that rent abatement occur only if the Premises become untenantable due to a service failure.

3. Lender's Perspective

Any abatement of rent and Tenant termination provisions may adversely affect the "mortgageability" of this Lease. Lender ordinarily would much rather limit Tenant's remedy to an action against Landlord for damages. However, abatement of rent and Lease termination for lengthy interruptions are fairly common and are generally acceptable to most Lenders.

4. Broker's Perspective

Landlord Broker has no need to raise this issue during the LOI stage. Tenant Broker should define during the up-front needs assessment phase of its assignment to determine how its client/tenant intends to use the Premises and what alternative arrangements/back up plans or facilities Tenant may need in the event the Premises becomes untenantable due to a diminution of services. The construction and location of the Property, quality and age of systems, and way the property management typically staffs the Property should all be evaluated in the context of Tenant selecting the Premises. Tenant Broker should support Tenant counsel to ensure that time frames to restore operations and any damages or rent abatement that might be secured are consistent with market standards and acceptable in light of Tenant's alternative arrangements.

C. COMPROMISES AND ALTERNATIVES

A savvy Tenant will endeavor to limit Landlord's rights under Paragraph 12 to a reasonable period of time. Here is a sample Tenant-friendly provision that would be added to the end of the existing Paragraph 12:

> *Notwithstanding the foregoing, if all or part of the Premises are rendered untenantable due to a diminution, interruption or cessation of any utilities or services required to be provided by Landlord under this Lease continuing beyond three (3) consecutive Business Days, then commencing on the fourth (4th) Business Day Tenant's Rent obligations shall proportionately abate for the remaining duration of such untenantable conditions, said abatement to reflect the portions of the Premises which are untenantable. Notwithstanding the foregoing, if such untenantable conditions arise at any time during the last year of the Term, and affect twenty percent or more of the rentable area of the Premises, or occur at any time during the Term and continue for more than twenty (20) Business*

Days, Tenant shall have the right to terminate the Lease, without liability, upon written notice to Landlord, in which case Landlord shall immediately return any prepaid Rent and Security Deposit.

Landlords endeavor to limit any Tenant Rent abatement or Lease termination rights in one or more of the following three (3) ways: (i) negotiating a longer time period before any Tenant Rent abatement or Lease termination right is exercisable by Tenant; (ii) limit Tenant's rights to only those untenantable conditions arising due to the negligence or willful misconduct of Landlord; or (iii) limit Tenant's rights to the diminution, interruption or cessation of just "Essential Services" rather than to all utilities or services required to be provided by Landlord under this Lease.

Following is another sample of how Paragraph 12 can be modified but, this time, in a more Landlord-friendly manner.

Notwithstanding the foregoing, if Tenant is unable to use the Premises for the ordinary conduct of Tenant's business due solely to an interruption of an Essential Service resulting from Landlord's willful misconduct, and such condition continues for a period in excess of ten (10) consecutive Business Days after (i) Tenant furnishes a notice to Landlord (the "Abatement Notice") stating that Tenant's inability to use the Premises is solely due to such condition, (ii) Tenant does not actually use or occupy the Premises during such period for the ordinary conduct of its business, and (iii) such condition has not resulted from the negligence or misconduct of Tenant, then Rent shall be abated on a per diem basis for the period commencing on the eleventh (11th) Business Day after Tenant delivers the Abatement Notice to Landlord and ending on the earlier of (x) the date Tenant reoccupies any portion of the Premises for the conduct of its business therein, and (y) the date on which such condition is substantially remedied. As used herein, "Essential Service" shall mean a service which Landlord is obligated under this Lease to provide to Tenant which if not provided shall (i) effectively deny access to the Premises, (ii) threaten the health or safety of any occupants of the Premises, or (iii) prevent the operation of Tenant's business in the Premises.

D. COMMENTS

Whether or not Tenant is successful getting any of the compromises or alternative provisions described above included in the Lease will generally depend on the relative leverage of Landlord and Tenant in the Lease transaction.

E. TYPICAL PARAGRAPH

12. **Diminution of Services. Landlord shall not be liable for the interruption, curtailment, stoppage, or suspension of services and utilities to be furnished by Landlord pursuant to this Lease when necessary by reason of accident or emergency or suspension of utility services or when necessary for repairs, alterations, replacements, or improvements desirable or necessary in the reasonable judgment of Landlord or for any cause beyond the control of**

Landlord, nor shall Landlord have any liability for damages sustained by Tenant resulting therefrom. In the event of any such interruption, curtailment, stoppage, or suspension, there shall be no diminution or abatement of Annual Base Rent, Additional Rent, or other charges due from Tenant to Landlord hereunder. Tenant's obligations hereunder shall not be affected or reduced, and Landlord shall have no responsibility or liability for any such interruption, curtailment, stoppage, or suspension; however, Landlord shall exercise reasonable diligence to restore any services or utilities so interrupted, curtailed, stopped, or suspended.

PARAGRAPH 13

Alterations

RISK RATING: 4

A. DESCRIPTION AND SCOPE

This Paragraph sets forth Tenant's rights to make improvements to the Premises and specific obligations of Tenant under the Lease with respect thereto.

Note that this Paragraph is typically meant to capture just those improvements made by Tenant after the Commencement Date and after any initial improvements made by or for Tenant for Tenant's initial occupancy of the Premises, as those initial improvements are typically governed by a separate section (in this case, in Part 1, Exhibit C), although those initial improvements may be subject to the terms of this Paragraph as well.

B. ANALYSIS

1. Landlord's Perspective

Landlord seeks to protect its investment in the Building, the look of the Building (to the extent any Tenant improvements can be seen outside of the Premises) and the operation of the Building (to the extent any Tenant improvements impact the Building systems or structure). Thus, this Paragraph 13 contains multiple Landlord protections to address Landlord's interests.

2. Tenant's Perspective

Tenant wants to ensure that it may alter the Premises so that the Premises reflects a configuration and aesthetic that is both functional and pleasing for the operation of Tenant's business therein.

This Paragraph is risk rated high due to the provisions of the Paragraph related to what Alterations need to be removed at the end of the Term. Tenant would be wise to carefully negotiate that provision.

3. Lender's Perspective

Lender will want Tenant's alteration rights to be limited in such a manner that they do not impact the value or marketability of the Building or result in any liens encumbering the Property.

4. Broker's Perspective

Landlord Broker should have little interest in raising this issue during the LOI stage unless Landlord has mandatory Alteration review fees that are prudent to document in the LOI. Tenant Broker should negotiate as part of the LOI that Landlord will permit Tenant to make reasonable alterations to the Premises using labor that is reasonably approved by Landlord without undue payments to Landlord for review, approval and performance in light of market norms. Tenant Broker may also wish to capture in the LOI that a certain level of Alternations that are minor or cosmetic should be permitted with notice to Landlord but without Landlord's consent or review fees. It is also important for Tenant Broker to negotiate into the LOI that Landlord can only require that nonstandard office Alterations (and possibly telecommunication cabling and wiring) be removed at the expiration of the Term and then only in the event that Landlord notifies Tenant of same at the time of Landlord's approval of the Alterations. Also, Tenant's Broker may wish to confirm for Tenant whether the Building is subject to union labor requirements.

C. COMPROMISES AND ALTERNATIVES

Paragraph 13 below contains comprehensive Landlord protections with respect to Alterations made Tenant. Tenant may wish to balance the Paragraph by proposing the following compromises:

Limited Alterations not Requiring Landlord Consent: Paragraph 13 below requires Landlord consent to all proposed Alterations. Tenants typically request and successfully achieve the right to make certain limited Alterations without Landlord consent. The following is a sample provision:

> *Notwithstanding anything contained herein to the contrary, Landlord's consent shall not be required for any Alteration which: (a) is of a cosmetic nature such as painting, wallpapering, hanging pictures and installing carpeting; (b) will not affect the Building Systems or the Building structure; and (c) does not require the preparation and filing of plans to obtain a building permit (a "Cosmetic Alteration").*

Limited Removal of Alterations at the Expiration Date: Paragraph 13 below permits Landlord to require removal of all Alterations upon the Expiration Date with notice of such removal only coming towards the end of the Term. Tenant often successfully negotiates (i) a limitation on the Alteration removal requirement to just those subset of Alterations that can be classified as Specialty Alterations, and (ii) that Landlord must notify Tenant of any removal requirement upon Landlord's approval of the Alteration and not at the end of the Term. The following is a sample provision:

Notwithstanding anything to the contrary contained in the Lease, Landlord may only require Tenant to remove Alterations that constitute Specialty Alterations (as hereinafter defined). In addition, Landlord must notify Tenant, simultaneously when Landlord notifies Tenant that it approves any proposed Alteration, that (i) any proposed Alteration constitutes a Specialty Alteration, and (ii) such Specialty Alteration is required to be removed the end of the Term or Landlord shall be deemed to have waived its right to require such removal. As used herein, "Specialty Alterations" shall mean Alterations which (i) materially affect the structure of the Building, (ii) materially and negatively affect any Building systems, (iii) establish a connection between any portions of the Premises which are not contiguous or are not on the same floor of the Building (such as staircases, dumbwaiters, and pneumatic tubes), (iv) constitute Alterations made to accommodate Tenant's particular technical installations (such as raised flooring for computer installation, any supplemental HVAC systems, or any satellite dishes and/or antennae) or to accommodate Tenant's subletting or assignment transactions, (v) constitute vaults or libraries. In no event, however, shall Specialty Alterations include Tenant's cable and wiring.

For extra protection on this issue, Tenant should endeavor to insert the following sentence into the Lease either here or in the surrender Paragraph of the Lease (Paragraph 33):

In no event shall Tenant be required to remove any improvements existing on the Commencement Date, any of Landlord's Work, and any Initial Alterations.

<u>Pre-Approval of Contractors, Designer and Labor Conflicts</u>: Paragraph 13 below requires any Tenant contractors and designers to be approved by Landlord. Tenant may wish to get any anticipated contractors or designers pre-approved by Landlord within the Lease before execution. Also, Tenant should inquire, prior to Lease execution, whether the Building is subject to union-labor contracts. If the Building is subject to union-labor contracts, Tenant should inquire further as to whether those contracts are just imposed upon Landlord or whether they extend to any Alteration made by Tenant. If the contracts extend to Alterations, the cost of any Alterations may be significantly higher than originally anticipated by Tenant. Interestingly, however, the labor contracts sometimes only apply to work performed by Landlord so using union labor can be evaded by Tenant although Tenant would likely be responsible for any disorder using non-union labor may, or may not, cause at the Building (i.e., picketing, etc.).

<u>Limiting Landlord's Expenses</u>. Paragraph 13 below permits Landlord to charge Tenant for costs and fees incurred by Landlord in connection with the Alterations plus a ten percent (10%) oversight fee. Tenant should, with the assistance of Tenant's Broker and counsel, understand the local market on these issues and revise the provision accordingly. Note that, nearly universally, Landlords get reimbursed for their "actual out-of-pocket" costs to review Tenant's plans and specifications for Alterations. Beyond that is generally negotiable. If Tenant is unable to remove the "oversight fee" in its entirety, it is sometimes able to get it waived (i) if Tenant agrees to use Landlord's designated contractors, or (ii) with respect to Tenant's Initial Alterations.

D. COMMENTS

Tenants who anticipate the necessity of certain Alterations before the Effective Date of the Lease, should endeavor to get such Alterations pre-approved by Landlord within the Lease before execution.

With increasing reliance on businesses operating on sophisticated and sometimes voluminous telecommunication and electrical wiring and cabling, the shaft, conduit, floor, ceiling, and walls spaces surrounding the Premises can easily get crowded and old wiring and cabling from preexisting tenants may be difficult to identify. Thus, increasingly, Landlords are endeavoring to require Tenant removal of its wiring and cabling at Lease expiration. Landlords may be less concerned if they anticipate a full demolition of the Premises at Lease expiration. In any event, this issue is typically now hotly negotiated. If Tenant ends up being required to remove their wiring and cabling, they should endeavor to limit the removal requirement to those wires and cables within the perimeter of the Premises and only to the point of connection to any data or communication closet on the floor of the Building but not beyond that.

Even if Tenant is not contemplating significant Alterations following the Commencement Date, care should go into balancing Paragraph 13 because a potential subtenant of Tenant may need Alterations and they would be inheriting the provisions of the Paragraph.

E. TYPICAL PARAGRAPH

13. Alterations.

(a) General. Tenant shall not make any improvements to the Premises ("Alterations") without Landlord's prior consent. Landlord shall not unreasonably withhold or delay its consent to Tenant's proposed Alterations, provided that such Alterations (i) are not visible, at street level, from the outside of the Building, (ii) do not require any alterations, installations, improvements, additions or other physical changes to be performed in or made to any portion of the Property other than the Premises, (iii) do not affect the proper functions of any Building system, (iv) do not affect the validity of the certificate of occupancy for the Building or any part thereof, and (v) do not constitute Alterations to the structural components of the Building.

(b) Procedure for Alterations. Tenant, before making any Alterations, shall submit to Landlord detailed plans and specifications therefor (including layout, architectural, mechanical, electrical, plumbing and structural drawings). If (x) Tenant is required to obtain Landlord's consent to an Alteration pursuant to this Paragraph 13, and (y) Landlord fails to disapprove Tenant's plans and specifications for such Alteration within fifteen (15) Business Days after Landlord's receipt thereof, then Landlord shall be deemed to have approved such plans and specifications. Landlord shall include with any disapproval of Tenant's aforesaid plans and specifications a statement of the reasons for such disapproval. Landlord

shall have the right to (i) disapprove any plans and specifications in part, (ii) reserve approval of items shown thereon pending Landlord's review and approval of other plans and specifications, or (iii) condition Landlord's approval on Tenant making revisions to the plans and specification or supplying additional information. Any review or approval by Landlord of any plans or specifications or any preparation or design of any plans by any architect or engineer designated by Landlord for any Alteration is solely for Landlord's benefit, and without any representation or warranty whatever with respect thereto.

(c) Permits and Insurance for Alterations. Tenant at Tenant's expense, shall obtain all permits, approvals and certificates required by any governmental authority in connection with each Alteration. Tenant, at Tenant's expense, shall also furnish to Landlord, in connection with each Alteration, duplicate original policies of worker's compensation insurance (covering all persons to be employed by Tenant, and Tenant's contractors and subcontractors, in connection with such Alteration) and commercial general liability insurance (including property damage coverage), in either case in such form, with such companies, for such periods and in such amounts (not to be less than Two Million Dollars ($2,000,000.00) in the aggregate with respect to general contractors and One Million Dollars ($1,000,000.00) with respect to subcontractors) as Landlord may reasonably approve, naming Landlord, Landlord's managing agent, any ground lessor and any mortgagee as additional insureds (it being agreed that Tenant, in lieu of providing Landlord with such insurance policies, may deliver to Landlord certificates thereof in form and substance reasonably acceptable to Landlord). Each insurance certificate (whether for insurance originally furnished or evidencing a renewal of insurance) shall include a standard "additional insured" endorsement naming the aforementioned parties as additional insureds. Tenant shall provide an Acord 27 form to evidence property insurance and an Acord 25 form to evidence liability insurance. Upon completion of each Alteration, Tenant, at Tenant's expense, shall obtain for each Alteration any certificates of final approval and/or certificates of occupancy required by any governmental authority and shall furnish Landlord with copies thereof, together with the "as-built" plans and specification for such Alterations (or, if "as-built" plans and specifications are not available, appropriate record drawings or shop drawings and specifications). Upon the request of Tenant, Landlord shall join in any applications for any permits, approvals or certificates required to be obtained by Tenant in connection with any permitted Alteration and shall otherwise cooperate with Tenant in connection with such applications, provided that (x) Landlord shall not be obligated to incur any cost or expense, including, without limitation, attorneys' fees and disbursements, or suffer any liability, in connection therewith, and (y) the applicable law requires Landlord to join in such application.

(d) Financial Integrity. Tenant shall not permit any materials or equipment to be incorporated in the Premises in connection with any Alterations to be subject to any lien, encumbrance, chattel mortgage or title retention or security agreement. Tenant shall not make any Alteration that: (i) is at a cost for labor and materials (as reasonably estimated by Landlord's architect, engineer or contractor) in excess of [AMOUNT] Dollars ($[AMOUNT]), either individually or in the aggregate with any other Alteration constructed in any twelve (12) month period, or (ii) causes Landlord to make any alterations, installations, improvements, additions or other physical changes to the Property under Paragraph 13(e) below ("Building Work"), without first delivering a performance bond and labor and materials payment bond (issued by a surety company and in form reasonably satisfactory to Landlord), each in an amount equal to such estimated cost.

(e) Effect on the Building. If, as a result of any Alterations performed by Tenant, any alterations, installations, improvements, additions or other physical changes are then required to be made to any portion of the building or the Property other than the Premises in order to comply with any applicable laws, which alterations, installations, improvements, additions or other physical changes would not otherwise have had to be made pursuant to applicable laws at such time, then (x) Landlord may make such alterations, installations, improvements, additions or other physical changes, and (y) Tenant shall pay to Landlord the reasonable costs incurred by Landlord in performing such alterations, installations, improvements, additions or other physical changes, not later than the tenth (10th) day after the date when Landlord gives to Tenant Landlord's statement therefor.

(f) Time of Performance of Alteration; Rules. Tenant shall not perform Alterations during the hours of 8:00 a.m. to 6:00 p.m. on Business Days to the extent such work disturbs other occupants of the Building or interferes with or interrupts the operation of the Property. Tenant, in connection with Tenant's performance of Alterations shall comply with reasonable rules adopted by Landlord from time to time to minimize the impact of the performance of Alterations on the operation of the Property and other tenants' use of the Building.

(g) Removal of Alterations and Tenant's Property. On or prior to the Expiration Date, Tenant, at Tenant's sole cost and expense, (i) shall remove Tenant's personal property from the Premises, and (ii) shall remove from the Premises all telecommunication, data and cabling equipment and wires installed in the Premises by Tenant. Tenant shall repair and restore in a good and workmanlike manner to good condition any damage to the Premises or the Building caused by such removal. Landlord may require Tenant to remove any Alterations, and to repair and restore in a good and workmanlike manner to good condition any damage to the Premises or the Building caused by such removal, by giving notice

thereof to Tenant not later than the thirtieth (30th) day before the Expiration Date, or, if the Expiration Date is not the scheduled Expiration Date, the thirtieth (30th) day after the Expiration Date. Tenant shall perform any work required by this subparagraph in accordance with the provisions of this Paragraph 13. The provisions of this subparagraph shall survive the expiration or earlier termination of the Term.

(h) Contractors; Architectural Supervision. Tenant shall perform Alterations using contractors, subcontractors or mechanics approved by Landlord (which approval shall not be unreasonably withheld or delayed); provided, however, that if any such Alteration affects a Building system, then (i) Tenant shall select a contractor therefor from a list of approved contractors furnished by Landlord to Tenant (containing at least three (3) contractors). All Alterations requiring the consent of Landlord shall be performed only under the supervision of an independent licensed architect approved by Landlord, which approval Landlord shall not unreasonably withhold or delay.

(i) Mechanic's Liens. Any mechanic's lien filed against the Premises or the Property for work claimed to have been done for, or materials claimed to have been furnished to, Tenant shall be discharged by Tenant within thirty (30) days after Tenant receives notice thereof, at Tenant's expense, by payment, filing the bond required by law, or making a deposit into a court of competent jurisdiction as provided by applicable law.

(j) Labor Conflicts. Tenant at any time prior to or during the Term, shall not directly or indirectly employ, or permit the employment of, any contractor, mechanic or laborer in the Premises if such employment interferes or causes any conflict with other contractors, mechanics or laborers engaged in the operation of the Property. Tenant shall use its best efforts to maintain harmony between any contractors, mechanics or laborers employed by Tenant and other contractors, mechanics or laborers engaged in the operation of the Property.

(k) Landlord's Expenses. Tenant shall pay to Landlord, from time to time, the actual, reasonable and out-of-pocket costs incurred by Landlord in connection with Alterations (including, without limitation, the reasonable out-of-pocket costs incurred by Landlord or a mortgagee or ground lessor in reviewing Tenant's plans and specifications for a proposed Alteration (or inspecting the construction of such Alteration) for which Landlord's consent is required hereunder). In addition, Tenant shall pay Landlord, as Additional Rent, within ten (10) Business Days after being billed therefor an administrative charge equal to 10% of the total hard costs of the Alterations to compensate Landlord for Landlord's oversight of the Alterations.

PARAGRAPH 14

Mechanic's Liens

RISK RATING: 3

A. DESCRIPTION AND SCOPE

This Paragraph obligates Tenant to discharge any mechanic's or materialmen's liens filed against the Premises. If not, Landlord has the right to do the same and charge Tenant as Additional Rent or subtract it from any amounts owed to Tenant by Landlord.

B. ANALYSIS

1. Landlord's Perspective

Depending upon the State where the Premises is located, Landlord may or may not be liable for the cost of work done for the benefit of Tenant. In any event Landlord has a vested interest, particularly if Landlord has mortgaged the Property as collateral to Lender, in seeing that the liens are satisfied and discharged.

2. Tenant's Perspective

Tenant's obligation to remove the lien could be troublesome particularly if Tenant questions the amount for which the lien was filed, or disputes that the work conformed to the requirements of the contract. In that case, Tenant may wish to bond the lien instead of discharge it and so Tenant should be sure that it has the right to bond the lien if the original mechanics lien paragraph of a lease does not include such a Tenant right.

Tenant wants to be careful that Tenant is only obliged to remove liens arising from Tenant's activity.

3. Lender's Perspective

Lender is particularly concerned if a mechanic's lien is placed on the Property that constitutes its collateral. It also may be deemed a default under Lender's loan documents if Landlord does not remove the liens within a specified period of time.

4. Broker's Perspective

When reviewing this Paragraph, Tenant Broker should ask Tenant's architect, engineer, and/or contractor whether the timeframes and provisions for Tenant's removal of mechanics liens in this Paragraph are realistic.

C. COMPROMISES AND ALTERNATIVES

Tenant may want to increase the time period given to Tenant to remove the lien. The Lease may also require that, as a condition for work or installation to commence, a completion bond must be provided by Tenant.

Below is a proposed compromise of Paragraph 14 that reflects protections that Tenant will want to secure (the underscored and stricken words reflect the changes made to the original Paragraph 14 below):

> *In the event any mechanic's or materialmen's lien shall at any time be filed against the Premises allegedly by reason of work, labor, services, or materials performed or furnished to Tenant or to anyone holding the Premises through or under Tenant for work or materials performed or used with respect to the Premises, Tenant shall within ~~ten (10)~~ thirty (30) days cause the same to be discharged of record or bonded to the satisfaction of Landlord. If Tenant shall fail to cause such lien forthwith to be so discharged or bonded after being notified of the filing thereof, then, in addition to any other right or remedy of Landlord, Landlord may discharge the same by paying the amount claimed to be due, and the amount so paid by Landlord and all costs and expenses, including reasonable attorneys' fees incurred by Landlord in procuring the discharge of such lien, shall be due and payable by Tenant to Landlord as Additional Rent on the first day of the next following month, or may, at Landlord's election, be subtracted from any sums owing to Tenant by Landlord.*

D. COMMENTS

If the lien is bonded, Landlord must make sure that it is written by a reputable company that has a sufficient net worth to protect Landlord against potential losses.

Tenant may not be able to remove or bond the lien within 10 days. A more reasonable period of time to deal with the lien is 30 days but even that time period may not be sufficient. This is because, in some jurisdictions, removing a lien by bond requires getting on a court calendar for the court to approve the bond and it can take in excess of 10 or even 30 days to get on a court calendar. That said, Landlord typically will not extend the date beyond 30 days because Landlords have 30-day lien removal requirements in their loan documents. What usually happens in such event, is that Tenant submits evidence to Landlord (who then submits evidence to Lender) that Tenant has submitted the necessary filings to get on the court's calendar and is diligently pursuing the bond, in which case Landlords (and Lenders) do not act on the Default provided Tenant continues to diligently pursue the removal by bond until completion.

E. TYPICAL PARAGRAPH

14. **Mechanic's Liens. In the event any mechanic's or materialmen's lien shall at any time be filed against the Premises, Tenant shall within ten (10) days cause the same to be discharged of record. If Tenant shall fail to cause such lien forthwith to be so discharged after being notified of the filing thereof, then, in addition to any other right or remedy of Landlord, Landlord may discharge the same by paying the amount claimed to be due, and the amount so paid by Landlord and all costs and expenses, including reasonable attorneys' fees incurred by Landlord in procuring the discharge of such lien, shall be due and payable by Tenant to Landlord as Additional Rent on the first day of the next following month, or may, at Landlord's election, be subtracted from any sums owing to Tenant by Landlord.**

PARAGRAPH 15

Floor-Load Limitations

RISK RATING: 3

A. DESCRIPTION AND SCOPE

This Paragraph establishes limits on Tenant's physical use of the Premises so that the design floor-load limits of the Building will not be exceeded.

B. ANALYSIS

1. Landlord's Perspective

Landlord is concerned about the type and extent of office equipment and fixtures Tenant proposes to install since it may adversely affect the structural integrity of the Building. Landlord also wants to approve the installation and placement of Tenant's machinery and electrical equipment so that it can consider the effects on electrical capacity, noise levels, other tenants, and the marketability of the Property.

2. Tenant's Perspective

Tenant wants to ensure that its contemplated use of the Premises is within the Property's stated structural capacity and can be conducted without additional cost and without interruption or requirement for subsequent consent.

3. Lender's Perspective

Lender wants to ensure that the structural integrity of the Property and the value of its security are protected, and that adjacent tenants have no cause to complain as a result of Tenant's operations.

4. Broker's Perspective

Landlord Broker should know the Building floor load to be able to respond to any questions regarding same by Tenant Broker. Tenant Broker should determine during the up-front needs assessment phase how the client/tenant intends to use the space and whether extraordinary floor loading may be required. Examples would be rolling files, a generator, fuel tank, certain other equipment, or heavy displays (storage, manufacturing, retail, medical use, etc.) to be placed within the Premises. Tenant Broker and Tenant should consult with an engineer who can verify the required floor load and help secure preapproval of the Landlord to reinforce the floor in some fashion prior to drafting the Lease (or certainly prior to signing the Lease), if applicable.

C. COMPROMISES AND ALTERNATIVES

Landlord might agree to share with Tenant the cost of strengthening and reinforcing the Premises where the modifications enhance the long-term value of the Property and improve its marketability. Alternatively, Landlord could allow Tenant to pay for the cost of any alterations over the remainder of the Lease Term rather than in one lump sum.

D. COMMENTS

Landlord should take care in making representations concerning the Premises, and ensure that breach of such representations should not be a default permitting termination or self-help by Tenant to correct the breach.

E. TYPICAL PARAGRAPH

15. **Floor-Load Limitations. Landlord represents that the floor space of the Premises will carry [AMOUNT] pounds per square foot of floor live load uniformly distributed. Tenant shall not place a load upon any floor of the Premises that exceeds [AMOUNT] pounds floor load per square-foot area that such floor was designed to carry. Landlord reserves the right to prescribe the weight and position of all business machines, mechanical equipment, and fixtures that shall be placed so as to distribute the weight. If Tenant shall desire a floor load in excess of [AMOUNT] pounds of floor load per square foot for which the floor and any portion of the Premises is designed, to the extent such excess is allowed by law, upon submission to Landlord of plans showing the location of and the desired floor live load for the area in question, Landlord, in its sole discretion, may strengthen and reinforce the same, at Tenant's sole expense, so as to carry the live load desired. Business machines and mechanical equipment used by Tenant that cause vibration or noise that may be transmitted to the Building or to any leased space to such a degree as to be reasonably objectionable to Landlord or to any tenants in the Building shall be placed and maintained by Tenant, at its expense, in settings of cork, rubber, or spring-type vibration eliminators sufficient to reduce such vibration or noise to an unobjectionable level.**

Tenant shall not move any safe, heavy machinery, heavy equipment, freight, bulky matter, or fixtures into, within, or out of the Premises without Landlord's prior written consent. If moving of such business machines, mechanical equipment, files, and/or fixtures require special handling, Tenant agrees to employ only persons holding a Master Rigger's License to do said work, and that all work in connection therewith shall comply with applicable laws and regulations. Any such moving shall be at the sole risk and hazard of Tenant, and Tenant will exonerate, indemnify, and save Landlord harmless against and from any liability, loss, injury, claim, or suit resulting directly from such moving. Tenant shall schedule such moving at such times as Landlord shall require for the convenience of the normal operations of the Building.

PARAGRAPH 16

Maintenance and Repairs

RISK RATING: 3

A. DESCRIPTION AND SCOPE

This Paragraph sets forth specific allocations of repair and maintenance responsibilities between Landlord and Tenant. Paragraph 16 below represents typical allocations made with respect to multi-tenant office or even retail Buildings wherein Tenant is taking just a portion of the Building. This Paragraph will look quite different in a "triple net" lease for a single occupant Building. Since "triple net" leases are most often used for industrial leases, that concept is discussed in Part 3, Paragraph 4.

B. ANALYSIS

1. Landlord's Perspective

Landlord seeks to ensure that (i) Tenant shall be responsible for maintaining the Premises, (ii) that the Building and Building systems will be appropriately maintained, and (iii) that the costs incurred by Landlord in performing its operation, maintenance and repair obligations under this Paragraph shall be subject to recoupment in Operating Expenses, to the extent permissible under and/or applicable with respect to the particular lease.

2. Tenant's Perspective

Tenant seeks to ensure that (i) Landlord will operate the Building in a first-class manner; (ii) that the Building, Building systems, and Common Area will remain in good working order and condition for the duration of the Term; and (iii) Tenant's repair and maintenance obligations shall be limited to the portions of the Premises within its control and any supplemental systems installed by Tenant. Tenant, of course, likely selected the Building to rent space within it, at least partly, due to the condition of the

Building on the Effective Date. Therefore, it is fair and reasonable that Tenant expects the condition to at least remain the same for the duration of the Term.

3. Lender's Perspective

Lender seeks to ensure that the Building remains in good condition so the value of the Property does not decline over the term of the loan. In addition, Lender will likely favor any Landlord covenant to operate the Building in a "first-class" manner that Tenant is able to negotiate into the Lease. Lender is concerned that its collateral, the Building, is maintained by Landlord in accordance with an objective standard. This will be one of the few instances in the Lease where interests of Lender and Tenant are aligned.

4. Broker's Perspective

Each Broker will want to consult with their respective client to determine any sensitivity to or any particular client need relating to this Paragraph that should be covered in the LOI. As an example, due to the nature of Tenant's business and corresponding confidentiality concerns, Tenant may wish to control maintenance and repairs in the Premises. If neither Landlord nor Tenant have any particular sensitivity to this issue, this Paragraph can be handled by the attorneys in Lease negotiations.

C. COMPROMISES AND ALTERNATIVES

This Paragraph requires Landlord to maintain the structural aspects of the Building and just those portions of Building systems outside of the Premises with Tenant being otherwise responsible for maintaining and repairing the Premises and those portions of the Building systems located with the Premises. This is a fairly typical allocation of maintenance and repair responsibilities between the parties.

However, the if Landlord built out the Premises (and the Building systems within it) as either pre-built space or in accordance with plans approved by Tenant, Tenant has an argument that Landlord should be responsible for the maintenance and repair obligations of all portions of the Building systems within the Premises including the distribution portions. Also, if Landlord performed any Landlord's Work, Tenant's maintenance and repair obligations should not commence with respect to same until after the expiration of any warranty of Landlord's Work that Tenant was able to negotiate into the Lease. See Part 1, Exhibit B, Alternate 2 on that issue.

If not already included in the Lease, Tenant should endeavor to incorporate a Landlord operational, repair and maintenance covenant into this Paragraph. An example of such a provision is as follows:

> *"Landlord covenants to operate, repair and maintain the Building in a 'first class manner' for the duration of the Term."*

In those situations where Landlord desires a standard narrower that a "first-class office building," a reference could be made to particular buildings in the geographic area where the Premises are located, or a general reference to similar buildings in the area where the Premises are located could be added. In addition, there may be situations where Landlord or Tenant will lease space in a Building other than a "first-class" Building; in those situations, a different standard will be appropriate.

D. COMMENTS

The allocation of responsibility for the repair and maintenance of the Building and Premises is generally based upon recognizing that Landlord owns the Property and has a long-term investment in the Property. Because of this, repair items that are structural or capital in nature, go to the operation of the Building or the Building systems or are otherwise out of the control of the Tenant, rightly belong with Landlord.

Tenant's repair and maintenance and obligations should not extend to a portion of the Building or the Building systems located outside of Tenant's control. As an example, if water main breaks between the street and the Building, that should be squarely within Landlord's obligation to repair. Thus, responsibility for Building systems are appropriately allocated to Landlord except for those portions of the Building systems that are located within the Premises and exclusively service the Premises. The fact that Tenant should only be responsible for the portion of the Building systems that exclusively serve the Premises is important to include because there may be Building systems that run through the Premises to service an adjacent tenant space and it is not appropriate for Tenant to be responsible for any portions of those systems.

An exception to the limitation on Tenant's repair and maintenance described herein is that a Tenant is also typically responsible to repair any damage outside the Premises caused by Tenant's negligence, willful misconduct or Alterations. See Subparagraph 16(c) for that typical expanded Tenant responsibility. Tenant must be exceptionally careful, however, that any such expanded Tenant repair and maintenance obligations be subject to and ultimately limited and trumped by the waiver of claims provision of the insurance Paragraph because the responsibility to repair portions of the Building should always lie with the party who has insured that portion of the Building despite who caused the damage.

Subparagraph 16(d) might not be included in a lease being reviewed by Tenant and, if it is missing, Tenant may wish to insert it.

E. TYPICAL PARAGRAPH

16. Maintenance and Repairs.

(a) Landlord's Repairs. Subject to casualty and condemnation provisions of the Lease, Landlord shall operate, maintain and make all necessary repairs or replacements to (i) the part of the Building systems located outside of the Premises which provide service to the Premises, and (ii) the structural portions, exterior portions and foundations of the Building (including the roof) and the public portions of the Building, both exterior and interior, in either case in conformance with standards applicable to [first-class] office buildings in the [City, State], area.

Notwithstanding anything to the contrary contained herein, unless Landlord elects otherwise, Landlord shall not be responsible for the repair of any Alteration made by Tenant or other installations made by or for Tenant which materially deviate from Building-Standard items or for any repairs caused by the negligence or misconduct of Tenant or Tenant's agents, employees, contractors, subcontractors, invitees or licensees. The cost of Landlord's operation, maintenance and repair obligations hereunder shall be included in Operating Expense.

(b) Tenant Repairs. Subject to casualty and condemnation provisions of the Lease, Tenant, at Tenant's sole cost and expense, shall take good care of the Premises and the fixtures, equipment and appurtenances therein, the distribution portions of the Building Systems located within and exclusively serving the Premises and any supplemental HVAC system installed by or on behalf of Tenant, and shall make all nonstructural repairs or replacements thereto as and when needed to preserve them in good working order and condition, except for reasonable wear and tear and obsolescence; provided, that in no event shall Tenant be obligated to improve the condition of the Premises from that which existed on the day possession thereof was delivered to Tenant. If there now is or shall be installed in the Building a "sprinkler system," and such system or any of its appliances shall be damaged or injured or not in proper working order by reason of any act or omission of Tenant, Tenant's agents, servants, employees, licensees or visitors, Tenant shall forthwith restore the same to good working condition at its own expense; and if any bureau, department or official of the state or city government, shall require or recommend that any changes, modifications, alterations or additional sprinkler heads or other equipment be made or supplied, Landlord shall, at Landlord's expense (subject to expense recoupment to the extent an Operating Expense), promptly make and supply such changes, modifications, alterations, additional sprinkler heads or other equipment. Tenant shall perform any repairs required to be performed by Tenant pursuant to this Paragraph 16 in accordance with the provisions of Paragraph 15 hereof. If Tenant fails after thirty (30) days' prior notice (or such shorter period as may be required due to an emergency) to proceed with due diligence to make repairs required to be made by Tenant, then Landlord may make such repairs, and the actual, out of pocket expenses thereof incurred by Landlord, with interest thereon at the Applicable Rate, shall be forthwith paid to Landlord as Additional Rent not later than the tenth (10th) day after Landlord gives Tenant an invoice therefor. Tenant shall give Landlord prompt notice of any defective condition in the Building or in any Building system located in, servicing or passing through the Premises that is known to Tenant.

(c) Limitations. Notwithstanding the provisions of Paragraph (a) and (b) above, (x) all damage or injury to the Premises or to any other part of

the Building and Building systems, whether requiring structural or nonstructural repairs, to the extent caused by or resulting from any negligence or willful misconduct or Alterations of Tenant (or Tenant's agents, employees, contractors or parties holding by, under or through Tenant), shall be repaired by Tenant, at Tenant's sole cost, to the reasonable satisfaction of Landlord (if the required repairs are nonstructural in nature and do not affect any Building System), or shall be repaired by Landlord, at Tenant's sole cost, (if the required repairs are structural in nature or affect any Building System), and (y) all damage or injury to the Premises, whether requiring structural or nonstructural repairs, to the extent caused by or resulting from the gross negligence or willful misconduct of Landlord, or repairs or replacements made by Landlord, shall be repaired, at Landlord's sole cost and expense, by Landlord to the reasonable satisfaction of Tenant; provided, however, that nothing contained in this Paragraph (c) limits the waivers of claims as provided in the insurance Paragraph.

(d) Landlord's Obligation to Minimize Interference. Landlord shall use commercially reasonable efforts under the circumstances to minimize interference with Tenant's use and occupancy of the Premises in making any repairs or replacements pursuant to this Paragraph 16; provided, however, that Landlord shall have no obligation to employ contractors or labor at overtime or premium pay rates or to incur any other overtime costs or expenses whatsoever, except that Landlord, at its expense, shall employ contractors or labor at overtime or other premium pay rates if necessary to make any repair required to be made by Landlord hereunder to remedy any condition that either (i) results in a denial of access to the Premises, (ii) threatens the health or safety of any occupant of the Premises, or (iii) materially interferes with Tenant's ability to conduct its business in the Premises.

PARAGRAPH 17

Assignment and Subleasing

RISK RATING: 4

A. DESCRIPTION AND SCOPE

This Paragraph prevents Tenant from assigning the Lease, subletting the Premises, sharing occupancy of the Premises or otherwise encumbering the Premises without Landlord's prior written consent, except under limited circumstances. This Paragraph states very specific criteria that Tenant must satisfy in order to obtain Landlord's consent.

This Paragraph is also drafted wide enough to encompass certain Tenant corporate transactions and deem them "assignments" so that the Landlords protections under this Paragraph 17 are extended to such corporate transactions even if no traditional subletting or assignment is proposed by Tenant.

In addition, this Paragraph also gives Landlord the option of taking back (or "recapturing") the space Tenant proposes to assign or sublet and permitting Landlord, at its election, to either (i) terminate the lease with respect to the proposed space or (ii) to "lease-back" the proposed space and re-lease it to a third party.

B. ANALYSIS

1. Landlord's Perspective

Generally, any right to assign or sublet favors Tenant and will thus diminish Landlord's rights to the Premises. From Landlord's point of view, it would prefer no transfers without its consent. However, many Tenants will request that Landlord not unreasonably withhold consent to assignment or subletting.

In some states, the courts will impose upon Landlord a "commercially reasonable" standard even though this standard is not so stated in the Lease. In such situations, it is preferable to Landlord to define, as in the case of the following proposed Paragraph 17, what is "reasonable" with respect to consenting to assignments and subletting.

Landlord wants to retain Tenant as the party liable under this Lease since Landlord has evaluated the financial condition of Tenant.

Landlord will likely insist that the right to "recapture" the Premises be retained in the Lease, since Landlord's ability to accept reconveyance enables Landlord to capture net gains due to increases in market rents and/or to accommodate the needs of another tenant of the Building.

2. Tenant's Perspective

This Paragraph should be reviewed very closely by a Tenant because, absent an express Tenant early termination right, Tenant's assignment and subletting rights are typically the only "exit" strategy a Tenant has should it wish or need to depart the Premises prior to the expiration of the Term without defaulting under the Lease.

This Paragraph is also important to a Tenant because it grants flexibility to Tenant in managing changes to its space needs.

3. Lender's Perspective

Lender wants to be able to analyze the income generated by the Lease. In the event that Tenant assigns or sublets, Lender wants assurances that (i) the assignee or sublessee will have the financial strength to meet its obligations under the Lease; (ii) the proposed assignee's or sublessee's business will not conflict with exclusive clauses in other tenants' leases; and (iii) the quality and character of such assignee's or sublessee's business is similar to that of other tenants of the Building.

Lender will likely insist that no Tenant be released of any liability in connection with any assignment or subletting without Lender's consent, since the credit of each Tenant in the Building is viewed by Lender as a potential source of repayment of Lender's mortgage loan so long as that Tenant is liable for the payment of rent under the Lease.

4. Broker's Perspective

Landlord Broker typically has little need to address this issue in the LOI. Tenant Broker will want to include in the LOI that Tenant will be permitted to sublet or assign to any Tenant Related Entity (as hereafter defined) without Landlord's prior consent and that Landlord shall not unreasonably withhold, condition or delay its consent to transfers to others who are not Related Entities. Also, Tenant Broker should inquire with Tenant whether Tenant has any special space sharing needs (e.g., the need to share the Premises with vendors or customers) so that any such need is addressed in the LOI.

Both Landlord Broker and Tenant Broker should actively support counsel in the negotiation of this Paragraph as there are a number of important elements of the Paragraph which may impact Landlord's leasing activity at the Building and Tenant's ability to market and sublet the Premises, if necessary.

C. COMPROMISES AND ALTERNATIVES

Typical Paragraph 17, as drafted below, intentionally reflects a strong Landlord position.

Tenants under long term leases and/or under leases wherein Tenant is leasing either the entire Property (especially tenants under net industrial leases) should negotiate Paragraph 17 aggressively to achieve the most flexibility possible.

To begin with, Tenant will want Landlord to agree not to unreasonably withhold, condition or delay its consent to any proposed assignment or sublease requiring Landlord's consent. Tenant should also request the following provision:

> *Landlord shall grant or withhold its consent in writing (with specific reasons for withholding its consent), within thirty (30) days after receiving Tenant's request therefor. Landlord's failure to so respond within said thirty (30)-day period shall be deemed a consent to said proposed assignment or sublease.*

Tenant may wish to trigger any Landlord "recapture" and/or "consent" right when an LOI is executed (versus when the sublease or lease assignment is executed) to have certainty of Landlord's position on the proposed transfer before finalizing the document. Although, oftentimes, Landlord's will insist that it not consider any assignment or sublease request before it has the final, fully executed document to review, and in such case the sublease or assignment agreement must contain a provision that is contingent upon receipt of Landlord's written consent thereto.

Tenant will not want the assignment and subletting provisions of the Lease to interfere with any potential corporate transaction that Tenant may contemplate during the Lease Term. Paragraph 17(d) below already contemplates this by permitting Tenant to sublet the Premises or assign the Lease, without Landlord's consent, in certain circumstances. If such a Tenant right is not already expressly included in any particular lease Tenant is entering into, Tenant may wish to propose the follow provision for insertion into the Lease:

> *Tenant shall have the right, upon prior notice to Landlord, but without obtaining Landlord's consent, to assign the Lease or sublet all or part of the Premises to any affiliate, parent, subsidiary, divisional entity, partner, joint venture entity or related business entity of Tenant, or to any entity arising by virtue of merger, consolidation or other business combination with Tenant or Tenant's parent entity, or to any purchaser of all or substantially all of Tenant's stock, membership or other ownership interests or assets, or to any entity under the ownership or control of Tenant's parent entity or holding entity (individually, a "Related Entity" and collectively, "Related Entities"). Notwithstanding anything to the contrary contained herein, no Landlord profit sharing, recapture or review fee rights shall apply to transfers to Related Entities permitted under this paragraph.*

Tenant may wish to "push back" on any net worth minimum thresholds for proposed subtenants or assignees and certainly with respect to any imposed upon Permitted Transfers to Related Entities. Permitted Transfers should be expressly exempt from any Landlord recapture or profit sharing rights.

Each of the Landlord's "reasonableness standards" for consent should be reviewed closely by Tenant and negotiated in the context of Tenant's leverage and the factual circumstances of the Lease. Landlord's "reasonableness standards" in Proposed Paragraph 17 can be found in Subparagraphs 17(e)(A) and 17(g)(A). For illustrative purposes, here are a few examples of where Tenant may wish to negotiate in Subparagraph 17(e)(A):

Subparagraph (1): Tenant should be able to "list" the Premises for subletting at a lower rent rate but not otherwise publicly advertise it.

Subparagraph (3): The necessary financial standing of the subtenant should just be enough to meet the obligations under the Lease as Tenant will not be released from its obligations under the Lease anyway.

Subparagraph (5): Tenant should be permitted to sublet less than the entire Premises if Tenant is taking more than a specified number of rentable square feet. Tenants leasing many rentable square feet should be able to sublet to multiple different subtenants resulting in the Premises being occupies by multiple occupants.

Paragraph 17 permits Landlord to recapture any space proposed to be sublet by Tenant through either, at Landlord's election, lease termination or lease-back of the space to be sublet. Tenant should resist granting Landlord the recapture rights under Paragraph 17, since a recapture by termination arguably limits Tenant's flexibility and also transfers to Landlord any increase in the value of the Premises. Thus, as a first position, Tenant wishes to strike from the Lease any Landlord recapture right. If Tenant is unsuccessful in eliminating the provision entirely, it may wish to limit it as much as the market conditions permit. As an example, Tenant may wish to argue that Landlord should only be permitted to recapture by termination if Tenant is proposing to assign the Lease or sublet all or a portion of the Premises for the remainder of the Lease Term, because, in that case, Tenant is voluntarily relinquishing any flexibility right it has to grow back into the space. However, if the term of any proposed sublease is for materially less than the remaining Term of the Lease, Tenant may be intentionally protecting its right to flexibility by a short sublease so that Tenant can regrow back into the Premises after the term of the sublease expires. Tenant may wish to argue against any provision limiting Tenant's flexibility in that manner. Also, Landlord recapturing by "lease back" can be a nuisance so Tenant may wish to limit any Landlord recapture right to Landlord terminating the Lease with respect to the portion of the Premises affected. In most cases, it will just be cleaner and easier for Tenant that way. If Tenant is unable to remove the Landlord recapture by "lease back" right, Tenant will want to be sure the Lease is clear that (i) Tenant has absolutely no obligations with respect to the leased-back premises during the term of the lease-back from Landlord (including any indemnity obligations); (ii) notwithstanding anything to the contrary contained in the Lease, Tenant shall not remain liable for the lease-back premises during the duration of the lease-back lease even in the event the occupant thereunder defaults under its lease with Landlord for the space; (iii) Landlord shall be responsible, as its cost, for returning to Tenant the leased-back premises in a condition agreed to by Landlord and Tenant, with certainly Tenant having no increased restoration obligations for the leased-back premises attributable to the lease-back and alterations made in connection therewith; and (iv) Landlord should expressly indemnify Tenant from and against any and all claims for damage to the Premises or the Building or bodily injury of whatever nature arising from or otherwise related to the lease-back lease or the use and occupancy of the lease-back premises.

The issue of "profit sharing" with respect to any proposed assignment or subletting (other than to Related Entities when typically, Tenant retains any "profits"), will likely be a negotiated point. Landlord may want 100% of the net gain from the transaction, particularly if any such subletting or assignment would directly compete with Landlord's efforts to lease the remainder of the Building. The Lease rights to the Premises could become very valuable if substantial increases in market rents occur during the Term of the Lease. Tenant may also argue that 100% of the excess rents received from any assignment or subletting should be retained by Tenant, since Tenant is assuming 100% of the risk that rents will decrease during the Term of the Lease. What happens most often, is Landlord and Tenant agree to share any "profit" or "net gain" in equal 50% part.

Tenants are more often "sharing space" with Related Entities or related vendors, partners or others with which they have a business or personal relationship. In the event Tenant may need such right, Tenant can add the following provision to the end of Typical Paragraph 17 below:

> *Notwithstanding anything in this Paragraph 17 to the contrary, Tenant shall be permitted from time to time, at its sole discretion and without the prior consent of Landlord and without triggering any Landlord profit sharing, review fees or recapture rights under the Lease, Tenant may permit portions of the Premises to be occupied, at any time and from time to time, by individuals who are not officers or employees of Tenant (such individuals who are permitted to occupy portions of the Premises pursuant to this subparagraph (m) being each referred to individually as a "Permitted Occupant," and collectively as the "Permitted Occupants"), without the consent of Landlord, provided that (i) no demising wall(s) are erected in the Premises separating the space used by a Permitted Occupant from the remainder of the Premises, (ii) the Permitted Occupants use the Premises (and Tenant's allocation of parking spaces) in conformity with all applicable provisions of this Lease, (iii) in no event shall the use of any portion of the Premises by any Permitted Occupant create or be deemed to create any right, title or interest of the Permitted Occupant in or to the Premises, (iv) the occupancy by a Permitted Occupant does not materially increase the traffic through the lobby or common areas of the Building, the Operating Expenses or the burden on the elevators serving the Premises, in each case beyond that which would reasonably be expected to occur if Tenant used the entire Premises for the normal conduct of its business, (v) the portion of the Premises used by all Permitted Occupants shall not exceed twenty percent (20%), (vi) each Permitted Occupant shall maintain, during their period of occupancy of the Premises, the insurance required by Tenant under this Lease and provide Landlord evidence of same, and (vii) at least ten (10) days prior to a Permitted Occupant taking occupancy of portion of the Premises, Tenant shall give notice to Landlord advising Landlord of (i) the name and address of such Permitted Occupant, (ii) the character and nature of the use and business to be conducted by such Permitted Occupant, (iii) the usable square footage to be occupied by such Permitted Occupant, and (iv) the duration of such occupancy. Within thirty (30) days after request by Landlord, Tenant shall provide Landlord with a list of the names of all Permitted Occupants then occupying any portion of the Premises.*

D. COMMENTS

Landlord may also want to limit the applicability of this Paragraph so that only the original Tenant and not any assignee or subtenant has assignment or subletting rights under the Lease. But Tenant's should be sure to extend its rights under Paragraph 17 to at least those Related Entities with rights pursuant to Permitted Transfers under Paragraph 17(d) below. Also, Tenants with Leases with long Terms should endeavor to remove any limitation out all together as any prospective subtenant will want to be able sub-sublet as an exit strategy and restrictive language would negatively impact the marketability of the space for the Tenant to sublease.

Finally, when a sublease or lease assignment is agreed to, Landlords typically enter into a written tri-party agreement with Tenant and the proposed subtenant or assignee when Landlord consents to such a transaction.

E. TYPICAL PARAGRAPH

17. **Assignment and Subleasing.**
    (a) **General Limitation. Except as expressly permitted herein, Tenant, without the prior written consent of Landlord in each instance, shall not (a) assign its rights or delegate it duties under this Lease (whether by operation of law or otherwise), or mortgage or encumber its interest in this Lease, in either case in whole or in part, (b) sublet or permit the subletting of, the Premises, or (c) permit the Premises or any part thereof to be occupied or used for desk space, mailing privileges or otherwise, by any Person (as hereinafter defined) other than Tenant. Either a transfer (including the issuance of treasury stock or the creation and issuance of new stock or a new class of stock) of a controlling interest in the shares of Tenant (if Tenant is a corporation or trust) or a transfer of a majority of the total interest in Tenant (if Tenant is a partnership, limited liability company or other entity) at any one time or over a period of time through a series of transfers, directly or indirectly, shall be deemed an assignment of this Lease and shall be subject to all of the provisions of this Paragraph 17; provided, however, that the transfer or issuance of shares of Tenant (if Tenant is a corporation or trust) for purposes of this Paragraph 17(a) shall not include the sale of shares by persons other than those deemed "insiders" within the meaning of the Securities Exchange Act of 1934, as amended, which sale is effected through the "over-the-counter market" or through any recognized stock exchange.**
    (b) **Landlord's Expenses. Tenant shall reimburse Landlord on demand for any reasonable out-of-pocket costs that Landlord incurs in connection with any proposed assignment of Tenant's interest in this Lease or any proposed subletting of the Premises, including, without limitation, reasonable attorneys' fees and disbursements and the reasonable costs of making investigations as to the acceptability of the proposed subtenants or the proposed assignee.**

(c) No Release. Neither an assignment of Tenant's interest in this Lease nor any subletting, occupancy or use of the Premises or any part thereof by any Person other than Tenant, nor any collection of Rent by Landlord from any Person other than Tenant shall, in any circumstances, relieve, release or discharge Tenant of its obligations under this Lease on Tenant's part to be observed and performed.

(d) Certain Permitted Transfers. Subject to the provisions of this Paragraph 17(d), Tenant, without first obtaining the prior written consent of Landlord (but upon at least thirty (30) days prior written notice to Landlord), shall have the right to assign its interest in this Lease (in whole but not in part) (i) to any corporation which is a successor to Tenant either by merger or consolidation, (ii) to a purchaser of all or substantially all of Tenant's assets (provided such purchaser also assumes substantially all of Tenant's liabilities), or (iii) to Tenant's Affiliate (as hereinafter defined) (any Person under (i), (ii) or (iii) a "Related Entity"). Subject to the provisions of this Paragraph 17(d), Tenant, without first obtaining the prior written consent of Landlord (but upon at least thirty (30) days prior written notice to Landlord), shall have the right to sublease all or any portion of the Premises to Tenant's Affiliate. Tenant shall not have the right to make an assignment of this Lease or sublease of all or any portion of the Premises without Landlord's consent pursuant to this Paragraph 17(d) unless either Tenant is then (i) the initially named Tenant under the Lease, (ii) a successor to the initially named Tenant under the Lease who acquired Tenant's interest in this Lease in a transaction approved by Landlord, or (iii) Tenant's Affiliate to the initially named Tenant under the Lease. Tenant shall not make an assignment of this Lease without Landlord's consent pursuant to this Paragraph 17(d) to any Person if (x) the principal purpose of the transaction comprising such assignment is to evade the Landlord consent requirements of Paragraph 17(a), or (y) the assignee has a net worth and annual net income and cash flow, determined in accordance with either generally accepted accounting principles or generally accepted auditing standards, in either case consistently applied, after giving effect to such assignment, less than Tenant's net worth and annual net income and cash flow on the day immediately preceding the effective date of any such assignment. If Tenant makes an assignment of this Lease without Landlord's consent pursuant to this Paragraph 17(d), then Tenant shall deliver to Landlord, on or prior to the fifth (5th) day after the effective date of such assignment, an instrument, in form and substance reasonably satisfactory to Landlord, duly executed by Tenant and the assignee, pursuant to which (I) Tenant makes such assignment to such assignee, and (II) such assignee assumes all of the obligations of Tenant arising hereunder from and after the effective date of such assignment. If Tenant makes any such assignment to any Person (other than Tenant's Affiliate), then Tenant shall also submit to Landlord, simultaneously with Tenant's submission of such instrument to Landlord, reasonable evidence to the effect that Tenant has complied with the provisions of clauses (x) and (y) above. If Tenant subleases all or any portion of the Premises without Landlord's consent pursuant to this Paragraph 17(d), then Tenant shall deliver to Landlord, on or prior to the fifth (5th) day after the date of such sublease, a copy of such sublease. Any transfer permitted under this Paragraph 17(d) shall be referred to as a "Permitted Transfer".

(e) Certain Rights to Sublease.

(A) Landlord shall not unreasonably withhold or delay its consent to any subletting of the Premises, provided that:

(1) the Premises has not been listed or otherwise publicly advertised for subletting at a rental rate less than the prevailing rental rate set by Landlord for comparable space in the Building or, if there is no comparable space, the prevailing rental rate which Landlord would charge reasonably determined by Landlord (Landlord having the right to reasonably approve any and all advertising relating to the Premises);

(2) no Default has occurred and is continuing;

(3) the proposed subtenant has a financial standing (taking into consideration the obligations of the proposed subtenant under the sublease) reasonably satisfactory to Landlord, and be of a character, be engaged in a business, and proposes to use the Premises in a manner in keeping with the standards in such respects of the other tenancies in the Building;

(4) if Landlord has or within six (6) months thereafter reasonably expects to have comparable space available in the Building, the proposed subtenant (or any Affiliate of the proposed subtenant) is neither a tenant or subtenant of any space in the Building, nor a Person with whom Landlord is engaged in negotiations regarding the leasing or subleasing of space in the Building;

(5) the subletting is not for less than the entire Premises;

(6) Tenant and the subtenant execute and deliver an agreement, in form and substance reasonably satisfactory to Landlord, pursuant to which Landlord grants Landlord's consent to such sublease on terms which are consistent with the provisions hereof; and

(7) such sublease expressly provides that it is subject and subordinate to this Lease (and all instruments to which this Lease may be subordinate), and further expressly provides that, in the event of termination of this Lease or reentry of the Premises by Landlord under this Lease, then Landlord may, at its option, take over all of the right, title and interest of Tenant, as sublessor under such

sublease, and such subtenant, at Landlord's option, shall attorn to Landlord pursuant to the then executory provisions of such sublease, except that Landlord shall not be:

(i) liable for any act or omission of Tenant under such sublease, or

(ii) subject to any defense or offsets which such subtenant may have against Tenant, or

(iii) bound by any previous payment which such subtenant may have made to Tenant of more than thirty (30) days in advance of the date upon which such payment was due, unless previously approved by Landlord, or

(iv) bound by any obligation to make any payment to or on behalf of such subtenant, or

(v) bound by any obligation to perform any work or to make improvements to the Premises, or portion thereof demised by such sublease, or

(vi) bound by any amendment or modification of such sublease made without its consent, or

(vii) bound to return such subtenant's security deposit, if any, until such deposit has come into Landlord's actual possession and such subtenant would be entitled to such security deposit pursuant to the terms of such sublease.

(B) Tenant hereby agrees that any sublease approved by Landlord shall not be modified without the prior written consent of Landlord, or assigned, encumbered or otherwise transferred, or the subleased premises further sublet by the subtenant in whole or in part, or any part thereof suffered or permitted by the subtenant to be used or occupied by others, without the prior written consent of Landlord in each instance.

(C) If Tenant seeks to sublease the Premises pursuant to this Paragraph 17(e), then, in connection with Tenant's request for Landlord's consent, Tenant shall submit to Landlord a statement containing the following information: (a) the name and address of the proposed subtenant, (b) a copy of the proposed sublease, duly executed by Tenant and the proposed subtenant, (c) the nature and character of the use and business of the proposed subtenant, (d) financial statements of the proposed subtenant prepared by a certified public accountant, and (e) any other information that Landlord may reasonably request.

(f) Sublease Profit. Tenant shall pay to Landlord from time to time an amount equal to one hundred percent (100%) of Sublease Profit (as hereinafter defined) promptly after Tenant receives funds that constitute Sublease Profit.

(g) Certain Rights to Assign.

(A) Landlord shall not unreasonably withhold or delay its consent to an assignment of this Lease in its entirety provided that:

(1) No Default has occurred and is continuing;

(2) The proposed assignee (i) has a net worth (determined in accordance with generally accepted accounting principles, or generally accepted auditing standards, in either case consistently applied, taking into consideration the obligations of the proposed assignee under the Lease) which is reasonably satisfactory to Landlord, and (ii) is of a character, is engaged in a business, and proposes to use the Premises in a manner in keeping with the standards in such respects of the other tenancies in the Building;

(3) If Landlord has or within six (6) months thereafter reasonably expects to have comparable space available in the Building, the proposed assignee (or any Affiliate of the proposed assignee) is neither a tenant or subtenant of any space in the Building, nor a person or entity with whom Landlord is engaged in bona fide negotiations regarding the leasing or subleasing of space in the Building; and

(i) The assignee agrees to unconditionally assume all of the obligations of Tenant under this Lease from and after the date of the assignment.

(B) If Tenant seeks to assign this Lease in its entirety pursuant to this Paragraph 17(g), then, in connection with Tenant's request for Landlord's consent, Tenant shall submit to Landlord a statement containing the following information (the "Assignment Statement"): (i) the name and address of the proposed assignee, (ii) the terms and conditions of the proposed assignment, including, without limitation, the consideration payable for such assignment and the value (including cost, overhead and supervision) of any improvements (including any demolition to be performed) to the Premises proposed to be made by Tenant to prepare the Premises for occupancy by such assignee, (iii) the nature and character of the use and business of the proposed assignee, and (iv) any other information that Landlord may reasonably request.

(C) If Tenant does not consummate any such assignment of this Lease (for which Landlord has granted Landlord's consent under this Paragraph 17(g)) within sixty (60) days after the delivery of the Assignment Statement to Landlord, then Tenant shall not have the right to thereafter consummate such assignment without first again complying with the provisions of this Paragraph 17(g).

(D) If Tenant assigns this Lease, then Tenant shall deliver promptly to Landlord, (x) a duplicate original instrument of assignment in form and substance reasonably satisfactory to Landlord, duly executed

by Tenant, and (y) an instrument in form and substance reasonable satisfactory to Landlord, duly executed by the assignee, in which such assignee assumes observance and performance of, and agrees to be personally bound by, all of the terms, covenants and conditions of this Lease on Tenant's part to be observed and performed from and after the date thereof.

(h) Assignment Profit. Tenant shall pay to Landlord from time to time an amount equal to one hundred percent (100%) of Assignment Profit (as hereinafter defined) promptly after Tenant receives funds that constitute Assignment Profit.

(i) Landlord's Recapture. Notwithstanding anything to the contrary contained in this Lease, if Tenant desires to assign this Lease or to sublet all or any portion of the Premises, it shall first submit in writing to Landlord all of the documents described in Paragraph 17(j) hereof, and Landlord shall have the option, to be exercised by written notice given to Tenant within thirty (30) days after Landlord's receipt of all such documents, to elect to cancel this Lease, without liability, with respect to the portion of the Premises proposed to be assigned or sublet (the "Leaseback Area"), said cancellation to be effective on the date specified in Landlord's notice (the "Effective Date"), which Effective Date shall be at least thirty (30) days after, but no more than one hundred eighty (180) days after, the date of Landlord's cancellation notice. If Landlord shall have elected to terminate this Lease pursuant to this Paragraph 17(i), such termination shall be effective as of the Effective Date and thereupon the Term of this Lease shall cease and come to an end on that day with the same force and effect as though that were the original date set forth as the Expiration Date, and Tenant shall deliver broom-clean possession of the Premises to Landlord, in accordance with the terms of this Lease. Thereafter, neither party shall have any obligation to the other hereunder, except for any Fixed Rent or Additional Rent due and owing to the Landlord up to and including the termination of this Lease, and except as the parties hereto may have agreed otherwise in this Lease or by a separate writing.

(j) Required Documents. Notwithstanding anything to the contrary contained in this Lease, if Tenant plans or proposes any specific assignment or subletting to any parties, it shall first submit in writing to Landlord (a) the name and address of the proposed assignee or subtenant, (b) a statement of the rent, Additional Rent and a description of the other material terms of the proposed transaction, (c) reasonably satisfactory information as to the nature of the business of the proposed assignee or subtenant, and as to the nature of its proposed use of the space, (d) financial statements of the proposed assignee or subtenant prepared by a certified public accountant, and (e) other information relating to the proposed assignee or subtenant, reasonably sufficient to enable Landlord to determine if such proposed assignee or subtenant satisfies

the relevant requirements of Subparagraphs 17(e) and 17(g) herein (provided, however, that this Subparagraph (d) shall not apply to any sublettings or assignments to any Tenant's Affiliate(s)).

(k) Definitions. As used herein, the following terms shall have the meanings ascribed below:

"Affiliate" shall mean a Person which (i) Controls, (ii) is under the Control of, or (iii) is under common Control with, the Person in question.

"Assignment Profit" shall mean all consideration payable to Tenant, directly or indirectly, by any assignee, or any other amount received by Tenant from or in connection with any assignment of this Lease (including but not limited to, sums paid for the sale or rental, or consideration received on account of any contribution, of Tenant's Property) after deducting therefrom: (i) in the event of a sale (or contribution) of Tenant's Property, the then unamortized or undepreciated cost thereof determined on the basis of Tenant's federal income tax returns, (ii) the reasonable out-of-pocket costs, concessions and expenses of Tenant in making such assignment such as brokers' fees, attorneys' fees, advertising fees paid to unrelated third parties, and any commercially reasonable free rent or construction allowance concessions, (iii) any payments required to be made by Tenant in connection with the assignment of its interest in this Lease pursuant to any real property transfer tax of the United States or the State or municipality where the Premises is located (other than any income tax), (iv) any sums paid by Tenant to Landlord pursuant to Paragraph 17(b) hereof, (v) the cost of improvements or alterations made by Tenant expressly and solely for the purpose of preparing the Premises for such assignment, as determined by Tenant's federal income tax returns, (vi) the unamortized or undepreciated cost of any Tenant's Property leased to and used by such assignee, and (vii) the then unamortized or undepreciated costs of the Alterations determined on the basis of Tenant's federal income tax returns. If the consideration paid to Tenant for any assignment is paid in installments, then the expenses specified above shall be amortized over the period during which such installments are paid.

"Control" shall mean ownership, directly or indirectly, of (x) more than fifty percent (50%) of the outstanding voting stock of a corporation, or (y) more than fifty percent (50%) of the equity interest in any other form of entity, and, in either case, the possession of power to direct or cause the direction of the management and policy of such corporation or other entity, whether through the ownership of voting securities, by statute or according to the provisions of a contract.

"Person" shall mean any natural person, a partnership, a corporation, limited liability company or any other form of business or legal association or entity.

"Sublease Expenses" shall mean, in connection with a Sublease, (i) in the event of a sale of Tenant's Property, the then unamortized or undepreciated cost thereof determined on the basis of Tenant's federal income tax returns, (ii) the reasonable out-of-pocket costs and expenses incurred by Tenant in connection with making such Sublease, such as brokers' fees, attorneys' fees, advertising fees paid to unrelated third parties, and any commercially reasonable free rent or construction allowance concessions, (iii) any sums paid to Landlord pursuant to Paragraph 17(b) hereof, (iv) the cost of improvements or alterations made by Tenant expressly and solely for the purpose of preparing the Premises for such Sublease, and (v) the unamortized or undepreciated cost of any Tenant's Property leased under such Sublease. In determining Sublease Rent, (a) the costs described in clauses (ii), (iii) and (iv) above shall be amortized on a straight-line basis over the term of such Sublease, and (b) the costs in clause (v) above shall be amortized on a straight-line basis over the greater of the longest useful life of such improvements, alterations or Tenant's Property (as permitted pursuant to the Internal Revenue Code) and the term of such Sublease.

"Sublease Profit" shall mean the product obtained by multiplying (x) the excess of (A) the Sublease Rent Per Square Foot, over (B) the Rent per square foot under the Lease, by (y) the number of rentable square feet by the Sublease in question.

"Sublease Rent" shall mean the excess of (a) any rent or other consideration paid by the subtenant, grantee or occupant under any Sublease (including, but not limited to, sums paid for the sale or rental, or consideration received on account of any contribution of Tenant's Property or sums paid in connection with the supply of electricity or HVAC), over (b) the Sublease Expenses.

"Sublease Rent Per Square Foot" shall mean the quotient obtained by dividing (x) the Sublease Rent, by (y) the number of rentable square feet covered by the Sublease in question.

"Tenant's Affiliate" shall mean an Affiliate of Tenant.

"Tenant's Property" shall mean Tenant's personal property, including, without limitation, furniture, furnishings and equipment.

PARAGRAPH 18

Compliance with Laws

RISK RATING: 4

A. DESCRIPTION AND SCOPE

This Paragraph seeks to allocate the risk and cost of compliance with laws and governmental mandates to the Tenant.

B. ANALYSIS

1. Landlord's Perspective

Landlord would like to allocate all of the compliance-with-laws risk relating to the Premises to Tenant, and this Paragraph does that. This is particularly true in industrial triple net lease situations. Some Landlords will reject any affirmative obligation or representation that the Property is in compliance with all laws or limit any representation and warranty to Landlord's actual knowledge. Landlord most likely believes that the Building is in compliance, but does not want to give Tenant the right to require Landlord to correct any nonconformities unless Landlord is so required to comply by a governmental authority. In addition, Landlord would prefer not to be responsible for costs or permits required as a result of Tenant's particular use of the Premises.

2. Tenant's Perspective

Tenant should take responsibility for the operation of its business in the Premises and any Alterations made by Tenant but does not want to pay to bring Landlord's Building (or the Premises) up to new standards. If a new law, regulation, or building code is enacted that requires a retrofit of the Building or Premises, Tenant wants to limit its costs to either noncapital expenditures or to an allocable share based on its Lease Term related to the useful life of the expenditures. See Compromises and Alternatives below for a Paragraph that favors Tenant.

3. Lender's Perspective

Lender wants to make sure the Property is always in compliance with laws and would prefer risks and costs shifted to Tenant.

4. Broker's Perspective

Each Broker will want to consult with their respective client to determine any sensitivity to or any particular client need relating to this Paragraph that should be covered in the LOI. If none exist, this Paragraph can be handled by the attorneys in Lease negotiations. Oftentimes the LOI will address responsibilities with respect to compliance with at least the Americans with Disabilities Act of 1991 which is addressed in Paragraph 19.

C. COMPROMISES AND ALTERNATIVES

Tenant will want to limit Tenant's legal compliance obligations under the Lease to consist solely of complying with those applicable laws, codes, statutes, ordinances, rules and regulations relating to Tenant's business in the Premises or to any Alterations made by Tenant subsequent to Landlord's Work (if applicable). Except as immediately set forth above, Tenant will want Landlord, at its sole cost and expense, to comply with all applicable laws, codes, statutes, ordinances, rules, and regulations relating to the Premises, the Building or the Property, including, without limitation, building, health, disability, and fire code requirements.

In an office Lease where Landlord is pushing to extend Tenant's compliance obligations to Tenant's use and occupancy of the Premises, Tenant should take responsibility ***only*** for its own particular manner of use of the Premises ***other than general office use***. If it is an office Building, it is fair that the Landlord take responsibility for Building modifications needed just for office use, provided the modifications are not prompted by any Tenant Alterations.

If Landlord pushes for Tenant to be responsible for compliance more broadly, another reasonable compromise that Tenant may wish to propose is that Tenant's compliance obligations shall be limited to non-structural (or non-capital) modifications to the Premises.

Depending upon Landlord's comfort level with its knowledge of the compliance of the Building (and Tenant's leverage), Landlord may give Tenant the requested protections above or offer compromises. As an example, Landlord may be willing to represent and warrant that Landlord has not received any notices of violation of any laws. Another compromise is that Landlord may agree to comply with laws outside the Premises but only to the extent that any violation would negatively impact Tenant's use and occupancy of Premises or the safety of Tenant's employees.

A Tenant who agrees to take on broad compliance obligations (like an industrial triple net tenant), may desire to have the express right to contest and appeal a particular law, statute or regulation affecting the Premises.

Lastly, it is always worth a Tenant endeavoring to include in the Lease that Landlord represents and warrants that, as of the Effective Date and the Commencement Date, the Premises and the Building shall be in compliance with all applicable laws.

In addition, if Landlord is performing work to the Premises for Tenant's initial occupancy thereof or the space is pre-built, Tenant should push for the Premises to have a valid certificate of occupancy as a precondition to the Commencement Date.

Below is an example of a reciprocal Landlord compliance obligation that Tenant may wish to add:

> *Upon issuance of a final non-appealable government order, Landlord shall, at its own expense, promptly observe and comply with all present and future laws, ordinances, requirements, orders, directions, rules, and regulations of federal, state, county, and city governments and of all other governmental authorities having or claiming jurisdiction, directly or indirectly, over the Property (excluding the Premises) or appurtenances or any part thereof (including governmental rules and regulations, and such regulations or standards as are or may be promulgated under the Federal Occupational Safety and Health Act of 1970 or similar federal, state, or local requirements), whether the same are in force at the commencement of the Term or may in the future be passed, enacted, or directed. Without limiting the generality of the foregoing, Landlord shall also procure each and every permit, license, certificate, or other authorization now or hereafter required in connection with the lawful and proper use of the Property. Tenant shall pay all costs of complying with laws, ordinances, requirements, orders, directions, rules, and regulations relating to the Premises. Under no circumstances shall Landlord be considered to be in default under this Lease, nor shall Tenant have the right to terminate this Lease as a result of Landlord's failure to comply with the provisions of this Paragraph 18.*

D. COMMENTS

Tenant should procure its own operating permits, such as food service or liquor licenses that are usually personal and transferable apart from the ownership of the real property.

All parties must be careful that costs of ADA and environmental compliance that may be substantial do not unintentionally get allocated by default under this paragraph.

See Paragraph 19 for ADA compliance and Paragraph 20 for Environmental Laws Compliance.

E. TYPICAL PARAGRAPH

18. Compliance with Laws. Tenant shall, at its own expense, promptly observe and comply with all present and future laws, ordinances, requirements, orders, directions, rules, and regulations of federal, state, county, and city governments and of all other governmental authorities having or claiming jurisdiction, directly or indirectly, over the Premises or any part thereof, whether the same are in force at the commencement of the Term or may in the future be passed, enacted, or directed. Without limiting the generality of the foregoing, Tenant shall also procure each and every permit, license, certificate, or other authorization now or hereafter required in connection with the lawful and proper use of the Premises.

PARAGRAPH 19

Americans with Disabilities Act Compliance

RISK RATING: 4

A. DESCRIPTION AND SCOPE

The Americans with Disabilities Act (ADA) prohibits discrimination against people with disabilities across various industries, including setting the regulatory standards for access to public accommodations. Businesses that are generally open to the public and commercial facilities like factories, warehouses, or office buildings are required to comply with the ADA standards for accessible design, and both Landlord and Tenant are responsible for ADA compliance.

This Paragraph requires that Landlord cause the Building and Common Areas to be in compliance with ADA and that Tenant cause the Premises to be in compliance with ADA. Each party provides an indemnity to the other for noncompliance with ADA.

B. ANALYSIS

1. Landlord's Perspective

Compliance with ADA requirements can be extremely expensive and all parties to a Lease should be aware of the costs and allocation of risk. Some ADA requirements are "use-specific," with greater accessibility required in places of public accommodation. This gives Landlord an incentive to narrowly define Tenant's permitted uses. Each party wants to shift costs to the other, but a reasonable Landlord should take responsibility for public Common Areas. For full-floor Tenants, hallways and bathrooms should be made a part of the Premises so that Tenant and not Landlord assumes responsibility for ADA compliance. As the ADA may be enforced by lawsuits brought by private persons or the U.S. Attorney General, a Landlord should add a requirement for Tenants to maintain insurance to cover ADA claims and include the right of Landlord to select defense counsel.

2. Tenant's Perspective

A Tenant should take responsibility for alterations required as a result of its own particular use of space (other than general office use), or special needs of its customers or employees, but not for bringing the base building to general accessibility standards. If Tenant is moving into space but not performing significant alterations, then Tenant may want to require that Landlord represent that the Premises are currently in compliance with ADA. If Landlord, rather than Tenant, is required to construct the improvements to the Premises, then Landlord should assure ADA compliance in connection with such improvements. Restrooms in particular can be expensive to retrofit for ADA compliance, and care should be taken in allocating responsibility for ADA compliance between Landlord and Tenant. As the majority of access impediments are visible to the naked eye, it may be presumed that both the Landlord and the Tenant were aware that the property was noncompliant at the time of executing the Lease, and knowingly failed to address any structural renovations in writing. Therefore, if the Landlord fails to make a representation, and if the ADA compliance risk is allocated to the Tenant, Tenant may wish to engage an Architect to conduct an independent evaluation of the Premises, to confirm whether the Premises meets the ADA.

3. Lender's Perspective

Lender wants to be assured that the Property is ADA compliant, so that the collateral value of the Property is maximized. Lender wants to make sure that as much of the future ADA compliance cost and risk as possible is shifted to Tenant. Lender may require an ADA compliance plan, if the Building or Premises do not currently comply with ADA.

4. Broker's Perspective

Brokers often address the allocation of ADA compliance obligations within the LOI and that is prudent. Tenant Broker may wish to seek in the LOI a Landlord representation or obligation that at least the common areas of the Building shall be compliance with ADA or will be brought into compliance by the Landlord. If the Premises is being leased with an existing installation, Tenant Broker should seek in the LOI a representation from Landlord that the Premises is also in compliance with ADA.

C. COMPROMISES AND ALTERNATIVES

Costs can be shifted in any manner acceptable to parties. A Tenant may be more willing to pay ADA improvement costs if Tenant's share is limited to a fraction based on the Lease Term over the useful life of the renovations.

If the Premises are being built-out, ADA compliance with the Premises should be allocated to the party performing the alterations.

This issue is worth negotiating at the LOI stage.

D. COMMENTS

Care should be taken not to allow this issue to be addressed by default through a "compliance with laws" clause that allocates the risk without considering the substantial cost and disruption this work can require. See Paragraph 18 for a discussion of compliance-with-laws issues.

E. TYPICAL PARAGRAPH

19. Americans with Disabilities Act Compliance.

(a) Landlord represents, warrants and agrees that the Building shell structure, Building common areas accessible by Tenant's employees and invitees, and core conditions will conform upon completion, to all applicable legal requirements, including, without limitation, the requirements of Title III of the Americans with Disabilities Act ("ADA"). Landlord agrees to indemnify and hold Tenant harmless from any claims, losses, costs, damages, or other expenses (including, without limitation, reasonable attorneys' fees) arising from any breach of the foregoing warranty and covenants; provided, however, that nothing herein shall require Landlord to indemnify Tenant for any noncompliance of the Premises with the ADA to the extent such noncompliance results from acts or omissions of Tenant or Tenant's breach of its obligations under this Paragraph.

(b) Tenant represents, warrants, and agrees that: (i) the placement of Tenant's furniture, fixtures, and equipment within the Premises and (ii) all Tenant Improvements and "Alterations" (both as that term is defined within the ADA and within this Lease) to the Premises undertaken by Tenant will comply, to the extent necessary, with the ADA. Further, in the event modifications are required to the Premises due to the nonconformity of the Premises to the requirements of the ADA regarding Tenant's disabled employees or access by disabled members of the public, including, without limitation, access standards relating to wheelchairs, doors, and entrances, Tenant shall promptly comply with the requirements of the ADA with respect thereto. Tenant agrees to indemnify and hold Landlord harmless from any claims, losses, costs, damages, or other expenses (including, without limitation, reasonable attorneys' fees) arising from any breach of the foregoing warranty and covenants.

PARAGRAPH 20

Environmental Compliance

RISK RATING: 4

A. DESCRIPTION AND SCOPE

This Paragraph prohibits Tenant from using, storing, generating, or disposing of Hazardous Substances at the Premises and requires Tenant to indemnify Landlord and remediate any Hazardous Substances brought onto the Premises by Tenant.

B. ANALYSIS

1. Landlord's Perspective

This paragraph seeks to protect the value of the Property by prohibiting Tenant's use, storage, generation, or disposal of Hazardous Substances at the Premises. Further, Landlord should seek indemnification from Tenant against all claims and losses arising out of Tenant's actions on the Property relating to Hazardous Substances and/or as may result in environmental conditions. It should be noted that in any event, Landlord would likely have continued environmental liability under CERCLA and other state and federal environmental laws.

2. Tenant's Perspective

Tenant should confirm that its contemplated use of the Premises and the operation of its business therein will not violate the prohibitions of this Paragraph pertaining to the use, storage, generation and disposal of Hazardous Substances. In office and retail leases, Tenant rarely anticipates triggering the prohibitions. Industrial Tenants, however, need to review this Paragraph more closely and tailor it as necessary to obtain pre-approval from Landlord to use any, store, generate or dispose of Hazardous Substances to the extent necessary for the operation of Tenant's business at the Premises. For this reason, the topic is explored in Part 3, Paragraph 8.

Tenant should seek to include in the Paragraph certain Landlord representations, covenants, and indemnifications as provided in the Compromises and Alternatives section below.

3. Lender's Perspective

A Lender will want environmental indemnities from its borrower, the Landlord, but is also interested in having Tenant be responsible for cleanup costs for environmental problems caused by Tenant. To this end, a Lender may require that Landlord provide Lender with a copy of any Environmental Site Assessment prepared on Landlord's behalf and may also seek issuance of a reliance letter to Lender by the environmental engineering firm that prepared the Assessment.

4. Broker's Perspective

Each Broker will want to consult with their respective client to determine any sensitivity to or any particular client need relating to this Paragraph that should be covered in the LOI. If none exist, this Paragraph can be handled by the attorneys in Lease negotiations. As an example, on occasion, Tenant will require in the LOI that Landlord representation and warrant in the Lease that no Hazardous Substances are in the Premises and that Landlord shall be responsible for any Hazardous Substances not introduced to the Premises by Tenant. Also, both Landlord Broker and Tenant Broker should be aware of whether the jurisdictions in which the Premises is located requires certain certifications of the Premises with respect to Hazardous Substances at Premises occupancy. If so, the allocation of responsibility for obtaining the certification should be included in the LOI.

C. COMPROMISES AND ALTERNATIVES

Tenant should request in office and retail leases (and require in industrial leases) that Landlord provide Tenant with a copy of any Environmental Site Assessment for the Property in Landlord's possession or otherwise prepared on Landlord's behalf. With respect to at least industrial leases, Tenant may also want to have such Assessment updated and a reliance letter issued to Tenant by the environmental engineering firm that prepared the Assessment, and may seek to obtain an indemnity from Landlord for environmental conditions and events, if any exist, that predate the term of the lease.

A Tenant who is accepting any Premises that are not in "raw" condition and who plan to demolish the Premises and rebuild it for Tenant's initial occupancy should consider the insertion of the following protective language:

> *Notwithstanding anything to the contrary contained herein, Tenant shall not be responsible for the presence of any Hazardous Substances existing at the Premises as of the Commencement Date in violation of Environmental Laws and Landlord agrees to remediate the same, at Landlord's sole cost and expense, in accordance with all applicable Environmental Laws. If asbestos or other Hazardous Substances are discovered in the Premises in*

> *connection with the performance of Tenant's initial Alterations to prepare the Premises for Tenant's occupancy or subsequent Alterations or otherwise, Landlord shall, at Landlord's expense, remove or otherwise encapsulate the asbestos or other Hazardous Substances to the extent required by, and in accordance with, all applicable Environmental Laws. Until the completion of any such work, Tenant's obligation to pay Base Rent and Additional Rent shall be postponed one (1) day for each day Tenant is delayed in performing the initial Alterations or Alterations until Landlord has completed such removal or other encapsulation. All such work shall be performed with reasonable diligence so as to minimize interference with the conduct of Tenant's business and access to the Premises. Landlord shall indemnify and hold Tenant and the Tenant Indemnities (as hereinafter defined) harmless against and from any and all claims of whatever nature arising wholly or in part from or in connection with the presence, removal or encapsulation of such asbestos or other Hazardous Substances in the Premises. The provisions of this Paragraph shall survive the expiration or termination of this Lease.*

All other Tenants may wish to insert the following protective language into a Lease that does not already include a Landlord representation and warranty with respect to Hazardous Substances (and many do not):

> *Landlord hereby warrants and represents that it has no knowledge of any Hazardous Substances in or about the Premises, the Building or the underlying Land, which are environmentally hazardous or harmful, or which violate any applicable Environmental Laws. Notwithstanding anything to the contrary contained herein, Tenant shall have no liability whatsoever in connection with any and all Hazardous Substances (and any related equipment such as, but not limited to, underground storage tanks) not deposited or created by Tenant. Landlord, at its sole cost and expense, shall promptly comply with all Environmental Laws in connection with any Hazardous Substances in or about the Building or the underlying Land not deposited or created by Tenant.*

Landlords may wish to resist the potential liability that Landlord warranties and representations contained above could create. Landlord may claim for existing construction that Landlord is not the original owner of the Property and has no specific knowledge regarding the acts of prior owners. In addition, if Landlord has had an Environmental Site Assessment Report prepared for the project, and such report indicates environmental problems that (i) have since been cleaned up or (ii) are exterior to the Building, Landlord may wish to take exception to the disclosures contained in the Environmental Site Assessment Report. In any event, any representations or warranties given by Landlord should be limited to Landlord's actual knowledge, and Landlord may seek to limit all such representations and warranties to actual knowledge regarding *material* compliance with all Environmental Laws.

D. COMMENTS

Federal and state laws will make owners and operators liable for contamination. These provisions contain, identify, and allocate the risk of those burdens between the Lease parties.

Real estate leasing practitioners representing office or retail Tenants who do not anticipate violating any of the prohibitions of the Paragraph can typically negotiate the Paragraph without environmental expertise by inclusion of the concepts above and otherwise carefully reviewing and appropriately balancing any environmental provisions in the Lease. However, with respect to industrial Tenants anticipating the use, storage, generation, or disposal of Hazardous Substances, it would be prudent for Tenant's counsel to have an environmental attorney weigh in on the environmental provisions of the Lease if such counsel does not have the expertise.

E. TYPICAL PARAGRAPH

20. Environmental Compliance.

(a) Tenant shall not cause or permit any Hazardous Substances (as hereinafter defined) to be used, stored, accumulated, generated, released or disposed of in, on or about the Property, Building or Premises by Tenant, its agents, employees, contractors, licensees or invitees. Tenant hereby agrees to indemnify, defend and hold harmless the Landlord Indemnitees (as hereinafter defined) from any and all claims, damages, fines, judgments, penalties, costs, expenses or liabilities (including, without limitation, any and all sums paid for settlement of claims or reasonable attorneys' fees, consultant and expert fees) arising before, during or after the Term from the use, storage, generation release or disposal of Hazardous Substances in violation of Environmental Laws (as hereinafter defined) in, on or about the Property, Building or Premises by Tenant, Tenant's agents, employees, contractors, licensees or invitees.

(b) Notwithstanding anything to the contrary stated hereinabove, the indemnification contained in Subparagraph (a) above shall expressly include, without limitation, subject to the terms of this Lease, any and all costs incurred due to any investigation of the site or any cleanup, removal, transportation, disposal or restoration mandated by or pursuant to any Environmental Laws. The indemnification contained herein shall survive any expiration or termination of the Term.

(c) Tenant shall notify Landlord immediately upon learning that any duty of Tenant described in this Article has been violated, that there has been any usage, release, discharge or disposal of any Hazardous Substances on a part of the Premises or the Building or the Land, or that the Premises are subject to any third party claim or action, or threat thereof, because of any environmental condition in or originating from the Premises or arising in connection with Tenant's operations at the Premises or at the Building or the Real Property. Tenant shall promptly provide Landlord with copies of all correspondence to or from third parties regarding such claims or actions or regarding environmental conditions in or originating from Tenant's operations in the Premises or at the Building or the Real Property.

(d) As used herein, "Hazardous Substances" means any unlawful substance which is toxic, ignitable, reactive, or corrosive or which is regulated by Environmental Laws (other than lawful substances normally or typically used at an office facility, such as, without limitation, cleaning solutions, landscaping fertilizers, etc.). The term "Environmental Laws" means applicable federal, state and local laws and regulations, judgments, orders and permits governing safety and health and the protection of the environment, including without limitation, (i) the Clean Air Act, the Federal Water Pollution Control Act of 1972, the Resource Conservation and Recovery Act of 1976, the Comprehensive Environmental Response, Compensation, and Liability Act of 1980, the Oil Pollution Act of 1990, 33 U.S.C. 2701 et seq., Emergency Planning and Community Right-to-Know Act of 1986, 42 U.S.C. 17001 et seq., Safe Drinking Water Act of 1974, as amended, 42 U.S.C. 300(f) et seq.,, and the Toxic Substances Control Act (including any amendments or extensions thereof, any rules, implementing regulations, standards, or guidelines issued pursuant to any of said Environmental Laws, and any State analog); and (ii) all other applicable environmental standards or requirements.

PARAGRAPH 21

Insurance; Waivers of Claims and Waiver of Subrogation

RISK RATING: 5

A. DESCRIPTION AND SCOPE

This Paragraph stipulates what insurance Tenant (and Landlord once the Lease is well negotiated) will be required to maintain during the Term and, with respect to property insurance, this Paragraph provides for certain waivers from Landlord and Tenant and corresponding waivers of subrogation from Landlord and Tenant's insurance carriers, respectively, in order to shift risk of property damage to the insured party and their insurance carrier.

B. ANALYSIS

1. Landlord's Perspective

By requiring certain insurance from Tenant, Landlord is endeavoring to guaranty that Tenant will have a source of funds to support Tenant's damage restoration obligations under the Lease as well as Tenant's indemnification obligations under the Lease with respect to property damage and personal injury.

Landlord wants to be sure that the insurance company will have the financial capacity to make good on claims, that Landlord is notified in advance before any lapse of insurance coverage, and that Tenant's deductible is small. In addition, Landlord will want an undertaking by Tenant either not to engage in any activity that could raise the rates of Landlord's insurance premiums, or to reimburse Landlord for the cost of such additional premiums.

2. Tenant's Perspective

Of critical importance, Tenant will want to confirm, prior to executing the Lease, that (i) Tenant has or can readily obtain the insurance required under the Lease; (ii) Tenant has property insurance on all portions of the Premises that Tenant is required to restore under the casualty section of the Lease, in an amount equal to the full replacement value thereof; and (ii) Tenant has the liability insurance required to cover Tenant's indemnification obligations under the Lease.

Tenant wants to keep its insurance obligations consistent with its own needs. If Tenant leases more than one property, Tenant may wish to confirm that all or some of Tenant's insurance requirements under the Lease may be satisfied by any blanket insurance policy or excess coverage policy carried by Tenant insuring other properties it leases. In addition, investment-rated credit Tenants may want to request the right to self-insure all risks so long as Tenant maintains an investment-grade credit rating. Coverage levels that are set at Landlord's discretion could lead to significantly increased premium costs for Tenant if the levels are increased.

If Tenant is leasing only a portion of a Building, then Tenant should limit its property insurance requirements to just those improvements that Tenant makes to the Premises and the Lease should so reflect Tenant is only obligated to restore such improvements to the Premises in the event or fire or other casualty. Tenant will also want to be protected that the Building and Premises (in the condition it received it) will be rebuilt by Landlord in the event of a casualty (subject to the terms and conditions of the casualty Paragraph of the Lease), and that Landlord has the source of funds to complete that work through appropriate insurance policies. Lastly, Tenant will want to confirm that Tenant shall not be responsible for damage to the Building even if Tenant accidentally causes it.

3. Lender's Perspective

Lender wants to see that its security is adequately protected against damage or destruction. Therefore, Lender is less interested in the level of Tenant's liability coverage. Whenever possible, Lender will want a clause providing that the Tenant's insurance coverage will be set as Landlord's mortgagee shall require.

4. Broker's Perspective

Each Broker will want to consult with their respective client to determine any sensitivity to or any particular client need relating to this Paragraph that should be covered in the LOI. If none exist, this Paragraph can be handled by the attorneys in Lease negotiations.

C. COMPROMISES AND ALTERNATIVES

To avoid unduly burdensome insurance requirements, Tenant may require that any coverage levels set by Landlord or Landlord's mortgagee shall be reasonable and not exceed the insurance requirements of landlords of comparable buildings in the geographical area of the Premises.

Landlord may wish to include in the Lease an express right to be able to increase the insurance amounts periodically and even require new types of insurance over a long Lease Term. Tenant will want to limit how often this can happen and limit Landlord in a manner that Landlord may never require insurance coverage in excess of comparable landlords of comparable buildings in the same geographical area of the Premises.

It is fairly typical that any first draft of a Lease only protects Landlord with respect to the insurance provisions. Every Tenant should find this unacceptable to the point of being a potential "deal breaker" if a Landlord will not include appropriate Tenant protections in the Lease. Except in true net leases used for single occupancy buildings (wherein a Tenant may insure the entire Building against damage because it is in control of the entire Building), it is impractical for Tenant to insure the Building against damage. In fact, Tenant pays Operating Expenses that expressly include Landlord's insurance costs. Thus, the insurance Paragraph of any lease including Paragraph 21 below (which is a typical "first draft" insurance paragraph), must be revised to protect Tenant and reflect the insurance that Tenant is paying for within Operating Expenses. Below is a sample provision incorporating the protections every Tenant of a multi-tenant Building should obtain:

> *Landlord shall carry and maintain throughout the Term, comprehensive special causes of loss form fire and casualty insurance covering the Building and other improvements on the Land in an amount equal to the full replacement value thereof, and commercial general liability insurance coverage in amounts held by reasonably prudent commercial landlords of comparable properties in the [CITY, STATE], area. Notwithstanding anything to the contrary contained in the Lease, (i) Landlord and Tenant hereby waive all rights to recover against each other for any loss or damage arising from any cost covered by any casualty insurance required under the Lease, or otherwise actually carried by each of them, and (ii) Landlord and Tenant hereby agree to look first to the proceeds of their respective insurance policies before proceeding against each other in connection with any claim relating to any matter covered by the Lease. Landlord and Tenant will cause their respective insurers to issue appropriate waiver of subrogation right endorsements to all policies and insurance carried in connection with the Premises or the contents of either of them.*

By achieving the inclusion of the above language within the Lease, the risk of property damage is appropriately on the party insured against the damage. Note that each sentence of the language is important. Landlord needs to agree to maintain insurance for the Term. For the risk of property damage to be appropriately allocated to the insured party, Landlord and Tenant need to give the "waivers" above between themselves and then the "waiver of subrogation" from their respective insurance carriers follows. Often times, a Lease will contain the waiver of subrogation but fail to include the equally necessary waivers between Landlord and Tenant.

Without this protective language, if a 3rd-floor Tenant accidentally sets fire that damages the rest of the Building, other language within the Lease might hold Tenant responsible for that damage. That is unacceptable because Landlord is the party holding the insurance policy for the Building and Tenant is paying for it through Operating Expenses.

Likewise, if Landlord fails to maintain the roof of the Building and a leak damages Tenant's computers, equipment and furnishings, Landlord should not be responsible for that damage because, under the Lease, Tenant is required to carry property insurance damage on Tenant's Property.

Some Landlords may claim that they "self-insure" all or a portion of casualty insurance. If this is indeed the case, Tenant should be certain that any damage risk is 100% expressly allocated to Landlord by the following language:

> *If Landlord elects to self-insure all or part of any risk that would be insured under the policies and limits described herein, and an event occurs that would have been a covered claim where insurance proceeds would have been available but for the election to self-insure, then Landlord shall make funds available to the same extent that they would have been available had such insurance policy been carried.*

Some Tenants have the credit allowing them to self-insure. Here is a sample of a Tenant self-insurance provision:

> *Notwithstanding anything to the contrary contained herein, Tenant may elect to self-insure the insurance requirements specified above in this Paragraph 21 ("Tenant's Self-Insurance Program"), provided: (i) Tenant's Self-Insurance Program is continuously maintained in accordance with prudent self-insurance principles as reasonably determined by Tenant, which includes procedures governing the investigation, litigation, processing, payment of insurance claims and adjustment of claims by a third-party administrator, and (ii) Tenant's net worth (exclusive of goodwill and other intangible assets) exceeds [AMOUNT]. If Tenant elects to self-insure all or part of any risk that would be insured under the policies and limits described herein, and an event occurs that would have been a covered claim where insurance proceeds would have been available but for the election to self-insure, then Tenant shall make funds available to the same extent that they would have been available had such insurance policy been carried.*

D. COMMENTS

Landlord should make sure the insurance they are requiring meets any insurance requirements under their loan documents.

Tenant should also have the insurance, casualty and indemnity sections of the Lease reviewed by their insurance professional and/or risk advisor to confirm that they have or can readily obtain the insurance being required. Often times, the insurance professional has comments to these sections and those comments should be incorporated into the Lease.

E. TYPICAL PARAGRAPH

21. Insurance; Waiver of Claims and Waiver of Subrogation.

(a) Tenant's Insurance. Tenant, at Tenant's sole cost and expense, shall maintain in force and effect throughout the Term, (i) a special causes of loss insurance policy for Tenant's Property (and any leasehold improvements installed by Tenant) at the Premises (in coverage amounts not less than one hundred percent (100%) of the full replacement cost therefor), and (ii) a policy of commercial general liability and property damage

insurance on an occurrence basis, with a broad form contractual liability endorsement (the insurance policy described in this clause (ii) being referred to herein as the "Liability Policy"), and (iii) worker's compensation (including employer's liability) policies, in statutory limits pursuant to all applicable Requirements, and (iv) if Tenant operates owned, hired or leased vehicles at the Real Property, a comprehensive automobile liability policy having coverage limits of not less than $1,000,000.00 per occurrence, combined bodily injury and property damage, and (v) a business interruption insurance policy having coverage limits of at least one hundred percent (100%) of Tenant's gross annual revenues. Such policies provided in subsections (i), (ii) and (iv) above shall name Tenant as the insured. Tenant's commercial general liability insurance policy shall be primary and non-contributory. Landlord and its agents, including, Landlord's Managing Agent, and any Lessors and any Mortgagees (whose names have been furnished to Tenant) shall be named as additional insureds on such policies, as their respective interests may appear. The Liability Policy shall contain a provision that (a) no act or omission of Tenant shall affect or limit the obligation of the insurer to pay the amount of any loss sustained, and (b) the policy shall be non-cancelable with respect to Landlord, Landlord's Managing Agent, and such Lessors and Mortgagees, unless written notice has been given to Landlord, which notice shall contain the policy number and the names of the insured and additional insureds, at least thirty (30) days prior to the effective date of any such cancellation for any reason other than the non-payment of premium, or at least ten (10) days prior to the effective date of any such cancellation by reason of non-payment of premium. If (x) any insurance obtained by Tenant covers Alterations, and (y) this Lease does not terminate after the occurrence of a fire or other casualty, then (a) Tenant, promptly after the occurrence of such fire or other casualty, shall make an appropriate claim against its insurer in respect thereof, (b) Tenant shall not settle, adjust or compromise any such claim without Landlord's prior approval, which approval Landlord shall not unreasonably withhold or delay, and (c) Tenant shall pay to Landlord any amounts recovered from Tenant's insurer for damage to such Alterations caused by such fire or other casualty, promptly after Tenant's receipt thereof from such insurer (it being agreed, however, that Landlord's obligation to restore such Alterations to the extent otherwise provided herein shall be unaffected by the inadequacy of such insurance to cover the cost of such restoration). Tenant shall deliver promptly to Landlord a copy of any notice of cancellation or any other notice from the insurance carrier which may adversely affect the coverage of the insureds under any policy of insurance described in this Subparagraph 21(a). The minimum amounts of liability under the Liability Policy shall be a combined single limit with respect to each occurrence in coverage amounts of $[AMOUNT] primary liability (with $[AMOUNT] in the aggregate), plus $[AMOUNT] of excess liability coverage, for injury (or death) to persons and damage to property, which amounts may be increased from time to time to those amounts of insurance which in Landlord's reasonable judgment are then being customarily required by prudent landlords of first-class buildings in the [COUNTY, STATE], area from tenants leasing space similar in size, nature and location to the Premises. All insurance required to be carried by Tenant pursuant to the terms of this Lease shall be effected under valid and enforceable policies issued by reputable and independent insurers permitted to do business in the State of [STATE], and rated in Best's Insurance Guide, or any successor thereto (or if there is none, an organization having a national reputation) as having a general policyholder rating of "A" or better and with a financial size category (FSC) of "X" or higher.

(b) Waiver of Subrogation. Subject to the provisions of this Subparagraph 21(b), Landlord and Tenant shall procure an appropriate clause in, or endorsement on, any fire or extended coverage insurance covering the Premises, the Building and personal property, fixtures and equipment located thereon or therein, pursuant to which the insurer waives subrogation, or consents to a waiver of right of recovery. Landlord and Tenant, having obtained such clauses or endorsements of waiver of subrogation or consent to a waiver of right of recovery, shall not make any claim against or seek to recover from the other for any loss or damage to its property or the property of others resulting from fire or other hazards covered by such fire and extended coverage insurance; provided, however, that the release, discharge, exoneration and covenant not to sue herein contained shall be limited by and be coextensive with the terms and provisions of the waiver of subrogation clause or endorsements or clauses or endorsements consenting to a waiver of right of recovery. If the payment of an additional premium is required for the inclusion of such waiver of subrogation provision, then each party shall advise the other of the amount of any such additional premium and such other party may, but shall not be obligated to, pay such additional premium. If such other party does not elect to pay such additional premium, then the first party shall not be required to obtain such waiver of subrogation provision. If either party is unable to obtain the inclusion of such clause even with the payment of an additional premium, then such party shall attempt to name the other party as an additional insured (but not a loss payee) under the policy. If the payment of an additional premium is required for naming the other party as an additional insured (but not a loss payee), then each party shall advise the other of the amount of any such additional premium and the other party at its own election may, but shall not be obligated to, pay such additional premium. If such other party does not elect to pay such additional premium or if it is not possible to have the other party named as an additional insured (but not loss

payee), even with the payment of an additional premium, then (in either event) such party shall so notify the first party and the first party shall not have the obligation to name the other party as an additional insured.

(c) Evidence of Insurance. On or prior to the date of such party's execution and delivery of this Lease, Tenant shall deliver to Landlord appropriate certificates of insurance, including evidence of waivers of subrogation required pursuant to Subparagraph 21(b) hereof. Evidence of each renewal or replacement of a policy shall be delivered at least twenty (20) days prior to the expiration of such policy. Each insurance certificate (whether for insurance originally furnished or evidencing a renewal of insurance) shall include a standard "additional insured" endorsement naming Landlord, Managing Agent, any Lessor and any Mortgagee as additional insureds. Tenant shall provide an Acord 27 form to evidence property insurance and an Acord 25 form to evidence liability insurance.

PARAGRAPH 22

Indemnification

RISK RATING: 4

A. DESCRIPTION AND SCOPE

This Paragraph sets forth the conditions under which Tenant agrees to indemnify Landlord. The indemnity is a broad, one-sided indemnity in favor of Landlord and it is, at least, a strong starting position for Landlord. The purpose of the one-sided indemnity is to require Tenant's insurance company to pay for damages relating to the Premises because the Premises are in Tenant's exclusive control.

B. ANALYSIS

1. Landlord's Perspective

This Paragraph protects Landlord against liability for the negligent acts, omissions, or failures of Tenant (even if Landlord is also negligent) for anything occurring in or about the Premises. Landlord does not want to use its time and resources in a legal fight over who was negligent, and if both Landlord and Tenant were negligent, each party's respective share of negligence. Landlord is also concerned with the out-of-pocket cost of the deductible amount of its insurance. With respect to Tenant's obligations to defend, Landlord may prefer to retain its own counsel and require a reimbursement of legal fees and expenses from Tenant.

Tenant may object that the indemnity is too one-sided in favor of Landlord and request a carve out from Tenant's indemnity claims relating to the negligence or willful misconduct of Landlord and/or an indemnification obligation back from Landlord.

Some minority of landlords, and most notably in New York City, have shown an ability to successfully resist carving out Landlord's negligence from Tenant's indemnification obligation and successfully avoid providing a Landlord indemnification obligation but such carve outs and even Landlord limited indemnification obligations have become predominantly acceptable in other markets.

The minority landlords who maintain an unqualified and one-sided Tenant indemnification obligation justify their position by arguing that (i) Landlord and Tenant should avoid dissipating their time and energy in legal proceedings determining whose liability insurance will pay for any given claim; and (ii) Tenant's insurance should pay for damage or injury arising in the areas which Tenant exclusively controls. The goal of both parties should be to create in the Lease clear demarcation lines as to which party's liability insurance will be responsible for any given third-party negligence claim. A demarcation line based on the standard of who is negligent does nothing to improve the status quo. If Tenant is paying Additional Rent, then Tenant is in effect paying for Landlord's insurance. Any increase in Landlord's insurance due to such claims will be passed on to Tenant. If Landlord and Tenant both are required to make claims against their respective insurance carriers, then Tenant will be the ultimate loser, since it will pay for any increase in its insurance premiums directly and for increases in Landlord's insurance premiums indirectly as Additional Rent.

2. Tenant's Perspective

Tenants generally accept that they will be required to indemnify Landlord from liability arising within the Premises since Tenants are, generally, in control of the Premises and the Lease requires Tenant to maintain the insurance to cover the indemnification liability.

That said, Tenant should endeavor to limit their indemnification provision and also seek to obtain a Landlord indemnification provision as discussed in the Compromises and Alternative sections below.

3. Lender's Perspective

Lender wants Tenant's indemnity to be broad enough to cover Lender in the event Lender takes control or possession of the Property either prior to or after foreclosure.

4. Broker's Perspective

Each Broker will want to consult with their respective client to determine any sensitivity to or any particular client need relating to this Paragraph that should be covered in the LOI. If none exist, this Paragraph can be handled by the attorneys in Lease negotiations.

C. COMPROMISES AND ALTERNATIVES

Nearly all Tenants in any jurisdiction can obtain the following carve out to their indemnification:

> *Tenant's indemnity of Landlord specifically excludes any losses, liabilities, claims, damages or expenses arising from the negligence or misconduct of Landlord or Landlord's agents, employees, contractors, or invitees, or arising from Landlord's breach of its obligations or representations under the Lease.*

In addition, Tenant should endeavor to have the following Landlord indemnification provision included in the Lease:

> *Landlord hereby agrees to indemnify, defend and hold Tenant harmless from and against any and all losses, liabilities, claims, damages or expenses (including, without limitation, reasonable attorneys' fees and costs), arising from or in connection with the negligence or misconduct of Landlord or Landlord's agents, employees, contractors or visitors, or arising from or in connection with Landlord's breach of its obligations or representations in the Lease. Any provisions in the Lease which purport to limit, waive or release Landlord for its negligence or misconduct (or the negligence or misconduct of Landlord's agents, employees, contractors, or visitors) shall be of no effect.*

D. COMMENTS

Even though Typical Paragraph 22 requires Tenant to carry insurance that covers Tenant's indemnity obligations, Landlord should carry its own insurance because Tenant may let its insurance lapse despite Landlord's monitoring Tenant's insurance. When a mutual indemnity is used, Landlord should resist naming Tenant as an additional insured on Landlord's policy unless Landlord can pass along to Tenant any additional premium caused thereby. Landlord should obtain separate indemnities from Tenant for matters not insurable at normal rates and for environmental matters caused by Tenant.

Due to the increase in the use of limited liability companies for the ownership of real estate, the possible "members" of Landlord should be an indemnified party.

Note that no Landlord general indemnification obligation included in the Lease should ever really be "reciprocal" to Tenant's indemnification obligation because Landlord is not able to control the Common Areas in the same manner that Tenant is able to control the Premises. Employees and invitees of all Building tenants have access to and use the Common Areas.

E. TYPICAL PARAGRAPH

22. <u>Indemnification</u>. Tenant shall indemnify and hold harmless Landlord and all ground lessors, superior mortgagees and its and their respective agents, employees, officers, directors, partners, members, and shareholders (collectively, "Landlord's Indemnities"), from and against any and all liabilities, judgments, demands, causes of action, claims, losses, damages, costs, and expenses, including, without limitation, reasonable attorneys' fees and costs arising out of or in any way connected with (a) the conduct or management of the Premises or any business therein, or any work or thing whatsoever done, or any condition created in or about the Premises during the Term or during the period of time, if any, prior to the Commencement Date that Tenant may have been given access to the Premises; (b) any act, omission, or negligence of Tenant or any of its subtenants or licensees or its or their partners, directors,

officers, agents, employees, invitees, or contractors (collectively, "Tenant's Indemnities"); (c) any accident, injury, or damage whatever occurring in, at, or upon the Premises; and (d) any breach or default by Tenant in the full and prompt payment and performance of Tenant's obligations under this Lease. In case any action or proceeding is brought against Landlord or any superior mortgagee or its or their agents, employees, officers, directors, parties, members, and shareholders and such claim is a claim for which Tenant is obligated to indemnify Landlord pursuant to this Paragraph 22, Tenant, upon notice from Landlord or such superior mortgagee, shall resist and defend such action or proceeding (by counsel reasonably satisfactory to Landlord or such superior mortgagee). Tenant shall carry insurance that covers its obligations under this Paragraph 22 and shall deliver evidence of such insurance to Landlord. The obligations of Tenant under this Paragraph 22 shall survive the expiration or earlier termination of this Lease.

PARAGRAPH 23

Casualty

RISK RATING: 4

A. DESCRIPTION AND SCOPE

This Paragraph sets out alternative responses and procedures in the event of casualty resulting in damage to the Property, including Landlord's obligation to restore, abatement of Annual Base Rent and Additional Rent, time limits for restoration, and termination of the Lease. The restoration and termination provisions are usually extensively negotiated by Landlord and Tenant.

B. ANALYSIS

1. Landlord's Perspective

Landlord wants to protect itself from having to repair or restore the Building or the Premises following a casualty if repair or restoration would not be in the best economic interest of Landlord. Landlord also wants to be able to terminate the Lease if restoration costs more than available insurance proceeds. Landlord should never agree to pay restoration costs in excess of insurance proceeds. Landlord does not want to be responsible for repair or replacement of Tenant's furnishings, removable fixtures and equipment or improvements to the Premises made by Tenant in the event of casualty damage. Landlord wants to lock Tenant into the Lease and not permit Tenant to rethink the economics of the deal. Provided the damage is restored within a year of the casualty, there is no economic loss to the parties because Tenant is protected by business interruption insurance and Landlord can obtain rent loss insurance to protect itself and assure its Lender that it will keep making its mortgage payments.

2. Tenant's Perspective

Tenant does not want to be inflexibly locked into the Lease when the Premises, Tenant's access thereto or the services provided to the Premises have been partially or totally damaged. Tenant may want to condition Landlord's right to terminate the Lease upon Landlord's election also to terminate the leases of all other tenants in the Building, in order to prevent Landlord from using casualty damage as an excuse for terminating an unfavorable lease. Tenant will want the same rights as Landlord to terminate the Lease. Tenant's rights to terminate should be limited, because Lender will object to unusual termination rights by Tenant (see Lender's Perspective below).

If Landlord will restore the Premises and the Building, Tenant will want Landlord to complete restoration within the shortest possible time period. In very large projects involving substantial damage, Landlord may require at least 180 to 365 days to complete restoration. Tenant will resist a long restoration time, since its operations at the site will be shut down or transferred to a temporary location during such restoration and typically business interruption insurance is limited to twelve (12) months from the date of casualty. If such restoration period is too long (e.g., beyond four (4) months), then it may be more appropriate for Tenant to negotiate a lease at a new location and terminate the Lease. Tenant will want a provision that permits Tenant to terminate the Lease for damage rendering the Premises untenantable during the last 6 or 12 months of the Lease Term. Landlord will likely resist such a provision if the Term is less than five years.

Tenant should pay careful attention to what level of Landlord restoration is required under the Lease as sometimes Landlord will resist restoring improvements made by Tenant and this could include all of Tenant's initial improvements if Tenant performed the initial buildout of the Premises. In this scenario, if Landlord is just required to restore the core and shell of the Premises, then Tenant should negotiate adequate time to rebuild its improvements on a "rent free" basis. So, the rent abatement period, following casualty, should commence on the date of casualty and not end on the date that Landlord meets its restoration obligations but rather after a reasonable time thereafter for Tenant to rebuild.

Tenant may also object to the following language in Subparagraph 23(a): **"If the damage is caused, directly or indirectly, by the fault, neglect, or negligence of Tenant, or its officers, contractors, licensees, agents, servants, employees, guests, invitees, or visitors, then there shall be no abatement of Annual Base Rent and Additional Rent, except to the extent Landlord receives proceeds from any applicable insurance policy of Tenant to compensate Landlord for loss of Annual Base Rent and Additional Rent."** Landlord should assure that it's rent loss insurance covers all causes for the damage, including any damage due to Ten-ant's negligence and therefore there is no need for this provision in the Lease.

3. Lender's Perspective

Lender will usually object to Tenant having the right to terminate the Lease as a result of damage to the Premises or the Building, if the damage can be repaired within a short period of time (e.g., less than six months). This is because termination of the Lease affects cash flow from the Property and may adversely affect Landlord's ability to pay debt service to Lender from the cash flow of the Property. Lender also wants to control insurance proceeds from any casualty.

Lender may require that casualty proceeds be used to reduce or pay off Landlord's indebtedness to Lender. In addition, requiring Landlord to use insurance proceeds to restore the Premises or the Building may not be acceptable to Lender, if (i) Tenant has the right to terminate the Lease if Landlord does not timely complete the restoration; or (ii) the abatement of rent following a casualty does not allow Landlord to pay debt service to Lender. Lender will want to make sure that Landlord has at least 12 months (some Lenders will require 18–24 months) of rent loss insurance so that debt service payments will not be interrupted during the restoration period.

It should be noted that any provision of the Lease that obligates Landlord to use insurance proceeds to restore the Building and Premises will likely be subordinate to Lender's rights to use insurance proceeds to pay down the mortgage loan by virtue of the automatic subordination provisions of the Lease or a separate Subordination, Nondisturbance, and Attornment Agreement that Lender requires Tenant to execute.

4. Broker's Perspective

Events of casualty are not typically address in the LOI, however, both Brokers should support legal counsel in negotiating this Paragraph.

C. COMPROMISES AND ALTERNATIVES

Variations in the language would require significant revision of the entire Paragraph and should only be undertaken on a comprehensive basis. Because Paragraph 23, as provided in Subparagraph E below, is written from arguably a Landlord's perspective, Tenant may wish to revise Paragraph 23 as follows (stricken and underscored words to indicate the proposed revisions to Paragraph 23 as originally drafted):

23. *Damage or Destruction of Premises.*

    (a) *If the Premises are destroyed or rendered untenantable, either wholly or in part, by fire or other casualty and restoration is estimated to require more than six (6) monthly, then Landlord may, at its option, (i) terminate this Lease effective as of the date of such damage or destruction, provided that Landlord terminates all other leases at the Building; or (ii) restore the Premises and all portions of the Building required for Tenant's access to the Premises to their previous condition, and in the meantime Annual Base Rent and Additional Rent shall abate in the same proportion as the untenantable portion of the Premises bears to the whole thereof from the date of casualty until Landlord and Tenant complete their restoration obligations, respectively, and this Lease shall continue in full force and effect.* ~~*If the damage is caused, directly or indirectly, by the fault, neglect, or negligence of Tenant, or its officers, contractors, licensees, agents, servants, employees, guests, invitees, or visitors, then there shall be no abatement of Annual Base Rent and Additional Rent, except to the extent Landlord receives proceeds from any applicable insurance policy of Tenant to compensate Landlord for loss of Annual Base Rent and Additional*~~

~~Rent~~. *Landlord, within sixty (60) days after the date of casualty, shall give to Tenant a statement prepared by a reputable and independent contractor setting forth such contractor's estimate in good faith as to the time required for Landlord to Substantially Complete the restoration described in Paragraph 23 (such statement that Landlord gives to Tenant being referred to herein as the "Casualty Statement"). If the estimated restoration time period noted in the Casualty Statement to repair the Premises and/or Tenant's access thereto exceeds six (6) months from the date of the applicable fire or other casualty, then Tenant may elect to terminate this Lease by giving notice to Landlord not later than the thirtieth (30th) day after the date that Landlord gives the Casualty Statement to Tenant.*

(b) *If the Building is destroyed or damaged by fire or other casualty insured against under Landlord's fire and extended coverage insurance policy to the extent that more than fifty percent (50%) thereof is rendered untenantable, or if the Building is materially destroyed or damaged by any other casualty other than those covered by such insurance policy, notwithstanding that the Premises may be unaffected directly by such destruction or damage, then Landlord may in its sole discretion terminate this Lease by giving written notice to Tenant within sixty (60) days after such destruction or damage, provided that Landlord terminates all other leases at the Building. Termination pursuant to such notice shall be effective thirty (30) days after receipt thereof by Tenant.*

(c) *Other than abatement of Annual Base Rent and Additional Rent as provided in Paragraph 23(a), no damages, compensation, or claim shall be payable by Landlord to Tenant for any inconvenience to or loss of Tenant's business arising from or in connection with any repair or restoration of the Property or portion thereof.*

(d) *If Landlord is required or otherwise elects to repair the Building or the Premises, then Landlord shall proceed with all reasonable diligence to start and complete such casualty restoration but Landlord's obligations shall be limited to the base Building and the Common Areas and improvements to the Premises existing on the Commencement Date. Anything herein to the contrary notwithstanding, if the Premises are destroyed or damaged in whole or in part during the last twelve (12) months of the Term, then Landlord or Tenant may, at its option, cancel and terminate this Lease as of the date of the occurrence of such damage, provided that Landlord's termination exercise shall be deemed void and invalid if Tenant exercises any remaining Tenant renewal option within twenty (20) days of Tenant receiving notice of Landlord's election to terminate the Lease.*

(e) *Tenant understands that Landlord will not carry insurance of any kind on Tenant's furniture and furnishings or on any fixtures or equipment removable by Tenant under the provisions of this Lease nor any improvements to the Premises other than the improvements existing on the Commencement Date and that Landlord shall not be obligated to repair any damage thereto or to replace the same.*

(f) *A total destruction of the Building shall, at Landlord's* <u>*or Tenant's*</u> *option, permit Landlord or* <u>*Tenant*</u> *to terminate this Lease.*

(g) *In the event of the termination of this Lease in accordance with the provisions of this Paragraph 23, any Annual Base Rent or Additional Rent paid in advance as of the date of such occurrence shall be immediately refunded to Tenant and this refund obligation shall survive such termination.*

(h) *Landlord and Tenant do each hereby release and discharge the other party and any officer, agent, employee, or representative of such party of and from any liability whatsoever hereafter arising from loss, damage, or injury caused by fire, or other insurable casualty for which insurance (permitting waiver of liability and containing waiver of subrogation) is required to be carried by the injured party by the terms of this Lease at the time of such loss, damage, or injury.*

(i) *Notwithstanding anything to the contrary contained herein, if neither Landlord nor Tenant elect to terminate this Lease pursuant to their express rights above and Landlord fails to Substantially Complete the performance of the restoration work either to the Premises and/or if access or services to the Premises or Building are restricted to the extent necessary for Tenant to access the Premises and operate its business therein, by the last day of the estimated time period set forth in the Casualty Statement, Tenant may elect to terminate this Lease by notice delivered to Landlord within twenty (20) days following the expiration of the restoration time period set forth in the Casualty Statement, in which event this Lease shall terminate fifteen (15) days following Tenant's termination notice unless Landlord Substantially Completes its restoration work prior to the expiration of such fifteen (15)-day period.*

D. COMMENTS

One important component to this Paragraph is that the parties should be sure that the restoration obligation should rest with the party required to insure the particular improvements. If Tenant is required to insure its own improvements but Landlord is obligated to restore the Premises fully, then Tenant should be required to remit its insurance proceeds to Landlord. It is prudent for Tenant to have its insurance professional review the casualty Paragraph of the Lease to confirm that Tenant is carrying the requisite insurance to cover any Tenant restoration obligation under the Lease.

E. TYPICAL PARAGRAPH

23. <u>Damage or Destruction of Premises.</u>

(a) If the Premises are destroyed or rendered untenantable, either wholly or in part, by fire or other casualty, then Landlord may, at its option, (i) terminate this Lease effective as of the date of such damage or destruction; or (ii) restore the Premises to their previous condition, and in the

meantime Annual Base Rent and Additional Rent shall abate in the same proportion as the untenantable portion of the Premises bears to the whole thereof, and this Lease shall continue in full force and effect. If the damage is caused, directly or indirectly, by the fault, neglect, or negligence of Tenant, or its officers, contractors, licensees, agents, servants, employees, guests, invitees, or visitors, then there shall be no abatement of Annual Base Rent and Additional Rent, except to the extent Landlord receives proceeds from any applicable insurance policy of Tenant to compensate Landlord for loss of Annual Base Rent and Additional Rent.

(b) If the Building is destroyed or damaged by fire or other casualty insured against under Landlord's fire and extended coverage insurance policy to the extent that more than fifty percent (50%) thereof is rendered untenantable, or if the Building is materially destroyed or damaged by any other casualty other than those covered by such insurance policy, notwithstanding that the Premises may be unaffected directly by such destruction or damage, then Landlord may in its sole discretion terminate this Lease by giving written notice to Tenant within sixty (60) days after such destruction or damage. Termination pursuant to such notice shall be effective thirty (30) days after receipt thereof by Tenant.

(c) Other than abatement of Annual Base Rent and Additional Rent as provided in Subparagraph 23(a), no damages, compensation, or claim shall be payable by Landlord to Tenant for any inconvenience to or loss of Tenant's business arising from or in connection with any repair or restoration of the Property or portion thereof.

(d) If Landlord elects to repair the Building or the Premises, then Landlord's obligations shall be limited to the base Building and the Common Areas and the improvements existing in the Premises on the Commencement Date. Anything herein to the contrary notwithstanding, if the Premises are destroyed or damaged in whole or in part during the last twelve (12) months of the Term, then Landlord may, at its option, cancel and terminate this Lease as of the date of the occurrence of such damage.

(e) Tenant understands that Landlord will not carry insurance of any kind on Tenant's furniture and furnishings or on any fixtures or equipment removable by Tenant under the provisions of this Lease nor any improvements to the Premises other than those existing on the Commencement Date and that Landlord shall not be obligated to repair any damage thereto or to replace the same.

(f) A total destruction of the Building shall, at Landlord's option, permit Landlord to terminate this Lease.

(g) In the event of the termination of this Lease in accordance with the provisions of this Paragraph 23, any Annual Base Rent or Additional Rent paid in advance as of the date of such occurrence shall be immediately refunded to Tenant and this refund obligation shall survive such termination.

(h) **Landlord and Tenant do each hereby release and discharge the other party and any officer, agent, employee, or representative of such party of and from any liability whatsoever hereafter arising from loss, damage, or injury caused by fire, or other insurable casualty for which insurance (permitting waiver of liability and containing waiver of subrogation) is required to be carried by the injured party by the terms of this Lease at the time of such loss, damage, or injury.**

PARAGRAPH 24

Condemnation

RISK RATING: 3

A. DESCRIPTION AND SCOPE

This Paragraph describes arrangements to be made in the event that any material portion of the Premises, the Building, or the Land is "taken" by a public authority under power of eminent domain (otherwise referred to as condemnation), including a proportionate reduction in Annual Base Rent and Additional Rent if the Lease is not terminated, and an allocation of the compensation award. This Paragraph under the Lease is typically entitled Condemnation but is also sometimes entitled Eminent Domain.

B. ANALYSIS

1. Landlord's Perspective

Landlord wants the Term to continue so long as the project remains economically viable after a taking. Landlord may therefore want to define a material taking by reference to some higher percentage of damage. Landlord also does not want to risk losing to Tenant a portion of Landlord's condemnation award.

2. Tenant's Perspective

Tenant does not want to be inflexibly obligated under the Lease when a material portion of the Premises, the Building, or the Land has been taken and wants protection against the risk of having to pursue its respective rights in the Premises against Landlord in an adversarial court action. Tenant will be concerned with the Landlord's termination clause, especially if Tenant is constructing or adding improvements in the Premises. In that case Tenant, in addition to its claim for moving expenses, will want the Lease to provide for Tenant's recovery of the unamortized cost of its improvements upon condemnation. An agreement to apportion the award may be made, perhaps capping Tenant's portion at Tenant's unamortized cost. If such agreement is not made subject to the rights of a Lender, a Lender will ordinarily object to it, since it might reduce the security (i.e., the condemnation award in lieu of the real property) available to Lender.

If the Lease is not terminated due to an immaterial taking, Tenant should require that Landlord reconstruct the Building, Premises, or Common Areas within a specified period of time after the taking. One hundred twenty (120) days would be a reasonable period of time for an immaterial taking.

3. Lender's Perspective

Lender wants (i) to be paid in full before any proceeds are available to Landlord, Tenant, or Tenant's leasehold mortgagee; and (ii) to hold the proceeds if a partial taking has occurred and reconstruction is to occur.

4. Broker's Perspective

Each Broker will want to consult with their respective client to determine any sensitivity to or any particular client need relating to this Paragraph that should be covered in the LOI. If none exist, this Paragraph can be handled by the attorneys in Lease negotiations.

C. COMPROMISES AND ALTERNATIVES

Tenant may be concerned if a portion of the parking area appurtenant to the Building is taken through condemnation. That is actually the most likely to occur of the possible condemnation scenarios, since a road widening could result in a loss of parking areas. In such case, Tenant may want to require that Landlord provide substitute parking either on site, if available, or off site if not. Should Landlord be unable to provide substitute parking, Tenant should have a right to terminate the Lease. Tenant may also want some definition of "material" and a right of Tenant to terminate the Lease if a "material" taking occurs. A "material" taking may be any taking that affects parking or Tenant's ingress and egress to the Property, Building, or Premises or any taking that affects any utilities or other services to the Building or Premises or any taking that materially and adversely impacts the operation of Tenant's business in the Premises.

Variations in the language would require significant revision of the entire Paragraph and should only be undertaken on a comprehensive basis. Because Paragraph 24, as provided in Subparagraph E below, is written from arguably a Landlord's perspective, Tenant may wish to revise Paragraph 24 as follows (stricken and underscored words to indicate the proposed revisions to Paragraph 24 as originally drafted):

> 24. *Eminent Domain. Landlord shall promptly notify Tenant of any contemplated condemnation of the Premises, Building or Land. If fifty percent (50%) or more of the Premises or of such portions of the Building or the Land as Landlord reasonably determines in good faith are material for Tenant's reasonable use of the Premises are taken by eminent domain or sale under threat of condemnation by eminent domain*

and Landlord is unable to relocate Tenant to another area of the Building, then this Lease shall, upon Landlord giving written notice to Tenant, terminate as of the date title vests in the condemning authority. In addition, if Tenant reasonably determines in good faith that the portion of the Premises, the Building or the Land taken will impair Tenant's ability to operate its business in the Premises, Tenant may elect to terminate this Lease upon giving written notice to Landlord and the Lease shall terminate as of the date title invests in the condemning authority. All Annual Base Rent and Additional Rent and other sums payable by Tenant hereunder shall accrue up to and including such date and shall be paid by Tenant to Landlord on such date. Landlord reserves all rights to any awards or damages in connection with any such full or partial taking by eminent domain. Tenant hereby assigns to Landlord any right Tenant may have to such damages or awards and waives all claims against Landlord and the condemning authority in connection with such taking, including all claims for termination of Tenant's leasehold interest hereunder and interference with Tenant's business. Notwithstanding the foregoing, Tenant shall have the right to claim and recover from the condemning authority compensation for any loss which Tenant may incur for Tenant's moving and relocation expenses or the taking of Tenant's personal property and trade fixtures and any loss of business (excluding Tenant's leasehold interest hereunder), provided such claim by Tenant does not reduce Landlord's claim. If this Lease does not terminate as aforesaid, then Landlord shall promptly proceed with due diligence to make all necessary repairs to the Property in order to render and restore the same to the condition they were in prior to the taking, but in no event shall Landlord be required to expend more than the condemnation proceeds received by Landlord with respect to such taking, and Tenant shall continue in possession of the portion of the Premises not so taken upon the same terms and conditions as are herein provided, except that Annual Base Rent and Additional Rent shall be reduced in direct proportion to the area of the Premises so taken.

D. COMMENTS

(i) The damage award will be property of Landlord.
(ii) Tenant may assert a separate claim for moving and relocation expenses as well as an award for Tenant's trade fixtures and loss of business.
(iii) If the Lease is not terminated, then Tenant will receive a proportionate abatement of Annual Base Rent and Additional Rent.

E. TYPICAL PARAGRAPH

24. Eminent Domain. If fifty percent (50%) or more of the Premises or of such portions of the Building or the Land as Landlord determines are material for Tenant's reasonable use of the Premises are taken by eminent domain or sale under threat of condemnation by eminent domain and Landlord is unable to relocate Tenant to another area of the Building, then this Lease shall, upon Landlord giving written notice to Tenant, terminate as of the date title vests in the condemning authority. All Annual Base Rent and Additional Rent and other sums payable by Tenant hereunder shall accrue up to and including such

date and shall be paid by Tenant to Landlord on such date. Landlord reserves all rights to any awards or damages in connection with any such full or partial taking by eminent domain. Tenant hereby assigns to Landlord any right Tenant may have to such damages or awards and waives all claims against Landlord and the condemning authority in connection with such taking, including all claims for termination of Tenant's leasehold interest hereunder and interference with Tenant's business. Notwithstanding the foregoing, Tenant shall have the right to claim and recover from the condemning authority compensation for any loss which Tenant may incur for Tenant's moving expenses or the taking of Tenant's personal property (excluding Tenant's leasehold interest hereunder), provided such claim by Tenant does not reduce Landlord's claim. If this Lease does not terminate as aforesaid, then Landlord shall proceed to make all necessary repairs to the Property in order to render and restore the same to the condition they were in prior to the taking, but in no event shall Landlord be required to expend more than the condemnation proceeds received by Landlord with respect to such taking, and Tenant shall continue in possession of the portion of the Premises not so taken upon the same terms and conditions as are herein provided, except that Annual Base Rent and Additional Rent shall be reduced in direct proportion to the area of the Premises so taken.

PARAGRAPH 25

Subordination (and SNDAs)

RISK RATING: 5

A. DESCRIPTION AND SCOPE

This Paragraph provides that the Lease, and Tenant's interest in the Lease, will be subordinate to any current and future mortgage, deed of trust, or underlying ground lease encumbering the Property. In other words, any such mortgage, deed of trust, or underlying ground lease is higher in priority than the Lease. This is the "subordination" portion of "subordination, nondisturbance, and attornment." Nevertheless, at the election of the mortgagee, the Lease can be made superior to the mortgage. Any such subordination of the Lease is conditioned on the mortgagee's and/or ground lessor's agreement that, in the event of the foreclosure of a mortgage or the termination of a ground lease, the Lease will not be terminated and that, so long as Tenant is not in default, Tenant's possession will not be disturbed. This is known as the "nondisturbance" language. Further, Tenant agrees to attorn to and recognize any successor to Landlord (including by foreclosure), which is the "attornment" portion of "subordination, nondisturbance, and attornment."

B. ANALYSIS

1. Landlord's Perspective

Where financing on the Property is not yet established or the Property may be refinanced in the future, this provision assists Landlord in obtaining financing for the Property from a Lender who is likely to require that its mortgage be superior in priority to all other interests, including the interests of Tenant under the Lease. Where there is existing financing for the Property, this subordination language is likely required by the Lender under the loan documents. Landlords should seek clear language providing that the Lease is automatically subordinate to any mortgages, deeds of trust, or underlying ground leases that may now or hereafter encumber or otherwise affect the Landlord or the Building or Landlord's leasehold therein.

Landlord should also consider limiting mortgagee's attornment obligations to make the Lease more attractive to Lenders, for example, to limit (or eliminate) a Lender's liability for acts of a prior landlord and to avoid binding a Lender to Tenant's prepayment of rent. This means Tenant will not be able look to Lender to satisfy unmet obligations of prior landlord.

2. Tenant's Perspective

Generally, Tenant agrees to subordinate its interest to that of Landlord's mortgagee or ground lessor but Tenant must recognize that Tenant is not protected from having the Lease or its right to possession of the Premises terminated by the foreclosure of a mortgage or by the termination of a ground lease that has priority over the Lease, unless (i) the Lease so provides for a nondisturbance of Tenant's possession, or (ii) Tenant obtains a Subordination, Nondisturbance, and Attornment Agreement (SNDA) from the current and any future mortgagees or ground lessors.

Tenant should require Landlord to disclose current mortgagees at the time of execution of the Lease or otherwise represent there are no current mortgagees. In situations where the Lease is being executed at a time when mortgage financing on the Property is already in place, Tenant will be motivated to ask for a SNDA because, without a SNDA, the Lease is automatically subordinate to any existing mortgage, and a foreclosure of such mortgage would permit the mortgage lender to terminate the Lease, even if Tenant is not in default under the Lease.

Whether a Tenant is likely to obtain, under the Lease, the right to a SNDA, is generally, based upon the leverage of the Tenant and certain factual circumstances. Generally, a Tenant entering into a lease for approximately 10,000 rentable square feet in a building or less will have little leverage to require the delivery of a SNDA from existing and future mortgagees and ground lessors but a Tenant taking more than about 10,000 rentable square feet of space will have much more leverage and should seek a SNDA and/or the protections outlined in the compromises and alternatives section below.

In addition, a Tenant who is making valuable leasehold improvements to the Premises with such improvements being paid for by Tenant, should aggressively pursue the right to a SNDA from the existing mortgagee or other holder of a superior leasehold interest upon the Effective Date or within a short period of time thereafter or otherwise Tenant risks losing the value of its improvements.

Additionally, a Tenant should push to obtain a SNDA if Tenant is expecting a large tenant improvement allowance, or is due a rent credit, and the attornment limitations in the Lease provide that mortgagee shall not be bound to make any payment to Tenant or honor any rent credit agreed to by a prior landlord. In such event, Tenant will need to strike any such limiting language or get rent offset rights for any Landlord failure to pay the tenant allowance (plus interest), which will protect Tenant in the event of a foreclosure or termination of a ground lease. Further, Tenant should carefully review the limitations of Lender's attornment as those limitations should not limit Tenant's rights for any Landlord defaults that continue after Lender succeeds to Landlord.

3. Lender's Perspective

A Lender wants to be sure that the lien of its mortgage or deed of trust has priority over all Leases. Lender does not want to be bound by prior acts of Landlord or by prepayment of rent by Tenant. This Paragraph serves two primary functions: (i) the rights of Tenant under a Lease when Tenant is in default beyond applicable notice, cure and grace periods may be extinguished by the Lender's exercise of its rights under the mortgage or deed of trust, and (ii) upon foreclosure, Tenant under a surviving Lease agrees to recognize Lender, or its purchaser or designee, as the successor to Landlord, without claim of offset or other damages due to prior acts of Landlord. Lender is assured of an uninterrupted source of income and avoids the assumption (by law or otherwise) of certain liabilities or obligations created by the prior Landlord. In some states foreclosure will extinguish the Lease, unless the Lease has an attornment clause or is made superior to the Mortgage. For that reason and others, in certain circumstances, it may be preferable under local foreclosure law to have the Lease superior to the mortgage in order to permit the Lease to survive the foreclosure. The Lender would prefer that the Lease survive foreclosure if the rent payable under the Lease is at or above market rent and/or the remaining term is a significant period of time.

4. Broker's Perspective

Tenant Broker should be sensitive to including in any LOI a Tenant right to an SNDA if the factual circumstances or Tenant's leverage make it prudent and reasonable. In determining whether Tenant Broker should include a Tenant SNDA right in the LOI, Tenant Broker should consider the size of the Premises, length of the Term, the amount of Tenant upfront investment in the Premises, Tenant's creditworthiness, and the current financing and financial performance of Landlord and of the Building (including occupancy levels). Tenant Broker should consider researching online data bases for the Property to evaluate the terms and conditions of the current debt on the Property.

C. COMPROMISES AND ALTERNATIVES

(i) Compromises and Alternatives to Paragraph 25 Generally

A Tenant's best protection against the provisions of this Paragraph is to require a SNDA from any current Mortgagee and/or superior Lessor with interest in the Property and conditioning its subordination to any future Mortgages or Superior Leases on obtaining a SNDA from the applicable parties. A sample provision affording Tenant such rights may look like the following and could be added to the end of Subparagraph 25(a) below.

> *Notwithstanding anything to the contrary contained herein, Tenant's subordination and attornment to any future Mortgages or Superior Leases shall be conditioned upon its receipt of reasonable and binding subordination, nondisturbance and attornment agreement (SNDA) protecting Tenant's tenancy as long as Tenant is not in Default of its obligations under the Lease. In addition, Landlord shall obtain, at no cost to Tenant, such SNDA(s) from any and all current Mortgagees and Lessors and provide same to Tenant on*

the Effective Date in the form attached hereto as Exhibit [__]. Landlord hereby represents and warrants that there are no defaults under any such current Mortgages or Superior Leases and that same permit Landlord to lease the Premises to Tenant as contemplated by the Lease.

Tenants who achieve the insertion of the language above should use the negotiation period for the Lease to also negotiate the SNDA with the applicable Mortgagee and/or Lessor during the same period so that the SNDA is simultaneously executed with the Lease. If Tenant will not be expending any money immediately upon the Effective Date to prepare the Premises for occupancy, it is reasonable to revise the above language to provide that Landlord has thirty (30) days from the Effective Date to deliver the fully executed SNDA to Tenant, provided that Tenant has a Lease termination right if the SNDA is not delivered prior to the expiration of the thirty (30)-day period.

Any lease provision requiring Tenant enter in a SNDA "in the Mortgagee's standard form" should be modified as follows "in the Mortgagee's standard form, *subject to reasonable revisions by Tenant.*"

As mentioned above, only Tenants taking substantial space within a Building (on a square feet or percentage basis) and/or expecting to expend substantial sums of money to prepare the Premises for Tenant's initial occupancy are likely to achieve the provision above. Landlord's loan documents may even include a provision that the Lender is not required to provide a SNDA to Tenants leasing less than approximately 10,000 rentable square feet. In such cases, it is common for Landlord to agree to add the following language only into the Lease:

Upon Tenant's written request of Landlord, Landlord shall use commercially reasonable efforts to obtain SNDA(s) from any and all current and future Mortgagees and/or Lessors, on such party's standard (but commercially reasonable) form(s), subject to reasonable Tenant revisions.

Finally, for Tenants leasing a more substantial portion of the Building, Lenders may actually prefer to have a SNDA in place with that Tenant anyway so Tenant's request is often accommodated.

(ii) Compromises and Alternatives to any SNDA Resulting from Paragraph 25

Standard form SNDAs vary greatly by Mortgagee in terms of how well balanced they are in protecting Mortgagee and Tenant with some forms being more Mortgagee-aggressive and some forms being fairer to the Tenant in the first draft. The following are concepts for Tenants to consider when reviewing, revising, and negotiating a SNDA.

Tenant should confirm that the SNDA provides clearly that (i) Tenant shall not be named as a party in any action or proceeding commenced by Lender for the foreclosure of the mortgage or sale of the Property (unless such joinder is required under law); (ii) the Lease shall not be terminated; and (iii) Tenant's possession or use of the Premises shall not be disturbed (Lender will like qualify this with the fact that Tenant is not in default under the Lease), in the case of (ii) or (iii), so long as Tenant is not in default under the Lease beyond applicable notice, cure and grace periods, ***and*** Tenant should try to extend these rights to Tenant's subtenants, successors, and/or assigns. Extending such Tenant rights to "subtenants" is very helpful because Landlords and Lenders often resist obtaining a separate SNDA for any subtenant and if

Tenant achieves subtenant protection in its SNDA, there is no need for subtenant to obtain a separate SNDA. This may help facilitate the finalization of a sublease.

Tenants should also request modifications of a form of SNDA in order to modify or reinstate certain Lease obligations for which Lender seeks exculpation. In particular, if Landlord is required to complete certain improvements to the Building or the Premises or the Property, or if Landlord is required to pay Tenant a tenant improvement allowance, or if Tenant is entitled to rent credit, Tenant should request that Lender honor any such negotiated terms or remain responsible for any such obligations and that the SNDA specifically reference the survival of these obligations.

Lastly, Tenant should confirm the SNDA is in recordable form for the jurisdiction in which the Property is located and Tenant should include in the SNDA an express right to record the SNDA on the applicable land records.

D. COMMENTS

In some instances, depending on factors such as state law, Landlord's mortgagee may desire to have a strong, credit Lease be superior rather than subordinate to its mortgage so that there is no question as to whether the Lease would survive in any foreclosure. See Part 4 of this Lease Manual for forms of Subordination, Nondisturbance and Attornment Agreements.

Mortgagees are more often charging an administration fee for the issuance of any SNDA together with legal fees if a Tenant seeks revisions to the SNDA that are negotiated with Lender's counsel. Who pays these fees as between Landlord and Tenant is often negotiated. A fair compromise is that Landlord pays the fees with respect to any SNDA being issued in connection with the execution of a Lease and, thereafter, for any SNDA being entered into at the request of Landlord (due to a Lender requirement in a Property refinance, etc.) and with Tenant paying for any SNDA being entered into at the request or right of Tenant.

When negotiating an SNDA, it is customary that Tenant's counsel be connected with Lender's counsel for direct negotiation and finalization of the SNDA as any revisions to the form SNDA typically have no impact on Landlord.

Finally, after explaining above the importance of Tenants obtaining a SNDA, it is worth evaluating the actual practical risk many Tenants are required to take if they are unable to obtain a SNDA. While there very much is a legal risk to Tenant embedded in Paragraph 25 as it permits a Mortgagee who succeeds to Landlord's position under the Lease to terminate the Lease, practically, does a Mortgagee actually have a motivation to terminate a Lease of non-defaulting Tenant? Generally, no. Mortgagees are, typically, not in the business of operating Properties. They are in the business of loaning money and collecting it back with interest to generate profit. If a Tenant is timely paying rent under a Lease, then Mortgagee stands to continue to collect money from Tenant. It is highly unlikely (although possible) a Mortgagee would risk a stable income stream from a non-defaulting Tenant under an existing Lease by terminating that Lease and endeavoring to upgrade that income stream though another tenant or otherwise. Therefore, many "small" Tenants accept the legal risk associated with Paragraph 25 by recognizing the practical risk is remote.

E. TYPICAL PARAGRAPH

25. Subordination.

(a) Subordination and Non-Disturbance. This Lease is subject and subordinate to each and every ground or otherwise superior lease ("Superior Lease") and to each and every mortgage encumbering the Property ("Mortgage"). This clause shall be self-operative and no further instrument of subordination shall be required to make the interest of any lessor under a Superior Lease ("Lessor") or mortgagee under a Mortgage ("Mortgagee") superior to the interest of Tenant hereunder; however, Tenant shall execute and deliver promptly any certificate that Landlord may request in confirmation of such subordination. If the date of expiration of any Superior Lease is the same day as the Expiration Date, then the Term shall end and expire twelve (12) hours prior to the expiration of the Superior Lease. If, in connection with the financing of the Property, the Building or the interest of the lessee under any Superior Lease, any lending institution shall request reasonable modifications of this Lease that do not materially increase the obligations or materially or adversely affect the rights of Tenant under this Lease, then Tenant promptly shall make such modifications, at no cost or expense to Tenant. Upon Tenant's written request of Landlord, Landlord shall use commercially reasonable efforts to obtain non-disturbance agreements from any and all future Mortgagees on such Mortgagee's standard form(s). Tenant shall be responsible for any actual administrative and legal fee imposed by Mortgagee for issuing such non-disturbance agreement.

(b) Attornment. If at any time prior to the expiration of the Term, any Superior Lease shall terminate or be terminated for any reason or any Mortgagee comes into possession of the Property or the Building or the estate created by any Superior Lease by receiver or otherwise, then Tenant, at the election and upon demand of any owner of the Real Property or the Building, or of the Lessor, or of any Mortgagee in possession of the Property or the Building, shall attorn, from time to time, to any such owner, Lessor or Mortgagee or any person acquiring the interest of Landlord as a result of any such termination, or as a result of a foreclosure of the Mortgage or the granting of a deed in lieu of foreclosure, upon the then executory terms and conditions of this Lease, subject to the provisions of this Paragraph 25, for the remainder of the Term, provided that such owner, Lessor or Mortgagee, as the case may be, or receiver caused to be appointed by any of the foregoing, shall then be entitled to possession of the Premises and provided further that such owner, Lessor or Mortgagee, as the case may be, or anyone claiming by, through or under such owner, Lessor or Mortgagee, as the case may be, including a purchaser at a foreclosure sale, shall not be:

(1) liable for any act or omission of any prior landlord (including, without limitation, the then defaulting landlord), or
(2) subject to any defense or offsets which Tenant may have against any prior Landlord (including, without limitation, the then defaulting Landlord), or
(3) bound by any payment of Rent which Tenant may have made to any prior landlord (including, without limitation, the then defaulting Landlord) more than thirty (30) days in advance of the date upon which such payment was due, or
(4) bound by any obligation to make any payment to or on behalf of Tenant, or
(5) bound by any obligation to perform any work or to make improvements to the Premises, except for (i) repairs and maintenance pursuant to the provisions of this Lease, the need for which repairs and maintenance first arises or continues after the date when such owner, Lessor, or Mortgagee succeeds to Landlord's interest in the Property, (ii) repairs to the Premises or any part thereof as a result of damage by fire or other casualty pursuant to Paragraph 13 hereof, but only to the extent the such repairs can be reasonably made from the net proceeds of any insurance actually made available to such Lessor or Mortgagee, and (iii) repairs to the Premises as a result of a partial condemnation pursuant to Partial 14 hereof, but only to the extent that such repairs can be reasonably made from the net proceeds of any award made available to such Lessor or Mortgagee, or
(6) bound by any amendment or modification of this Lease made without the consent of such Mortgagee or Lessor, as the case may be.

The provisions of this Subparagraph (b) shall inure to the benefit of any such owner, Lessor or Mortgagee, shall apply notwithstanding that, as a matter of law, this Lease may terminate upon the termination of any Superior Lease, and shall be self-operative upon any such demand, and no further instrument shall be required to give effect to said provisions. Tenant, however, upon demand of any such owner, Lessor or Mortgagee, shall execute, from time to time, instruments, in recordable form, in confirmation of the foregoing provisions of this Subparagraph (b), reasonably satisfactory to any such owner, Lessor or Mortgagee, acknowledging such attornment and setting forth the terms and conditions of its tenancy.

(c) Rights to Cure Landlord's Default. If (i) a Mortgage or Superior Lease is in effect, and (ii) Tenant has theretofore received notice thereof and of the address for each Mortgagee or Lessor, then Tenant shall not seek to terminate this Lease by reason of Landlord's default hereunder until the thirtieth (30th) day after the date when Tenant has given written notice of such default to such Lessors and Mortgagees at such addresses;

provided, however, that if, during such thirty (30) day period, any such Lessor or Mortgagee either (a) remedies such default, or (b) in respect of any such default by Landlord which can be remedied but cannot with due diligence be remedied during such thirty (30)-day period, institutes action to remedy such default (and thereafter diligently prosecutes such remedy to completion), then Tenant shall not have the right to terminate this Lease by reason of such default.

PARAGRAPH 26

Estoppel Certificate

RISK RATING: 4

A. DESCRIPTION AND SCOPE

This Paragraph obligates Tenant to deliver an estoppel certificate to Landlord upon ten (10) days' prior written notice, setting forth certain facts with respect to the status of the Lease and the tenancy.

B. ANALYSIS

1. Landlord's Perspective

This provision is primarily an aid to Landlord in financing or selling the Property, since mortgage lenders and purchasers typically require estoppel certificates from Tenant to identify issues that may impact the cash flow generated by the Lease.

2. Tenant's Perspective

A Tenant requirement to provide an estoppel certificate, within a reasonable period of time from Landlord request, which certificate is limited to a reasonable set of facts that a lender or purchaser would be otherwise unable to ascertain by a mere review of the Lease, is a customary and generally uncontroversial obligation of Tenant under the Lease.

3. Lender's Perspective

A Lender will require estoppel certificates from Tenants of the Property, because it provides Lender with assurances that there are no claims or issues that may impact the income generated by the Leases.

4. Broker's Perspective

Each Broker will want to consult with their respective client to determine any sensitivity to or any particular client need relating to this Paragraph that should be covered in the LOI. If none exist, this Paragraph can be handled by the attorneys in Lease negotiations. As an example, a retail franchisee Tenant may need the right to obtain a Landlord estoppel for its franchisor. Each Broker should support their respective legal counsel to ensure that the negotiated terms and this Paragraph are commercially reasonable and protective of their respective clients' needs.

C. COMPROMISES AND ALTERNATIVES

Tenants may request that Landlord provide Tenant with a similar estoppel certificate for Tenant's financing, Premises subletting or Lease assignment purposes.
Tenant may also ask that the number of Landlord requests for estoppels be limited to not more than one or two per year.

Tenant may also be able to insert the below protective language at the end of any estoppel certificate:

Nothing contained in this certification shall constitute or be deemed to constitute an amendment, modification, or waiver of any term or condition of the Lease or any right or remedy of Tenant thereunder. In the event of a conflict between the Lease and this certificate, the Lease shall control.

D. COMMENTS

Landlord will want to make sure there is no long notice and cure period (or no notice and cure period at all) on Tenant's obligation to deliver an estoppel certificate and/or the Lease should provide that any non-response by Tenant shall be deemed an approval by Tenant to the Tenant statements within the estoppel certificate.

Tenant should be careful to review the statements within the estoppel certificate for accuracy and limit the statements to Tenant's actual knowledge, where appropriate. Tenant wants to be especially careful not to waive its claims of offset against Annual Base Rent or Additional Rent by inadvertently failing to disclose such claims in the estoppel certificate. Tenant can protect against this by specifying in its certificate those ways, if any, in which Landlord is in default, and Landlord may be required by a Lender or a purchaser to cure the default before financing or sale.

In addition, Tenant should only be required to stipulate to facts in the estoppel certificate that cannot be ascertained by a mere review of the Lease and any statements beyond that should be stricken. The risk of any lease due diligence should not be shifted from any potential lender or buyer to Tenant. Also, Tenant should not agree to make any changes to the Lease or take on any obligations within the estoppel certificate (like notifying Lenders of any Landlord default). If Lender wants Tenant to be obliged to Lender in any way, those obligations are more properly contained in a SNDA.

Tenant will want to strike any provision in the Lease that names Landlord as Tenant's "attorney in fact" for the execution of the estoppel certificate in the event that Tenant does not timely deliver the estoppel certificate.

Tenant should note that Landlords are often anxious to obtain an estoppel certificate from Tenant for a financing or a potential purchaser and that provides Tenant with some surprise leverage and potentially its best opportunity during the Term to get Landlord to address any operational concerns raised by Tenant (including of any failure of Landlord to meet its maintenance, repair, or operational obligations) because Landlord will be anxious for Tenant to not include any such issues or defaults in the estoppel certificate. Tenant should be careful to include any such issues or defaults in any first draft of the estoppel certificate and Tenant should not be surprised if Landlord addresses the issues and then asks Tenant for a follow-up estoppel certificate excluding those issues or defaults that Landlord has then cured or otherwise satisfactorily addressed.

Most Lenders request estoppel certificates in advance of closing on a mortgage loan. See Part 4 of this Lease Manual for forms of Tenant Estoppel Letters.

E. TYPICAL PARAGRAPH

26. Estoppel Certificate. Tenant shall, upon ten (10) days' prior written request by Landlord, execute, acknowledge, and deliver to Landlord or its designee, which may include any mortgagee or purchaser of the Property, a written statement stating, to the reasonable knowledge of Tenant as of the date made: (a) the date this Lease was executed; (b) the Commencement Date, the Rent Commencement Date, and the Expiration Date; (c) the amount of monthly installment Annual Base Rent and the date to which the latest installment Annual Base Rent has been paid; (d) that this Lease is in full force and effect, that neither Landlord nor Tenant is in default under the Lease, and the Lease has not been assigned, modified, supplemented, or amended in any way (or specifying the date and terms of any agreement so affecting this Lease); (e) that this Lease represents the entire agreement between the parties as to this lease transaction (or identifying those other documents that, together with this Lease, form the entire agreement between the parties as to this lease transaction); (f) that all conditions under this Lease to be performed by Landlord have been satisfied (or specifying those conditions that Landlord has not satisfied); (g) that all required contributions by Landlord to Tenant on account of Tenant's improvements have been received (or specifying those required contributions which Landlord has not made); (h) that as of the date of said statement there are no existing defenses or offsets that Tenant has against the enforcement of this Lease by Landlord except as set out by Tenant; (i) that no Annual Base Rent has been paid for more than one (1) month in advance except as set out by Tenant; (j) that no security has been deposited with Landlord (or the amount of such deposit, if any); and (k) any other matter relating to the Lease that Landlord may request. Any such statement may be relied upon by a prospective purchaser or any mortgagee of Landlord's interest in the Property.

PARAGRAPH 27

Bankruptcy

RISK RATING: 4

A. DESCRIPTION AND SCOPE

This Paragraph describes the changes in the financial condition of Tenant or any guarantor of Tenant's obligations that constitute a default under the Lease, as well as Landlord's remedies with respect to such a default.

B. ANALYSIS

1. Landlord's Perspective

The automatic stay that arises under the Federal Bankruptcy Code upon the filing of a bankruptcy petition will prevent the Landlord from recovering possession or obtaining immediate satisfaction of a monetary award granted against the Tenant. However, all rents and other charges that accrue after filing of the petition become an administrative charge against the debtor's estate entitled to priority against all other unsecured claims, irrespective of whether the Lease is assumed or rejected. It should be noted that much of Paragraph 27 may not be enforceable under the current Bankruptcy Code. However, these provisions should remain in the event that during the Term the Bankruptcy Code is changed.

2. Tenant's Perspective

Tenant may not want a change in the financial condition of any Guarantor to constitute a default under the Lease, since Tenant is meeting its obligations.

3. Lender's Perspective

Same as Landlord's Perspective.

4. Broker's Perspective

Events of bankruptcy are not typically addressed in the LOI and this Paragraph is typically negotiated between legal counsel for the respective parties.

C. COMPROMISES AND ALTERNATIVES

The time period for failure to discharge an involuntary bankruptcy petition is generally negotiable.

D. COMMENTS

None.

E. TYPICAL PARAGRAPH

27. Bankruptcy. In the event that any of the following events occur, Landlord may terminate this Lease and pursue any and all remedies set forth in this Lease or available at law or in equity:

(a) Any sale of Tenant's interest in the Premises created by this Lease as a result of any bankruptcy, insolvency, execution, or similar legal process;

(b) Tenant or any guarantor of Tenant's obligations under this Lease (a "Guarantor") shall make an assignment for the benefit of its creditors or shall admit in writing the inability to pay its debts generally as they become due;

(c) Tenant or any Guarantor files or consents to the filing of any petition, or commences or consents to the commencement of, any proceeding, action, petition, or filing under the Federal Bankruptcy Code or any similar state or federal law now or hereafter in effect relating to bankruptcy, reorganization, or insolvency, or the arrangement or adjustment of debts (a "Bankruptcy Proceeding") with respect to Tenant or Guarantor;

(d) Any petition shall have been filed against Tenant or Guarantor in connection with a Bankruptcy Proceeding and the same is not withdrawn, dismissed, canceled, or terminated within sixty (60) days of such filing;

(e) Tenant or Guarantor is adjudicated bankrupt or insolvent or a petition for reorganization of Tenant or Guarantor is granted;

(f) A receiver, liquidator or trustee of Tenant or Guarantor or of any of the properties of Tenant or Guarantor shall be appointed and the same not be dismissed or terminated within sixty (60) days thereafter; or

(g) Tenant's interest under this Lease shall pass to another by operation of law or in any manner other than as may be permitted by Paragraph 17 of this Lease.

PARAGRAPH 28

Default by Tenant

RISK RATING: 4

A. DESCRIPTION AND SCOPE

This Paragraph describes the conditions under which Tenant may be in default under the Lease (including failure to pay rent, bankruptcy, and failure to comply with Lease covenants) and establishes a notice and cure period for certain defaults.

B. ANALYSIS

1. Landlord's Perspective

This Paragraph enables Landlord to take appropriate remedial action should Tenant fail to comply with its Lease obligations. The Paragraph does not require Landlord to give written notice for rental defaults. Since Landlord's mortgage loan obligation likely would be due on the first day of the month, requiring Landlord to give Tenant written notice of default each month would cause delay in the payment of Landlord's mortgage loan obligation and perhaps subject it to default interest, late charges, or foreclosure. Such an argument may be countered by the Tenant, depending upon its credit rating and its history of paying its obligations when due. The Paragraph also sets an outside date on nonmonetary defaults that Tenant is not capable of curing within thirty (30) days.

2. Tenant's Perspective

This Paragraph clearly identifies for Tenant what act or omission of Tenant can trigger Landlord's right to pursue remedies against Tenant. Tenant should seek to modify the default Paragraph so that Tenant is afforded reasonable notice and cure periods for all Tenant breaches under the Lease before they become actionable by Landlord.

3. Lender's Perspective

The notice and cure periods are reasonable and should not be objectionable to Lender.

4. Broker's Perspective

Brokers would not typically address Tenant defaults in the LOI but Tenant Broker should review this Paragraph and have an understanding of what circumstances and events may trigger a Tenant default and whether Tenant prior written notice to Tenant is required for a Default to exist in any particular circumstance. Tenant Broker should identify any concerns with respect to a Tenant notice of Default and cure periods in its initial review of the Paragraph and share those concerns with Tenant legal counsel and support Tenant legal counsel in negotiating reasonable terms and conditions in this Paragraph.

C. COMPROMISES AND ALTERNATIVES

In all cases, Tenant should revise the Default Paragraph to provide a reasonable notice and cure period for monetary default. Up to ten (10) days is typical and reasonable since most Lenders will give Landlord similar notice or grace period and Tenant should not risk a forfeiture of the Lease if the check truly was "lost in the mail" or, through oversight or inadvertence, Tenant fails to make a timely rental payment. Landlord's may wish to limit how often Landlord needs to provide a notice and cure period for monetary defaults within a 12-month period. This is to protect Landlord from the chronic defaulter.

Tenant cure periods for nonmonetary defaults are typically thirty (30) days but are subject to extension to the extent the default cannot be reasonably cured by Tenant to within the thirty (30) days, but Tenant commences curative action within such thirty (30)-day period and continues to diligently pursue a cure for such nonmonetary default. Tenant should resist any cap to such cure period and whatever time period is reasonably needed should be provided as long as Tenant is diligently pursuing to cure the default.

With respect to Subparagraph 28(c), Tenant should request a ninety (90)-day period to dismiss an involuntary bankruptcy.

With respect to Subparagraph 28(e) and (g), Tenant should not be in default for failing to occupy nonretail Premises as long as Tenant continues to pay rent.

The experience of COVID-19 taught both Landlord and Tenant that there are now reasons for which a Tenant might vacate the Premises for extended periods of time. If Tenant is paying rent for the office space and otherwise meeting its repair and maintenance obligations under the Lease, in no event shall an office Tenant (versus a retail Tenant) be deemed to be in default under the Lease for not commencing occupancy or for vacating the Premises for extended periods of time. Thus, typical default Paragraphs need to be revised accordingly.

D. COMMENTS

Since procedures for declaring and enforcing a Lease default are State specific, Landlord should discuss with local counsel the validity of this Paragraph in the jurisdiction where the Property is located.

E. TYPICAL PARAGRAPH

28. **Default by Tenant. The occurrence of any of the following events shall constitute a "Default" under this Lease: (a) the failure of Tenant to pay when due any installment of Annual Base Rent, Additional Rent, or other charge due under this Lease; or (b) the failure of Tenant to fulfill any of the other covenants or provisions of this Lease on its part to be performed and such default is not remedied within thirty (30) days (or if such default cannot reasonably be remedied within such thirty (30) days, within such time as may reasonably be required to remedy the default up to an aggregate of ninety (90) days, provided Tenant diligently commences curing such default within the first thirty (30) days and diligently proceeds to cure such default) after Landlord shall have given Tenant written notice of such default; or (c) any bankruptcy, insolvency, or similar proceeding shall be filed by or against Tenant and the same shall not be dismissed within thirty (30) days; or (d) if Landlord shall give to Tenant within any period of twelve (12) consecutive months during the term of this Lease, three (3) notices of Default; or (e) if Tenant shall abandon or fail to occupy the Premises for a period of thirty (30) consecutive days and fails to pay rent therefor; or (f) if Tenant shall fail to take possession of the Premises on the Commencement Date; or (g) if Tenant assigns the Lease or sublets the Premises in violation of the assignment and subletting Paragraph of this Lease.**

PARAGRAPH 29

Remedies of Landlord

RISK RATING: 4

A. DESCRIPTION AND SCOPE

This Paragraph describes Landlord's remedies upon Tenant's default and permits Landlord to pursue concurrently any remedy provided under the Lease, at law or in equity. The Lease remedies include terminating the Lease, recovery of the present value of the rental and other charges payable by Tenant for the remainder of the Lease term, or collection of the monthly rent and charges as and when due less the proceeds of reletting the Premises.

B. ANALYSIS

1. Landlord's Perspective

Since remedies for a Lease default are State-specific, Landlord should discuss with local counsel the enforceability of this Paragraph in the jurisdiction where the Property is located. In many States, this Paragraph will provide Landlord with an adequate choice of remedies for a Default by Tenant under the Lease. Generally, a Landlord will be reluctant to negotiate or alter the remedies provisions of the Lease as it is not reasonably expected that Landlord needs to protect Tenant from its bad behavior. In Subparagraph 29(e) Landlord has a right to relet the Premises, but should not be obligated to do so. Landlord should generally not agree to mitigate damages since if Tenant so chooses, Tenant can locate a subtenant and mitigate Tenant's damages. However, some states do require that Landlord use commercially reasonable efforts to re-lease the Premises and mitigate damages. An additional remedy that Landlord may want to add is the right to take possession of the Premises without terminating the Lease, since in some jurisdictions, recovery of damages may be limited if the Lease is terminated.

Landlord's damages in Paragraph 29 below expressly include any Abated Base Rent and if Landlord provided any improvement allowance to Tenant or spent significant sums of money preparing the Premises for Tenant's occupancy, Landlord should revise the language to expressly include those amounts in Landlord's collectable damages as well.

2. Tenant's Perspective

Tenant needs to understand that, unless they have an express early termination right under the Lease, Tenant is committing to unconditionally fulfill their obligations under the Lease when Tenant executes the Lease on the Effective Date. If the Premises or Tenant's business operating therein does not work well for Tenant, Tenant's options are to endeavor to sublet the Premises or assign the Lease, endeavor to negotiate an early termination agreement with Landlord or Default under the Lease. Should Tenant Default under the Lease, Tenant will be subject to Landlord's remedies under the Lease, at law and in equity.

Tenant has little leverage in negotiating Landlord's remedies in the event of a Tenant Default. Those limited options are set forth in the Compromises and Alternatives below. Tenant may also have the ability to file bankruptcy proceedings. In such case, any legal action against Tenant by Landlord may be suspended and in a bankruptcy reorganization, Tenant may have the ability to reject the Lease and terminate or limit future Lease obligations.

3. Lender's Perspective

Since Lender may become the future Landlord should Lender foreclose on the Property, Lender will want to make sure the Lease contains strong Landlord remedies.

4. Broker's Perspective

Brokers would not typically address Landlord remedies for Tenant Defaults in the LOI but Tenant Broker should review this Paragraph and share any concerns with Tenant legal counsel and support Tenant legal counsel in negotiating reasonable terms and conditions in this Paragraph.

C. COMPROMISES AND ALTERNATIVES

Credit Tenants or other Tenants with significant leverage may be in a position to negotiate some changes to the remedies of Landlord. In such case, Tenant may want Landlord to covenant to mitigate Landlord's damages. In the jurisdictions where Landlords may be required to mitigate damages under local law, adding an express provision to the Lease for any Tenant may not be objectionable.

Also, all Tenants should push back on (and Landlords should accept) the nearly unqualified acceleration of Rent provision contained in Subparagraph 29(d) below. It is much more reasonable, fair and market that Landlord's remedy after taking possession or termination be limited to an alternative definition of "Liquidated Final

Damages," which is the then discounted present value of the difference, if any, between (a) the then remaining Rent reserved under the Lease, and (b) the fair market rental value of the Premises for the then balance of the Term. The discount factor for calculating "present value" is sometimes negotiated.

The practical application of Landlord's remedies under the Lease result most often in Landlords suing for or collecting month to month Rent and then only accelerating damages if and when a replacement tenant has been identified as that definitively establishes the fair market rent value of the Premises. Thus, it is at that time when Landlord switch from month-to-month damages to terminating the Lease and pursing their Liquidated Final Damages.

In addition, with respect to Subparagraph 29(b), Tenant should object to any recovery of the Premises "by force." The appropriate modification to this provision to is to insert "lawful" before "force." This results in Landlord only being permitted to recover the Premises by lawful action.

With respect to Subparagraph 29(f), credit Tenant may want to limit liability for Landlord's reletting costs, since if the Lease Term had expired normally at the end of the Lease Term, Tenant would not have been liable for Landlord's reletting costs, and since Tenant will be liable for the economic equivalent of the Annual Base Rent due for the remainder of the Term, Tenant should not be also liable for such reletting costs.

Lastly, Tenant should not allow Landlord to limit utilities, Tenant's parking rights, or other Building services in the event of a Default. Tenant should also not unilaterally lose its extension options under the Lease in the event of Default unless Landlord terminates Tenant's possession to the Premises or terminates the Lease due to the Default.

D. COMMENTS

None.

E. TYPICAL PARAGRAPH

29. Remedies of Landlord.

(a) In the event of any Default under this Lease, Landlord may, at Landlord's option and without prejudice to its rights hereunder, terminate this Lease upon notice to Tenant or terminate Tenant's right to possession to the Premises without terminating the Lease. No act by Landlord other than its giving written notice to Tenant shall terminate this Lease. Acts of maintenance, efforts to relet the Premises, or the appointment of a receiver on Landlord's initiative to protect Landlord's interest under this Lease shall not constitute a termination of this Lease or Tenant's right to possession of the Premises. In the event of such termination, all of the right, title, and interest of Tenant under this Lease, including any

renewal or extension privileges, shall end, and Tenant shall quit and surrender the Premises to Landlord. Tenant's liability under all of the provisions of this Lease shall continue notwithstanding any termination or surrender, and notwithstanding Landlord's pursuit of any other remedy under this Lease, at law or in equity.

(b) Upon termination of this Lease pursuant to this Paragraph 29, Landlord may recover possession of the Premises by summary proceedings, by force, by any suitable action or proceeding at law, or otherwise. Landlord may also enter the Premises and execute reentry of the Premises at any time after such termination and remove all persons and property therefrom without being deemed guilty of trespass or becoming liable for any loss or damage that may be occasioned thereby and may have, hold, and enjoy the Premises.

(c) If this Lease is terminated pursuant to this Paragraph 29, Tenant shall pay to Landlord, in addition to all Abated Base Rent, Annual Base Rent, Additional Rent and other charges due and payable by Tenant on the date of such termination, as current damages for Tenant's default, the equivalent of the amount of Annual Base Rent, Additional Rent, and all other charges Tenant would have been required to pay until the date this Lease would have expired had such termination not occurred, minus the proceeds of any reletting. Tenant shall pay such current damages (the "Deficiency Damages") to Landlord monthly on the days on which rent would have been payable under this Lease if this Lease were still in effect and Landlord shall be entitled to recover each month from Tenant Deficiency Damages as the same shall arise. Any suit brought to collect the Deficiency Damages for any month shall not prejudice in any way the right of Landlord to collect Deficiency Damages for any subsequent month by a similar proceeding.

(d) If this Lease is terminated pursuant to this Paragraph 29, and if Landlord so elects at any time , in lieu of Landlord's damages under Subparagraph (c) above, Tenant shall pay in addition to all Abated Base Rent, Annual Base Rent, Additional Rent and all other charges due and payable by Tenant on the date of such termination, "Liquidated Final Damages." As used herein, "Liquidated Final Damages" shall mean the present value of an amount equivalent to the Annual Base Rent, Additional Rent, and other charges that would have been payable by Tenant from the date of such election to the date this Lease would have expired had it not been so terminated. Said Liquidated Final Damages shall become due and payable to Landlord immediately upon Landlord's notice to Tenant of such election.

(e) In the event of termination of this Lease or a reentry into the Premises pursuant to this Paragraph 29, Landlord may relet the whole or any part of the Premises in the name of Landlord, Tenant, or otherwise, for a period equal to, greater, or less than the remainder of the then term of this Lease, at such rental and upon such terms and conditions as

Landlord shall deem reasonable, including, without limitation, concessions of free rent. In no event shall the making of any alterations to and/or remodeling of the Premises operate or be construed to release Tenant from liability hereunder as aforesaid. Landlord's failure to relet the Premises or in the event of such reletting, Landlord's failure to collect the rent thereunder, shall not release or affect Tenant's liability for damages hereunder, and Landlord in any event shall not be liable in any way whatsoever for said failures. Any sums received by Landlord on a reletting shall belong to Landlord.

(f) Tenant hereby indemnifies Landlord for all of Landlord's expenses incurred or paid in connection with repossessing or reletting the Premises in the event of Tenant's Default hereunder, including, without limitation, the costs of recovering possession of the Premises; the costs of removing and storing the property of Tenant or any other occupant; the costs of repairing, altering, remodeling, cleaning, or otherwise putting the Premises into condition acceptable to a new tenant or tenants; brokerage and management fees; operating and security expenses of the Premises; and reasonable attorneys' fees and disbursements.

(g) In the event of any Default or any threatened default by Tenant of any of the agreements, terms, covenants, or conditions contained in this Lease, Landlord shall be entitled to enjoin such Default or threatened default and shall have the right to invoke any right and remedy allowed at law or in equity or by statute or otherwise even if not specifically provided for in this Lease.

(h) The rights and remedies of Landlord set forth herein shall be in addition to any other right and remedy now or hereafter provided by law or in equity. All rights and remedies shall be cumulative and not exclusive of each other. Landlord may exercise its rights and remedies at any time, in any order, to any extent, and as often as Landlord deems advisable without regard to whether the exercise of one right or remedy precedes, concurs with, or succeeds the exercise of any other. A single or partial exercise of a right or remedy shall not preclude a further exercise thereof or the exercise of another right or remedy from time to time. No delay or omission by Landlord in exercising a right or remedy shall exhaust or impair the same or constitute a waiver of, or acquiescence to, any Default by Tenant. No waiver of any Default by Tenant shall extend to or affect any other Default or impair any right or remedy with respect thereto. No action or inaction by Landlord shall constitute a waiver of any Default by Tenant. No waiver of any Default by Tenant shall be effective, unless it is in writing and signed by both Landlord and Tenant.

(i) Tenant hereby expressly waives its right to any notice to quit under any statutes relating to summary process or any statutes that may be enacted for recovery of possession of leased premises or other formalities of any nature.

PARAGRAPH 30

Self-Help

RISK RATING: 2

A. DESCRIPTION AND SCOPE

This Paragraph describes the conditions under which Landlord may invoke self-help remedies and establishes Tenant's obligation to reimburse Landlord for expenses in connection therewith.

B. ANALYSIS

1. Landlord's Perspective

This Paragraph enables Landlord, without notice to Tenant, to take appropriate remedial action should Tenant fail to comply with its Lease obligations.

2. Tenant's Perspective

In the event that Tenant does not comply with its obligations under the Lease, it will be liable to Landlord for the costs incurred by Landlord in ensuring compliance. However, Tenant is usually able to negotiate that Landlord may not exercise its self-help rights prior to the expiration of any applicable notice and cure period.

Tenant would also like a reciprocal paragraph that would permit Tenant to have self-help rights should Landlord fail to perform its Lease obligations. Both Landlord and Lender typically object to granting Tenant such self-help rights. However, a Tenant with strong leverage may be able to obtain such self-help rights together with a Rent offset right if Landlord fails to timely reimburse Tenant for costs incurred by Tenant in the exercise of Tenant's self-help rights.

3. Lender's Perspective

Lenders like this Paragraph for the additional leverage it provides as well as the ability to recoup the costs associated with remedial expenses.

Lenders will typically object to any reciprocal self-help rights granted to Tenant. However, if such rights are granted to Tenant, Lender will want notice of Tenant's intended self-help and an opportunity to cure.

4. Broker's Perspective

Brokers would not typically address Tenant self-help rights in the LOI but Tenant Broker should review this Paragraph and share any concerns with Tenant legal counsel and support Tenant legal counsel in negotiating reasonable terms and conditions in this Paragraph.

C. COMPROMISES AND ALTERNATIVES

If Tenant requests that Landlord give notice prior to remedying the default, alternatives would be a short notice period and/or that Landlord shall not be required to give such notice in an emergency or more than twice in any twelve-month period. The parties may also negotiate the rate at which interest accrues on Landlord's expenditures. A reciprocal Tenant self-help right might look like the following:

> *To the extent Landlord fails to perform any of its obligations under the Lease, and such failure continues beyond two (2) business days' notice to Landlord from Tenant, except in the event of emergencies (in which case no prior notice shall be required to Landlord, but Tenant shall use reasonable efforts to notify Landlord as soon as practicable) then Tenant shall have the right to cure such non-performance for the account of Landlord, and any amount of reasonable costs so incurred by Tenant shall be reimbursed by Landlord to Tenant within ten (10) days following Tenant's statement therefor, failing which, Tenant shall have the right to offset such reasonable costs against its Rent next coming due and payable.*

D. COMMENTS

None.

E. TYPICAL PARAGRAPH

30. Self-Help. In the event Tenant defaults in fulfilling any of Tenant's covenants or provisions of this Lease on its part to be performed, Landlord may, at Landlord's sole option, at any time, without notice, cure such default for the account and at the expense of Tenant. If Landlord at any time so elects, or is compelled, to cure any such default and incurs any expense in connection therewith or is compelled to incur any other expense because of any such default (including, without limitation, reasonable attorneys' fees and

disbursements in instituting, prosecuting, or defending any suits, actions, or proceedings to enforce Landlord's rights under this Lease or otherwise), the sum or sums so paid by Landlord plus all costs and damages, with interest at the lesser of the maximum legal rate of interest or [AMOUNT] percent ([AMOUNT]%) per annum from the date Landlord incurs any expense under this Paragraph 30 until Landlord has been reimbursed by Tenant for all such expenses, costs, and damages, shall be paid by Tenant to Landlord, as Additional Rent, upon demand therefor by Landlord.

PARAGRAPH 31

Lien Rights of Landlord

RISK RATING: 1

A. DESCRIPTION AND SCOPE

This Paragraph establishes a lien in favor of Landlord on all property Tenant now or hereafter placed in or upon the Premises. This Paragraph can often times be found in a first draft of Lease prepared by Landlord.

B. ANALYSIS

1. Landlord's Perspective

This Paragraph enables Landlord to enjoy the status of a secured creditor on Tenant's equipment, trade fixtures, inventory and other personal property as additional security for the performance of Tenant's obligations under the Lease, provided Landlord takes steps to perfect the lien, such as the filing of a UCC-1 Financing Statement in the appropriate filing offices. This Paragraph does not work in all jurisdictions. In some states, purchase money liens will take priority over Landlord's lien.

2. Tenant's Perspective

This Paragraph is nearly universally rejected in commercial office leases but may be appropriate in certain retail or industrial leases wherein Landlord's lien rights may be acceptable to Tenant and may even result in Tenant being permitted to post a smaller Security Deposit under the Lease. However, for Tenants who finance or lease from a third party equipment, trade fixtures or other personal property in the operation of their business, this Paragraph will likely conflict with other credit facilities maintained by Tenant. In such a case, Tenant's creditors may have a blanket lien on all of Tenant's fixtures, equipment, inventory and other personal property, and Tenant may be prohibited from granting any other liens on such property. For further discussion of this topic for retail and industrial leases, Part 3, Paragraph 10 should be reviewed instead of this Paragraph.

If Tenant does grant a Landlord's lien and Landlord files a UCC-1 Financing Statement, upon expiration of the Lease Term, Tenant will need to obtain a UCC-3 Termination Statement from the Landlord in order to extinguish Landlord's lien, and a provision should be added to this Paragraph requiring Landlord to execute such a Termination Statement.

3. Lender's Perspective

Lenders like this Paragraph for the additional collateral it can provide to secure Tenant's obligations under the Lease.

4. Broker's Perspective

Each Broker will want to consult with their respective client to determine any sensitivity to or any particular client need relating to this Paragraph that should be covered in the LOI. If none exist, this Paragraph can be handled by the attorneys in Lease negotiations.

C. COMPROMISES AND ALTERNATIVES

This Paragraph should be removed from all office leases by Tenant.

D. COMMENTS

For retail and industrial leases, Part 3, Paragraph 10 should be reviewed instead.

E. TYPICAL PARAGRAPH

31. Lien Rights of Landlord. In consideration of the mutual benefits arising under this Lease, Tenant hereby grants to Landlord a lien on all property Tenant now or hereafter placed in or upon the Premises, and such property shall be and remain subject to such lien of Landlord for payment of all rent and other sums agreed to be paid by Tenant herein. Said lien shall be in addition to and cumulative upon Landlord's liens provided by law.

PARAGRAPH 32

Security Deposit

RISK RATING: 4

A. DESCRIPTION AND SCOPE

This Paragraph sets forth Tenant's obligation to maintain a Security Deposit and Landlord's right to apply the Security Deposit in the event of a default under or breach of the Lease by Tenant. It also establishes the Landlord's duties with respect to the Security Deposit.

B. ANALYSIS

1. Landlord's Perspective

It is advisable for Landlords to obtain a security deposit because they often take a very substantial upfront risk when entering into a Lease as typically brokerage commissions are due upon Lease execution and Landlords are often performing initial alterations and/or providing Tenant with an allowance for initial alterations to prepare the Premises for Tenant's initial occupancy. Also, Tenants often have free-rent periods at commencement of the Lease so it may, under many leases, take Landlord several years to recoup its upfront investment in a Lease and start seeing a profit its initial investment. Beyond that, Landlord wants a source of funds to repair damage to the property or to offset nonpayment of rent by Tenant. Landlord, however, wants the option of enforcing other remedies it has against a defaulting Tenant and saving the Security Deposit for future application. Landlord also wants a Security Deposit to assure Tenant's performance of its obligations at the end of the Lease Term, including any restoration obligations of Tenant.

Landlords may wish to hold any substantial security deposit in the form of a letter of credit instead of in the form of cash. Under current bankruptcy law, a cash security deposit held by a Landlord is considered property of the debtor's estate. As such,

Landlords must obtain a court order prior to using cash security deposit if the Tenant has declared bankruptcy.

On the other hand, some courts view letters of credit as enforceable third-party agreements between Landlords (or beneficiaries) and the issuing banks and not as property of the Tenant's bankruptcy estate. In such cases, Tenant's collateral used to obtain the letter of credit may be subject to the jurisdiction of bankruptcy courts, but the issuing bank assumes that risk, not the Landlord.

2. Tenant's Perspective

Tenant wants to ensure that the Security Deposit held by Landlord is not subject to claims by the Landlord's creditors, and that it will be returned to Tenant at expiration of the Lease Term. Tenant may also want the option to substitute a letter of credit for cash as the Security Deposit. If Tenant has any concern about the financial health of the Landlord, it may wish to provide the security deposit in the form of a letter of credit to minimize the risk of Landlord not returning the security deposit.

3. Lender's Perspective

Lender's perspective is aligned with Landlord's perspective.

4. Broker's Perspective

For both Landlord Broker and Tenant Broker it is important, when possible, that Tenant's financial statements are delivered to Landlord for review prior to finalization of the LOI so that the amount and form of any security for Tenant's performance of its obligations under the Lease are agreed to prior to the Lease being drafted. Considerations when negotiating and establishing the amount and form of any security include the creditworthiness of the Tenant, the amount of free rent granted to Tenant, the amount of any renovation allowance provided to Tenant and Landlord's expenses associated with preparing Premises for Tenant's initial occupancy, any Tenant options under the Lease (most notably to either expand, contract or terminate early) and the customs in the particular market area of the Premises. If a security deposit is requested by Landlord, Tenant Broker should endeavor to have such amount reduced or "burned down" after a specified period of time.

Landlord Broker and Tenant Broker should review this Paragraph closely to ensure that it conforms with any agreement on this issue in the LOI.

C. COMPROMISES AND ALTERNATIVES

Security Deposits are held in the form of cash or letters of credit. Because of this, two alternative Paragraph 32s are provided below to reflect both options.

Tenant will want Landlord to segregate any cash Security Deposit from Landlord's general funds so as to protect the funds from any bankruptcy proceeding against Landlord. Tenant may also want the funds to be placed in an interest-bearing account. However, it should be noted that these Tenant requests are rarely accommodated.

Tenant may be able to negotiate that the Security Deposit shall be phased out or "burned down" over time if Landlord has recouped the cost of improvements, leasing commissions, or incentives, or if Tenant has established a solid history of default-free performance. Typically, a "burning down" of the Security Deposit will occur on an anniversary of the Commencement Date or Rent Commencement Date. If Tenant is posting a letter of credit, it should endeavor to have any "burn down" language included in the initial letter of credit so the burn-down happens automatically if Tenant has not defaulted prior to the burn down date(s) but Landlords often resist this.

Finally, Tenant's obligations under the Lease can also be "secured" through a guaranty in addition to or in lieu of a Security Deposit. Guarantors range from the principals of the Tenant to the corporate parent of the Tenant. Personal guarantees should be avoided by Tenant guarantors if possible and/or limited in time or amount or even by a "good guy clause." Typically, a "good guy guaranty" is a limited guaranty wherein the Guarantor guarantees a defaulting Tenant's obligations under the Lease until the Tenant vacates and surrenders the Premises. This motivates a defaulting Tenant to vacate and surrender the Premises because it extinguishes the "good guy guaranty." This is helpful to Landlord because Landlord's worst case scenario is a "squatting defaulting Tenant" which is a Tenant who is failing to pay rent but refusing to vacate the Premises. This precludes Landlords from mitigating its damages.

D. COMMENTS

Information in this Paragraph pertaining to the rights and obligations concerning the Security Deposit should be as specific as possible to avoid questions when a default occurs and Landlord seeks to apply the Security Deposit.

E. TYPICAL PARAGRAPH

32. <u>Security Deposit (Cash Alternative)</u>

Tenant has deposited with Landlord on the signing of this Lease by Tenant the sum of [AMOUNT] (the "<u>Security Deposit</u>"), as security for the faithful performance and observance by Tenant of the terms, provisions and conditions of this Lease. Tenant agrees that in the event of the occurrence of a Default, Landlord may draw the amount of the Security Deposit to the extent required for the payment of any Base Rent, Additional Rent, or any other sum as to which Tenant is in default, or for any sum that Landlord may expend or may be required to expend by reason of the such default (including any damages or deficiency accrued before or after summary proceedings or other re-entry by Landlord). If Landlord applies or retains any portion or all of the proceeds of the Security Deposit, Tenant shall forthwith restore the amount so applied or retained by delivering additional cash so that, at all times, the amount of the Security Deposit shall be the then required full amount. Provided there is no uncured Default, any balance of the proceeds of the Security Deposit held by Landlord and not used, applied or retained by Landlord as above provided,

and any remaining Security Deposit, shall be returned to Tenant within thirty (30) days after the Expiration Date and after delivery of possession of the entire Premises to Landlord in accordance with the terms of this Lease. Any cash Security Deposit shall be held by Landlord without liability for interest.

32. Security Deposit (Letter of Credit Alternative)

(a) Tenant has deposited with Landlord on the signing of this Lease by Tenant the sum of [AMOUNT] Dollars ($[AMOUNT]) (the "Security Deposit") by Letter of Credit (as defined and further described in Paragraph 32(b)), as security for the faithful performance and observance by Tenant of the terms, provisions and conditions of this Lease. Tenant agrees that in the event (i) of the occurrence of a Default or (ii) Tenant has defaulted in the performance of any of its obligations under this Lease, including the payment of any item of Rent, and the transmittal of a notice of default by Landlord is barred by applicable law, Landlord may draw the entire amount of the Letter of Credit and use, apply or retain the whole or any part of such proceeds, to the extent required for the payment of any Base Rent, Additional Rent, or any other sum as to which Tenant is in default, or for any sum that Landlord may expend or may be required to expend by reason of the such default (including any damages or deficiency accrued before or after summary proceedings or other re-entry by Landlord). If Landlord applies or retains any portion or all of the proceeds of the Letter of Credit, Tenant shall forthwith restore the amount so applied or retained by delivering an additional or new Letter of Credit so that, at all times, the amount of the Security Deposit shall be the then required full amount. Provided there is no uncured Default, any balance of the proceeds of the Letter of Credit held by Landlord and not used, applied or retained by Landlord as above provided, and any remaining Letter of Credit, shall be returned to Tenant after the Expiration Date and after delivery of possession of the entire Premises to Landlord in accordance with the terms of this Lease.

(b) Tenant shall deliver to Landlord a clean, irrevocable and unconditional letter of credit (such letter of credit, and any replacement thereof as provided herein, is called a "Letter of Credit") issued by and drawn upon any commercial bank approved by Landlord with offices for banking purposes in the State of [X] ("Issuing Bank"), which Letter of Credit shall have a term of not less than one year, be in form and content satisfactory to Landlord, be for the account of Landlord and be in the amount $[X]. The form of letter of credit annexed to this Lease as Exhibit [X] is satisfactory. The Letter of Credit shall provide that:

(1) The Issuing Bank shall pay to Landlord or its duly authorized representative an amount up to the face amount of the Letter of Credit upon presentation of the Letter of Credit and a sight draft in the amount to be drawn;

(2) The Letter of Credit shall be deemed to be automatically renewed, without amendment, for consecutive periods of one year each during the Term, unless the Issuing Bank sends written notice (the "Non-Renewal Notice") to Landlord by certified or registered mail, return receipt requested, at least thirty (30) days prior to the expiration date of the Letter of Credit, to the effect that it elects not to have such Letter of Credit renewed;

(3) The Letter of Credit delivered in respect of the last year of the Term shall have an expiration date of not earlier than sixty (60) days after the Expiration Date; and

(4) The Letter of Credit shall be transferable by Landlord as provided in Subparagraph 32(d).

(c) Landlord, after receipt of the Non-Renewal Notice, shall have the right to draw the entire amount of the Letter of Credit and to hold the proceeds as a cash Security Deposit. Landlord shall release such proceeds to Tenant upon delivery to Landlord of a replacement Letter of Credit complying with the terms hereof.

(d) In the event of the sale or lease of the Building or the Property, Landlord shall have the right, at no cost to Landlord, to transfer the Security Deposit, without charge for such transfer, to the purchaser or lessee, and Landlord shall thereupon be released by Tenant from all liability for the return of such Security Deposit. In such event, Tenant agrees to look solely to the new landlord for the return of said Security Deposit. It is agreed that the provisions hereof shall apply to every transfer or assignment made of the Security Deposit to a new Landlord. Tenant shall execute such documents as may be necessary to accomplish such transfer or assignment of the Letter of Credit. If Landlord does not so transfer the Security Deposit, then Tenant will not be obligated to post a new (i.e., duplicate) Security Deposit with the transferee until such time as Tenant receives the originally-posted Security Deposit, it being the intent of the parties that Tenant will not be required to post two of the Security Deposit at the same time.

(e) Tenant covenants that it will not assign or encumber, or attempt to assign or encumber, the Security Deposit held hereunder, and that neither Landlord nor its successors or assigns shall be bound by any such assignment, encumbrance, attempted assignment, or attempted encumbrance. In the event that any bankruptcy, insolvency, reorganization or other debtor-creditor proceedings shall be instituted by or against Tenant, its successors or assigns, or any guarantor of Tenant hereunder, the security shall be deemed to be applied to the payment of the Base Rent and Additional Rent due Landlord for periods prior to the institution of such proceedings and the balance, if any, may be retained by Landlord in partial satisfaction of Landlord's damages.

PARAGRAPH 33

Surrender of the Premises

RISK RATING: 5

A. DESCRIPTION AND SCOPE

This Paragraph sets forth a specific obligation of Tenant to surrender the Premises to Landlord in good condition on the Expiration Date and sets forth any restoration obligations of Tenant. This Paragraph should be read in conjunction with Paragraph 15 (Alterations) which discusses the Alterations that need to be Tenant removed at the expiration of the Term. This Paragraph also serves to clarify the title of any abandoned property of Tenant.

B. ANALYSIS

1. Landlord's Perspective

Landlord wants to protect itself from having to restore or repair the Premises as each new Tenant gains possession. Landlord wants the authority to dispose of any of Tenant's abandoned property in order to minimize the time period that the Premises is not leased.

2. Tenant's Perspective

Removal of Alterations and restoration at the end of a Term can be quite costly so a Tenant will want to pay particular attention to the requirements of this Paragraph and Paragraph 15 (Alterations) which discusses the Alterations that need to be removed by Tenant at the expiration of the Term. Tenant would like its obligations to be set forth precisely to protect Tenant against a claim for damages by Landlord. Tenant also should seek to have the condition of the Premises upon surrender remain "as is" so that Tenant does not have to restore or remove any alterations or additions made by Tenant during the Term.

3. Lender's Perspective

Lender will want to see that Tenant fulfills its obligation to restore the Premises and to surrender the Premises in "broom-clean condition," thereby minimizing the cost of repair or restoration to Landlord as well as minimizing the amount of time the Premises is not leased.

4. Broker's Perspective

Landlord Broker and Tenant Broker would be prudent to discuss Premises surrender condition requirements with their clients and then endeavor to come to agreement within the LOI as to the required Premises surrender condition. Tenant Broker should endeavor to negotiate that Tenant shall not be required to remove any improvements existing on the Commencement Date, Alterations other than Specialty Alterations or any Tenant cabling and wiring. Landlord Broker may wish to specify in the LOI whether Tenant will be required to remove any Tenant cabling, Specialty Alterations, signage and/or outside business equipment (e.g., generators and roof-top equipment installed by Tenant).

C. COMPROMISES AND ALTERNATIVES

Tenant may want to limit its restoration obligation to nonstructural or nonstandard alterations or may want to exclude those alterations and additions approved by Landlord.

Here is a Tenant friendly surrender Paragraph and any surrender provision in a Lease (including Paragraph 55 below) should be modified to reflect these changes:

> *Tenant's surrender obligations under the Lease shall consist solely of returning the Premises to Landlord vacant and in reasonably good order and repair, reasonable wear and tear, damage by casualty and condemnation, and Landlord's maintenance, repair and replacement obligations, excepted. Tenant shall have no obligation to remove or pay for the removal of Landlord's Work or the initial fit-up of the Premises, or any subsequent alterations which Landlord has approved during the Term. Nothing in the Lease shall preclude Tenant from removing its trade fixtures, personal property or business equipment from the Premises, provided Tenant reasonably repairs any portions of the Premises affected by such removal.*

D. COMMENTS

See Paragraph 13 about removal requirements for Specialty Alterations (versus all Alterations).

Landlord may wish to include that any failure surrender the Premises in the condition required under this Paragraph (versus just the delivery of possession of the Premises) be deemed a "holdover." Tenant should avoid this because Subparagraph 33(b) provides Landlord with an appropriate remedy if Tenant fails to remove its personal property from the Premises.

E. TYPICAL PARAGRAPH

33. Surrender of the Premises.

(a) Tenant, on the Expiration Date (or earlier termination, if this Lease is terminated prior to the Expiration Date), shall peaceably surrender the Premises, including the leasehold improvements, in broom-clean condition, and Tenant shall, at the request of Landlord, restore the Premises and return the Premises to Landlord in as good condition as when Tenant took possession, except for: (i) reasonable wear and tear; (ii) loss by fire or other casualty; and (iii) loss by condemnation. Tenant shall, on Landlord's request, remove Tenant's property on or before the termination date and pay the cost of repairing all damage to the Premises or the Building caused by such removal.

(b) If Tenant abandons or, without the consent of Landlord, surrenders the Premises, or is dispossessed by process of law, or otherwise, any of Tenant's property (except money, securities, and other like valuables) left on the Premises shall be deemed abandoned; and, at Landlord's option, title shall pass to Landlord under this Lease as by a bill of sale, or, if Landlord elects to remove all or any part of such Tenant's property, the cost of such removal, including repairing any damage to the Premises or Building caused by such removal, shall be paid by Tenant within ten (10) days of Landlord's demand therefore; this obligation shall survive the termination of this Lease. On the Expiration Date (or such earlier termination), Tenant shall surrender to Landlord all keys to the Premises.

PARAGRAPH 34

Holding Over

RISK RATING: 2

A. DESCRIPTION AND SCOPE

If Tenant continues in occupancy of the Premises, without the consent of Landlord, after the expiration of the Term, this Paragraph states that such occupancy shall be upon the same terms and conditions, except that monthly amount of Annual Base Rent will be a multiple of the last monthly rental payment of the Term.

B. ANALYSIS

1. Landlord's Perspective

Landlord may hold Tenant to the terms of the Lease during any holdover period, and Landlord may terminate Tenant's continued occupancy upon appropriate notice under state law. Landlord wants Tenant to be considered a Tenant at will or a Tenant at sufferance to facilitate eviction of Tenant if so needed. As a disincentive for Tenant to hold over, Tenant must pay an increase in the monthly amount of Annual Base Rent and Additional Rent for the holdover period. Landlord desires this, since Landlord may have already relet the Premises to a third party and may be liable to such third party if the Premises are not available.

2. Tenant's Perspective

Holding over is typically not a choice Tenant elects lightly but Tenant holding over may often be required due to reasons outside of Tenant's control, including that any new space Tenant is moving into is not yet ready for Tenant's occupancy. Thus, Tenant should negotiate this Paragraph with care.

3. Lender's Perspective

This Paragraph protects Lender, since it ensures increased cash flow during the holdover period and requires Tenant to comply with the terms and provisions of the Lease upon which Lender relied in providing financing.

4. Broker's Perspective

Brokers often include negotiated hold over penalties within the LOI. Brokers should note that there are many circumstances, outside the control of Tenant, that might require Tenant to remain in the Premises after the Term expires, and so any increase in Annual Base Rent for the holdover period should be reasonable for the first thirty (30) or preferably sixty (60) days (e.g., 125% to 150% increase) with Tenant not being subject to additional Landlord damages. It is typical that a higher amount (150% or as much as 200%) would follow any initial holdover period and then it is difficult for Tenant to avoid being subject to Landlord damages as well.

C. COMPROMISES AND ALTERNATIVES

Landlord may wish to slip into the paragraph subtly that if Tenant surrenders possession of the Premises but not in the condition required (meaning with personal property and any required alterations to be removed) that such event shall be deemed a holdover. Of course, Tenant should be on guard and resist by arguing that Landlord's typically have self-help rights for any failure of Tenant to meet its removal and restoration obligations and so Landlord should look at Tenant's failure as a "default" allowing for typical default remedies and not punitive holdover rent. Tenant must be careful though because if it enters the space after the expiration date to remove and restore, then Landlord can argue that behavior is a regaining of possession and holdover penalties are appropriate.

Holdover rent is negotiable and sometimes starts at 125% for a short period upon Tenant giving Landlord written notice, but more often 150%, and sometimes Landlord's negotiate an escalation to 200% after 30 or 60 days of Tenant holding over. From a Tenant's perspective this harsh percentage increase in rent for the holdover period should only be on Base Rent and Tenant should continue to pay any Operating Expenses and Real Estate Taxes on only a 100% basis.

In addition to escalated holdover rent, Landlord may wish to include a Tenant indemnification obligation for any damages incurred by Landlord due to the Tenant's holdover. Such an indemnification provision subjects Tenant to an unquantifiable risk (including consequential damages) and should be avoided to the extent possible. If Tenant is unable to remove any such indemnification provision, Tenant should push for a period of time (at least 30 days) before the indemnification provision is triggered.

D. COMMENTS

By permitting Tenant to hold over, Landlord impliedly assents to Tenant's continued tenancy (at will) thereby permitting Tenant to avoid liability to Landlord or any other new third-party tenant claiming the right to occupy the Premises. Landlord must account for Tenant's holdover rights before entering into a Lease of the space with a new Tenant. Tenant's status during the holdover will vary from State to State. In some jurisdictions, Tenant may be considered a Tenant at will, in others a Tenant at sufferance or a Tenant with a month-to-month occupancy. Local counsel should be consulted on this matter.

E. TYPICAL PARAGRAPH

34. Holding Over. If Tenant remains in possession of the Premises after the expiration or earlier termination of the Term without Landlord's express written consent, (A) its tenancy shall be on a month-to-month basis and shall be subject to all of the terms, conditions, provisions, and obligations of this Lease (excluding any expansion or renewal option or other similar right or option), except that the monthly Base Rent due and payable hereunder shall be equal to [150%–200%] of the monthly amount of Annual Base Rent and Additional Rent payable as of the last month of the Term, pro-rated on a daily basis, and (B) Tenant shall be responsible for all damages suffered by Landlord resulting from or occasioned by Tenant's holding over, including consequential damages. Tenant shall be considered a Tenant at will during any such holdover period. No holding over by Tenant, with or without consent of Landlord, shall operate to extend this Lease except as otherwise expressly provided, and this Paragraph 34 shall not be construed as consent for Tenant to retain possession of the Premises. Acceptance by Landlord of Rent after the expiration of the Term or earlier termination of the Lease shall not result in a renewal or reinstatement of the Lease. Notwithstanding any provision to the contrary contained herein, (a) Landlord expressly reserves the right to require Tenant to surrender possession of the Premises upon the expiration of the Term of this Lease or upon the earlier termination hereof, the right to reenter the Premises, and the right to assert any remedy at law or in equity to evict Tenant and collect damages in connection with any such holding over, and (b) Tenant shall indemnify, defend and hold Landlord harmless from and against any and all claims, demands, actions, losses, damages, obligations, costs and expenses, including, without limitation, attorneys' fees incurred or suffered by Landlord by reason of Tenant's failure to surrender the Premises on the expiration or earlier termination of this Lease in accordance with the provisions of this Lease.

PARAGRAPH 35

Landlord Access to Premises and Reservation of Landlord Rights

RISK RATING: 3

A. DESCRIPTION AND SCOPE

This Paragraph permits Landlord to enter the Premises with prior notice to Tenant at reasonable times to inspect, make repairs, bring in materials for the purpose of making such repairs and, during the last twelve (12) months of the Term, to show the Premises to prospective tenants and other interested parties. Emergency repairs do not require prior notice to Tenant.

The second portion of the Paragraph reserves certain rights to Landlord including the right to duct and conduit space surrounding the Premises and the right to make changes to the Common Areas of the Building.

B. ANALYSIS

1. Landlord's Perspective

Landlord wants authority to enter the Premises at all times to maintain, inspect, or show the Premises as well as immediate access without prior notice in the event of emergency. Landlord should resist having to obtain Tenant's prior consent to enter the Premises, and if Landlord does agree to obtain Tenant's consent, then Tenant's consent should not be unreasonably withheld or delayed.

In addition, Landlord wants to preserve flexibility and reserve the right to access and use space immediately surrounding or running through the Premises (such as duct space and the space above Tenant's ceiling tiles) so that it can accommodate any future needs of adjacent tenants as tenants immediately above the Premises may need to run telecommunication wiring and cabling below their floor and/or reinforce their floors for their needs.

Finally, Landlord wants the right the make changes to the Common Areas of the Building should upgrades be desirable to keep the Building marketable.

2. Tenant's Perspective

With respect to Landlord access right to the Premises, Tenant desires protection against Landlord's unwarranted intrusions and protection against damages and disruption from Landlord's warranted intrusions. Accordingly, Tenant will want (i) Landlord to obtain Tenant's consent prior to Landlord entering the Premises (except for emergencies); and (ii) to restrict Landlord's entry to after normal business hours. If Landlord's entry is required during normal business hours, then Tenant will want Landlord to use its best efforts not to materially interfere with Tenant's use of the Premises or normal business routine. Tenant may also wish to require that any Landlord non-emergency access be performed in a manner consistent with Tenant's reasonable security requirements (including having a Tenant representative be present during any Landlord access). Tenant may also object that the twelve (12)-month period allowed to show the space to new or prospective tenants is too long.

With respect to Landlord access and use rights to space immediately surrounding or running through the Premises, Tenant will want to limit Landlord rights so that they do not materially and negatively impact Tenant.

Finally, with respect to Landlord's right to change the Common Areas of the Building, Tenant will want to make sure any changes made are at least the quality of existing improvements and that no changes will negatively impact Tenant's access to the Premises or Tenant's rights under the Lease.

3. Lender's Perspective

Lender will want to ensure that the parties permitted to inspect the Premises include Lender. Also, in the event Lender forecloses and takes title to the Premises, Lender will want to assure there is access to the Premises in order to make any repairs to the Building and Premises that were neglected by Landlord.

Lender is aligned with Landlord having the remaining reserved rights under the Paragraph as they support Landlord in operating the Building and upgrading the Building to market standards and, thus, protecting the Building's value.

4. Broker's Perspective

Each Broker will want to consult with their respective client to determine any sensitivity to or any particular client need relating to this Paragraph that should be covered in the LOI. If none exist, this Paragraph can be handled by the attorneys in Lease negotiations.

C. COMPROMISES AND ALTERNATIVES

Landlord may agree to use reasonable efforts not to enter the Premises during Tenant's normal business hours, and if Landlord enters the Premises during Tenant's normal business hours, not to unreasonably interfere with Tenant's business routine. If the Premises and the market is such that it could take less than twelve months to market and lease the space, then Landlord may agree that a period of nine, six, or even three months may be a more reasonable period during which Landlord may show the Premises. This time period should "dovetail" with the amount of lead time provided for exercise of any Option to Renew.

Tenant should clarify in the Lease that Landlord's installation of any pipes, ducts, or conduits should not reduce the usable area of the Premises beyond a de minimis amount. In addition, any work to be performed above Tenant's ceiling tiles should be completed outside of normal business hours as such work is nearly guaranteed to interfere with the operation of Tenant's business within the Premises.

D. COMMENTS

If Landlord anticipates any possible need to subdivide the Property and/or convert the Property into a common interest community (such as a condominium), Landlord should include additional reservation of rights paragraph(s) to address these issues. It is not uncommon to see Landlord condominium conversion rights within leases spanning a variety of contexts, including, leases pertaining to large commercial office buildings (such as in New York City), leases pertaining to buildings that are a part of a larger multi-building suburban "complex" or "park" (either an office complex or an industrial park), and leases pertaining to a mix-use buildings or projects (where the street level of the building may be retail and other portions of the building (or buildings in a related "complex" or "park") are dedicated to office, residential, industrial, hotel, or other use).

E. TYPICAL PARAGRAPH

35. **Landlord Access Rights and Reservations of Rights.**

    (a) **Landlord Access Right. Tenant shall permit Landlord and its agents, representatives, and contractors to enter the Premises at all reasonable times with prior notice for any reasonable purpose, including to (a) inspect the same; (b) show the Premises to prospective tenants or interested parties such as prospective lenders and purchasers; (c) enforce the rules and regulations, clean, repair, alter, or improve the Premises or the Building; (d) discharge Tenant's obligations when Tenant has failed to do so within a reasonable time after written notice from**

Landlord; (e) post notices of non-responsibility and similar notices or "For Sale" signs, and (f) place "For Lease" signs upon or adjacent to the Building or the Premises at any time within twelve (12) months of the expiration of the Term. Tenant shall permit Landlord and its agents to enter the Premises at any time and without prior notice in the event of an emergency. When reasonably necessary for repair of the Premises or Building; Landlord may temporarily close entrances, doors, corridors, elevators, or other facilities in the Premises or the Building, all without liability to Landlord. Landlord shall have no liability for disrupting Tenant's business if Landlord or its agents enter the Premises as provided above.

(b) <u>Landlord Reservation of Rights</u>. Landlord shall have the right at any time to change the arrangement or location of entrances or passageways, doors and doorways, and corridors, elevators, stairs, toilets, or other public parts or common areas or other aspects of the Building, provided that any such change does not (a) unreasonably reduce, interfere with or deprive Tenant of access to the Building or the Premises, or (b) reduce the rentable areas of the Premises. All parts (except surfaces facing the interior of the Premises) of all walls, windows and doors bounding the Premises (including exterior Building walls, exterior core corridor walls, exterior doors and entrances), all balconies, terraces and roofs adjacent to the Premises, all space in or adjacent to the Premises used for shafts, stacks, stairways, chutes, pipes, conduits, ducts, fan rooms, heating, air cooling, plumbing and other mechanical facilities, service closets and other Building facilities are not part of the Premises and Landlord shall have the use thereof, as well as reasonable access thereto through the Premises for the purposes of operation, maintenance, alteration and repair. Landlord shall have the right to change the name, number or designation by which the Building is commonly known from time to time.

PARAGRAPH 36

Building Amenities

RISK RATING 3

A. DESCRIPTION AND SCOPE

Increasingly, Landlords are constructing new buildings or retrofitting existing buildings to include more "amenity space" or amenity services to attract and retain companies who employ younger generations expecting more creature comforts within their greater work environments and/or companies who support the recently emerged "sharing economy" philosophy that encourages certain space needs (like conference rooms) be shared with other Building tenants.

Available Building amenities vary widely from none, to common amenities (like gym space, conference rooms, and cafeterias) to more inventive amenities (like roof top terraces, beer gardens, and golf simulation rooms). This Paragraph focuses on the common amenities but the concepts explored herein extend to any amenity provided by Landlord.

B. ANALYSIS

1. Landlord's Perspective

Landlord seeks to balance the need to provide the amenities that attracted Tenant to the Building with the ability to retain flexibility to amend, expand, or terminate any amenity.

2. Tenant's Perspective

Tenant seeks to ensure that all Building amenities (or at least any amenity that was a deciding factor in choosing the Building) continue for the Term of the Lease.

3. Lender's Perspective

Lender has the same perspective as Landlord and likely desires an express limitation that the amenities are not guaranteed or at least not guaranteed beyond the ownership of the original named Landlord under the Lease because Lender may not wish to continue all or any particular amenity if it succeeds to Landlord under the Lease.

4. Broker's Perspective

Landlord Broker should be aware of all Building amenities as they are often what sets the Building apart from other options being considered by Tenant. Landlord Broker should be clear on what amenities, if any, Landlord will obligate itself in the LOI to provide for the duration of the Term. As part of the negotiation of the LOI, Tenant Broker should expect Landlord to outline in the LOI the various amenities of the Building. Tenant Broker should push to include in the LOI the terms and costs of Tenant's use of those amenities. It may not be realistic to expect that all amenities existing on the date of the LOI will be maintained throughout the entire Term, but Tenant Broker should consult with Tenant and make sure the LOI provides that any amenities particularly important to Tenant (e.g., potentially a cafeteria, gym or conference facilities) will be maintained by Landlord throughout the Term. Both Brokers should review this Paragraph to confirm it conforms to what was agreed to in the LOI.

C. COMPROMISES AND ALTERNATIVES

Compromises will be centered around the scope of Amenities expressly included in the Lease and language surrounding Landlord's rights to amend, expand, restrict, or even terminate an amenity. Landlord should lead with strong optionality language for all Amenities but expect sophisticated Tenants to negotiate this point.

One way the parties compromise on this issue is to bifurcate which Amenities Landlord must guarantee for the Term of the Lease and which Amenities Landlord has flexibility on to restrict or terminate. As an example, suburban office parks with no restaurants or food providers in proximity to the Building, can expect that a Tenant will require the operation of a cafeteria at the Building for the Term and this is a fair position as the existence of the cafeteria was likely a deciding factor in Tenant selecting the Building. In that case, Subparagraph 36(c) can be modified by the following:

> *provided, however, in no event shall the foregoing Landlord reserved right be applicable to the cafeteria and, for the sake of clarity, Landlord confirms that Landlord shall operate the cafeteria (consistent with the standards existing on the Effective Date) through the entirety of the Term.*

Another compromise is that Landlord will agree to provide the Amenities but only so long as it owns the Building. In that case Subparagraph 36(c) can be replaced with the following:

> *Landlord agrees to provide the Amenities for the duration of the Term for as long as the initial named Landlord under this Lease ([NAME]) remains the fee owner of the Building. No successor Landlord shall have any responsibilities to maintain the Amenities at the Building.*

Lastly, another compromise is that Landlord agrees to provide the Amenities to the extent that they are being reasonably utilized. In that case Subparagraph 36(c) can be replaced with the following:

> *Landlord agrees to provide the Amenities for the duration of the Term, except to the extent that Landlord, in its sole but reasonable judgment, determines any Amenity is being underutilized in which case Landlord may elect, without liability to Tenant, to terminate the Amenity.*

D. COMMENTS

The Operating Expense Paragraph of the Lease should be appropriately modified to expressly include any operating expenses incurred with respect to the Amenities. That said, Landlord may wish to charge Tenant separately, as Additional Rent, for the use of certain amenities like gym use (on a per employee basis based upon a membership system) or conference room use (on a per day or per hour basis based upon a reservation system).

In addition, certain amenities, like the use of a gym or physical fitness center within the Building, may elevate Landlord's liability under the Lease. In such cases, Landlord may wish to consider obtaining waivers of liability from each Tenant employee who uses the gym to endeavor to shift use risk from Landlord to the Tenant employee.

Tenant may wish to add clarifying language to the Amenities paragraph that the manner in which the Amenities are operated and maintained shall remain consistent during the Term by providing that the Amenities will continue to be operated in the manner existing on the Effective Date. This may be particularly important with respect to the cafeteria as different cafeteria operators operate at different qualities levels and at different hours. A Tenant taking a large percentage of a Building may even be able to negotiate the right to terminate any existing cafeteria operator for poor service and approve any replacement cafeteria operator.

E. TYPICAL PARAGRAPH

36. Amenities.

(a) Landlord, at its sole election, shall provide the following amenities (the "Amenities") for the benefit of all tenants at the Building:

(i) at least two (2) electric vehicle charging stations, on a first-come, first-served basis;

(ii) sundry shop;

(iii) ATM machine;

(iv) conference facilities, on a first-come, first-served reservation basis to be coordinated with the Building manager;

(v) cafeteria; and

(vi) fitness center/health club, subject to prior written membership agreement for each user.

(b) The costs and expenses incurred by Landlord in connection with the Amenities shall be included in Operating Expenses, except for the amenities described in Subparagraphs 36(a)(i), (iv) and (vi), which will be subject to Building-standard use fees, subject to change from time to time during the Term, which shall be payable by Tenant, as Additional Rent, for individual use of such amenities.

(c) Landlord reserves the right to amend, restrict, expand or eliminate Amenities at its sole discretion during the Term with no liability to Tenant.

PARAGRAPH 37

Tenant Signage

RISK RATING: 2

A. DESCRIPTION AND SCOPE

This Paragraph assures Tenant that Landlord will provide appropriate signage to Tenant at the Building.

B. ANALYSIS

1. Landlord's Perspective

By providing adequate Tenant signage (including directory information), Landlord can ensure that a Tenant's visitors and clients locate Tenant with a minimum of inconvenience. Landlord further ensures an orderly flow of traffic through the lobby and reduces visitors' requests for information. Landlord must have the ability to control both interior and exterior signage.

2. Tenant's Perspective

Tenant wants to have Tenant information prominently posted so that clients and visitors can locate Tenant with a minimum of inconvenience. Tenant may request that the directory include the names of Tenant's principal departments, sections, employees, and agents. Tenant may also request that the elevator lobby on each floor contain a directory of tenants on that floor. If Tenant will be one of the largest tenants in the Building, then this Paragraph becomes much more important, and Tenant may wish to negotiate for additional exterior signage (i.e., on the exterior Building façade signage, on an exterior monument, ornamental flags on flag poles, etc.) and lobby signage rights, and, perhaps, naming rights to the Building.

3. Lender's Perspective

Lender wants to ensure that the Landlord offers services consistent with those found in a first-class office building.

4. Broker's Perspective

Brokers should negotiate all Tenant signage rights in the LOI with specificity. Tenant Broker should endeavor to include in the LOI, at a minimum, that Tenant (and any Related Entities) are entitled to standard signage in the Building lobby directory, on the floor of the Premises and at the entry to the Premises. The cost of such signage may be at the expense of Landlord or Tenant depending upon the Building and market conditions. A relatively larger Tenant might also be able to secure exterior signage on the Building or on monuments surrounding the Building. Both Brokers should review this Paragraph to confirm it conforms to what was agreed to in the LOI.

C. COMPROMISES AND ALTERNATIVES

Tenant may agree that based on the number of tenants per floor, a floor directory may not be necessary. If Tenant requests that all employees be listed on the Building directory, Landlord could negotiate that only a certain number of employees or employees above a certain title be listed.

A Tenant taking extensive space in a Building may be able to negotiate exterior Building signage rights. Such rights may include the right for Tenant to be named on a "monument" or even the exterior façade of the Building. Here is a sample provision:

> *In addition to Tenant's other signage rights under this Paragraph 37, Tenant shall have the nonexclusive right, at Tenant's sole cost and expense, to install a single exterior, commercially reasonable identification sign on the exterior façade of the Building (the "Exterior Signage"), the design and location of which is subject to prior written approval by Landlord and any governmental authority having jurisdiction to approve such signage. Such signage shall comply in all respects with Landlord's Building-wide specifications and standards. Landlord shall permit Tenant to install such Exterior Signage, subject to Tenant's compliance with the terms of the Lease, including compliance with all applicable Laws. Tenant's right to the Exterior Signage shall be exclusive to the original named Tenant herein (i.e., [TENANT NAME]) and shall only continue for the period of time that the original named Tenant herein is in occupancy of [an entire floor of the Building]. Tenant shall be responsible at Tenant's cost and expense for the maintenance of the Exterior Signage. Landlord shall provide Tenant with reasonable access to the façade of the Building, including reasonable access and use of the Building's electrical power supply, in order to install, maintain and light the Exterior Signage, at Tenant's cost and expense. Tenant agrees, upon Landlord's request, to remove, at Tenant's cost and expense, the Exterior Signage upon failing to meet the occupancy standard, and if later, at the expiration or sooner termination of the Lease, and to reasonably repair and restore any areas damaged by such sign's installation or removal. Tenant's obligations under this Paragraph shall survive the expiration or earlier termination of the Lease.*

The above sample paragraph can be modified to define "Exterior Signage" in a manner which substitutes exterior Building façade signage with (or additionally includes) exterior monument signage or even ornamental flags on flag poles located outside the Building.

D. COMMENTS

Some Landlords now place electronic information kiosks in the entrance to the building that can display Tenant's location and provide a list of Tenant's employees. If an electronic kiosk is available, then Tenant will want to list all employees.

In the event Landlord grants Tenant any special signage rights (like the Exterior Signage provision above), Landlord will want to limit any such special signage right to the originally named Tenant and, since these more expansive signage rights are only typically given to tenants taking large portions of a building, Landlord may wish to condition these special signage rights to Tenant continuing to lease and be in possession of all of the initial Premises (although this may be negotiated to a certain percentage of the initial premises). Of course, Tenant will want to make sure any special signage rights remain for any corporate assignees or successors or affiliates.

E. TYPICAL PARAGRAPH

37. Tenant Signage. Landlord shall, as an Operating Expense, list Tenant on any Building-standard directory in the lobby of the Building [and on the Building-Standard floor directory on the Building floor on which the Premises is located]. Tenant shall be permitted, at Tenant's option and expense, to install a single Building-standard identifying sign on the entrance doors to the Premises, said sign to be subject to Landlord's prior approval, which approval shall not be unreasonably withheld or delayed.

PARAGRAPH 38

Parking

RISK RATING: 3

A. DESCRIPTION AND SCOPE

This Paragraph establishes a fixed number of parking spaces for Tenant's use in the parking facilities appurtenant to the Building. Note that in some intensely densified urban locations (such as Manhattan, New York), parking rights are not routinely granted to Tenant. In Paragraph 38 below, two alternative parking provisions are provided to reflect typical parking provisions in different geographical areas.

B. ANALYSIS

1. Landlord's Perspective

Landlord generally allocates parking spaces in order to provide Tenant with its proportionate share of the available parking spaces based on the rentable square feet of the Premises (e.g., three (3) parking spots per 1,000 square feet of the Premises). In certain circumstances, Landlord reserve a fixed number of parking spaces to be used by visitors or to be leased by Tenant at an additional cost.

2. Tenant's Perspective

Tenant may assign a certain number of employees to the Premises, in part, based on the availability of parking spaces. In the event that the required number of parking spaces exceeds Tenant's allocation, Tenant may need to make alternative parking arrangements, which may include leasing additional parking spaces at the Building and/or contracting with a third party.

3. Lender's Perspective

Lender, as a potential owner of the Building, will want to confirm that there is parking available on-site for all tenants and that parking fees may be collected at Landlord's discretion in appropriate locations.

4. Broker's Perspective

Brokers should negotiate all Tenant parking rights in the LOI with specificity. Tenant Broker should determine the importance and quantity of parking required by Tenant as part of the up-front needs assessment phase of its assignment to acquire space. Tenant Broker should inquire into such details as the type of vehicles required by Tenant to park as well as requirements for security, indoor versus outdoor parking space needs, reserved versus unreserved parking needs (including for any Tenant visitors) and whether any costs associated with the parking shall be paid by Tenant or passed through to Tenant's employees. Tenant Broker should be sure to include in the LOI whatever minimum parking that Tenant will need for the Term and any extensions thereof. In some circumstances, and in some markets, not having an adequate number of parking spaces for employees and/or visitors can be a limiting factor in fully utilizing the Premises. Lastly, it is also important for Tenant Broker to include in the preliminary financial projections for the Lease the cost of parking as part of total occupancy expenses for Tenant.

Both Brokers should review this Paragraph closely to confirm it conforms to the parking terms agreed to in the LOI.

C. COMPROMISES AND ALTERNATIVES

Alternatives will depend largely upon the available supply of parking spaces and whether Tenant agrees to an additional charge for parking; however, this Paragraph should be included to establish a fixed number of parking spaces for each Tenant and to provide Landlord with the right to institute parking rules.

Paragraph 38 below provides two Alternatives with Alternative 1 being useful for those geographical areas where parking spaces are not a scarce resource and Landlord's grant parking rights to Tenant in parking areas appurtenant to the Property (often outside surface lots) without any charge to Tenant and Landlord "operates" those parking areas.

Alternative 2 is useful for those geographical areas where parking spaces are at a premium (typically urban locations) and Landlord's grant parking rights to Tenant in the Building's garage with a separate Tenant charge and Landlord engages a third-party operator that "operates" the Garage.

D. COMMENTS

Depending on whether the Building is located in a suburb or downtown (where paid parking is the norm), parking requirements vary considerably. Tenant's allocation of reserved parking spaces should be shown on the diagram attached as an Exhibit to the Lease. In buildings with more than one tenant, or with one major tenant, Landlord must ensure that the number of spaces provided in each Tenant's Lease does not cumulatively total more spaces than are available. In addition, Landlord may desire to designate certain parking spaces reserved for visitors.

Tenant should be careful that any parking provision is indeed granting Tenant a right to parking and not a revocable license to parking spaces.

Landlord may desire, and in some geographical locations Landlord may be required by law, to provide electric vehicle charging spaces. These spaces are sometimes granted to Tenant on a reserved basis but more often when the Tenant pays for the installation itself. Otherwise, such spaces are typically granted to all Building tenants on a first come, first served basis.

E. TYPICAL PARAGRAPH

Alternative 1: Rural or Suburban Parking Provision

38. Parking.

(a) Tenant shall have access, during the Term, to [NUMBER] unreserved parking spaces (on a first come, first served basis) at the surface parking areas of the Building and [NUMBER] reserved parking spaces located in the garage of the Building as designated in Exhibit "[X]" attached hereto, on a Rent-inclusive basis (all Tenant's visitor parking included in such total).

(b) Notwithstanding anything to the contrary contained herein, Tenant's parking spaces under this Lease shall be subject to Landlord's reasonable rules and regulations as same may be promulgated and changed from time to time, provided Tenant has notice of same. Furthermore, notwithstanding anything to the contrary contained herein, Landlord shall not be in default of any of its obligations under this Lease if parking spaces are periodically unavailable for Tenant's use and Landlord shall have no obligation to police Tenant's reserved parking spaces.

(c) Landlord shall not be responsible for money, jewelry, automobiles or other personal property lost in or stolen from the Building's parking areas. Except as caused by the negligence or willful misconduct of Landlord and without limiting the terms of the preceding sentence, Landlord shall not be liable for any loss, injury or damage to persons using the Building's parking areas or other property therein, it being agreed that, to the fullest extent permitted by law, the use of the Building's parking areas shall be at the sole risk of Tenant and its employees and invitees.

Alternative 2: Urban Parking Provision

38. Parking.

(a) During the Term, Tenant agrees to lease [NUMBER] of unreserved parking spaces at the surface parking areas of the Building [and [NUMBER] reserved parking spaces located in the garage of the Building ("Garage") as designated in Exhibit "[X]" attached hereto] (collectively,

the "Spaces") for the use of Tenant and its employees and visitors [at no additional cost] or [at cost of [$[X] per space per month]. Except for the reserved spaces, the Spaces shall be leased on an unreserved basis. No deduction or allowances shall be made for days when Tenant or any of its employees does not utilize the parking facilities or for Tenant utilizing less than all of the Spaces.

(b) **The Garage is managed by a third-party operator ("Garage Operator"). Tenant, upon request of Landlord, shall enter into a commercially reasonable parking agreement with the Garage Operator, and Landlord shall have no liability for claims arising through acts or omissions of the Garage Operator unless caused by Landlord's negligence or willful misconduct. It is understood and agreed that the identity of the Garage Operator may change from time to time during the Term. In connection therewith, any parking lease or agreement entered into between Tenant and a Garage Operator shall be freely assignable by such Garage Operator or any successors thereto.**

(c) **During the Term, if Tenant desires to lease additional parking spaces, it may do so subject to availability and the terms, conditions and rates then imposed by the Garage Operator.**

(d) **Except for particular spaces and areas designated by Landlord for reserved parking, all parking in the Garage and surface parking areas serving the Building shall be on an unreserved, first-come, first-served basis.**

(e) **Landlord shall not be responsible for money, jewelry, automobiles or other personal property lost in or stolen from the Garage or the surface parking areas regardless of whether such loss or theft occurs when the Garage or other areas therein are locked or otherwise secured. Except as caused by the negligence or willful misconduct of Landlord and without limiting the terms of the preceding sentence, Landlord shall not be liable for any loss, injury or damage to persons using the Garage or the surface parking areas or automobiles or other property therein, it being agreed that, to the fullest extent permitted by law, the use of the Spaces shall be at the sole risk of Tenant and its employees.**

(f) **Landlord shall have the right from time to time to reasonably designate the location of the Spaces and to promulgate reasonable rules and regulations regarding the Garage, the surface parking areas, if any, the Spaces and the use thereof, including, but not limited to, rules and regulations controlling the flow of traffic to and from various parking areas, the angle and direction of parking and the like. Tenant shall comply with and cause its employees to comply with all such rules and regulations as well as all reasonable additions and amendments thereto.**

(g) **Tenant shall not store or permit its employees to store any automobiles in the Garage or on the surface parking areas without the prior written consent of Landlord. Except for emergency repairs, Tenant and its employees shall not perform any work on any automobiles while** located in the Garage or on the Property. If it is necessary for Tenant or its employees to leave an automobile in the Garage or on the surface parking areas overnight, Tenant shall provide Landlord with prior notice thereof designating the license plate number and model of such automobile.

(h) Landlord shall have the right to temporarily close the Garage or certain areas therein in order to perform necessary repairs, maintenance and improvements to the Garage or the surface parking areas, if any.

(i) Tenant shall not assign or sublease any of the Spaces without the consent of Landlord; provided that Tenant may transfer its right to use some or all of the Spaces in connection with an assignment of this Lease or sublease of any portion of the Premises entered into pursuant to the terms of this Lease.

(j) Landlord may elect to provide cards or keys to control access to the Garage or surface parking areas, if any. In such event, Landlord shall provide Tenant with one card or key for each Space that Tenant is leasing hereunder, provided that Landlord shall have the right to require Tenant or its employees to place a deposit on such access cards or keys and to pay a fee for any lost or damaged cards or keys.

PARAGRAPH 39

Notices

RISK RATING: 3

A. DESCRIPTION AND SCOPE

This Paragraph sets out the addresses and method of delivery for any notices or copies of notices required under the Lease.

B. ANALYSIS

1. Landlord's Perspective

This Paragraph protects against notices being sent to the incorrect address or without record of timely posting. Landlord wants to ensure that both Landlord and its designated representative receive copies of all notices. Landlord should refuse a request by Tenant that the notice is effective only upon receipt unless a clause is added stating that a notice shall be deemed to have been received upon attempted delivery so as to negate the situation where Tenant refuses to accept delivery.

2. Tenant's Perspective

Tenant may desire that both it and its legal counsel receive copies of all notices or just default notices.

3. Lender's Perspective

A Lender is concerned that adequate provision for notice be made so that it can give and receive appropriate notices in cases where the Lender has succeeded to the interests of Landlord under the Lease.

4. Broker's Perspective

Brokers would not typically detail notice provisions as part of the LOI. That said, Brokers maintaining long relationships with their clients should assist in confirming that the notice addresses in this Paragraph remain current and accurate at all times during the Term, as such addresses will be needed when exercising Landlord and Tenant rights and options under the Lease.

C. COMPROMISES AND ALTERNATIVES

An alternative would be to use a post office box number; the risk is that overnight delivery services usually will not deliver to post office boxes (U.S. Postal Service overnight delivery will). Other alternatives include delivery via e-mail. The concern with both of these alternatives is verification of receipt. One alternative is to require that a confirming original hard copy of the e-mail be delivered overnight the next day, but that the notice is deemed received upon sending the e-mail.

D. COMMENTS

The COVID-19 pandemic found many Landlord and Tenant offices (and the offices of their legal counsel) nearly empty, and written notices not being timely reviewed. From this experience, e-mail copies of all written notices to Landlord, Tenant, and their respective counsel is advised.

E. TYPICAL PARAGRAPH

39. <u>Notices</u>. Except as otherwise expressly provided in this Lease, any bills, statements, consents, notices, demands, requests, or other communications required or desired to be given under this Lease shall be in writing and shall be deemed sufficiently given or rendered if delivered by hand (against a signed receipt) or if sent by a nationally recognized overnight mail carrier or registered or certified mail (return receipt requested) addressed as follows:

if to Tenant (a) at Tenant's address set forth in this Lease, if mailed prior to Tenant's taking possession of the Premises, or (b) at the Building, if mailed subsequent to Tenant's taking possession of the Premises, or (c) at any place where Tenant or any agent or employee of Tenant may be found if mailed subsequent to Tenant's vacating, deserting, abandoning or surrendering the Premises, in each case with a copy to [TENANT'S COUNSEL ADDRESS with a simultaneous copy via e-mail to [E-MAIL ADDRESS FOR TENANT'S COUNSEL], or

if to Landlord (a) at [LANDLORD ADDRESS], with a copy to [LANDLORD'S COUNSEL with a simultaneous copy via e-mail to [E-MAIL ADDRESS FOR LANDLORD'S COUNSEL], and (c) each Mortgagee and Lessor which shall have requested same, by notice given in accordance with the provisions of this Paragraph 39 at the address designated by such Mortgagee or Lessor, or

to such other address or addresses as Landlord, Tenant or any Mortgagee or Lessor may respectively designate as its new address or addresses for such purpose by notice given to the other in accordance with the provisions of this Paragraph 39. Any such bill, statement, consent, notice, demand, request, or other communication shall be deemed to have been rendered or given on the date when it has been hand delivered, or if given by overnight express mail or by national overnight delivery service, one (1) day after deposit in the mail or with such service or three (3) Business Days from when it has been mailed by certified or registered mail. Notices sent by counsel representing Landlord or Tenant, respectively, shall be deemed notices sent by Landlord or Tenant, as applicable.

PARAGRAPH 40

Rules and Regulations

RISK RATING: 2

A. DESCRIPTION AND SCOPE

This Paragraphs sets forth the obligation of Tenant to comply with the Rules and Regulations for the Building. Violation of the rules and regulations is a default under the Lease. An inclusion of Rules and Regulations further clarifies the relationship between Landlord and Tenant and prevents disputes as prohibited behavior is expressly set forth.

B. ANALYSIS

1. Landlord's Perspective

Landlord wants to prevent any activities that may damage the Premises or disturb other tenants. Landlord wants to retain as much control over the operation of the Property as possible.

Landlord should retain the right to amend the Rules and Regulations during the Term. Also, to avoid any possible Landlord exposure to Tenant for another tenant failing to abide the Rules and Regulations, Landlord should reserve the express right not to enforce the Rules and Regulations.

2. Tenant's Perspective

Tenant should be sure that no Rules or Regulations interfere with Tenant's expected uses since a breach of the rules is a default.

3. Lender's Perspective

By clarifying the Rules and Regulations of the Premises, Lender is assured that disruptions and disputes at the Property are minimized.

4. Broker's Perspective

Each Broker will want to consult with their respective client to determine any sensitivity to or any particular client need relating to this Paragraph that should be covered in the LOI (e.g., does the Tenant need a "pet friendly" Building?). If none exist, this Paragraph can be handled by the attorneys in Lease negotiations.

C. COMPROMISES AND ALTERNATIVES

Tenant may want to alter this sample Paragraph to provide that the Rules and Regulations will not be amended without Tenant's consent or that Tenant will not be subject to any such amendments unless Tenant's consent thereto has been obtained. Landlord may resist this change since any change to the Rules and Regulations would have to be approved by all tenants having such approval rights. A customary compromise is the following:

> *No such rules and regulations shall materially impair Tenant's leasehold interest in the Premises or increase Tenant's Rent obligations.*

Tenant may also want assurance that Rules will be the same for all tenants of the Building and will be enforced in a nondiscriminatory manner. Since Landlords may include provisions in the Rules and Regulations that are in direct conflict with provisions of the Lease, in such case, Tenant should request the addition of the following sentence:

> *In the event of any conflict between the other provisions of the Lease and the Rules and Regulations, the other provisions of the Lease shall prevail.*

D. COMMENTS

Most often the Rules and Regulations are attached as an Exhibit to the Lease. See Part 4 for sample Rules and Regulations for a multi-tenant office Building.

E. TYPICAL PARAGRAPH

40. <u>Rules and Regulations</u>. Tenant shall comply with the rules and regulations attached hereto as Exhibit [X] (the "<u>Rules and Regulations</u>"). Nothing in this Lease shall impose upon Landlord any duty to enforce the Rules and Regulations against any other tenant in the Building. Upon notice to Tenant, Landlord may amend, modify, delete, or add new and additional Rules and Regulations for the use and care of the Property. Landlord shall not enforce any Rule or Regulation against Tenant which Landlord is not then enforcing against other office tenants in the Building using space similar in size and configuration to the Premises. If a conflict or inconsistency exists between the Rules and Regulations and the provisions of the remaining portion of this Lease, then the provisions of the remaining portion of this Lease shall control.

PARAGRAPH 41

Sustainable Building Operations

RISK RATING: 2

A. DESCRIPTION AND SCOPE

This Paragraph sets forth the Building's sustainability protocols and Tenant's responsibilities with respect thereto. This Paragraph is typically only included in a Lease if the Building has achieved or is seeking to achieve certification under the U.S. EPA's Energy Star® rating and/or Design to Earn Energy Star, the Green Building Initiative's Green Globes™ for Continual Improvement of Existing Buildings (Green Globes™-CIEB), the U.S. Green Building Council's Leadership in Energy and Environmental Design (LEED) rating system, and/or the International WELL Institute.

B. ANALYSIS

1. Landlord's Perspective

If Landlord has achieved or is seeking the certifications described above, this Paragraph is necessary so that Tenant does not threaten the Building's certifications (or ability to achieve certifications).

2. Tenant's Perspective

Being located in Buildings with nationally recognized sustainability certifications is of importance to some Tenants if their internal corporate objectives require or encourage it. Tenant will want to confirm that their operations will not run afoul of any sustainability protocols under the Lease and that compliance with such protocols will not unreasonably impact Tenant's operations or cause unexpected expenses.

3. Lender's Perspective

Achieving and maintaining nationally recognized sustainability certifications can add value to the Property and, thus, Lender has an interest in the Building maintaining any certifications achieved.

4. Broker's Perspective

Each Broker will want to consult with their respective client to determine any sensitivity to or any particular client need relating to this Paragraph that should be covered in the LOI. Landlord Broker should be well versed in any certifications of the Building. Tenant Broker should consult with Tenant to understand Tenant's sustainability requirements and/or objectives. As described above, there are many designations that run the spectrum of what may be considered environmentally conscious. If Tenant has specific sustainability requirements, Tenant Broker should consider consulting with Tenant's architect, engineer and/or project manager early in the Premises identification process so that Tenant Broker has all information necessary to identify properties meeting Tenant's sustainability requirements. In addition, Tenant Broker should identify at the onset of the assignment (and with support from Tenant's architect, engineer, and/or project manager), any incremental costs associated with Tenant achieving its sustainability requirements.

C. COMPROMISES AND ALTERNATIVES

Tenant may wish to have any sustainability or recycling rules and regulations attached to the Lease so that they can be reviewed and approved prior to Lease execution.

D. COMMENTS

None.

E. TYPICAL PARAGRAPH

41. Sustainable Building Operations.

(a) Sustainability Requirements. Tenant will comply with any reasonable Sustainability Requirements (as hereinafter defined) that apply to the Premises, Tenant and/or Tenant's business operations.

(b) Compliance with Sustainability Objectives. Tenant will operate its business within the Premises and maintain the Premises in a manner consistent with the Sustainability Objectives (as hereinafter defined). The Building is, or may become in the future, certified under the U.S. EPA's Energy Star® rating and/or Design to Earn Energy Star, the Green Building Initiative's Green Globes™ for Continual Improvement of Existing

Buildings (Green Globes™-CIEB), the U.S. Green Building Council's Leadership in Energy and Environmental Design (LEED) rating system. All construction and maintenance methods and procedures, material purchases, and disposal of waste must be in compliance with the Sustainability Objectives.

(c) Energy Conservation Measures. Tenant shall use proven energy and carbon reduction measures, including energy efficient bulbs in task lighting; use of lighting controls; daylighting measures to avoid over-lighting interior spaces; closing shades to avoid overheating the space, unless an automated shade system is installed in the Building; turning off lights and equipment at the end of the work day; and purchasing Energy Star® qualified equipment, including but not limited to, lighting, office equipment, commercial and residential quality kitchen equipment, vending and ice machines; purchasing products certified by the U.S. EPA Water Sense® program.

(d) Recycling and Waste Management. Tenant covenants and agrees, at its sole cost and expense: (i) to comply with all laws or orders by any governmental authorities having jurisdiction over the Property regarding the collection, sorting, separation, and recycling of garbage, trash, rubbish and other refuse; (ii) to comply with the Building's recycling policy, and any applicable Laws relating to recycling of materials; (iii) that Landlord reserves the right to refuse to collect or accept from Tenant any waste that is not separated and sorted as required by Law, and to require Tenant to arrange for such collection at Tenant's sole cost and expense, utilizing a contractor satisfactory to Landlord; and (iv) that Tenant shall pay all costs, expenses, fines, penalties or damages that may be imposed on Landlord or Tenant by reason of Tenant's failure to comply with the provisions of this Paragraph.

(e) Utility Consumption Data. In the event electricity, propane, natural gas, or water is separately metered to the Premises and Tenant pays utility charges directly to the utility provider, Tenant shall submit to Landlord electricity, water, and other utility consumption data in a format deemed reasonably acceptable by Landlord on a quarterly basis on or before the first day of January, April, July, and October.

(f) Definitions:

"Sustainability Objectives" mean a gold level status for the Building in accordance with the U.S. Green Building Council's Leadership in Energy and Environmental Design (LEED) rating system and any other designations sought or obtained by Landlord, including, but not limited to, the U.S. EPA's Energy Star® rating and/or Design to Earn Energy Star, the Green Building Initiative's Green Globes™ for Continual Improvement of Existing Buildings (Green Globes™-CIEB), and any additional designations under the U.S. Green Building Council's Leadership in Energy and Environmental Design (LEED) rating system.

"Sustainability Requirements" mean any laws, requirements, standards or goals established by any Authority that imposes upon the Building or Landlord any requirement to make any alterations or improvements to the Building, including, any action or activity that may be required to avoid or minimize the imposition of any Carbon Offset Costs or Carbon Tax or any other tax, charge, fee, fine, or penalty that may be imposed upon the Building or Landlord.

PARAGRAPH 42

Relocation of Premises

RISK RATING: 4

A. DESCRIPTION AND SCOPE

This Paragraph gives Landlord the right to move Tenant to other space in the Building. Notwithstanding any relocation of Tenant, the Lease remains in full force and effect except for the recalculation of Annual Base Rent and Additional Rent for the substituted space. Landlord will be obligated to pay for the build-out of the new Premises together with Tenant's costs and expenses for such relocation.

Larger tenants are nearly always able to successfully remove this Landlord right from the Lease.

B. ANALYSIS

1. Landlord's Perspective

Landlord wants to have the ability to relocate Tenant to (i) make the space available for a more desirable tenant, or (ii) to consolidate space in the Building for a potential Tenant that is a large user of space. This is particularly important for new Buildings or a Building that Landlord intends to expand. If Property is an office park where Landlord owns multiple Buildings, Landlord may also want to extend this relocation right to any Building owned by Landlord in the Office Park.

2. Tenant's Perspective

Tenant should be assured that it receives (i) comparable space (e.g., same views or floor level, comparable layout, improvements, fixtures and window lines or amount of windows), (ii) no increase rent or other liabilities (even if the substitute space is larger), and (iii) no decrease in rights under the Lease. The expense of tenant improvement costs, IT installation, moving, and decorating the new space should fall on the Landlord as should the cost of new stationery and business cards, if needed. Many Tenants will not agree to this provision since such a move will generally cause significant disruption to Tenant's business.

3. Lender's Perspective

Landlord's quest for financing can be enhanced if Landlord has the ability to relocate Tenant, making the Premises available to a more desirable or "key tenant" that offers an economic anchor to the Building.

4. Broker's Perspective

Each Broker will want to consult with their respective client to determine any sensitivity to or any particular client need relating to this Paragraph that should be covered in the LOI. Both Brokers should address the specter of a Landlord relocation of Tenant when negotiating the LOI. Each Broker should be aware that, as the size of prospective tenancy gets larger, the relatively higher proportion of Tenant's own capital is likely to be expended for initial renovations of the Premises resulting in the greater likelihood of Tenant refusing the inclusion of this Paragraph in the Lease. For smaller tenancies occupying more generic space in lager multi-tenant Buildings, this Paragraph might be appropriate and unavoidable. If this Paragraph is included in the LOI, Tenant Broker should endeavor to include as many rights as possible as further described below. Both Brokers should confirm this Paragraph in the Lease conforms to any applicable terms and conditions agreed to in the LOI.

C. COMPROMISES AND ALTERNATIVES

Tenant may want the ability to relinquish part of its space, or take additional space in connection with a relocation, depending on its needs. Tenant's right to more space, however, may be contingent on the additional space being available. A mechanism to determine the rent for the additional space must be included in such a provision.

Tenant should in no event have to pay more rent even if the substitute premises is larger. Tenant may wish to negotiate a rent abatement period after the move to help off-set the cost of disruption to Tenant's business.

Tenant should make sure relocation cannot happen prior to the first anniversary of the Commencement to avoid any "bait and switch" activity by Landlord. Relocation should also be limited to only one time during the term. The substitute premises needs to be completed by Landlord prior to the relocation. Tenant may wish to have its own architect and furniture designer plan out the substitute premises at Landlord's cost especially if Tenant carefully designed the original premises. Tenant will need sufficient notice (likely significantly more than the 30 days proposed) as IT installation could take longer. Tenant may want to control when the move happens so not to disrupt its business operations (i.e., over the weekend, etc.).

Here is an example of a fully negotiated Relocation clause:

Landlord reserves the one-time right to be exercised upon no less than one hundred twenty (120) days' prior notice delivered not prior to the first anniversary of the Commencement Date, to relocate Tenant from time to time to comparable space in another part of the Building ("Substitute Premises"). The Substitute Premises shall have improvements and number of exterior windows and views comparable to those in the Premises and shall be comparable to the Premises in size, layout and access and shall be on the [NUMBER] floor or above in the Building. From and after the date of any such relocation, the term "Premises" as used herein shall mean the Substitute Premises, and Landlord and Tenant shall execute an appropriate amendment to this Lease describing the Substitute Premises. Promptly following receipt of notice from Landlord that Landlord is exercising its relocation option hereunder, Tenant shall, at Landlord's sole expense, have plans and specification prepared by an architect chosen by Tenant for the build-out of the Substitute Premises, which build-out shall be for improvements and alterations comparable to those existing in the original Premises as of the date of such relocation. Landlord, at its sole cost and expense, shall complete the build-out of the Substitute Premises prior to Tenant relocating into the Substitute Premises. Landlord shall bear Tenant's actual out-of-pocket expenses in moving Tenant's furnishings and equipment from the occupied Premises to the Substitute Premises (including the cost of (i) installation in the Substitute Premises of Tenant's then-existing telephone system and telecommunications cabling, (ii) the hard and soft costs of such improvements and alterations to be made to the Substitute Premises as required hereunder, and (iii) up to $500.00 of the cost of replacing a reasonable amount of Tenant's stationery made obsolete by the relocation of the Premises). If the Substitute Premises are smaller than the original Premises (unless the smaller area is requested by Tenant), Annual Base Rent and Tenant's Pro Rata Share shall be adjusted on a per square foot basis effective as of the date the relocation is accomplished; but if the Substitute Premises is larger than the Premises (unless the larger area is requested by Tenant), Landlord agrees that there shall be no increase to the Annual Base Rent or Tenant's Pro Rata Share notwithstanding the increase in the rentable area. Notwithstanding the foregoing, Tenant shall not be required to take space that is more than 1% smaller than the Premises. Tenant's relocation shall transpire over one (1) weekend to minimize any disruption to Tenant's business. Following the relocation, the next [AMOUNT] full months of Base Rent next coming due shall be abated.

D. COMMENTS

Landlord's right to relocate Tenant, and the exercise of this right, have been held not to destroy the concept of exclusive possession and control of the Premises.

E. TYPICAL PARAGRAPH

42. <u>Relocation of Premises</u>. Tenant covenants and agrees that Landlord shall have the absolute and unqualified right upon at least thirty (30) days' written notice to Tenant to require Tenant move to other space in the Building. Such

notice shall specify and designate the space to which Tenant shall be required to move. Notwithstanding said substitution of space, this Lease and all terms, provisions, covenants, and conditions, contained herein shall remain and continue in full force and effect, except that Landlord shall recalculate the rent for the substituted space based upon the number of square feet in the substituted space and Annual Base Rent and Additional Rent shall be deemed amended to reflect said recalculation. Landlord shall move Tenant to the substituted space without cost or charge to the Tenant.

PARAGRAPH 43

Quiet Enjoyment

RISK RATING: 2

A. DESCRIPTION AND SCOPE

This Paragraph sets out Landlord's covenant that, so long as Tenant is not in default under its Lease, Tenant is entitled to uninterrupted use of the Premises during the Term.

B. ANALYSIS

1. Landlord's Perspective

The Paragraph establishes the obligation of Landlord to provide Tenant with quiet enjoyment of the Premises. Contrary to popular belief, that Paragraph has nothing to do with the level of noise that may be generated by Tenant's neighbors in the Building. Rather "quiet enjoyment" refers to quality of Landlord title to the Premises and the Property. In this Paragraph, Landlord is covenanting that Landlord has good title to the Premises and that no other person or entity has any interest in the Premises that could interfere or interrupt Tenant's use of the Premises.

2. Tenant's Perspective

The Paragraph protects against Tenant having to enforce its rights under the Lease against third parties claiming an interest in or legal title to the Premises.

3. Lender's Perspective

Lender will want any quiet enjoyment covenant to be subject to the other terms and conditions of the Lease because the subordination Paragraph of the Lease contains several important Lender protections that Lender wants to supersede the quiet enjoyment covenant.

4. Broker's Perspective

Brokers should not expect to negotiate this Paragraph in the LOI or the Lease as legal counsel to Landlord and Tenant typically negotiate the Paragraph.

C. COMPROMISES AND ALTERNATIVES

Tenant should be careful that the quiet enjoyment covenant remain in place through the expiration of any applicable notice and cure period for Tenant defaults under the Lease and extends to claims by, under and through Landlord. So, the following revision to Paragraph 43 below should be proposed (underscored words indicating changes made to the original Paragraph 43 below):

> *43. Quiet Enjoyment. Subject to the terms and conditions of this Lease, so long as Tenant is not in default under this Lease <u>beyond any applicable notice and cure period</u>, Landlord covenants and agrees that Tenant is entitled to quiet enjoyment of the Premises during the Term <u>free from claims of any parties claiming by, under or through Landlord</u>.*

D. COMMENTS

Generally, this Paragraph should not be controversial.

E. TYPICAL PARAGRAPH

43. <u>Quiet Enjoyment</u>. Subject to the terms and conditions of this Lease, so long as Tenant is not in default under this Lease, Landlord covenants and agrees that Tenant is entitled to quiet enjoyment of the Premises during the Term.

PARAGRAPH 44

Brokers

RISK RATING: 3

A. DESCRIPTION AND SCOPE

This Paragraph specifies the broker or brokers, if any, involved in negotiating the Lease (or clearly states no brokers were involved) and states which party shall be responsible for any fees or commissions payable to the broker(s) involved. Landlord is typically responsible for any fees or commissions payable to the broker(s) pursuant to a separate agreement between Landlord and broker(s). The Paragraph also provides an indemnification by both parties for commissions owed to any brokers who are not named.

B. ANALYSIS

1. Landlord's Perspective

This Paragraph protects Landlord by requiring Tenant to identify all brokers with which Tenant has had any dealings regarding the Lease. The Paragraph further requires that Tenant indemnify Landlord in the event any unspecified brokers with whom Tenant has had dealings should make any claims after the execution of the Lease.

2. Tenant's Perspective

Generally, Tenant expects that Landlord will pay the cost of all brokers involved in the Lease transaction. However, this can be a negotiated point. Tenant knows that Landlord usually has a budget for broker fees and that the amount of these fees factor into the Annual Base Rent calculation that is offered by Landlord. Any broker retention letter or agreement entered into between Tenant and Tenant's broker or representative should indicate that the broker will look to Landlord for payment of the broker fees and should set a maximum amount or percentage of Annual Base Rent that Tenant's broker will seek to obtain from Landlord. It is then incumbent upon Tenant's broker to negotiate a satisfactory arrangement with Landlord that is within the parameters set by Tenant's retention letter or agreement with its broker. Tenant needs to be careful in its interaction with multiple brokers since Landlord will likely be unwilling to compensate more than a single Tenant broker. There should be no circumstances where there is more than one broker claiming to be the "procuring cause" of Tenant's new lease, unless an agreement exists among multiple brokers to share the fees.

This Paragraph also protects Tenant by requiring Landlord to confirm the brokers with whom Landlord has had any dealings regarding the Lease. The Paragraph further requires that Landlord indemnify Tenant in the event any unspecified brokers with whom Landlord has had dealings should make any claims after the execution of the Lease.

3. Lender's Perspective

This Paragraph benefits Lender by specifying the responsibility of each party to pay the claims of named and unnamed brokers.

4. Broker's Perspective

Brokers will want to review this Paragraph closely for accuracy including confirming that all involved Brokers (and their firms) are named within the Paragraph accurately. Brokers should also obtain a written compensation agreement from Landlord prior to Lease execution. Many states restrict enforceability of broker's commission to that specified in a written agreement. In addition, Brokers would be well advised to include in the LOI that should the transaction contemplated by the LOI be fully executed and delivered, that Broker will be paid a full market rate commission by the Landlord pursuant to a separate agreement between the parties.

C. COMPROMISES AND ALTERNATIVES

None.

D. COMMENTS

A modified version of this paragraph should be used even if no broker or tenant representative is involved. If a broker or tenant representative is not involved, both Landlord and Tenant will want a representation from the other party to that effect and an indemnification in the event the representation made is untrue.

E. TYPICAL PARAGRAPH

44. Brokers. The parties hereby represent and warrant that the only real estate broker involved in the negotiation and execution of this Lease is [NAME OF LANDLORD'S BROKER] and [NAME OF TENANT'S BROKER] (collectively, the "Broker") and that no other party is entitled, as a result of the actions of the respective party, to a commission or other fee resulting from the execution of this Lease, and that Landlord is solely responsible for commissions payable to the Broker hereunder in accordance with, and subject to, the terms of a separate agreement. Each party shall protect, defend, indemnify, and hold the other harmless from and against any and all claims for the breach of this representation and warranty on its part (including, without limitation, the obligation to pay any compensation to any other broker or person who may be entitled thereto).

PARAGRAPH 45

Recording of Lease and Notice (Memorandum) of Lease

RISK RATING: 4

A. DESCRIPTION AND SCOPE

Nearly all leases provide an express prohibition of recording of the Lease and both Alternatives for Paragraph 45 below provide for same. However, in some jurisdictions, a short form of lease (typically referred to as a notice of lease or memorandum of lease) (herein, a "Notice of Lease") must by law be recorded or otherwise customarily are recorded in the land records so as to ensure that the Lease is enforceable against any party other than the Landlord or Tenant. Because of the foregoing, Paragraph 45 contains Alternative provisions with Alternative 2 permitting the recording of a Notice of Lease under certain conditions.

Note that some states have statutory forms for Notices of Leases, and each jurisdiction should be reviewed on this subject.

B. ANALYSIS

1. Landlord's Perspective

Landlord does not want a Lease recorded because it encumbers the Property and reveals to the public what business terms Landlord agreed to in the Lease. This would negatively impact Landlord's negotiating leverage in all subsequent leases.

As for any Notice of Lease, Landlord may not want the Notice of Lease to contain any information other than the basic lease terms (and, as applicable, statutory minimums). In jurisdictions where Notices of Lease are neither required by law or customary practice, Landlord may object to recording a Notice of Lease so as to avoid encumbering the title of the Property. It will be difficult for Landlord to clean up title should an early termination of the Lease occur because of a Tenant default.

2. Tenant's Perspective

Tenant may want to have the Lease or Notice of Lease recorded, as recordation puts the world on notice as to Tenant's interest in Premises. With a recorded Notice of Lease, any purchaser will take the Premises subject to Tenant's Lease. In addition, recording a Notice of Lease will establish Tenant's priority relative to any future Lender, if the Lease does not contain an automatic subordination provision.

If Tenant has any important rights (for example, rights of renewal, expansion, or first refusal, or an option to purchase) it is important that these rights are expressly provided in the recorded Notice of Lease.

3. Lender's Perspective

Lender may object to having a Notice of Lease recorded, as this creates an encumbrance on the title. If the Notice of Lease is recorded before Lender's mortgage, Lender will most likely require an SNDA from Tenant, particularly if there is no automatic subordination provision.

4. Broker's Perspective

Brokers do not typically include this Paragraph in the LOI or help negotiate it in the Lease.

C. COMPROMISES AND ALTERNATIVES

When not required by local law or in accordance with local custom, Landlord will resist any Tenant request for the recoding of a Notice of Lease. However, Landlords often compromise and permit the recording of a Notice of Lease if a Release or Discharge of Notice of Lease is simultaneously executed and delivered to Landlord to be held in escrow by Landlord under the terms of the Release. Tenant is typically willing to simultaneously execute and delivery a Release or Discharge of Notice of Lease to be held in escrow by Landlord in exchange for the ability to record a Notice of Lease. Alternative 2 for Paragraph 45 addresses this circumstance.

Thus, when Landlords are willing to permit the recording of Notices of Lease, they typically condition it upon Tenant simultaneously delivering an executed Release or Discharge of Notice of Lease to be held in escrow by the terms of the Release by Landlord until expiration of the Lease Term, or an early termination of the Lease.

D. COMMENTS

It is suggested that the Notice of Lease be executed at the same time as the Lease itself and recorded immediately. The Notice or Memorandum of Lease may also have to be modified to take into account any particular legal requirements of the state in which the Premises are located.

The cost of recording a Notice of Lease is typically borne by Tenant.

See Part 4 of this Lease Manual for a form of Notice of Lease and Release of Notice of Lease.

E. TYPICAL PARAGRAPH

Alternative 1: No Recording at All

45. No Recordation. Neither Landlord nor Tenant shall record this Lease.

Alternative 2: No Recording of Lease but Recording of Memorandum of Lease.

45. Recording. This Lease shall not be recorded, however, upon Tenant's request, Landlord shall execute in recordable form and deliver to Tenant a Notice of Lease prepared by Tenant, provided that Tenant simultaneously executes and delivers to Landlord in recordable form a Release of Notice of Lease, which Landlord agrees to hold until the expiration or earlier termination of Term and, thereafter, record.

PARAGRAPH 46

Force Majeure

RISK RATING: 3

A. DESCRIPTION AND SCOPE

This Paragraph excuses performance of Lease obligations (except for the payment of Annual Base Rent or Additional Rent or any other monetary amount due under the Lease) by either party for a certain period of time, if performance is made impossible by events outside the control of the nonperforming party. Failure to perform during such period is not a default under the Lease.

In the wake of the COVID-19 pandemic, both Landlords and Tenants were reviewing their existing "Force Majeure" clauses carefully to find any relief in the timing requirements of their Lease obligations because the pandemic caused widespread delays in unexpected ways. Force Majeure clauses for new leases were revised in response to the lessons learned from the pandemic, and Paragraph 46 reflects those revisions.

B. ANALYSIS

1. Landlord's Perspective

This Paragraph protects Landlord against default under the Lease obligations when events beyond the control of Landlord make compliance impossible. However, as to Tenant Defaults, Landlord will want to exclude from the applicability of this Paragraph the payment of Annual Base Rent, Additional Rent, or any other amount due Landlord under the Lease.

2. Tenant's Perspective

This Paragraph protects Tenant from being in Default under the Lease if it is unable to comply with its Lease obligations (other than the obligations to pay Annual Base

Rent, Additional Rent, or other amounts due Landlord under the Lease) due to events beyond Tenant's control. However, as to Landlord defaults, Tenant may want to exclude from the provisions of this Paragraph, or at least modify the consequences and timing of, Landlord's obligation to complete any required tenant improvements and Landlord's work to prepare the Premises by the Commencement Date or to make repairs.

3. Lender's Perspective

Lender will require that obligations requiring Tenant to pay money, such as the rental obligation and the obligation to pay property taxes and operating expenses, be excluded from this Paragraph since inclusion potentially obstructs Property cash flow available for debt service.

4. Broker's Perspective

This Paragraph is not typically addressed in the LOI, however, both Brokers should support legal counsel in negotiating this Paragraph as it may relate to critical initial Landlord and Tenant obligations at the outset of the Term, including Premises delivery requirements.

C. COMPROMISES AND ALTERNATIVES

If Tenant is moving to the Premises from another location with a lease expiration date that cannot be extended, Tenant may require that Landlord's delivery requirement of the Premises be excluded from this Paragraph. This will likely be resisted by Landlord if Landlord is performing any initial construction to the Premises prior to Premises delivery since construction delays are common and were even more so during the COVID-19 pandemic.

One compromise is to limit the amount of days Landlord can delay delivering the Premises to Tenant without penalty by reason of Force Majeure conditions (e.g., to no more than sixty (60) days) even if the Force Majeure conditions continue beyond such 60-day time period. This is just an allocation of Force Majeure risk between the two parties. This limitation can be imposed on any time-sensitive obligation under the Lease.

D. COMMENTS

Obligations involving solely the payment of money by Tenant are often carved out of this Paragraph. Similarly, any Landlord monetary obligations (e.g., the payment of an improvement allowance or the refund of an overpayment in Operating Expenses or Real Estate Taxes) should be carved out of this Paragraph.

E. TYPICAL PARAGRAPH

46. Force Majeure. If, by reason of strike, lockouts or other labor or industrial troubles; governmental pre-emption in connection with a national, state or local emergency; any rule, order or regulation of any governmental agency applicable to the Building or the Premises, or either party hereto in connection with a national, state or local emergency; conditions of supply or demand that are affected by war or other national, state or municipal emergency including inability to obtain or shortages in labor or materials or reasonable substitutes therefor; governmental restrictions, governmental regulations, governmental controls, governmental orders or directives, delay in issuance of permits, inspections or approvals, utility company delays; fire or other casualty (not due to the negligence or willful misconduct of the party claiming same); acts of God such as (by way of example only) tornado, earthquake, flood, hurricane, windstorm, washout or storm, civil disturbance, act of the public enemy, riot, sabotage, blockade, embargo, explosion (not due to the negligence or willful misconduct of the party claiming same); pandemic (including, without limitation, COVID-19), epidemics, endemics, or government-imposed quarantines; or any other cause beyond the relevant party's reasonable control, whether or not similar to any of the causes hereinabove stated (each of the foregoing, called "Force Majeure"), Landlord or Tenant shall be unable to perform any obligation that such party is obligated to perform, then such party's obligation to perform shall be excused for the duration of such Force Majeure, and, except as otherwise expressly set forth in the Lease, the Lease and all rights and obligations of the parties thereunder shall not be affected, impaired, or excused. However, and notwithstanding anything to the contrary contained in this provision, a Force Majeure event shall not, in any case, excuse any monetary obligations of Landlord or Tenant hereunder including, without limitation, Tenant's obligation to pay rent, when same is due and payable hereunder. In addition, each party agrees to resume its performance delayed by a Force Majeure event as promptly as is commercially reasonable under the circumstances. A party claiming Force Majeure must give notice to the other party within ten (10) days of the occurrence of the event describing with reasonable detail the events giving rise to a claimed Force Majeure.

PARAGRAPH 47

Time Is of the Essence

RISK RATING: 2

A. DESCRIPTION AND SCOPE

This Paragraph provides that "time is of the essence" and obligates both parties to perform their obligations under the Lease in a strictly timely manner.

B. ANALYSIS

1. Landlord's Perspective

This statement protects Landlord against untimely performance by Tenant of its obligations including payment of Annual Base Rent and Additional Rent. Landlord may object to the application of this clause as it relates to Landlord completion of Tenant Improvements or to the scheduled Commencement Date. Tenant may demand that the clause apply, as these are areas of great concern to Tenant. Landlord may want to limit this Paragraph to Tenant's obligations under the Lease. If there are any renewal options, rights of first refusal, or purchase option under the Lease, Tenant will be held strictly to the precise dates in exercising such rights and options.

2. Tenant's Perspective

This statement may protect Tenant from the untimely completion by Landlord of required Tenant improvements, delivery of the Premises at a date later than the scheduled Commencement Date, and other untimely performance by Landlord. The existence of this Paragraph should cause Tenant to pay close attention to the timing of the exercise of any renewal or extension rights of Tenant or any expansion options of Tenant under the Lease. Tenant may want to require that Landlord notify Tenant prior to the expiration of any such rights.

3. Lender's Perspective

Lender generally wants to ensure that all obligations under the Lease, whether by Landlord or Tenant, are performed in a strictly timely manner.

4. Broker's Perspective

This Paragraph is not typically addressed in the LOI, however, both Brokers should support legal counsel in negotiating this Paragraph as it may relate to critical initial Landlord and Tenant obligations at the outset of the Term, including Premises delivery requirements.

C. COMPROMISES AND ALTERNATIVES

In light of Landlords and Tenants experiencing unexpected delays and interruptions to their non-monetary obligations under the Lease due to COVID-19, it is now advisable that both Landlord and Tenant should seek to except from the applicability of this Paragraph, Force Majeure events. Thus, Landlord and/or Tenant may wish to revise Paragraph as follows:

> *47. Time Is of the Essence. Subject to Paragraph 46 [which is Force Majeure], Landlord and Tenant agree that, in fulfilling all terms and conditions of this Lease, time is of the essence.*

D. COMMENTS

If "time is of the essence" is included in the Lease, mutually agreed-upon extensions on any time-defined provisions must be in writing and signed by all parties.

E. TYPICAL PARAGRAPH

47. Time Is of the Essence. Landlord and Tenant agree that, in fulfilling all terms and conditions of this Lease, time is of the essence.

PARAGRAPH 48

Attorneys' Fees

RISK RATING: 3

A. DESCRIPTION AND SCOPE

This Paragraph provides for the awarding of reasonable attorneys' fees to the prevailing party in a lawsuit concerning a default under the Lease.

B. ANALYSIS

1. Landlord's Perspective

Landlord may want Tenant to pay Landlord's legal fees regardless of who prevails and regardless of whether or not Landlord actually institutes an action. Landlord may consider expanding Tenant's obligation to the amount of all legal fees incurred by Landlord arising out of or resulting from any act or omission by Tenant with respect to the Lease, the Premises, or from any bankruptcy case involving Tenant.

2. Tenant's Perspective

Tenant wants this provision to be mutual so that Landlord must pay Tenant's legal fees if Tenant prevails and Tenant must pay Landlord's legal fees if Landlord prevails. This Paragraph benefits Tenant as well as Landlord in that it encourages compliance with the terms of the Lease and promotes cooperative resolution of disputes. It also discourages frivolous litigation.

3. Lender's Perspective

Lender wants a mechanism promoting dispute resolution but would prefer the clause ran in favor of its borrower, the Landlord, rather than benefiting Tenant and Landlord mutually.

4. Broker's Perspective

This Paragraph is not typically included in the LOI and it is typically negotiated in the Lease through legal counsel.

C. COMPROMISES AND ALTERNATIVES

If Landlord objects to Tenant's right to obtain attorneys' fees, or cannot accept a reciprocal arrangement on the payment of legal fees, Tenant may find it more beneficial to delete the Paragraph entirely than to attempt to negotiate any changes to Tenant's rights. This would be particularly true for a Tenant that does not have significant credit or financial support.

D. COMMENTS

None.

E. TYPICAL PARAGRAPH

48. **Lawyer Expenses. If either party shall at any time be in default hereunder, and if either party shall institute an action or summary proceeding against the offending party based upon such default, then the losing party will reimburse the prevailing party for the expense of attorneys' fees and disbursements thereby incurred by the prevailing party, so far as the same are reasonable in amount. In addition, if Tenant makes any requests of Landlord hereunder and Landlord consults with or seeks the advice of a lawyer in connection therewith, Tenant shall immediately reimburse Landlord for all reasonable attorneys' fees incurred by Landlord.**

PARAGRAPH 49

Partial Invalidity

RISK RATING: 4

A. DESCRIPTION AND SCOPE

In the event one clause of the Lease is held to be invalid or unenforceable, this Paragraph allows the remainder of the Lease to remain in effect and enforceable. This Paragraph negates a legal rule that would permit a court in some situations to declare that if one clause of a Lease is invalid, the entire Lease is invalid.

B. ANALYSIS

1. Landlord's Perspective

This Paragraph protects Landlord in that it permits the Lease from being invalidated as a result of one, perhaps minor, clause being held invalid. Landlord may request that if any clause, which Landlord deems essential to Landlord's interests, is held invalid, Landlord has the right to terminate the Lease. If requested, Tenant must give careful consideration to the provisions marked for such treatment.

2. Tenant's Perspective

This Paragraph similarly protects Tenant from determining that the whole Lease must fall if any one provision is deemed invalid or unenforceable. If Landlord is granted rights to terminate the Lease for material provisions of the Lease being declared invalid, Tenant should similarly obtain such rights.

3. Lender's Perspective

Lender is interested in keeping the Lease in force so that the rental income stream is not affected; therefore, the partial invalidity clause benefits both Landlord Lender.

4. Broker's Perspective

This Paragraph is not typically included in the LOI and it is typically negotiated in the Lease through legal counsel.

C. COMPROMISES AND ALTERNATIVES

Generally, it would be best not to modify this provision. Any modifications should be reviewed by legal counsel.

D. COMMENTS

This Paragraph is rarely the subject of much negotiation.

E. TYPICAL PARAGRAPH

49. Partial Invalidity. If any provision of this Lease, or its application to any situation, shall be invalid or unenforceable to any extent, the remainder of this Lease, or the application thereof to situations other than that as to which it is invalid or unenforceable, shall not be affected thereby, and every provision of this Lease shall be valid and enforceable to the fullest extent permitted by law.

PARAGRAPH 50

Successors and Assigns

RISK RATING: 4

A. DESCRIPTION AND SCOPE

This paragraph binds the heirs, executors, administrators, successors, and permitted assigns of Landlord and Tenant and requires that they perform their predecessor's obligations under the Lease.

B. ANALYSIS

1. Landlord's Perspective

This Paragraph protects Landlord from a claim that a transfer of Tenant's interest in the Lease has terminated Landlord's rights under the Lease against the original Tenant or that a permitted successor Tenant is not bound by the terms of the Lease.

2. Tenant's Perspective

This Paragraph similarly protects Tenant from a claim that a transfer of the Premises by Landlord has terminated Tenant's rights under the Lease or that a successor Landlord is not bound by the terms of the Lease.

3. Lender's Perspective

This Paragraph protects Lender by preventing the termination or impairment of rights and obligations resulting from an assignment of the Lease, which rights and obligations were relied upon by Lender in providing financing.

4. Broker's Perspective

This Paragraph is not typically included in the LOI and it is typically negotiated in the Lease through legal counsel.

C. COMPROMISES AND ALTERNATIVES

None.

D. COMMENTS

Landlord will generally require that Tenant obtain Landlord's written consent to an assignment of Tenant's interest, while permitting Landlord to freely assign its interest in the Lease.

E. TYPICAL PARAGRAPH

50. Successors and Assigns. This Lease shall be binding upon and shall inure to the benefit of the parties hereto, their heirs, executors, administrators, successors, and permitted assigns.

PARAGRAPH 51

No Partnership or Joint Venture

RISK RATING: 5

A. DESCRIPTION AND SCOPE

This Paragraph sets forth the statement that Landlord and Tenant are not associated as partners in any respect.

B. ANALYSIS

1. Landlord's Perspective

This statement will serve as evidence of an intent not to create any form of legal association between Landlord and Tenant. Such a statement is necessary to limit Landlord's liability for the acts of Tenant that are done in the course of Tenant's business.

2. Tenant's Perspective

Tenant will be equally concerned that it not bear responsibility for the acts of Landlord, and therefore, Tenant is unlikely to resist the inclusion of this Paragraph in the Lease.

3. Lender's Perspective

Lender has the same concerns as Landlord regarding this Paragraph. If Lender succeeds to Landlord's interest under the Lease, Lender will desire an affirmative statement in the Lease concerning the nonexistence of any legal association between Lender and Tenant.

4. Broker's Perspective

This Paragraph is not typically included in the LOI and it is typically negotiated in the Lease through legal counsel.

C. COMPROMISES AND ALTERNATIVES

None.

D. COMMENTS

This clause occurs in many office and retail leases. It is probably most important in those retail leases requiring the payment of percentage rent since rent derived from a percentage rent clause may be viewed as giving Landlord a form of participation in Tenant's revenues. This clause should also be used with any other provisions that give Landlord some rights to exercise control over Tenant's operations. In such situations, it is advisable to include a clause in the Lease to indicate that the parties do not intend the establishment of a partnership or joint venture.

E. TYPICAL PARAGRAPH

51. **No Partnership or Joint Venture. Landlord shall in no event be construed, held, or become in any way or for any purpose a partner, associate, or joint venturer of Tenant or any party associated with Tenant in the conduct of its business or otherwise.**

PARAGRAPH 52

Merger

RISK RATING: 5

A. DESCRIPTION AND SCOPE

This paragraph provides that only the terms and provisions of the written Lease (which can only be modified by a written amendment) and any Exhibits, Riders, or Addenda attached to it are binding on the parties.

B. ANALYSIS

1. Landlord's Perspective

This paragraph protects Landlord against any representations, statements made in negotiation, oral agreements, or extraneous agreements being construed as part of the Lease.

2. Tenant's Perspective

Tenant wants to ensure that its only obligations under the Lease are those specifically described in the Lease. Similarly, Tenant needs to be aware that all of Landlord's obligations need to be specifically described or else they will not be enforceable. Verbal understandings or agreements with the Landlord will not be upheld if they are not contained in the Lease.

3. Lender's Perspective

Lender is relying on the written Lease as being the entire Agreement between Landlord and Tenant. Therefore, for example, an oral agreement between Landlord and Tenant to reduce rent payments would not be valid. As a result, Lender is assured that the relationship between its borrower/Landlord and Tenant is clear. Lender will want to specify in the Subordination, Nondisturbance, and Attornment Agreement that any written amendment to the Lease is not valid without Lender's written consent.

4. Broker's Perspective

This Paragraph is not typically included in the LOI and it is typically negotiated in the Lease through legal counsel.

C. COMPROMISES AND ALTERNATIVES

None.

D. COMMENTS

This Paragraph should not be controversial.

E. TYPICAL PARAGRAPH

52. Merger. This Lease and the Exhibits, Riders, and/or Addenda, if any, attached hereto, set forth the entire agreement between the parties. Any prior conversations or writings are merged herein and extinguished. No subsequent amendment to this Lease shall be binding upon Landlord or Tenant unless reduced to writing and signed by the parties.

PARAGRAPH 53

Limitations of Liability

RISK RATING: 4

A. DESCRIPTION AND SCOPE

This Paragraph limits the Landlord's liability to Tenant to the value of Landlord's interest in the Property where the Premises are located. Additionally, it expressly specifically excludes the assets of any individuals having an interest in Landlord as well as any other assets owned by Landlord.

B. ANALYSIS

1. Landlord's Perspective

Landlord wants to limit its potential liability to Tenant as much as possible. In particular, potential liability of individuals who control Landlord should be limited.

2. Tenant's Perspective

Tenant wants to have the largest possible pool of assets to pursue in the event it has a claim against Landlord. Tenant may therefore object to this paragraph entirely. This will particularly be the case if Landlord has little or no equity in the Property. It is unlikely that Tenant will prevail in removing the paragraph entirely so Tenant should seek to have the limitation extended to Landlord's interest in the Property (versus the Premises) and extended to any and all proceeds derived therefrom (including, sales, insurance, and rental proceeds).

3. Lender's Perspective

Lender has an interest in seeing that the damages against Landlord are minimized since Landlord is Lender's borrower and Landlord's assets may provide additional security for Lender's loan.

4. Broker's Perspective

This Paragraph is not typically included in the LOI and it is typically negotiated in the Lease through legal counsel. Tenant Broker should be apprised as to any current financing encumbering the Property.

C. COMPROMISES AND ALTERNATIVES

A prospective tenant who is in a strong negotiating position might seek to increase the assets that it might pursue upon Landlord's default by removing some of the restrictions noted in this Paragraph. Because many Landlords are single-purpose entities whose sole assets are often the property being leased, the practical effect of these efforts may be limited.

Tenant should revise Paragraph 53 as follows (with the underscored words representing the modified language):

> *. . . Tenant shall be limited for the satisfaction of said money judgment solely to Landlord's interest in the Building and Land and any and all proceeds derived thereto (including, but not limited to, all sales, insurance, and rental proceeds) and no other property or assets of Landlord . . . .*

The extension of the limitation to "sales proceeds" is particularly important because, without the proposed language, if the Landlord sells the Property, it will have no further interest in the Property and, therefore, no assets/liability for any unfulfilled obligations accruing prior to the date of transfer. This is an unacceptable situation for Tenant.

In addition, it is fair and reasonable for Tenant to request a reciprocal liability limitation with respect to the second portion of the Paragraph 53. Below is a sample of mutual language that Tenant would be prudent to request:

> *Likewise, only Tenant shall be responsible for its obligation under this Lease and no other property or assets of the individual partners, members, directors, officers, or shareholders of Tenant shall be subject to levy, execution, or other enforcement procedure whatsoever for the satisfaction of any judgment against Tenant.*

D. COMMENTS

Tenant will want to make sure that the limitation is indeed to Landlord's interest in the Property (meaning the Building and underlying Land where the Premises is located) and not just Landlord's interest in the Premises.

E. TYPICAL PARAGRAPH

53. <u>Limitations of Landlord's Liability</u>. If Landlord becomes obligated to pay Tenant a money judgment arising out of any failure by Landlord to perform or observe any of the terms, covenants, conditions, or provisions to be performed or observed by Landlord hereunder, Tenant shall be limited for the satisfaction of said money judgment solely to Landlord's interest in the Building and Land and no other property or assets of Landlord or the individual partners, members, directors, officers, or shareholders of Landlord shall be subject to levy, execution, or other enforcement procedure whatsoever for the satisfaction of said money judgment.

PARAGRAPH 54

Transfer of Landlord's Interest

RISK RATING: 4

A. DESCRIPTION AND SCOPE

This Paragraph provides that both the obligations of and the benefits to Landlord that arise under this Lease can be transferred, and that only the person or entity in Landlord's position at a given time has the rights and responsibilities of Landlord.

B. ANALYSIS

1. Landlord's Perspective

This provision benefits Landlord since it will be relieved of further responsibility to the Tenant after Landlord sells the Property.

2. Tenant's Perspective

Tenant wants to be sure that any subsequent Landlord is required to fulfill the current Landlord's obligations. In addition, Tenant would like the original Landlord to remain liable after the transfer of the Lease for acts committed during the time that the then-Landlord was lessor of the Property. To accomplish this, Tenant may insert language that provides that any provisions in the Lease that purport to release Landlord of its Lease obligations upon any transfer of Landlord's interest in the Property shall only release Landlord for said obligations accruing on and after such transfer. If there are outstanding obligations in the past of Landlord, such as a return of a security deposit, the payment of a Tenant Allowance, or the completion of Tenant Improvements, Tenant may want to condition the current Landlord's release of liability upon the new Landlord's assumption of and completion of the obligations and liabilities.

3. Lender's Perspective

Lender wants to be sure that whoever is in the position of Landlord is entitled to receive rent payments from Tenant in order to maintain the income stream of the Property.

4. Broker's Perspective

This Paragraph is not typically included in the LOI and it is typically negotiated in the Lease through legal counsel.

C. COMPROMISES AND ALTERNATIVES

Although a Landlord is unlikely to want any impediments to its ability to sell or otherwise transfer the Lease and the Premises, a prospective Tenant might seek to use a similar rationale to negotiate less-restrictive terms in the Assignment and Subletting clause. For example, Tenant might request that Tenant should have no further liability under the Lease after an assignment to and assumption of Tenant's interest in the Lease by a credit-worthy replacement Tenant. However, Tenant should expect resistance from both Landlord and Lender to such a provision.

Paragraph 54, as drafted below, is typical of first drafts of Leases and can be read to release Landlord entirely from its past, present, and future obligations under the Lease, which is inappropriate as new owners will likely only assume obligations under the Lease on and after the date of transfer. Thus, when Tenant is faced with language such as Paragraph 54, it should add the following modification:

> *Notwithstanding the foregoing, any provisions in the Lease which purport to release Landlord of its Lease obligations upon any transfer of Landlord's interest in the Property shall only release Landlord for said obligations accruing on and after such transfer.*

D. COMMENTS

None.

E. TYPICAL PARAGRAPH

54. <u>Transfer of Landlord's Interest</u>. The term "Landlord" as used in this Lease, so far as covenants or agreements on the part of Landlord are concerned, shall be limited to mean and include only the owner or owners of Landlord's interest in this Lease at the time in question. Upon any transfer or transfers of such interest, Landlord herein named (and in case of any subsequent transfer, the then-transferor) shall thereafter be relieved of all liability for the performance of any covenants or agreements on the part of Landlord contained in this Lease.

PARAGRAPH 55

Arbitration

RISK RATING: 4

A. DESCRIPTION AND SCOPE

If a dispute arises between Landlord and Tenant, each party may seek their respective rights and remedies under the Lease, at law and in equity. Because seeking remedies in a court of law is oftentimes cost prohibitive and inefficient, the Lease will incorporate a variety of dispute resolution remedies within the Lease itself and many have been discussed within other Paragraphs of this Lease (for example, Tenant rent abatement rights for late Premises delivery or interruptions of services, self-help rights for maintenance defaults, specified dispute resolution processes for disputes in Operating Expense charges or the determination of rent for a renewal term, etc.).

Paragraph 55 or a variation thereof is sometimes (but certainly not always) included in a Lease to address other common disputes that may arise during the Lease but for which Landlord and Tenant do not want to litigate in order to resolve.

B. ANALYSIS

1. Landlord's Perspective

Landlord wants to ensure that relatively minor disputes (not worthy of Lease termination) be decided in an efficient and fair manner, and that the arbitrator's decision will be binding so that the dispute is conclusively resolved.

2. Tenant's Perspective

Tenant wants to ensure that relatively minor disputes (not worthy of a full law suit) will be decided in an efficient and fair manner, and that the arbitrator's decision will be binding so that the dispute is conclusively resolved.

3. Lender's Perspective

Lender's perspective is the same as Landlord's since Lender will want a limited scope arbitration that can be readily decided so as not to interrupt the rental income from Tenant.

4. Broker's Perspective

Each Broker will want to consult with their respective client to determine any sensitivity to or any particular client need relating to this Paragraph that should be covered in the LOI. If none exist, this Paragraph can be handled by the attorneys in Lease negotiations.

C. COMPROMISES AND ALTERNATIVES

The types of disputes that will be subject to arbitration are negotiable between the parties and will vary from lease to lease.

D. COMMENTS

The parties should ensure that the types of disputes that will be subject to arbitration are clearly spelled out in the appropriate sections of the Lease.

In some jurisdictions, arbitration can be just as costly and time-consuming as litigation within a court. In that event, arbitration clauses such as Paragraph 55 are not included within a Lease.

E. TYPICAL PARAGRAPH

55. <u>Arbitration</u>. If there is a dispute between Landlord and Tenant as to (i) the reasonableness of Landlord's refusal to consent to any subletting or assignment with respect to which Landlord agreed herein to be reasonable, (ii) the reasonableness of Landlord's refusal to give any approval relating to an Alteration with respect to which Landlord agreed herein to be reasonable, or (iii) the reasonableness of any Rule or Regulation adopted by Landlord from and after the date of this Lease; or (iv) the accuracy of any remeasurement of the Premises as permitted under the Lease, or (v) the date of the Rent Commencement Date and/or the amount of any Landlord Delays or Tenant Delays, then Tenant or Landlord may submit the dispute to binding arbitration by an arbiter in [COUNTY, STATE] in accordance with the rules in effect of the American Arbitration Association (or any successor organization). Landlord and Tenant shall cooperate with each other to conclude such arbitration on an expedited basis. The arbiter shall have no right whatsoever to alter the provisions of this Lease (including, without limitation, the provisions of this paragraph). Landlord and Tenant shall each pay one half of

the costs of the arbitration (other than the fees and disbursements of their respective experts and attorneys which each shall be solely responsible for). With respect to a dispute concerning the reasonableness of Landlord's refusal to consent to a subletting or assignment or the reasonableness of a Rule or Regulation, the arbiter shall have at least ten (10) years' experience in the business of managing real estate or acting as a real estate broker dealing with first-class office buildings in the [COUNTY, STATE], area. With respect to a dispute concerning the reasonableness of Landlord's refusal to give any approval of any Alteration with respect to which Landlord agreed to be reasonable, the arbitrator shall be an architect or engineer with at least ten (10) years' experience in designing and performing alterations in first-class office buildings in the [COUNTY, STATE], area similar in size, quality, and character to the alteration which is the subject of the dispute.

PARAGRAPH 56

Governing Law

RISK RATING: 3

A. DESCRIPTION AND SCOPE

This Paragraph sets forth the applicable law that will control construction and the enforceability of the terms of the Lease and the rights, remedies, and duties of the parties thereto.

B. ANALYSIS

1. Landlord's Perspective

Landlord wants to establish the controlling law so it can evaluate, at the inception and throughout the term of the Lease, the enforceability of the Lease's terms and its rights and remedies.

2. Tenant's Perspective

Generally, Tenant will want the controlling law to be that of the State where the Property is located. If Landlord specifies a different jurisdiction, this will be a red flag for Tenant's attorney.

3. Lender's Perspective

Lender's interest would be served by the laws of a jurisdiction that favors the rights of secured parties and imposes the least restrictions on the enforcement of Lender's rights under its mortgage.

4. Broker's Perspective

This Paragraph is not typically included in the LOI and it is typically negotiated in the Lease through legal counsel.

C. COMPROMISES AND ALTERNATIVES

If Landlord includes in the Lease a choice of law other than the jurisdiction where the Premises is located, then Landlord will also want to include in the Lease specific provisions that grant it rights not otherwise granted by the controlling law should a local court in any dispute determine that the law where the Property is located is the controlling law. Alternatively, Landlord could seek a waiver by Tenant, where permitted by the applicable jurisdiction, of Tenant rights that are adverse to Landlord's interests.

D. COMMENTS

Careful drafting of specific lease provisions can mitigate the effect of rights and remedies granted to Tenant by controlling law. Since leases are contracts affecting land, they will be construed in accordance with local law absent provisions to the contrary. Consumer protection aspects of local lease law may not be waivable directly or by choice of law of another jurisdiction.

E. TYPICAL PARAGRAPH

56. Governing Law. This Lease and the rights and obligations of Landlord and Tenant hereunder shall be governed by and construed in accordance with the laws of the jurisdiction in which the Premises are located.

PARAGRAPH 57

Name of Building

RISK RATING: 2

A. DESCRIPTION AND SCOPE

This Paragraph establishes that Landlord has the unilateral right to change the name and/or address of the Building and exterior signage of the Building.

B. ANALYSIS

1. Landlord's Perspective

Landlord wants the option of renaming the Building to enhance the Building's image, and, it is hoped, its marketability, and as a mechanism for attracting an anchor Tenant by agreeing to name the Building after that Tenant.

2. Tenant's Perspective

Tenant wants to avoid confusion on the part of its customers and clients as to its business address. Additionally, to the extent that Tenant may have incorporated the Building name or address into its stationery and promotional materials, Tenant may incur expenses if the name is changed. Larger Tenants will also be concerned about Landlord changing the name of the Building to a name that reflects one of Tenant's competitors. Tenant may want to request that this process be modified so that Tenant receives at least 30 days' prior written notice of any name change.

3. Lender's Perspective

Lender is most likely indifferent to a name change provision unless it adversely affects the value of the Property. If a new name has marketing appeal and can be trademark protected, Lender will want to be sure it has rights to use that name if it takes over Property.

4. Broker's Perspective

Brokers have no particular interest in this Paragraph other than to be aligned with the position of their respective client. Occasionally a Tenant has a particular sensitivity to the possibility that a Building might be named after one of Tenant's competitors should they become a tenant of the Building. Therefore, it is prudent for Tenant Broker to discuss this issue with its client/tenant during the LOI stage.

C. COMPROMISES AND ALTERNATIVES

Landlord may agree to compensate Tenant for any costs involved in changing stationery and other materials that mention the previous Building name or address. Landlord might also agree to run newspaper advertisements announcing the change of name or address and/or share Tenant's cost incurred notifying its customers and clients.

D. COMMENTS

If a Landlord agrees to name the Building after an anchor tenant, it should retain the right in the lease with such anchor tenant to change the name if that tenant fails or ceases to occupy the anticipated amount of leasable space in the Building (subject to reasonable Force Majeure events interrupting anchor tenant's occupancy).

See Paragraph 37 for additional discussion regarding name of Building and signage.

E. TYPICAL PARAGRAPH

57. **Name and Address of Building. Landlord reserves the right at any time after the execution of this Lease to name or change either or both the name and address of the Building or the exterior signs to be affixed to the Building or located on the Property.**

PARAGRAPH 58

Right of First Refusal; Right of First Offer to Lease Additional Space

RISK RATING: 4 for Rights of First Refusal; 3 for Rights of First Offer

A. DESCRIPTION AND SCOPE

This Paragraph sets forth the terms of Tenant's right of first refusal or right of first offer to lease additional space in the Building. A right of first refusal provides that Tenant shall have the preferential right to accept or refuse Landlord's offer to lease additional space on the terms that Landlord has already negotiated with a proposed tenant. A right of first offer provides that Tenant shall have the first opportunity to respond to Landlord's offer to lease the additional space prior to Landlord offering the additional space to the general public.

B. ANALYSIS

1. Landlord's Perspective

Landlord and prospective tenants do not want to expend time and money to negotiate potential lease terms only to have Tenant exercise its right of first refusal with respect to such terms. Therefore, Landlord's should strongly resist giving rights of first refusal. Landlord would prefer to grant a right of first offer, because if Tenant fails to exercise the same within the allotted time, Landlord may proceed to lease the additional space to any prospective tenant. Landlord must be careful to survey other Tenants' Lease options to avoid conflicts with other Lease terms. Landlord wants to limit the space for which Tenant has the right of first refusal/offer because Landlord wants to have the ability to lease space to others. Landlord therefore wants to designate specific space, rather than the entire Building. For example, Landlord might designate space on a certain floor or floors or in a certain elevator bank, for which Tenant has the right of first refusal/offer. If Tenant has the right to lease space contiguous to the Premises, Landlord should make sure that "contiguous" is narrowly defined in the Lease or Tenant may argue that contiguous means space that is both horizontally and vertically contiguous. To avoid confusion, an exhibit that shows the space subject to the right of first refusal/offer is often attached to the Lease. In addition, the Tenant Work or Tenant Improvement Allowance in connection with Right of First Refusal/First Offer Space should be addressed as should any increase in the Pro Rata Share, change in Base Years, Security Deposit and any allocated parking spaces, as may be applicable. Landlord may wish to condition Tenant's right on Tenant meeting certain financial criteria. Also, Landlord would be prudent to limit Tenant's expansion rights to the initial named Tenant so it can control who grows within its building and how much they can grow.

2. Tenant's Perspective

Tenant wants the flexibility to expand to meet its future needs. Tenant would prefer to have the right to refuse rather than a right of first offer to lease. Tenant may also request longer time periods to respond to Landlord's notice. Tenant will also be concerned if Landlord does not complete a lease transaction or materially modifies the terms of a lease transaction that is the subject of a right of first refusal or right of first offer. In such case, Tenant will again want a right to lease the space before Landlord proceeds with a lease transaction with a third party. With respect to the right of first offer, Tenant will want to require that the Landlord again offer the space to Tenant if Landlord intends to offer the space to a third party at a rent that is less than that offered to Tenant or on terms materially more advantageous than those offered to Tenant or if Landlord does not lease the space to a third party within a designated period of time such as four months, as Tenant's needs may change over time.

3. Lender's Perspective

Lender wants the period within which the option may be exercised to be limited. For the reasons stated above, Lender also would prefer a right of first offer.

4. Broker's Perspective

Both Tenant Broker and Landlord Broker play an instrumental role in negotiating the terms of any Tenant Right of First Refusal or Right of First Offer. Tenant Broker will want to fully understand, during the needs assessment phase of its assignment, the space flexibility needs of Tenant so Tenant Broker can negotiate all required options as the result thereof may play an instrumental part of Tenant's Building selection process. Any such Tenant space flexibility needs should be well negotiated and memorialized in the final LOI. Landlord Broker will want to understand which other tenants in the Building have superior rights to any rights being granted to Tenant as Tenant Broker will likely request such information.

Both Brokers will want to understand the nuances of how Rights of First Refusal and Rights of First Offer are negotiated so that they can capture the best possible terms and conditions within the LOI with respect to the options and then review this Paragraph closely to confirm that it conforms to the agreed upon terms of the LOI. Brokers should also support legal counsel through the negotiation of this Paragraph.

Finally, Brokers will want to make sure their brokerage agreement provides for a commission payment in the event Tenant exercises its rights to acquire additional Premises pursuant to this Paragraph.

C. COMPROMISES AND ALTERNATIVES

General (Applicable to Both Options):

If any offer space is vacant on the Effective Date, Landlord may wish to provide that Tenant's right of first refusal or first offer shall not be triggered on such offer space until after the initial lease up of the offer space. The argument for this position is that the space is already available for lease, and Tenant should negotiate for it presently if it wants it and not wait until Landlord has a deal in hand.

Tenant may object to the requirement that Landlord approve Tenant's financial condition. However, Landlord must be able to confirm Tenant's ability to meet its obligations with respect to the additional space. A reasonable compromise is that Tenant shall limit Landlord's ability to reject Tenant's financial condition to those situations where there has been a material adverse decline in Tenant's financial condition since the inception of the original Lease Term.

Landlord and Tenant should be clear about whether the right of first refusal and/or the right of first offer is a "one time" Tenant right or a "continuing" Tenant right during the Term and revise the provisions accordingly.

With respect to any right of first refusal or first offer being limited to the initial named Tenant, Tenant will want to be careful to extend its rights to any affiliates or permitted successors of Tenant. The justification for this position is that if Tenant is purchased by or merges with another entity, it should not be at risk of losing its expansion rights.

Tenant may wish to negotiate that any leasing of the additional space either through a right of first refusal or a right of first offer shall be on the terms provided by Landlord ***except*** for the fact that the term shall be coterminous with the term of leasing of Tenant's original Premises. This protects Tenant from having to vacate the original Premises and the additional space at differing times. This can be problematic for Landlord as it may wish to lease the additional space for a longer term. A typical compromise is that Tenant's right of first refusal or right of first offer will sunset a few years prior to the expiration of the Lease unless Tenant has the option to renew the Term and elects to do so. Compromise language may look like the following:

> *The terms and conditions of the Lease shall apply to the offer space, provided, however that the term of the Lease for the offer space shall be coterminous with the existing Premises except that if the Expiration Date of the Lease would occur within twenty-four (24) months prior to the expiration of the term of the offer space as set forth in the offer notice,*

Tenant may not exercise its option unless Tenant has one or more remaining renewal options available under the original Lease and concurrently exercises its renewal option under this Paragraph 58.

Landlord will want to be careful that the terms of any right of first offer or right of first refusal do not preclude Landlord from extending a lease for an existing tenant of the offer space or entering into a new lease with a then existing tenant of the offer space or a portion thereof whether or not that existing tenant has an express extension right under the Lease.

Tenant may wish for the Lease to specify which tenants of the Building, if any, have superior rights to Tenant and to which Tenant is expressly subordinating its rights.

Tenant may also wish to strike any "occupancy" requirement conditioning Tenant's right to exercise any Right of First Offer or Right of First Refusal (and really any other Tenant right under the Lease conditioned upon Tenant's occupancy) as we have experienced Tenants not "occupying" their Premises for significant periods of time in response to pandemics. Arguably any such traditional "occupancy" requirement as provided in the Paragraphs below have become antiquated by recent experiences and both Landlord and Tenant should reconsider the inclusion of such language.

Right of First Offer:

Paragraph 58(c) for Right of First Offer Paragraph below is typical in the way it provides if Tenant rejects, or is deemed to have rejected, Landlord's offer, Landlord shall be free to lease such First Offer Space to any party upon any terms and conditions that Landlord may determine. This is unfair to Tenant because it may offer the First Offer Space to Tenant upon one set of terms which Tenant may reject because they appear out of market. If the terms change or if a lease for the First Offer Space is not entered into within a specified period of time, Landlord should be forced to re-offer the space to Tenant. Here is how Paragraph 58(c) is typically negotiated to protect Tenant (with the <u>underscored words</u> showing the changes made to the original Paragraph 58(c) below:

If Tenant rejects, or is deemed to have rejected, Landlord's offer, Landlord shall be free to lease such First Offer Space to any party upon any terms and conditions that Landlord may determine from time to time during the Term, with no further obligation to Tenant under this Paragraph and this Paragraph 58 shall be automatically deemed null and void<u>; provided, however, if (i) Landlord intends to enter into a lease for the First Offer Space on net economic terms differing and more favorable to Tenant by more than five percent (5%) percent of the economic terms contained in the First Offer Notice and/or the non-economic terms materially differ from those contained in the First Offer Notice, and/or (ii) Landlord does not enter into a lease for the First Offer Space within six (6) months from the date of the First Offer Notice, Landlord must re-offer the First Offer Space to Tenant on the revised terms in an updated First Offer Notice to Tenant</u>.

Note that the percentage change in the economic terms and the time period requirement in the underscored language above is typically negotiated with the percentage generally not ever being more than ten percent (10%). Landlord may wish to add an exculpation provision to the six-month time deadline for any lease actively being negotiated and reasonably expected to be executed within thirty (30) days of expiration of the six-month deadline.

Right of First Refusal

Because any right of first refusal is based upon final agreed-upon business terms, there should be no risk that the terms of the lease for the offer space should be different from the terms provided to Tenant in the offer notice, however, the same timing issue applies. Therefore, here is how Paragraph 58(a)(i) is typically negotiated to protect Tenant (with the underscored and stricken words showing the changes made to the original Paragraph 58(a)(i) below:

> *Tenant's Right of First Refusal shall be exercised as follows: At any time that Landlord receives an offer that Landlord intends to accept for all or a portion of the First Refusal Space that is then vacant or to become vacant, Landlord shall advise Tenant of the terms of such offer (the "ROFR Notice") and Tenant shall thereafter have ten (10) Business Days to waive or exercise its Right of First Refusal (the "Notice of Exercise"). Time shall be of the essence with respect to Tenant's Notice of Exercise, and Tenant's failure to give such notice within the ten Business Day period shall be deemed a rejection of Landlord's offer, any principles of law or equity to the contrary notwithstanding. A ROFR Notice may only be accepted in whole, not in part. Should Tenant not match the terms and conditions of the proposed new lease ~~the Landlord may execute the lease on terms substantially similar to the terms in the ROFO Notice~~ (or if Tenant waives its Right of First Refusal or if Tenant does not timely respond to Landlord) the Landlord has a six (6) month period to execute the lease on the terms set forth in the ROFR Notice, after which Tenant will again have a Right of First Refusal as to such First Refusal Space. If Landlord does not enter into a lease with a third party within the above-described six (6) month period and/or on the same terms as set forth in the ROFR Notice, Landlord shall again offer the First Refusal Space to Tenant on the terms set forth in this Paragraph 58.1(a).*

D. COMMENTS

A Tenant taking a substantial portions of a Building may be able to negotiate "continuing" rights of first refusal and rights of first offer on the same or differing portions of the Building. Beyond that, in rare circumstances, they may be able to even obtain a straight "right to expand" on a date certain and that Tenant right is discussed in Paragraph 59.

E. TYPICAL PARAGRAPHS

58. Right of First Refusal

(a) Grant of Option; Conditions. Tenant shall have a [one time] [continuing] right of first refusal (the "Right of First Refusal") with respect to any portion of the [NUMBER] floor[S] of the Building [that is contiguous to the Premises] (the "First Refusal Space").

(i) Tenant's Right of First Refusal shall be exercised as follows: At any time that Landlord receives an offer that Landlord intends to accept for all or a portion of the First Refusal Space that is then vacant or to become vacant, Landlord shall advise Tenant of the terms of such offer (the "ROFR Notice") and Tenant shall thereafter have ten (10)

Business Days to waive or exercise its Right of First Refusal (the "Notice of Exercise"). Time shall be of the essence with respect to Tenant's Notice of Exercise, and Tenant's failure to give such notice within the ten Business Day period shall be deemed a rejection of Landlord's offer, any principles of law or equity to the contrary notwithstanding. A ROFR Notice may only be accepted in whole, not in part. Should Tenant not match the terms and conditions of the proposed new lease the Landlord may execute the lease on terms substantially similar to the terms in the ROFR Notice.

(ii) Tenant may lease such First Refusal Space in its entirety only, under such terms, by delivering its Notice of Exercise to Landlord for responding to the ROFR Notice, except that Tenant shall have no such Right of First Refusal and Landlord need not provide Tenant with a ROFR Notice and any attempted exercise shall be void and of no effect, if:

(1) A Default shall have occurred and such Default shall not have been cured (a) at the time that Landlord would otherwise be obligated to give the ROFR Notice or, if such Default occurs after Tenant's attempted exercise of its Right of First Refusal, or (b) at the time of the proposed commencement of the lease of the First Refusal Space; or

(2) Any part of the Premises is sublet (other than as permitted under the Lease) at the time that Landlord would otherwise deliver the ROFR Notice; or

(3) Tenant has assigned the Lease (other than as permitted under the Lease) at the time that Landlord would otherwise deliver the ROFR Notice; or

(4) Tenant (or a Related Party or Affiliated Entity) is not occupying the Premises on the date that Landlord would otherwise deliver the ROFR Notice; or

(5) The existing tenant in the First Refusal Space is interested in extending or renewing its lease for the First Refusal Space or entering into a new lease for the First Refusal Space; or

(6) The original Term (or any Renewal Term, if applicable) shall have expired.

(b) Notwithstanding anything to the contrary contained herein, Tenant's Right of First Refusal is subject and subordinate to the rights and options of other parties (if any) with respect to the First Refusal Space predating this Lease. This section shall not preclude Landlord from extending a lease for an existing tenant in any portion of the First Refusal Space or entering into a new lease with a then existing Tenant in any portion of the First Refusal Space for such portion of the First Refusal space,

(c) Terms for First Refusal Space for Tenant's Right of First Refusal
   (i) If Tenant exercises its rights hereunder, the term for the First Refusal Space shall commence on the commencement date stated in the ROFR Notice and thereupon such First Refusal Space shall be considered part of the Premises, provided that all of the terms stated in the ROFR Notice shall govern Tenant's leasing of the First Refusal Space.
   (ii) Tenant shall pay Base Rent and Additional Rent for the First Refusal Space in accordance with the terms and conditions of the ROFR Notice.
   (iii) The First Refusal Space (including improvements and personalty, if any) shall be delivered in the condition provided in the ROFR Notice but otherwise accepted by Tenant in its condition and as-built configuration existing on the earlier of the date Tenant takes possession of the First Refusal Space or as of the date the term for such First Refusal Space commences, unless the ROFR Notice specifies any work to be performed by Landlord in the First Refusal Space, in which case Landlord shall perform such work in the First Refusal Space. If Landlord is delayed in delivering possession of the First Refusal Space due to the holdover or unlawful possession of such space by any party, Landlord shall use reasonable efforts to obtain possession of the space, and the commencement of the term for the First Refusal Space shall be postponed until the date Landlord delivers possession of the First Refusal Space to Tenant free from occupancy by any party in the condition described in the ROFR Notice.

(d) Termination of Right of First Refusal. The rights of Tenant hereunder with respect to the First Refusal Space and the ROFR Notice shall terminate on the earlier to occur of: (i) twenty-four (24) months prior to the Expiration Date (unless Tenant exercises a Renewal option); (ii) Tenant's failure to exercise its Right of First Refusal within the time frame provided in Paragraph 58(a) above; and (iii) the date Landlord would have provided Tenant a ROFR Notice should Tenant not have been in violation of one or more of the conditions set forth in Paragraph 58(a) above, if applicable.

(e) ROFR Amendment. If Tenant is entitled to and properly exercises its Right of First Refusal, Landlord shall prepare an amendment (the "ROFR Amendment") adding the First Refusal Space to the Premises on the terms set forth in the ROFR Notice and reflecting the changes in the Annual Base Rent, rentable square footage of the Premises, Tenant's Pro Rata Share and other applicable business terms. The ROFR Amendment shall be sent to Tenant within a reasonable time after Landlord's receipt of the Notice of Exercise executed by Tenant and Tenant shall execute

and return the ROFR Amendment to Landlord within fifteen (15) days after Tenant's receipt of same, but an otherwise valid exercise of the Right of First Refusal shall be fully effective whether or not the ROFR Amendment is executed.

58. Right of First Offer

(a) As used herein, "First Offer Space" shall mean any of space on the [NUMBER] floor[S] of the Building [that is contiguous to the Premises]. If any such First Offer Space not available for lease on the Commencement Date subsequently becomes available for lease to the general public and Landlord desires to lease same, Landlord shall first offer to lease the First Offer Space to Tenant, as set forth in a notice to Tenant ("First Offer Notice") which identifies the First Offer Space, describes the length of term, commencement date and all other material business terms acceptable to Landlord and Landlord shall offer to lease the First Offer Space to Tenant upon the business terms set forth in the First Offer Notice. Such terms shall represent Landlord's good faith estimate of fair market rental terms for such First Offer Space.

(b) Tenant shall have a period of ten (10) Business Days after receipt of the First Offer Notice to give to Landlord notice that Tenant (i) accepts Landlord's offer, or (ii) rejects Landlord's offer. Time shall be of the essence with respect to Tenant's notice, and Tenant's failure to give any such notice within the ten (10) Business Day period shall be deemed a rejection of Landlord's offer, any principles of law or equity to the contrary notwithstanding. A First Offer Notice may only be accepted in whole, not in part.

(c) If Tenant rejects, or is deemed to have rejected, Landlord's offer, Landlord shall be free to lease such First Offer Space to any party upon any terms and conditions that Landlord may determine from time to time during the Term, with no further obligation to Tenant under this Paragraph and this Paragraph 58 shall be automatically deemed null and void.

(d) Anything herein to the contrary notwithstanding, Landlord shall not be obligated to give a First Offer Notice, Tenant shall have no right to exercise its option to lease the First Offer Space, and any attempted exercise shall be void and of no effect, if: (i) the initial named Tenant herein has assigned the Lease or has at any time subleased any portion of the Premises; or (ii) a Default shall have occurred and such Default shall not have been cured at the time that Landlord would otherwise be obligated to give the First Offer Notice or, if such Default occurs after Tenant's attempted exercise of its option, at the time of the proposed commencement of the lease of the First Offer Space. Notwithstanding anything to the contrary contained herein, Tenant's Right of First Offer is subject and subordinate to the tenancies, rights and options of other parties (if any) predating this Lease.

(e) **This Paragraph 58 shall not preclude Landlord from extending a lease for an existing tenant of the First Offer Space or entering into a new lease with a then existing tenant of the First Offer Space for the First Offer Space or a portion thereof.**

(f) **If Tenant accepts the First Offer Notice, Landlord shall prepare an amendment (the "Offering Amendment") adding the First Offer Space to the Premises on the terms set forth in the First Offer Notice and reflecting the changes in Annual Base Rent, Tenant's Pro Rata Spare, and other appropriate terms. A copy of the Offering Amendment shall be sent to Tenant within a reasonable time after Landlord's receipt of Tenant's acceptance of the First Offer Notice and Tenant shall deliver to Landlord within fifteen (15) days thereafter the Offering Amendment executed by Tenant. In the event that Tenant fails to timely execute and deliver the Offering Amendment to Landlord, an otherwise valid exercise of the Right of First Offer shall be fully effective whether or not the Offering Amendment is executed.**

PARAGRAPH 59

Unilateral Tenant Option to Lease Additional Space

RISK RATING: 4

A. DESCRIPTION AND SCOPE

This Paragraph provides Tenant with the option to increase the area of the Premises. As opposed to a right of first refusal or a right of offer, an expansion option is a unilateral right of Tenant to expand the Premises at a determined time (or within a defined time period) within the Lease term.

B. ANALYSIS

1. Landlord's Perspective

This Paragraph protects Landlord against Tenant outgrowing the Premises and seeking to terminate the Lease in favor of a lease in a building better suited to its spatial needs. That said, Landlord should give such expansion right judiciously and, to the extent possible, tied to the timing of the expiration of a lease of an existing tenant in the space otherwise Landlord is at risk of having to hold space vacant until Tenant's option date expires. If Landlord has previously granted other tenants options for additional space, Landlord must be careful when choosing the potential additional space to accommodate the rights of other tenants. Landlord also wants the rental and other terms applicable to the lease of such space to be specifically identified. Options to Lease Additional Space have many of the same concerns and problems as Rights of First Refusal and Rights of First Offer. See Landlord's Perspective in Paragraph 58 for a more complete discussion of these issues.

2. Tenant's Perspective

This Paragraph provides Tenant with guaranteed flexibility against the possibility that it will outgrow the Premises during the Term. Tenant may want to specify the condition of the additional space and any Tenant Improvement Allowance that Tenant is to receive and the rental rate for the space. Tenant would prefer to fix the rent for the Additional Space (including rent at the same per square foot rate as the existing premises), rather than pay a market rent. If parking spaces are allocated, Tenant will want a proportional increase in the number of allocated parking spaces. For larger Tenants a series of expansion options with sequential exercise windows may be appropriate. If Landlord subordinates Tenant's expansion rights to any rights of existing tenants of the building or project, Tenant should endeavor to get Landlord to represent in the Lease what rights of existing tenants exist.

3. Lender's Perspective

A Lender wants the terms of the option to be clearly defined, and the time for the exercise of such option to be limited, so that Lender may analyze the present and potential income generated by the Project.

4. Broker's Perspective

Brokers play an instrumental role in negotiating the terms of Tenant expansion options. Tenant Broker will want to fully understand, during the needs assessment phase of its assignment, the Term flexibility needs of Tenant so Tenant Broker can negotiate required option(s) as the result thereof may play an instrumental part of Tenant's Building selection process. Any such Tenant Term flexibility needs should be well negotiated and memorialized in the final LOI.

Landlord Broker will want to understand what other tenants in the Building may have superior rights to any right being granted to Tenant under this Paragraph and whether granting such a unilateral right to Tenant may negatively impact the long-term leasing strategy developed between Landlord and Landlord's Broker. Tenant Broker should inquire regarding the details of tenant right superior to that of Tenant.

Both Brokers should review this Paragraph closely to confirm that it conforms to the agreed upon terms of the LOI. Brokers should also support legal counsel through the negotiation of this Paragraph.

Brokers will want to make sure their brokerage agreement provides for a commission payment in the event Tenant exercises its rights under this Paragraph.

C. COMPROMISES AND ALTERNATIVES

This provision is negotiated on an individual-deal basis, depending upon Tenant's projected need for additional space and its desire to maintain flexibility, and Landlord's ability to accommodate Tenant's projected needs.

D. COMMENTS

This Paragraph should set forth all of the terms of Tenant's option to lease additional space. Landlord wants the "window period" during which the option may be exercised to be limited so that Landlord has the flexibility to lease such space to other tenants. Landlord may wish to protect itself from failure to deliver the additional space if an existing tenant holds over and prevents Landlord from timely delivering the additional space after Tenant exercises its option.

If any particular Tenant unilateral right to lease additional space in the Building does not have specific and well defined terms as provided in Paragraph 59 below, then many of Landlord's and Tenant's perspectives, concerns and compromises contained in Paragraph 58 may be applicable to the expansion option being reviewed and Paragraph 58 should be reviewed for a more complete discussion of these issues.

E. TYPICAL PARAGRAPH

59. Option to Lease Additional Space. Provided that Tenant is not in Default of its obligations under this Lease, Tenant shall have the option (the "Option") during the period commencing on [DATE] and ending on [DATE] (the "Option Period") to lease [AMOUNT] rentable square feet of additional space on the [NUMBER] floor of the Building as more particularly described in Exhibit [X] hereto (the "Option Space"). The Annual Base Rent for the Option Space shall be $[AMOUNT] payable in monthly installments of $[AMOUNT] per month. The term of the Option Space shall be coterminous with the Term of the original Premises and shall end on the Expiration Date of the Lease, provided that to the extent this Lease permits Tenant to extend the Term, then the term of the Option Space shall also be extended.

Tenant must exercise the Option, if at all, by delivering written notice to Landlord of Tenant's exercise of the Option during the Option Period. Time shall be of the essence with respect to Tenant's exercise of the Option. Should Tenant exercise the Option, then the Option Space shall become part of the Premises and Annual Base Rent on the Option Space shall commence on [DATE]. Tenant shall accept the Option Space in an "as-is" "where-is" condition, and Landlord shall have no obligation to improve the Option Space.

PARAGRAPH 60

Option to Renew

RISK RATING: 3

A. DESCRIPTION AND SCOPE

This Paragraph sets forth Tenant's right to renew the Lease at a rental rate equal to the greater of the Annual Base Rent that Tenant is then paying or the fair-market rental value of the Premises as determined by Landlord.

B. ANALYSIS

1. Landlord's Perspective

Depending on Landlord's perspective regarding long-term market rental rates, Landlord may or may not agree to a renewal option. The rent that Tenant is willing to pay during the renewal term, if not fixed, should be a market rate. Landlord may want to have a "floor" to the market rate equal to the rental rate in the last year of the initial term of the Lease. If such an option is included in the Lease, Landlord will require that Tenant exercise its right to renew by a specific date (at least 6 months and possibly 12 months prior to the expiration of the initial Term) so that Landlord may find other tenants should Tenant elect not to renew. Renewal rights shift the power to Tenant to control space in the Building over time. In an effort to mitigate the power shift, Landlord may wish to condition Tenant's right to renew based upon the conditions provided in Paragraph 60(a).

2. Tenant's Perspective

The concept of an option to renew protects Tenant against being burdened with long-term commitments to space that it no longer requires or is unsuitable, while providing the flexibility to remain for a long period in space that is still needed and remains acceptable. If the rental for the option period is fixed, the provision also protects Tenant against the risks of an uncertain rent in the future. If a market rate rent is used, Tenant will want to participate in the selection of the market rate and/or an appraiser or use arbitration rather than having Landlord determine the market rental rate. In addition, Tenant may want the right to revoke the option to renew if it is not satisfied with the market rate although it may be difficult for Tenant to obtain such a right. Tenant may also desire to specify a Tenant Improvement Allowance. Tenant may also want to pay only a percentage of a market rent rate (e.g., 90%) to reflect the lower cost to Landlord of the renewal (e.g., no broker's fees, no down time, and lower Tenant Allowances to the extent they apply). Tenant may also want several sequential options to renew, for example, three 5-year renewal options.

3. Lender's Perspective

A Lender wants the ability to evaluate the income generated by the Lease during the Renewal Term.

4. Broker's Perspective

Brokers play an instrumental role in negotiating the terms of any Tenant option such as the option in this Paragraph. Tenant Broker will want to fully understand the Term flexibility needs of Tenant at the outset of their engagement so that they can negotiate for Tenant's required options as an instrumental part of Tenant's Building selection process. Any such Tenant Term flexibility needs should be well negotiated and memorialized in the final LOI.

Brokers will want to understand the nuances of how this Paragraph is negotiated so that they can capture the best possible terms and conditions within the LOI with respect to the renewal options, including whether any Annual Base Rent rate for the renewal term based upon fair rental value shall be subject to a "floor" or not.

Finally, Brokers want to make sure their brokerage agreement provides for a commission payment in the event Tenant exercises its rights under this Paragraph.

C. COMPROMISES AND ALTERNATIVES

If Landlord is unwilling to grant an option to renew, Tenant may propose that it be given a right of first refusal or right of first offer in the event that Landlord elects to re-let the Premises. This alternative gives both Landlord and Tenant the opportunity to assess current market rental rates.

Tenant should endeavor to remove any Annual Base Rent floor for the renewal term because it should not be allocated the risk of protecting Landlord from market fluctuations in the rental value of the Premises for the renewal term. Also, the definition of the fair rental value for the Premises for the renewal term should expressly include all relevant factors.

For Tenants paying Operating Expenses and Real Estate Taxes on a Base-Year Model, they may wish to update the Base Year for the renewal term. Also, Tenant may wish to try to negotiate a limited tenant improvement allowance for renewal terms so that they can "refresh" the Premises with at least fresh paint and carpeting.

Tenant should negotiate the conditions which Landlord endeavors to impose upon Tenant's option to renew. While it is fair that Tenant should not be in default under the Lease beyond any applicable notice and cure period on the date Tenant exercises its option, such condition should not apply on the first day of the renewal period. Tenant losing its renewal option is arguably too punitive as it can be exercised by Landlord for immaterial defaults. Landlord should seek its default protections in the Lease. Also, Tenant should be able to extend the Term provided it is for some significant portion of the Premises (60%) rather than the entire portion of the Premises. Tenant should not lose its option if it has sublet a portion of the Premises and is exercising its option with respect to the entire Premises. Finally, Tenant will want to be careful to extend its renewal rights to any affiliates or permitted successors of Tenant. If Tenant is purchased by or merges with another entity, it should not be at risk of losing its renewal rights.

D. COMMENTS

The parties should be aware that Lease provisions that state that the parties will agree to negotiate renewal terms in good faith may be deemed unenforceable in many states. Thus, a well-drafted renewal option clause should identify specifically all pertinent terms, including the rent to be paid during the extended Term.

Landlord and Tenant may expend significant energy negotiating the terms of Paragraph 60, but it is prudent for all parties to recognize, as they pick their battles of negotiation within the Lease, that the reality is that the original Term of the Lease is often renewed outside of the terms and conditions of Paragraph 60 and the dispute resolution process contained within Paragraph 60 to determine the Annual Base Rent for the renewal term is rarely, if ever, actually followed. What happens in practice, more typically, is that well before the deadline for Tenant to exercise its option under Paragraph 60, Tenant approaches Landlord to negotiate the terms of any renewal of the Lease. The parties then negotiate the renewal terms based upon market conditions and, nearly always, the parties finalize the terms of the renewal outside of the terms, conditions and processes contained within Paragraph 60. Paragraph 60 remains important, however, for the protection of Tenant against one risk. If there is a much larger tenant or otherwise more important tenant to Landlord within the Building (or shortly coming to the Building) and that tenants wants Tenant's Premises, Landlord may not act reasonably in a normal negotiation process outside of Paragraph 60 as it may actually be looking for Tenant to vacate the Premises. In that case, Tenant can force Landlord's hand and protect its right to the Premises for the renewal term by exercising its right in strict accordance with Paragraph 60.

Tenant may also wish to strike any "occupancy" requirement conditioning Tenant's right to exercise its renewal option (and really any other Tenant right under the Lease conditioned upon Tenant's occupancy) as we have experienced Tenants not "occupying" their Premises for significant periods of time in response to pandemics. Arguably any such traditional "occupancy" requirement as provided in the Paragraphs below have become antiquated by recent experiences and both Landlord and Tenant should reconsider the inclusion of such language.

E. TYPICAL PARAGRAPH

60. Option to Renew.

(a) Provided no Default has occurred and is continuing under this Lease at the time same is exercised, Tenant shall have a [one-time] option to renew the initial Lease term demised hereunder (hereinafter in this Paragraph 60, the "Original Term") for one (1) additional term of [(NUMBER)] years (the "Renewal Term"). Such Renewal Term, if exercised, would start on the next day following the last day of the Original Term, and end on the date which is the [(NUMBER)] anniversary of the last day of such Original Term. Such extension would be on the same terms and conditions as are set forth in (and are last applicable under) this Lease, except that, during such Renewal Term: (i) Tenant's Annual Base Rent shall be as provided in Paragraph 60 (b) immediately following; (ii) there shall be no fit-up or construction or other work or allowance or concessions relating to preparing the Premises for Tenant's occupancy; and (iii) there shall be no further option to renew. The exercise of such option to renew the Lease must be completed not later than the date which is twelve (12) months prior to the last day of the Original Term (time being of the essence). Tenant, if it wishes to exercise such option, must notify Landlord in writing that Tenant elects to renew for such [YEAR]-year Renewal Term, or be deemed to have waived Tenant's option to renew. Notwithstanding anything to the contrary contained in this Lease: (a) Tenant's option to renew shall apply only with respect to the entire Premises as then constituted, and not to a portion or portions of the Premises as then constituted; (b) if Tenant fails to properly and timely exercise its option to renew hereunder, said option shall be null and void; (c) Tenant's option to renew shall be limited to Initial Tenant (or any Affiliate of Initial Tenant succeeding to Initial Tenant's interest hereunder pursuant to the terms of this Lease) only, and shall not be transferred or assigned to any other party; and (d) Tenant must be in occupancy of the entire Premises, as then constituted under this Lease, at the time of the exercise of such option.

(b) The Annual Base Rent for the Renewal Term provided above shall be the greater of: [$AMOUNT] per rentable square foot of the Premises per year; or the annual "Fair Rental Value of the Premises" determined as follows: Upon Landlord's receipt of Tenant's timely notice of Tenant's election to renew and commencing on or about the start of the calendar month which is twelve (12) months before the end of the Original Term, Landlord and Tenant shall have a period of fifteen (15) days within which to enter into a written agreement fixing the annual rate of Base Rent for the Renewal Term at the greater of: [$AMOUNT] per rentable square foot of the Premises per year, or the Fair Rental Value of the Premises as of the Expiration Date, which Fair Rental Value of the Premises shall be based on the annual fair rental value for comparable, first-class commercial office space (including any available in the Building) on comparable terms and conditions in the [CITY, STATE] area as of such applicable date (Landlord and Tenant agreeing, however, that the Fair Rental Value of the Premises shall not be reduced due to the presence or lack of any vacancy periods, renewal commissions or fit-up contributions). If the parties agree in writing to the Annual Base Rent for the Premises for the Renewal Term within such fifteen (15) day period, the Annual Base Rent for the Renewal Term shall be governed by such agreement. If the parties are unable to agree on the Annual Base Rent for the Renewal Term, then such figure shall be determined as follows: Each party shall, within ten (10) days after the expiration of such fifteen (15) day period, appoint a reputable, independent, commercial MAI appraiser, commercial real estate broker or commercial real estate consultant, which, as to any such selected party, has had not less than ten (10) years' experience appraising and/or leasing comparable, first-class commercial properties in the [CITY, STATE], area (an "Advisor"). On the failure of either party to appoint such Advisor within ten (10) days after notification of the appointment by the other party, the person appointed as an Advisor shall appoint an advisor to represent the party who has not so appointed an Advisor. The two (2) Advisors appointed in either manner above provided shall then proceed to act to determine such figure equaling such Fair Rental Value of the Premises as of such applicable date, in accordance with the above definition. In the event of their inability to reach an agreement between them within ten (10) days, they shall, within ten (10) days, appoint a third similarly qualified Advisor who has had not less than ten (10) years' experience appraising comparable, first-class commercial properties in the [CITY, STATE], area. If the three (3) Advisors are then unable to reach an agreement within ten (10) days thereafter, the decision of the third Advisor shall determine such figure equaling such Fair Rental Value of the Premises,

in accordance with the above definition (which decision shall be made by the third Advisor picking one of the two such submitted figures by the other Advisor(s)). The final decision of the Advisors shall be delivered to the parties in writing not later than ten (10) months before the expiration of the Original Term (the "Decision Date"), time being of the essence. Landlord and Tenant agree to each pay the expenses and fees of their own Advisor and one-half (1/2) the expenses and fees of any third Advisor and to be bound by their final decision. Notwithstanding anything to the contrary contained herein, in no event shall the Annual Base Rent for the Renewal Term, however determined, be less than [$AMOUNT] per rentable square foot of the Premises per year.

(c) **If for any reason by the commencement of the Renewal Term, the Annual Base Rent for such period shall not have been finally determined, Tenant shall, until such determination, pay the Annual Base Rent at the annual rate of [$AMOUNT] per rentable square foot of the Premises per year. Upon such final determination, Tenant shall thereafter pay such Annual Base Rent for a rate which is based upon the Annual Base Rent for the Renewal Term as so determined and shall pay Landlord the balance, if any, which shall be owing for the period preceding such determination. Whenever the Annual Base Rent for the Renewal Term shall have been determined, the parties hereto, on request of either of them, shall enter into a Lease amendment setting forth the amount of the Annual Base Rent for the Renewal Term.**

PARAGRAPH 61

Early Termination Option

RISK RATING: 3

A. DESCRIPTION AND SCOPE

This Paragraph sets out the right of Tenant to terminate the Lease early upon advance notice to Landlord and the payment of a termination fee. This is not a typical Tenant right but is sometimes negotiated at the LOI stage of the transaction.

B. ANALYSIS

1. Landlord's Perspective

Landlord is concerned with any Tenant early termination option that Landlord obtains sufficient notice from Tenant prior to the early termination date so that Landlord has time to market the Premises for re-leasing. Also, Landlord will want to make sure that the amount of any termination fee is sufficient to at least permit Landlord to recoup its "up front" investment costs incurred with respect to the Lease (including, the unamortized brokerage fees, improvement costs, allowances paid, legal fees, etc.).

2. Tenant's Perspective

This Paragraph offers Tenant an additional exit strategy (beyond Tenant's typical subletting and assignment rights) if Tenant determines the Premises no longer meets its needs.

3. Lender's Perspective

Lender's Perspective is aligned with Landlord's Perspective above.

4. Broker's Perspective

Brokers play an instrumental role in negotiating the terms of any Tenant early termination option. Tenant Broker will want to fully understand the Term flexibility needs of Tenant at the outset of their engagement so that they can negotiate for Tenant's required options as an instrumental part of Tenant's Building selection process. Any such Tenant Term flexibility needs should be well negotiated and memorialized in the final LOI.

Brokers will want to understand the nuances of how this Paragraph is negotiated, as described below, so that they can capture the best possible terms and conditions within the LOI with respect to the option, including what costs are included in any termination fee. Both Brokers should review this Paragraph closely to confirm that it conforms to the agreed upon terms of the LOI. The Brokers should also support legal counsel through the negotiation of this Paragraph.

Finally, Brokers will want to understand how this option may impact their commission under their brokerage agreement.

C. COMPROMISES AND ALTERNATIVES

Instead of Tenant having a "one time right" to terminate the Lease as of a particular date, Tenant may have a "rolling" termination right after a particular date (usually the anniversary of a Rent Commencement Date) to terminate the Lease at any time upon substantial advance notice to Landlord.

If the actual amount of the termination fee can be calculated prior to the Effective Date, it is preferable for all parties to stipulate the amount to avoid any disagreement about the calculation later. Any interest factor used in the calculation of the Termination Fee may be negotiable.

If the termination fee cannot be determined by the Effective Date, Tenant may wish to modify Paragraph 61 by adding the last sentence to Paragraph 61 below:

> *At any time following the first (1st) anniversary of the Commencement Date, within thirty (30) days of Tenant's written request to Landlord, Landlord shall provide Tenant with the determination of the Termination Fee, as determined by Landlord in accordance with this Paragraph 61.*

Sometimes the Termination Fee is payable 50% at Tenant exercise with the remaining 50% being paid six (6) months later or at Lease termination.

D. COMMENTS

Tenant's notice obligation with respect to exercising its early termination right should be "time is of the essence."

E. TYPICAL PARAGRAPH

61. Early Termination Option. Tenant shall have the one time right to terminate the Lease as of the expiration of the [NUMBER] Lease Year, provided (a) Tenant is not in default under the terms of the Lease, and (b) Tenant provides Landlord with a minimum of [AMOUNT] months prior written notice of its exercise of this right (time being of the essence). In addition, in the event Tenant exercises this termination option, Tenant shall pay to Landlord at the time Tenant notifies Landlord of the exercise of its option a sum equal to the unamortized portion of (i) the initial Abated Base Rent, (ii) the amount of improvement Allowance paid to Tenant, (iii) the cost of Landlord's Work performed by Landlord, (iv) [AMOUNT] of months of Monthly Base Rent at the rate payable on the date of early termination, and (v) the brokerage commission and legal costs paid by Landlord on account of the Lease; all amortized (using a [AMOUNT%] interest factor) on a straight-line basis over the Term (collectively, the "Termination Fee").

PARAGRAPH 62

Storage Space

RISK RATING: 1

A. DESCRIPTION AND SCOPE

This Paragraph sets out the occasional agreement of Tenant to lease Storage Space from Landlord and the agreement of Landlord to lease Storage Space to Tenant during the Term. This Paragraph describes the location and square footage of the Storage Space and provides that Tenant will accept the Storage Space in its "as-is" condition. The monthly rent for the Storage Space is due on the first business day of every month during the Term.

B. ANALYSIS

1. Landlord's Perspective

Landlord is concerned with having a clear and accurate description of the Storage Space. Landlord is also concerned with having a clear and accurate statement of the rent for the Storage Space, stating exactly when each installment of rent is due. The provision of this Paragraph providing that Tenant takes the Storage Space in its "as-is" condition protects the Landlord from having to install shelving or otherwise prepare the storage space for use as a storage area.

2. Tenant's Perspective

Tenant is concerned with having a clear and accurate description of the Storage Space for space planning purposes. Tenant is also concerned with having a clear and accurate statement of the rent to be charged for the Storage Space, stating exactly when each installment of rent is due.

3. Lender's Perspective

Lender is concerned with preserving the cash flow generated by the Property that is, in part, produced through lease of Storage Space. This is the operative paragraph that binds Landlord and Tenant to the lease of Storage Space.

4. Broker's Perspective

Brokers play an instrumental role in negotiating the terms of any Tenant right to lease storage space. Tenant Broker will want to fully understand, during the needs assessment phase of its assignment, the storage space needs of Tenant so Tenant Broker can negotiate the required rights as such storage rights may play an instrumental part of Tenant's Building selection process. Any such Tenant storage needs should be well negotiated and memorialized in the final LOI. Landlord Broker will want to understand which other tenants in the Building have superior rights to any rights being granted to Tenant as Tenant Broker will likely request such information.

Brokers will want to endeavor to include any Rent attributable to the Storage Space in the Rent for the purposes of calculating their commission, however this may be difficult if Tenant has the right to terminate the Lease as to the Storage Space at any time.

C. COMPROMISES AND ALTERNATIVES

The Rent and improvements to the Storage Space are subject to negotiation.

To maintain flexibility, Landlord may wish to have any express right to relocate the storage space within the Building.

Likewise, Tenant may wish to achieve some flexibility, with a right to terminate the lease with respect to only the Storage Space at any time in order to cease incurring any additional expense with respect to storage space it no longer needs.

D. COMMENTS

The location of the Storage Space should be attached as an Exhibit.

Tenant should confirm and inspect what, if any, utilities and services will be provided to the storage space (i.e., electricity and/or HVAC) should the stored items be temperature sensitive.

E. TYPICAL PARAGRAPH

62. Storage Space. In addition to the Premises, Tenant agrees to lease from Landlord, and Landlord agrees to lease to Tenant during the Term, approximately [AMOUNT] rentable square feet of Storage Space (the "Storage Space") on the [NUMBER] floor. Tenant accepts the Storage Space in its "as-is" condition. The Storage Space shall be located as shown on Exhibit [X] attached hereto.

The monthly rent for the Storage Space shall be $[AMOUNT], computed as one-twelfth (1/12th) of the product of $[AMOUNT] multiplied by the total rentable square footage of the Storage Space. The monthly rent for the Storage Space shall be due on the first business day of each month during the Term on the same terms and conditions of Monthly Base Rent.

PARAGRAPH 63

Outside Business Installations

RISK RATING: 3

A. DESCRIPTION AND SCOPE

This Paragraph sets out any rights Landlord is willing to grant to Tenant for the installation of Tenant business equipment (such as supplemental HVAC systems, a generator or a satellite dish) located outside of the Premises.

B. ANALYSIS

1. Landlord's Perspective

Landlord recognizes that Tenant may need business equipment to be located on the Building roof or land adjacent to the Building in order to support Tenant's business operations from the Premises. Landlords are generally open to this on a reasonable basis, provided Tenant does not interfere with the operation of the Building or other tenants at the Building.

2. Tenant's Perspective

Tenant should identify, in advance of executing a Lease, any outside business equipment rights it may need and make sure they obtain express rights under the Lease to address their needs. Telecommunication needs may be essential to Tenant's business operations, and, if so, Tenant should assure that any needed Outside Business Installations cannot be altered or terminated by Landlord during the Term of the Lease.

3. Lender's Perspective

Lender's perspective is aligned with Landlord's Perspective above.

4. Broker's Perspective

Brokers play an instrumental role in negotiating the terms of any Outside Business Installations. Tenant Broker will want to fully understand, during the needs assessment phase of its assignment, the Outside Business Installation needs of Tenant so Tenant Broker can negotiate all required terms as such needs may play an instrumental part of Tenant's Building selection process. Any such Tenant needs should be well negotiated and memorialized in the final LOI. Landlord Broker will want to understand which other tenants in the Building have superior rights to any rights being granted to Tenant as Tenant Broker will likely request such information.

Brokers will want to understand the nuances of how this Paragraph is negotiated so that they can capture the best possible terms and conditions within the LOI with respect to the right, including whether Tenant will be charged a separate fee for the installation and use of business equipment located outside of the Premises.

Both Brokers should review this Paragraph closely to confirm that it conforms to the agreed upon terms of the LOI. Broker should also support legal counsel through the negotiation of this Paragraph.

C. COMPROMISES AND ALTERNATIVES

The Typical Paragraph was drafted to include supplemental HVAC, communication equipment, and a generator to be located on the roof of the Building. This should be revised accordingly to reflect Tenant's actual needs.

Note sometimes the equipment is located in areas other than the Building roof such as the Building's garage. In that case, Tenant is typically required to lose parking rights equivalent to the amount of parking spaces impacted.

Landlord sometimes elects to charge Tenant for the space used for Tenant's equipment.

D. COMMENTS

None.

E. TYPICAL PARAGRAPH

63. <u>Outside Business Installation</u>.

Subject to the terms and conditions contained herein, Tenant shall have the nonexclusive right to install, at its sole cost and expense, a commercially reasonable [supplemental HVAC, and/or two (2) commercially reasonable satellite and/or microwave dish or other communications device, and/or a generator] exclusively to service Tenant's business operations in the Building, along with such commercially reasonable roof-to-Premises cable routing in the Building's available conduits and/or available riser space as are necessary therefor (said equipment, together with such cable routing and conduits,

collectively constituting Tenant's supplemental equipment (collectively, the "Outside Business Installation"). The Outside Business Installation shall not, collectively, exceed [AMOUNT] square feet of space on the Building's roof. Such Outside Business Installation devices shall be permitted to remain and/or be installed, as the case may be, on the Building's rooftop during the duration of the Term and be connected to the Premises, provided that Tenant, at its cost and sole expense, satisfies all of the following conditions:

(a) Except as otherwise provided herein, there shall be no Additional Rent charge imposed by Landlord upon Tenant to lease space on the roof of the Building (the "Roof Space") for the purpose of operating and maintaining the presently existing Outside Business Installation devices. Landlord reserves the right, at Landlord's sole cost and expense, and upon reasonable advance notice to Tenant, to relocate the Roof Space during other than Building Service Hours as reasonably necessary during the Term provided such location meets line of sight requirements for the Outside Business Installation devices. Tenant shall be solely responsible for obtaining all necessary governmental and regulatory approvals and for the cost of operating, maintaining and removing the Outside Business Installation. If at any time Landlord, in its sole discretion, deems it necessary, Tenant shall provide and install, at Tenant's sole cost and expense, appropriate and reasonable aesthetic screening, reasonably satisfactory to Landlord, for the Outside Business Installation (the "Aesthetic Screening").

(b) Landlord agrees that Tenant and its employees, contractors and vendors, upon reasonable prior notice to Landlord, shall have access to the roof of the Building and the Roof Space for the purpose of maintaining, repairing and removing the Outside Business Installation, its appurtenances and installing, maintaining, repairing and removing the Aesthetic Screening, if any, all of which shall be performed by Tenant or Tenant's authorized representative or contractors, which shall be approved by Landlord, at Tenant's sole cost and risk. It is agreed, however, that only authorized engineers, employees or properly authorized contractors of Tenant, FCC (defined below) inspectors, or persons under their direct supervision will be permitted to have access to the roof of the Building and the Roof Space. Tenant further agrees to exercise control over the people requiring access to the roof of the Building and the Roof Space in order to keep to a minimum the number of people having access to the roof of the Building and the Roof Space and the frequency of their visits.

(c) It is further understood and agreed that the installation, maintenance, operation and removal of the Outside Business Installation, the appurtenances and the Aesthetic Screening, if any, is not permitted to damage the Building or the roof thereof, or interfere with the use of the Building and roof by Landlord. Tenant agrees to be responsible for any damage caused to the roof or any other part of the Building, which may be caused by Tenant or any of its agents or representatives.

(d) Tenant agrees to only operate equipment of types and frequencies which will not cause interference to Landlord or existing tenants of the Building. In the event Tenant's equipment causes such interference, Tenant will change the frequency on which it transmits and/or receives and take any other steps necessary to eliminate the interference. If any equipment on the roof interferes with Tenant's Outside Business Installation devices, Landlord shall cause the owner of such equipment to take steps necessary to eliminate such interference. If said interference within any equipment located on the roof as of the date hereof cannot be eliminated within a reasonable period of time, in the reasonable judgment of Landlord, then Tenant agrees to remove the Outside Business Installation from the Roof Space. If any interference with Tenant's Outside Business Installation devices caused by equipment installed on the roof from and after the date hereof cannot be eliminated within a reasonable period of time, in the reasonable judgment of Landlord, then Landlord shall remove or cause to be removed such equipment from the roof.

(e) Tenant shall, at its sole cost and expense, and at its sole risk, operate and maintain the Outside Business Installation in a good and workmanlike manner, and in compliance with all Building, electric, communication, and safety codes, ordinances, standards, regulations and requirements, now in effect or hereafter promulgated, of the Federal Government, including, without limitation and as applicable, the Federal Communications Commission (the "FCC"), the Federal Aviation Administration ("FAA") or any successor agency of either the FCC or FAA having jurisdiction over radio or telecommunications, and of the state, city and county in which the Building is located. Landlord and its agents assume no responsibility for the licensing, operation and/or maintenance of Tenant's equipment, as same shall be the sole responsibility of Tenant. Tenant has the responsibility of carrying out the terms of its FCC license in all respects, as applicable.

(f) The Outside Business Installation shall be connected to Landlord's power supply, at Tenant's expense, in strict compliance with all applicable Building, electrical, fire and safety codes. Neither Landlord nor its agents shall be liable to Tenant for any stoppages or shortages of electrical power furnished to the Outside Business Installation or the Roof Space because of any act, omission or requirement of the public utility serving the Building, or the act or omission of any other tenant, invitee or licensee or their respective agents, employees or contractors, or for any other cause beyond the reasonable control of Landlord, and, Tenant shall not be entitled to any rental abatement for any such stoppage or shortage of electrical power. Neither Landlord nor its agents shall have any responsibility or liability for the conduct or safety of any of Tenant's representatives, and repair, maintenance and engineering personnel, while in or on any part of the Building or the Roof Space. In the event that Tenant installs any Outside Business Installation Tenant shall, at its sole cost and expense, install separate electric meters to measure electrical consumption by the such Outside Business Installation(s) and pay when due all electricity charges reflected on such meters.

(g) The Outside Business Installation, the appurtenances and the Aesthetic Screening, if any, shall remain the personal property of Tenant, and shall be removed by Tenant at its sole expense at the expiration or earlier termination of the Lease or Tenant's right to possession hereunder. Tenant shall repair any damage caused by such removal, including the patching of any holes to match, as closely as possible, the color surrounding the area where the equipment and appurtenances were attached. Tenant agrees to maintain, at its sole expense, all of the Tenant's equipment placed on or about the roof or in any other part of the Building in proper operating condition and maintain same in satisfactory condition as to appearance and safety in Landlord's reasonable discretion. Such maintenance and operation shall be performed in a manner to avoid any interference with any other tenants or Landlord. Tenant agrees that at all times during the Term, it will keep the roof of the Building and the Roof Space free of all trash or waste materials produced by Tenant or Tenant's agents, employees or contractors.

(h) In light of the specialized nature of the Outside Business Installation, Tenant shall be permitted to utilize the services of its choice for operation, removal and repair of the Outside Business Installation, the appurtenances and the Aesthetic Screening, if any, subject to the approval of Landlord. Notwithstanding the foregoing, Tenant must provide Landlord with prior notice of any such installation, removal or repair and coordinate such work with Landlord in order to avoid voiding or otherwise adversely affecting any warranties granted to Landlord with respect to the roof. If necessary, Tenant, at its sole cost and expense, shall retain any contractor having a then existing warranty in effect on the roof to perform such work (to the extent that it involves the roof), or, at Tenant's option, to perform such work in conjunction with Tenant's contractor. In the event the Landlord contemplates roof repairs that could affect Tenant's Outside Business Installation, or which may result in an interruption of the Tenant's telecommunication service, Landlord shall formally notify Tenant at least thirty (30) days in advance (except in cases of an emergency) prior to the commencement of such contemplated work in order to allow Tenant to make other arrangements for such service.

(i) Tenant shall not allow any provider of telecommunication, video, data, or related services ("Communication Services") to locate any equipment on the roof of the Building or in the Roof Space for any purpose whatsoever unrelated to Tenant's business operations within the Premises, nor may Tenant use the Roof Space and/or Outside Business Installation to provide Communication Services to an unaffiliated tenant, occupant or licensee of another building, or to facilitate the provision of

Communication Services on behalf of another Communication Services provider to an unaffiliated tenant, occupant or licensee of the Building or any other building.

(j) Tenant acknowledges that Landlord may at some time require Tenant to enter into a License Agreement with respect to the use of roof space. Tenant, upon request of Landlord, shall enter into such License Agreement with Landlord provided that such agreement does not materially alter the rights or obligations of Tenant hereunder with respect to the Roof Space.

(k) Tenant specifically acknowledges and agrees that the terms and conditions of Paragraph 22 of the Lease (Indemnity and Waiver of Claims) shall apply with full force and effect to the Roof Space and any other portions of the roof accessed or utilized by Tenant, its representatives, agents, employees or contractors.

(l) If Tenant defaults under any of the terms and conditions of this Paragraph, and Tenant fails to cure said default within the time allowed by Paragraph [__] of the Lease, Landlord shall be permitted to exercise all remedies provided under the terms of the Lease, including removing the Outside Business Installation, the appurtenances and the Aesthetic Screening, if any, and restoring the Building and the Roof Space to the condition that existed prior to the installation of the Outside Business Installation, the appurtenances and the Aesthetic Screening, if any. If Landlord removes the Outside Business Installation, the appurtenances and the Aesthetic Screening, if any, as a result of an uncured default, Tenant shall be liable for all costs and expenses Landlord incurs in removing the Outside Business Installation, the appurtenances and the Aesthetic Screening, if any, and repairing any damage to the Building, the roof of the Building and the Roof Space caused by the installation, operation or maintenance of the Outside Business Installation, the appurtenances, and the Aesthetic Screening, if any.

PARAGRAPH 64

Miscellaneous

RISK RATING: 1

A. DESCRIPTION AND SCOPE

This Paragraph contains provisions that aid in the interpretation of the Lease and therefore minimize disputes between Landlord and Tenant and otherwise contains "miscellaneous" provisions to a Lease that typically require little-to-no negotiation.

B. ANALYSIS AND COMMENTS

The provisions below are presented in generally a balanced manner as between Landlord and Tenant and, therefore, only limited analysis and commentary is being included where reasonably warranted per particular provision of this Paragraph.
The contents of this Paragraph should be tailored to any individual lease.

Limited Analysis and Commentary:

Paragraph 69(a): Execution: Note that nearly all Lease documents (where land recording of the document is not required) typically now expressly permits both the electronic signature and the electronic delivery of documents. This concept was emerging in the years before the COVID-19 pandemic but has become a nearly universal standard in the wake of the pandemic as electronic signatures and electronic delivery allow for a more efficient document execution process.

Paragraph 69(c): Landlord's Consents and Approvals: The [bracketed and underscored language] in the proposed Paragraph is typically not in a first draft of a Lease prepared by Landlord but such language is fair and reasonable to be negotiated into the Lease by Tenant. If a Landlord pushes back on the proposed language, Tenant should explain that the "finally determined" words within the provision mean "finally determined by a court of law." If Landlord's actions are egregious enough for Tenant to seek legal action and a court finds that Landlord has acted "maliciously or capriciously, or in bad faith," Landlord should be responsible for monetary damages. The inclusion of the language is meant to incentivize Landlord to never act in such a manner.

Paragraph 69(l): OFAC: Tenant may wish a reciprocal paragraph from Landlord. If Landlord, Tenant or their respective parent companies are complex (such as REITS or funds) and/or large international companies, it would be prudent for Landlord and Tenant to make sure any representation given is narrowly drafted (as it is below). Some other versions of this Paragraph are drafted to extend beyond Landlord and Tenant to their parent entities and their respective owners, principals, partners, members, shareholders, related entities, etc. Making a representation this wide can be difficult and should be avoided when appropriate.

Paragraph 69(o): Tenant's Waiver: This Paragraph may not be in a first draft of a Lease prepared by Landlord but it is fair and reasonable for any Tenant to include it as it is a reciprocal provision to Paragraph (n).

Paragraph 69(p): Financial Statements: This Paragraph is "sample" and may or may not be included in a Lease. Tenants that are publicly traded companies may delete this Paragraph as their financial statements are publicly available and even if Tenant sublets or assigns the Lease, Tenant will remain primarily liable under the Lease. However, the provision is sometimes caveated to "spring up" if Tenant is no longer a publicly traded company. In other cases where Tenant is required to deliver financial statements during the Term, Tenant should try to limit (i) the frequency of delivery of such financial statements (such as no more than once annually or only if Tenant Defaults or only if Landlord is contemplating a sale or refinance of the Property, etc.), and (ii) the form of the financial statements. Sometimes the Paragraph requires "audited" financial statements and Tenant may not prepare their financial statements in that manner. In that case, Tenant may wish to say the form of any future financial statements shall be substantially similar to the form initially provided to Landlord at the outset of the Lease. Finally, Tenant may wish to condition their obligation to deliver financial statements upon Landlord first entering into a reasonable nondisclosure agreement with Tenant.

C. TYPICAL PARAGRAPH

69. Miscellaneous.

(a) Not Binding Until Execution; Execution. This Lease shall not be binding upon Landlord or Tenant unless and until Landlord and Tenant have each executed and unconditionally delivered a fully executed copy of this Lease to the other. This Lease may be executed in any number of counterparts, each of which shall be deemed an original, and all of such counterparts shall constitute one agreement. To facilitate execution of this Lease, the parties may electronically execute (including, without limitation, by DocuSign or PDF) and/or electronically exchange counterparts of the signature pages by e-mail or facsimile and e-mail or facsimile counterparts shall serve as originals.

(b) Survival. Tenant's liability for all items of Rent due under this Lease shall survive the Expiration Date.

(c) Landlord's Consents and Approvals. Tenant hereby waives any claim against Landlord which Tenant may have based upon any assertion that Landlord has unreasonably withheld or unreasonably delayed any consent or approval requested by Tenant (in respect of which Landlord agreed herein to not unreasonably withhold or delay such consent or approval), and Tenant agrees that its sole remedy shall be an action or proceeding to enforce the applicable provision or for specific performance, injunction or declaratory judgment, or an arbitration to the extent provided under the Lease. In the event of a determination that such consent or approval has been unreasonably withheld or delayed, the requested consent or approval shall be deemed to have been granted; however, Landlord shall have no liability to Tenant for its refusal or failure to give such consent or approval [(except to the extent that it is finally determined that Landlord maliciously or capriciously, or in bad faith, refused or failed to give such consent or approval)]. Tenant's sole remedy for Landlord's unreasonably withholding or delaying consent or approval shall be as provided in this Paragraph.

(d) Submission to Jurisdiction. Tenant (and any guarantor of Tenant's Lease obligations) hereby (a) irrevocably consents and submits to the jurisdiction of any federal, state, county, or municipal court sitting in the State of [STATE] in respect to any action or proceeding brought therein by Landlord against Tenant concerning any matters arising out of or in any way relating to this Lease; (b) irrevocably waives all objections as to venue and any and all rights it may have to set a change of venue with respect to any such action or proceeding; (c) agrees that the laws of the State of [STATE] shall govern in any such action or proceeding and waives any defense to any action or proceeding granted by the laws of any other country or jurisdiction unless such defense is also allowed by the laws of the State of [STATE]; and (d) agrees that any final judgment rendered against it in any such action or proceeding shall be conclusive and may be enforced in any other jurisdiction by suit on the judgment or in any other manner provided by law. Tenant further agrees that any action or proceeding by Tenant against Landlord in respect to any matters arising out of or in any way relating to this Lease shall be brought only in the State of [STATE] and County of [COUNTY].

(e) Captions. The captions are inserted herein only for reference and in no way define, limit, or describe the scope of this Lease or the intent of any provision hereof.

(f) Parties Bound. The covenants, conditions and agreements contained in this Lease shall bind and inure to the benefit of Landlord and Tenant and their respective legal representatives, successors, and, except as otherwise provided in this Lease, their assigns.

(g) Exhibits. All of the Exhibits attached hereto are incorporated in and made a part of this Lease, but, in the event of any inconsistency between the terms and provisions of this Lease and the terms and provisions of the Exhibits hereto, the terms and provisions of this Lease shall control.

(h) Divisibility. If any term, covenant, condition, or provision of this Lease, or the application thereof to any person or circumstance, shall ever be held to be invalid or unenforceable, then in each such event the remainder of this Lease or the application of such term, covenant, condition or provision to any other Person or any other circumstance (other than those as to which it shall be invalid or unenforceable) shall not be thereby affected, and each term, covenant, condition and provision hereof shall remain valid and enforceable to the fullest extent permitted by law.

(i) Waiver of Trial By Jury, Etc. THE RESPECTIVE PARTIES HERETO HEREBY WAIVE TO THE FULLEST EXTENT PERMITTED BY LAW, TRIAL BY JURY IN ANY ACTION, PROCEEDING OR COUNTERCLAIM BROUGHT BY EITHER OF SUCH PARTIES AGAINST THE OTHER ON ANY MATTERS WHATSOEVER ARISING OUT OF OR IN ANY WAY CONNECTED WITH THIS LEASE, THE RELATIONSHIP OF LANDLORD AND TENANT, TENANT'S USE OR OCCUPANCY OF THE DEMISED PREMISES, OR FOR THE ENFORCEMENT OF ANY REMEDY UNDER ANY STATUTE, EMERGENCY OR OTHERWISE. IF LANDLORD COMMENCES AGAINST TENANT ANY SUMMARY PROCEEDING OR OTHER ACTION TO RECOVER POSSESSION OF THE DEMISED PREMISES OR TO RECOVER ANY RENT, THEN TENANT SHALL NOT INTERPOSE ANY COUNTERCLAIM OF WHATEVER NATURE OR DESCRIPTION IN ANY SUCH PROCEEDING OR ACTION OTHER THAN COMPULSORY COUNTERCLAIMS.

(j) No Surrender. Tenant acknowledges that Landlord shall be deemed to have accepted a surrender of the Premises by Tenant only if Landlord executes and delivers to Tenant a written instrument providing therefor.

(k) Adjacent Excavation, Shoring. If an excavation shall be made upon land adjacent to the Premises, or shall be authorized to be made, Tenant shall, upon reasonable advance notice, afford to the Person causing or authorized to cause such excavation, license to enter upon the Demised Premises for the purpose of doing such work as said Person shall deem necessary to preserve the wall of the Building from injury or damage and to support the same by proper foundations without any claim for damages or indemnity against Landlord, or diminution or abatement of Rent, provided that Tenant shall continue to have access to the Premises and the Building.

(l) OFAC. Tenant represents, warrants, and covenants that Tenant is not (i) listed on the Specially Designated Nationals and Blocked Persons List maintained by the Office of Foreign Asset Control, Department of the Treasury ("OFAC") pursuant to Executive Order No. 13224, 66 Fed.

Reg. 49079 (Sept. 25, 2001) ("Order") and all applicable provisions of Title III of the USA Patriot Act (Public Law No. 107-56 (October 26, 2001)); (ii) listed on the Denied Persons List and Entity List maintained by the United States Department of Commerce; (iii) listed on the List of Terrorists and List of Disbarred Parties maintained by the United States Department of State; (iv) listed on any list or qualification of "Designated Nationals" as defined in the Cuban Assets Control Regulations, 31 C.F.R. Part 515; (v) listed on any other publicly available list of terrorists, terrorist organizations or narcotics traffickers maintained by the United States Department of State, the United States Department of Commerce or any other governmental authority or pursuant to the Order, the rules and regulations of OFAC (including without limitation the Trading with the Enemy Act, 50 U.S.C. App. 1-44; the International Emergency Economic Powers Act, 50 U.S.C. §§ 1701–06; the unrepealed provision of the Iraq Sanctions Act, Publ. L. No. 101–513; the United Nations Participation Act, 22 U.S.C. § 2349 as-9; The Cuban Democracy Act, 22 U.S.C. §§ 6001–10; The Cuban Liberty and Democratic Solidarity Act, 18 U.S.C. §§ 2332d and 233; and The Foreign Narcotic Kingpin Designation Act, Publ. L. No. 106–120 and 107–108, all as may be amended from time to time); or any other applicable requirements contained in any enabling legislation or other Executive Orders in respect of the Order (the Order and such other rules, regulations, legislation, or orders are collectively called the "Orders"); (vi) engaged in activities prohibited in the Orders; or (vii) (and has not been) convicted, pleaded nolo contendere, indicted, arraigned or custodially detained on charges involving money laundering or predicate crimes to money laundering, drug trafficking, terrorist-related activities, or other money laundering predicate crimes or in connection with the Bank Secrecy Act (21 U.S.C. §§ 5317 et seq.). Tenant further represents, warrants and covenants that Tenant shall conduct its business operations in compliance with the foregoing laws, rules, orders and regulations. Tenant hereby agrees to defend, indemnify, and hold harmless Landlord from and against any and all claims, damages, losses, risks, liabilities, and expenses (including attorney's fees and costs) arising from or related to any breach of the foregoing representations, warranties and covenants. The breach of any of the above representations, warranties and covenants in this Subparagraph (l) by Tenant shall be a Default under the Lease.

(m) Modifications in Writing. This Lease may not be changed, modified, terminated or discharged, in whole or in part, except by a writing, executed by the party against whom enforcement of the change, modification, termination, or discharge is to be sought.

(n) No Waiver by Landlord. Landlord's failure to seek redress for violation of, or to insist upon the strict performance of, any covenant or condition of this Lease, or any of the Rules and Regulations, shall not prevent a subsequent act, which would have originally constituted a violation of

the provisions of this Lease, from having all of the force and effect of an original violation of the provisions of this Lease. The receipt by Landlord of Rent with knowledge of the breach of any covenant of this Lease shall not be deemed a waiver of such breach. No provision of this Lease shall be deemed to have been waived by Landlord, unless such waiver is in writing signed by Landlord. No payment by Tenant or receipt by Landlord of a lesser amount than the Rent herein stipulated shall be deemed to be other than on account of the earlier stipulated Rent, or as Landlord may elect to apply same, nor shall any endorsement or statement on any check or any letter accompanying any check or payment of Rent be deemed an accord and satisfaction, and Landlord may accept such check or payment without prejudice to Landlord's right to recover the balance of such Rent or to pursue any other remedy provided in this Lease.

(o) No Waiver by Tenant. Tenant's failure to seek redress for violation of, or to insist upon the strict performance of, any covenant or condition of this Lease on Landlord's part to be performed, shall not be deemed a waiver of such breach or prevent a subsequent act which would have originally constituted a violation of the provisions of this Lease from having all of the force and effect of an original violation of the provisions of this Lease. The payment by Tenant of Rent or performance of any obligation of Tenant hereunder with knowledge of any breach by Landlord of any covenant of this Lease shall not be deemed a waiver of such breach, and payment of the same by Tenant shall be without prejudice to Tenant's right to pursue any applicable remedy against Landlord.

(p) Financial Statements. Upon written request by Landlord (but not more than once per calendar year unless Tenant is in default of this Lease beyond any applicable notice and cure period), Tenant shall furnish to Landlord the most recent annual consolidated financial statements of Tenant, and its consolidated subsidiaries, as at the end of the then prior fiscal year of Tenant in the same form as previously delivered to Landlord, which such financials shall be certified to Landlord as true, correct, and complete by the chief financial officer of Tenant or other authorized officer or manager of Tenant having financial responsibilities therefor.

Premises

RISK RATING: 4

A. DESCRIPTION AND SCOPE

Exhibit A invariably identifies the Premises. For office and retail leases wherein Tenant is just leasing a portion of the Building, Exhibit A typically identifies the Premises through a schematic depiction of the Premises. Further identification of the Building/Property is not usually necessary because the Building/Property is identified in the body of the Lease by street address and that is sufficient.

For corporate headquarters leases, big box retail leases or industrial leases wherein Tenant is a single occupant of the Property (and the Premises may even be the entirety of the Property), Exhibit A may identify the Premises through a metes and bounds legal description of the Land (if the Premises includes the Building and the Land) or through a survey of the Property (showing boundaries of the Land and the Building). Sometimes, as noted in Paragraph 2, Exhibit A will show the Premises (of the Building), and an additional Exhibit will be attached to the Lease to include the metes and bounds legal description of the property lines for the Land.

B. ANALYSIS

1. Landlord's Perspective

An accurate and readily understandable description of the Premises is a requirement for the enforceability of a Lease.

2. Tenant's Perspective

Tenant's Perspective is aligned with Landlord's Perspective.

3. Lender's Perspective

Lender's Perspective is aligned with Landlord's Perspective.

4. Broker's Perspective

If possible, it is helpful to have Exhibit A attached to the LOI but it can certainly be circulated later with the Lease.

C. COMPROMISES AND ALTERNATIVES

See Description and Scope above about how Exhibit A may take different forms for certain office, retail, and industrial leases.

D. COMMENTS

If a schematic is being used to identify the Premises, care should be taken to make sure the schematic shows the demising walls of the Premises and the placement of the Premises on the floor of the Building on which it is located. Improvements (or a "test fit") showing actual or proposed improvements to the Premises should not be included in Exhibit A as it may lead to confusion as to who is responsible for completing the improvements shown. Any such "test fit" depiction will likely be attached to the Lease as a separate Exhibit in connection with describing Landlord's Work (as further described in Part 1, Exhibit B) or Tenant's Work (as further described in Part 1, Exhibit C).

E. TYPICAL EXHIBIT

See next page for a "sample" of an Exhibit A (in schematic form) to be used when Tenant is taking a portion of a floor in a multi-tenanted office Building, sometimes further indicating the Premises by hatching and indicating that the Premises means the hatched area.

Exhibit A: Premises

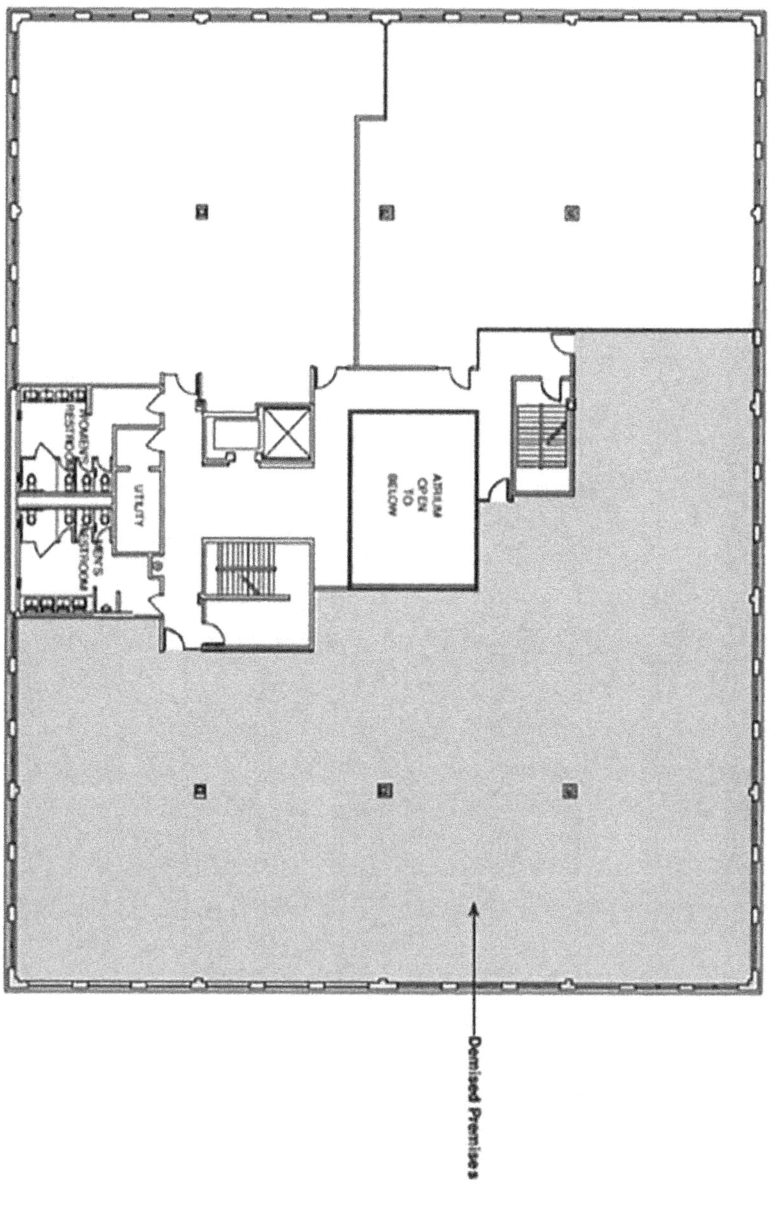

Floor 3

EXHIBIT B (ALTERNATIVE 1: LANDLORD PERFORMING LIMITED WORK FOR PREMISES DELIVERY)

Landlord's Work

RISK RATING: 2

A. DESCRIPTION AND SCOPE

Exhibit B identifies the improvements to be performed by Landlord, at Landlord's cost and expense, to the Premises (or, in some cases, to areas of the Building outside of the Premises) prior to Landlord's delivery of the Premises to Tenant ("Landlord's Work"). The scope of Landlord's Work may be limited or expansive depending upon the condition of the Premises on the Effective Date and Tenant's needs.

Exhibit B, Alternative 1 should be used when the Premises are in near deliverable condition and Landlord is obligated to perform only a very limited scope of work to get the Premises into the condition required under the Lease for delivery to Tenant. This is often the case when the Premises have been "pre-built" by Landlord for marketing purposes or when the existing improvements at the Premises (likely installed for a previous tenant) are suitable (or nearly suitable) for Tenant's needs, subject to Landlord completing a few minor construction items comprising Landlord's Work.

Alternatively, Exhibit B, Alternative 1 may also be used if Landlord has agreed to perform some work (potentially demolishing the existing improvements to the Premises or performing other work pertaining to the structure or systems of the Building), at its sole cost and expense, in order to prepare the Premises for delivery to Tenant so that Tenant may commence its own "build-out" of the Premises upon the completion of Landlord's Work.

B. ANALYSIS

1. Landlord's Perspective

Exhibit B is important because it sets forth all work that Landlord needs to complete in order for the Premises to be in the condition required under the Lease for delivery to Tenant.

When Landlord's Work is limited in scope, as it is in this Alternative 1, Landlord is likely funding the cost of Landlord's Work itself (versus using funds yet to be disbursed by the Lender) and, therefore, Landlord is not subject to or otherwise concerned with any terms and conditions of loan documents encumbering the Property.

2. Tenant's Perspective

Tenant should confirm that the definition or description of Landlord's Work accurately and sufficiently describes the entirety of the improvements Tenant is expecting Landlord to perform.

3. Lender's Perspective

Lender is likely not concerned with the terms and conditions of Exhibit B, Alternative 1, because the scope of Landlord's Work is limited and very likely being funded by Landlord itself. Also, if Lender succeeded to Landlord's position under the Lease prior to the completion of Landlord's Work, such limited work would likely not concern lender.

4. Broker's Perspective

Brokers will want to fully and accurately capture the scope of Landlord's Work in the LOI.

Note that what follows is applicable, in part, to Exhibit B, Alternatives 1 through 3 as well as Exhibit C (as applicable) but Broker's perspective is described in this Alternative 1 due to the order of the Alternatives and Exhibits and for efficiency. In all cases, Landlord Broker will need to have a clear understanding as to what condition of the Premises Landlord prefers to deliver the Premises to Tenant. Because some Landlords have related construction companies (which may be profit centers for Landlord) and/or may be sensitive as to who performs construction work in their Building, some Landlords prefer to control all or a portion (e.g., any work that may impact the Building structure or Building systems) of any initial alterations required to prepare the Premises for Tenant's initial occupancy. Other Landlords prefer not to perform any construction work but may require Landlord oversight or administration of any Tenant work and may charge Tenant a fee for same. Landlord Broker should negotiate the LOI with all of these Landlord preferences and requirements in mind. In either case, Landlord Broker should know whether Landlord maintains a written set of "Building-standard" materials, fixtures, and finishes that Landlord will construct the Premises to or require Tenant to adhere to if Tenant is performing the initial alterations to the Premises.

Tenant Broker will want to fully understand, during the needs assessment phase of its assignment, Tenant's preferences with respect to the condition of the Premises at delivery to Tenant (e.g., does Tenant prefer an existing "pre-built" space, prefer for Landlord to perform all or any portion of the necessary initial build-out of the Premises or prefer to design and build out the Premises itself). Should Tenant wish for Landlord to perform all initial alterations to the Premises, will Tenant want the space delivered "turnkey" (i.e., by Landlord with no cost exposure to Tenant) or with Landlord funding a portion of the work (either to a defined "Building-standard" or to a monetary cap of Landlord's investment (typically expressed on a dollar amount on a per rentable square foot basis of the Premises) with Tenant investing its own capital to the extent Tenant desires for the Premises to be constructed above "Building standard" or otherwise. Should Tenant wish to build out the Premises, Tenant Broker should inquire how Tenant prefers to finance the construction (e.g., entirely or partly through an allowance provided by Landlord and/or entirely or partly through a Tenant funded capital investment or some mixture of the two). It is, of course, very important that Tenant Broker include all relevant costs that will be attributable to Tenant for the initial construction of the Premises in its financial projections of the Lease so the same is understood by Tenant before a Lease draft is even requested.

The amount of any Tenant allowance, the cost of any Landlord's Work, the amount of any Tenant contribution toward the cost of Landlord Work and/or the cost of any Tenant initial work to prepare the Premises for Tenant's initial occupancy (performed in lieu of Landlord) will directly impact the amount of Annual Base Rent agreed to by the parties so both Brokers will need to define these amounts with as much specificity as possible and it is advisable that both Brokers work with Landlord's or Tenant's design and construction team, as applicable, in order to best understand both the known and estimated construction costs. To the extent possible, Brokers should help facilitate their respective clients closing or narrowing any estimated cost exposure through the preparation and bidding of design plans prior to Lease execution.

Brokers should will want to understand the particular nuances of Exhibit B, Alternatives 1 through 3 as well as Exhibit C so that they can capture the best possible terms and conditions in the LOI for their respective clients. Of course, both Brokers will then want to review the applicable Exhibits to the Lease to carefully confirm that terms and conditions therein conform to what the parties agreed to in the LOI.

Lastly, Brokers often act as liaisons between Landlord and Tenant's respective design and construction teams and should expect to actively support legal counsel (and legal counsel should actively include the Brokers) during the negotiation of all of the terms and conditions of the applicable Exhibit.

C. COMPROMISES AND ALTERNATIVES

Landlord's Work when limited in scope, as it is in this Alternative 1, is typically completed prior to the Commencement Date (i.e., the date exclusive possession of the Premises is delivered to Tenant) but sometimes the parties negotiate that Landlord's Work and any Tenant's work (i.e., the Initial Alterations covered in Exhibit_C, if applicable) will be performed simultaneously following the Commencement Date. This happens most often when Tenant is time pressured to accept delivery of the Premises to either start operating its business in the Premises or to start construction of its

Initial Alterations and, in either case, is not concerned about interruption from Landlord's Work due to its limited scope. When this is the case, Exhibit B may be revised to provide:

> *Landlord, at its sole cost and expense, shall install into the Premises, simultaneously during the construction of the Initial Alterations, the following work . . .*

There is little for Tenant to negotiate in this Alternative of Exhibit B because Landlord's Work is limited and straightforward, provided, however, that Tenant has confirmed that the description of Landlord's Work accurately and sufficiently describes the entirety of the improvements Tenant is expecting Landlord to perform.

D. COMMENTS

Note that this version of Exhibit B is meant only to define Landlord's Work. The issues surrounding the timing of the completion of the Landlord's Work and how completion of Landlord's Work interplays with the Commencement Date, are covered in Part 1, Paragraph 5.

E. TYPICAL EXHIBIT

See next page for a "sample" of an Exhibit B, Alternative 1.

Exhibit B (Alternative 1): Landlord's Work

Prior to the Commencement Date, Landlord, at Landlord's sole cost and expense, shall complete the following work at the Premises (collectively, "Landlord's Work"):

[DRAFTING NOTE: THE FOLLOWING IS FOR EXAMPLE PURPOSES ONLY]

(1) replace the seven (7) stained ceiling tiles with new ceiling tiles matching the rest of the ceiling tiles in the Premises;
(2) paint all interior walls of the Premises with Building-standard white paint; and
(3) professionally clean the carpet located within the Premises.

EXHIBIT B (ALTERNATIVE 2: LANDLORD DELIVERING PREMISES "TURNKEY")

Landlord's Work

RISK RATING: 4

A. DESCRIPTION AND SCOPE

Exhibit B identifies the work or improvements to be performed by Landlord, at Landlord's cost and expense, to the Premises prior to Landlord's delivery of the Premises to Tenant ("Landlord's Work").

Exhibit B, Alternative 2 is used when Landlord is delivering the Premises to Tenant on a "Turnkey" basis meaning that Landlord is performing all of the improvements to the Premises (although often not Tenant equipment and furniture installation) necessary for Tenant's initial occupancy of the Premises. The sample Exhibit B, Alternative 2 attached assumes that certain "Plans" and "Building-Standard methods, materials and finishes" defining Landlord's Work have been agreed to by parties prior to Lease execution and are attached to the Lease, at Lease execution, as Exhibit B-1 and Exhibit B-2, respectively. If plans and specifications are not expected to be agreed to until after Lease execution, the attached sample can be revised with the applicable language and concepts contained in Exhibit B, Alternative 3.

Typically, all costs associated with Landlord's Work made on a "Turnkey" basis are paid by Landlord except for costs attributable to any "Extra Work" and "Change Orders" if same are permitted and requested by Tenant, as further described in the sample Exhibit B, Alternative 2 attached. When Landlord's liability for the cost of Landlord's Work are subject to a "cap" with Tenant paying any excess costs above the "cap," Exhibit B, Alternative 3 should be used instead of this Exhibit B, Alternative 2.

Note that while Landlord is responsible for Landlord's Work (i.e., the improvements to the Premises), the attached sample contemplates that Tenant shall be solely responsible for the installation into the Premises of furniture, security system, IT wiring, telephone installation, other computer and communication equipment, and all business equipment ("Tenant's Installations"). Tenant is nearly always responsible for the installation of Tenant's Installations, as these are not "improvements" to the Premises.

B. ANALYSIS

1. Landlord's Perspective

Landlord is interested in ensuring that the scope of Landlord's Work, including the fixtures, materials, and finishes are sufficiently defined to avoid dispute with Tenant over whether Landlord has Substantially Completed Landlord's Work.

If Landlord is funding all or a portion of the cost of Landlord's Work through Lender disbursed funds, Landlord will want to confirm that Landlord strictly conforms to the construction requirements under the loan documents.

Landlord will want the Rent Commencement Date accelerated for each day the Substantial Completion of Landlord's Work is delayed due to a Tenant Delay.

2. Tenant's Perspective

Tenant's Perspective is aligned with Landlord's Perspective in terms of the importance of confirming that the definition or description of Landlord's Work accurately and sufficiently describes the entirety of the improvements Tenant is expecting Landlord to perform.

In any "Turnkey" build-out, Tenant is typically not anticipating that it will expend much money in advance of the Commencement Date, so it not overly concerned about whether Landlord has the funds to complete Landlord's Work. Tenant will likely have protected itself against such an event through abatement and termination rights under Part 1, Paragraph 5 in the event that Landlord fails to Substantially Complete Landlord's Work by a date certain and this is typically enough protection for Tenant.

Tenant will want some protections against any Landlord right to accelerate the Rent Commencement Date due to Tenant Delays.

3. Lender's Perspective

Lender's perspective will vary depending upon whether Landlord is performing Landlord's Work with funds provided by Landlord (in which case it will not be overly concerned) or with funds to be disbursed by Lender to Landlord under applicable loan documents. In the event of the latter, Lender will want all required documentation and processes required under the loan documents to be strictly followed by Landlord.

Lender will want to protect against being obligated to complete Landlord's Work in the event Lender succeeds to the position of Landlord under the Lease prior to Landlord's Work being completed. Lender may insist on protective language in the Subordination Paragraph in the Lease or in any SNDA entered into by the parties. If Tenant has appropriately negotiated rights into Part 1, Paragraph 5, it will not be concerned with Lender's Perspective because Tenant will have the right to terminate the Lease if Landlord's Work is not Substantially Completed within the negotiated time period.

4. Broker's Perspective

See Broker's Perspective to Exhibit B, Alternative 1 for insight and guidance. Such section is not repeated here only for sustainability and efficiency purposes.

C. COMPROMISES AND ALTERNATIVES

In any "Turnkey" Lease, Landlord's Work is universally performed prior to the Commencement Date as delivery of exclusive possession of the Premises to Tenant with Landlord's Work Substantially Completed is typically the triggering event to the Commencement Date.

The attached sample Exhibit B is drafted in a Landlord favorable manner. Below are concepts/provisions that Tenant may wish to try to include in any Exhibit B similar to the sample attached.

> *Performance Standards: Said Landlord's Work shall be performed promptly and diligently until completion, by supervised, experienced personnel. Said Landlord's Work shall be performed in a first-class manner as to workmanship, installation, and materials, and in accordance with [Exhibit B-1 (Plans) and Exhibit B-2 (Material, Fixture and Finish Specifications). Landlord shall perform Landlord's Work in compliance with all applicable federal, state and local laws, codes, statutes, ordinances, guidelines, rules, and regulations.*
>
> *Change Orders: Tenant shall have the right to make change orders to said approved plans, upon Landlord's prior written consent, which consent shall not be unreasonably withheld, conditioned, or delayed. Landlord shall provide Tenant with the details of any and all resulting cost increases and/or time delays associated with said change orders upon approving same.*
>
> *Claimed Delays: During the course of construction, Landlord shall keep Tenant duly apprised of the progress of Landlord's Work and any claimed delays, including Tenant Delays. No act or omission of Tenant shall be deemed a Tenant Delay unless Landlord notifies Tenant of such claimed Tenant Delay and Tenant does not cure the act or omission giving rise to such claimed Tenant Delay within two (2) business days of notice of such claimed Tenant Delay; provided, however, no notice and cure period shall be applicable to any failure of Tenant to meet an express time obligation contained in Exhibit B. Also, Landlord shall be deemed to have waived the right to claim a Tenant delay if Landlord does not notify Tenant of any claimed Tenant Delay within two (2) business days of the action or omission giving rise to such Tenant Delay.*
>
> *Warranty: Landlord hereby warrants and represents that Landlord's Work shall be free from defects in workmanship, installation and materials for a period of one (1) year from the Commencement Date, and Landlord, at its sole cost and expense, shall promptly perform any corrective work arising from said warranty.*
>
> *Punch-list Period. Within sixty (60) days after the Commencement Date, Tenant shall have the right to submit to Landlord a "punch list" of any Landlord's Work items which need to be finished or corrected, and Landlord, at its sole cost and expense, shall promptly complete and/or correct same.*
>
> *Substantial Completion. Notwithstanding anything to the contrary contained herein, Landlord's Work shall not be deemed "Substantially Completed" unless and until it meets*

> *the definition under this Exhibit B and a final and unconditional certificate of occupancy permitting lawful occupancy has been duly issued for the Premises such that Tenant may reasonably commence its business operations therein.*

If any "Turnkey" provision or Work Letter attached to the Lease does not include an early access right for Tenant to install Tenant's Alterations, then Tenant should propose language similar to the language already included in Exhibit B, Alternatives 2 and 3.

D. COMMENTS

Note that this Exhibit B is limited to describing Landlord's Work and the construction process. The issues surrounding the timing of the completion of the Landlord's Work and how completion of Landlord's Work interplays with the Commencement Date, are covered in Part 1, Paragraph 5.

E. TYPICAL PARAGRAPH

See next page for a "sample" of an Exhibit B, Alternative 2.

Exhibit B (Alternative 2): Landlord's Work

1. As used herein, "Landlord's Work" shall mean the work described in the plans attached hereto as Exhibit "B-1" (the "Plans"). Landlord's Work shall be performed by a general contractor selected by Landlord (the "General Contractor") using Building-Standard methods, materials and finishes and in accordance with Exhibit "B-2." It is agreed that the cost of the design, engineering, permitting, and construction of Landlord's Work (collectively, "Work Cost") shall be paid for by Landlord except as otherwise expressly provided herein. Any work requested by Tenant that deviates from either the Building-Standard methods, materials, and finishes and/or the Plans shall be deemed "Extra Work" and, subject to Landlord's reasonable consent thereto, shall be performed by Landlord in connection with Landlord's Work but shall paid for by Tenant within thirty (30) days upon invoice therefor by Landlord. Landlord's Work shall be performed in a good and workmanlike manner in accordance with all applicable legal requirements.
2. Landlord and Tenant agree to cooperate with each other in order to enable Landlord's Work and Tenant Installations (as hereinafter defined) to be performed in a timely manner. Notwithstanding anything herein to the contrary, any delay in the completion of Landlord's Work or inconvenience suffered by Tenant during the performance of Landlord's Work due to a Tenant Delay shall not delay the Commencement Date nor shall it subject Landlord to any liability for any loss or damage resulting therefrom or entitle Tenant to any credit, abatement, or adjustment of Rent or other sums payable under the Lease.

   The term "Tenant Delay" shall mean any actual delay in the performance of Landlord's Work directly by reason of any act, neglect, failure, or omission of Tenant, its agents, servants, employees, contractors, or subcontractors, or in the performance of Tenant's obligations under this Exhibit or this Lease, including, but not limited to:

   (i) Any actual delay due to Tenant's failure to meet any scheduled items in this Exhibit;
   (ii) Any actual delay due to Extra Work or Tenant's Installations: or
   (iii) Any actual delay due to Tenant's actions or omissions.

Notwithstanding anything to the contrary contained in this Lease, for each one (1) day of a Tenant Delay, the Rent Commencement Date shall be accelerated one (1) day (resulting in one (1) day of Base Rent abatement being lost for each day of Tenant Delay).

3. (a) Tenant shall be solely responsible for the installation into the Premises of furniture, security system, IT wiring, telephone installation, other computer and communication equipment and all business equipment ("<u>Tenant's Installations</u>"). Landlord agrees to afford Tenant reasonable access to the Premises and the Building following execution of the Lease but prior to the Commencement Date for the purpose of making inspections, taking measurements and making Tenant's Installations (all of which are to be paid for by Tenant), provided that such Tenant's Installations will not require any structural changes, and further provided that the construction of the Landlord Work and all installations required to be made by the Landlord therein shall have reached a point which in Landlord's sole but reasonable judgment, exercised in good faith, will not delay or hamper Landlord in the completion of the Landlord Work. This Paragraph shall permit Tenant to make only installations or improvements in the Premises, prior to the Commencement Date, which do not unreasonably interfere with, or delay, the Substantial Completion of the Landlord's Work. All of the Tenant's Installations shall be installed and completed in accordance with applicable Requirements. Tenant shall have the right to select telecommunication service providers from those providers already serving the Building, in Tenant's sole discretion, provided that service provider connection, installation and use shall be at Tenant's sole cost and expense. Tenant may not bring new telecommunication service providers to the Building without Landlord's prior written consent.

(b) Prior to the commencement of Tenant's Installations, Tenant shall submit to Landlord complete detailed plans and specifications thereof for Landlord's prior written approval, which approval shall not be unreasonably withheld, conditioned, or delayed.

(c) Any entry by Tenant in or on the Premises shall be at Tenant's sole risk and upon request of Landlord, Tenant, or its contractors, shall pay for and deliver to Landlord, certificates of insurance (except for worker's compensation) in amounts and with such companies as otherwise required pursuant to the Lease.

(d) All Tenant's Installations shall be in accordance with applicable laws, and shall not conflict with or be in violation of, or cause any violation of Landlord's basic building plans and/or the construction of the Building, and all Tenant's Installations shall be completed free of all liens and encumbrances. All permits which may be required by Tenant for Tenant's Installations shall be procured and paid for by Tenant only after having obtained Landlord's written approval of such work. No plans and/or specifications required to be filed by Tenant pursuant to any work contemplated to be performed by it within the Premises shall be filed or submitted to any governmental authority having jurisdiction thereover without first having obtained Landlord's approval to the same not to be unreasonably withheld.

(e) Notwithstanding anything to the contrary contained hereinabove, Landlord reserves the right to deny Tenant or its contractor access to the Premises and/or to request Tenant to withdraw therefrom and cease all work being performed by it or on its behalf by any person, firm or corporation other than Landlord, if Landlord shall, in its sole but reasonable judgment, to be exercised in good faith, determine that the commencement and/or the continuance of Tenant's Installations shall interfere with, hamper or prevent Landlord from proceeding with the completion of Landlord's Work.

(f) Tenant agrees that should Tenant enter upon the Premises for the purposes of performing any work, the labor employed by Tenant or anyone performing such work for or on behalf of Tenant shall always be harmonious and compatible with the labor employed by Landlord or any contractors or subcontractors of Landlord. Should such labor be incompatible with such Landlord's labor as shall be determined by the reasonable judgment of Landlord to be exercised in good faith, Landlord may require Tenant to withdraw from the Premises until the completion of the Building or Premises by Landlord. Notwithstanding the foregoing, in no event shall Tenant be required to utilize union labor.

(g) Any costs for services incurred or repairs required due to Tenant's contractors or Tenant's Installations shall be paid for by Tenant.

4. This Exhibit shall not be deemed applicable to any additional space added to the Premises at any time or from time to time, whether by any options under the Lease or otherwise, or to any portion of the original Premises or any additions to the Premises in the event of a renewal or extension of the original Term of the Lease, whether by any options under the Lease or otherwise, unless expressly so provided in the Lease or any amendment or supplement to the Lease.

5. As used herein, "Substantial Completion" or "Substantially Completed" or words of similar import shall mean that the applicable work has been substantially completed, it being agreed that such work shall be deemed substantially completed notwithstanding that minor or insubstantial details or construction or demolition and/or mechanical adjustment and/or decorative items remain to be performed.

EXHIBIT B (ALTERNATIVE 3: LANDLORD PERFORMING LANDLORD'S WORK SUBJECT TO COST CAP)

Landlord's Work

RISK RATING: 5

A. DESCRIPTION AND SCOPE

Exhibit B identifies the work or improvements to be performed by Landlord to the Premises prior to Landlord's delivery of the Premises to Tenant ("Landlord's Work"). Exhibit B, Alternative 3 is used when Landlord's liability for the cost of Landlord's Work is capped with Tenant being responsible for the cost of Landlord's Work in excess of the "cap." The sample Exhibit B, Alternative 3 attached assumes only preliminary plans for Landlord's Work will be available and attached to the Lease at Lease execution and that final construction drawings and the budget for Landlord's Work will be developed after the Effective Date.

Given the complexities described above, Alternative 3 is more detailed and more highly negotiated than Alternatives 1 and 2.

Note that while Landlord is responsible for Landlord's Work (i.e., the improvements to the Premises), the attached sample contemplates that Tenant shall be solely responsible for the installation into the Premises of furniture, security system, IT wiring, telephone installation, other computer and communication equipment, and all business equipment ("Tenant's Installations"). Tenant is nearly always responsible for the installation of Tenant's Installations as these are not "improvements" to the Premises.

B. ANALYSIS

1. Landlord's Perspective

With respect to this Exhibit B, Alternative 3, Landlord has both timing and funding concerns with respect to the completion of Landlord's Work because both completion of the design and construction of Landlord's Work will be partly dependent on Tenant meeting its timing and monetary obligations under this Exhibit.

If the portion of the cost of Landlord's Work that Landlord is responsible for paying (i.e., the portion up to the "cap") is partly or entirely being funded through Lender disbursed funds, Landlord will want to confirm that it strictly conforms to the construction and funding requirements under the loan documents.

Landlord will want the Rent Commencement Date accelerated for each day the Substantial Completion of Landlord's Work is delayed due to a Tenant Delay.

2. Tenant's Perspective

With respect to this Exhibit B, Alternative 3, Tenant has an interest in participating in the bidding and budget approval process as Tenant is responsible for the cost of Landlord's Work in excess of the "cap."

If Tenant expects to expend significant funds in excess of the "cap" and is required to deliver those funds prior to Landlord's Work being Substantially Completed, then it will be interested in having additional remedies if Landlord fails to Substantially Complete Landlord's Work because the remedies of additional rent abatement and Tenant Lease termination provided in Part 1, Paragraph 5 will be insufficient to address Tenant's risks as it is unlikely that any Tenant would exercise a termination option for late or failed completion and delivery of the Premises if Tenant stands to walk away from funds it has delivered toward completion of Landlord's Work.

Tenant will want some protections against any Landlord right to accelerate the Rent Commencement Date due to Tenant Delays.

Depending upon the amount of money Tenant may be contributing to the cost of Landlord's Work, Tenant may also seek written protections from Lender, under a SNDA, expressly recognizing any remedies that Tenant is successfully able to achieve in negotiating this Exhibit B.

3. Lender's Perspective

Lender's perspective will vary depending upon whether Landlord is performing Landlord's Work with funds provided by Landlord (in which case it will not be overly concerned) or with funds to be disbursed by Lender to Landlord under applicable loan documents. In the event of the latter, Lender will want all required documentation and processes required under the loan documents to be strictly followed by Landlord.

Lender will want to protect against being obligated to complete Landlord's Work in the event Lender succeeds to the position of Landlord under the Lease prior to Landlord's Work being completed. Lender may insist on protective language in the Subordination Paragraph in the Lease or in any SNDA entered into by the parties. If the facts indicate that Tenant will be expending significant sums toward the cost of Landlord's Work, Lender and Tenant will likely hotly negotiate the SNDA, with Lender likely ultimately yielding to Tenant if the lease will provide a meaningful rent stream benefiting Lender or otherwise significantly increase the value of the Property.

4. Broker's Perspective

See Broker's Perspective to Exhibit B, Alternative 1 for insight and guidance. Such section is not repeated here only for sustainability and efficiency purposes.

In addition, the Brokers will want to fully and accurately capture the scope of Landlord's Work in the LOI and the amount of any "cap."

C. COMPROMISES AND ALTERNATIVES

In Exhibit B, Alternative 3, Landlord's Work is universally performed prior to the Commencement Date as delivery of exclusive possession of the Premises to Tenant with Landlord's Work Substantially Completed is typically the triggering event to the Commencement Date.

The attached sample Exhibit B is drafted in a Landlord favorable manner. Below are concepts/provisions that Tenant may wish to try to include in any Exhibit B similar to the sample attached.

> *Performance Standards: Said Landlord's Work shall be performed promptly and diligently until completion, by supervised, experienced personnel. Said Landlord's Work shall be performed in a first-class manner as to workmanship, installation, and materials, and in accordance with the approved Plans and the Approved Budget, subject to approved Change Order. Landlord shall perform Landlord's Work in compliance with all applicable federal state and local laws, codes, statutes, ordinances, guidelines, rules, and regulations.*

> *Claimed Delays and Tenant Delays: During the course of construction, Landlord shall keep Tenant duly apprised of the progress of Landlord's Work and any claimed delays, including Tenant Delays.*

> *No act or omission of Tenant shall be deemed a Tenant Delay unless Landlord notifies Tenant of such claimed Tenant Delay and Tenant does not cure the act or omission giving rise to such claimed Tenant Delay within two (2) business days of notice of such claimed Tenant Delay; provided, however, no notice and cure period shall be applicable to any failure of Tenant to meet an express time obligation contained in Exhibit B. Also, Landlord shall be deemed to have waived the right to claim a Tenant delay if Landlord does not notify Tenant of any claimed Tenant Delay within two (2) business days of the action or omission giving rise to such Tenant Delay.*

> *Warranty: Landlord hereby warrants and represents that Landlord's Work shall be free from defects in workmanship, installation, and materials for a period of one (1) year from the Commencement Date, and Landlord, at its sole cost and expense, shall promptly perform any corrective work arising from said warranty.*

> *Punch-list Period. Within sixty (60) days after the Commencement Date, Tenant shall have the right to submit to Landlord a "punch list" of any Landlord's Work items which need to be finished or corrected, and Landlord, at its sole cost and expense, shall promptly complete and/or correct same.*

> *Substantial Completion. Notwithstanding anything to the contrary contained herein, Landlord's Work shall not be deemed "Substantially Completed" unless and until it meets the definition under this Exhibit B and a final and unconditional certificate of occupancy permitting lawful occupancy has been duly issued for the Premises such that Tenant may reasonably commence its business operations therein.*

In addition to the above, Tenant may also wish to negotiate: (i) the time period Tenant gets to "value engineer" the Work Cost after the bids come in, (ii) whether

Tenant may be present for the opening of the bids and have a part of selecting the contractors and subcontractors and otherwise approving the budget before Landlord's Work is commenced, (iii) stipulating that the bids will be "fixed" or "guaranteed" as to price to guard against unexpected charges to Tenant for amounts above the "cap," (iv) the timing of Tenant paying its contribution towards the Work Cost (which is paid "pari passu" pursuant to the attached sample Exhibit B but Tenant may wish to pay its contribution upon Substantial Completion (for ultimate protection) or on a different schedule), (v) the amount of any Landlord Construction Management Fee, (vii) a potential capping of Landlord's design fees so that the amount of Landlord's funds to the "cap" are not excessively used for Landlord's design fees.

If the estimated Work Cost exceeds the Cap by a certain percentage, Tenant may wish to have the option to terminate the Lease without liability or with liability (e.g., with the payment of some reasonable fee for design and bidding costs incurred by Landlord).

If the estimated Work Costs exceeds the Cap by a significant amount, Tenant may wish to protect itself by obtaining the express "self-help" right to take over the construction of Landlord's Work and to offset Rent by any amounts expended by Tenant in completing Landlord's Work.

Additionally, Tenant may wish to protect its investment by requiring a SNDA with the Lender wherein Lender expressly (i) agrees to complete any portion of Landlord's Work not completed in the event Lender succeeds to Landlord's position under the Lease and/or, (ii) expressly accepts any self-help and Rent offset right Tenant successfully negotiates in the Lease.

If any Landlord's Work provisions contained in or attached to the Lease do not include an early access right for Tenant to install Tenant's Alterations, then Tenant should propose language similar to the language already included in Exhibit B, Alternative 2 and 3.

Landlord may wish Tenant to pay its contribution to Work Costs upon the approval of the Budget and prior to commencing Landlord's Work instead of "pari passu" as provided in the sample Exhibit B to protect itself against Tenant failing to pay its portion of the Work Cost later. The timing of Tenant's payment will likely be highly negotiated.

D. COMMENTS

Note that this Exhibit B is limited to describing Landlord's Work and the construction process. The issues surrounding the timing of the completion of the Landlord's Work and how completion of Landlord's Work interplays with the Commencement Date, are covered in Part 1, Paragraph 5.

All terms in [Brackets] in Exhibit B are meant to indicate negotiable terms.

E. TYPICAL PARAGRAPH

See next page for a "sample" of an Exhibit B, Alternative 3.

Exhibit B (Alternative 3): Landlord's Work

1. (a) Landlord shall perform improvements to the Premises ("Landlord's Work") in accordance with the Plans (as hereinafter defined). Subject to Paragraph 3 below, Tenant shall work with [NAME OF ARCHITECT] ("Landlord's Architect") and an engineer approved by Landlord to prepare and submit to Landlord final construction drawings (the "Plans") by the date which is [AMOUNT OF DAYS] days following the Effective Date (the "Plan Delivery Date"). The Plans shall be consistent with the space plan and specifications attached hereto as Exhibit "B-1" (collectively, the "Preliminary Plans") and shall be subject to Landlord's prior written approval only to the extent the Plans are not consistent with the Preliminary Plans, which approval shall not be unreasonably withheld, conditioned or delayed. Any such approval shall be given or denied within [five (5)] Business Days after receipt of the Plans. If Landlord denies such approval, Landlord's denial shall specify in reasonable detail the reasons for such disapproval, and if such denial is permitted hereunder, Tenant shall revise the Plans in accordance with Landlord's objections and submit to Landlord the revised Plans for its review and approval within [five (5)] Business Days. Landlord shall notify Tenant in writing whether it approves of the resubmitted Plans within [three (3)] Business Days after receipt. This process shall be repeated until the Plans have been finally approved by Landlord. Landlord shall advise Tenant if the Plans contain any lead-time items that could constitute a Tenant Delay or otherwise are reasonably expected to result in a delay in Substantial Completion at the time of its approval or disapproval of the Plans or any resubmitted Plans.

   (b) It is agreed that the cost of the design, permitting and construction of Landlord's Work, [together with the Construction Management Fee] (collectively, "Work Cost") shall not cost Landlord more than $[AMOUNT] per rentable square foot of the Premises (the "Landlord Contribution"). Landlord shall have the right to select and/or approve any subcontractors used in connection with Landlord's Work. Landlord's supervision or performance of any work for or on behalf of Tenant shall not be deemed a representation by Landlord the improvements constructed in accordance with the approved

Plans and any revisions thereto will be adequate for Tenant's use, it being agreed that Tenant shall be responsible for all elements of the design of Tenant's plans (including, without limitation, functionality of design, the configuration of the Landlord's Work within the Premises and the placement of Tenant's furniture, appliances and equipment). Landlord's Work shall be performed in a good and workmanlike manner in accordance with all Requirements. [As used herein, "Construction Management Fee" shall mean the [AMOUNT] percent ([AMOUNT]%) fee on the hard construction cost of Landlord's Work which shall be paid to Landlord for managing the construction of Landlord's Work.]

(c) **Landlord shall, with reasonable promptness following Landlord's approval of the Plans, competitively bid the construction of Landlord's Work to at least [three] reputable general contractors and at least [three] reputable subcontractors in each major trade selected by Landlord (at least one of whom must be an independent third party [and one selected by Tenant]). Landlord shall submit to Tenant a cost estimate of the Work Cost based upon the bids received promptly after receipt, which estimate shall be in reasonable line item format allowing Tenant to reasonably value engineer and which shall include an estimated construction schedule detailing all major construction milestones (the "Schedule"). Tenant shall have [ten (10)] Business Days from receipt of the estimate (the "Plan and Budget Approval Date") to alter or approve the Work Cost and/or the Plans, subject to Landlord's reasonable approve. At the end of the such [10-Business Day] period, the then current Plans (as revised, if applicable) and the Work Cost (as revised, if applicable) shall be deemed approved by Tenant (collectively, the "Approved Budget"). Landlord shall keep Tenant reasonably informed as to the bidding process and Landlord's selection of the general contractor (the "General Contractor") and notify Tenant in writing as soon as reasonably practicable after Landlord's bidding procedure is completed (including providing copies of all bid materials related thereto).**

(d) **The General Contractor shall perform Landlord's Work pursuant to a guaranteed maximum price construction contract** (the "GMP Contract"), which shall (i) be between Landlord and General Contractor, (ii) provide for payment on the basis of the Approved Budget (subject to adjustments otherwise permitted under the contract and Tenant having an approval right over any costs above the guaranteed maximum price amount), and (iii) shall otherwise be in a commercially reasonable form as determined in Landlord's reasonable discretion.

(e) In the event that the Work Costs are, in the aggregate, in excess of the Landlord Contribution, Landlord and Tenant shall fund the Work Costs on a pari passu basis (with Landlord paying based upon a fraction, the numerator of which is the Landlord Contribution and the denominator of which is the amount of the Work Costs as set forth in the GMP Contract, and with Tenant paying the balance ("Tenant's WC Payment") for each installment of Work Costs paid during the construction of Landlord's Work, which installments shall not be more frequent than monthly. Tenant shall pay any and all installments of Tenant's WC Payment no later than the date Landlord is required to pay its installment of Work Costs, provided that Tenant shall have at least [twenty (20)] days to pay such amount upon receipt of invoice and reasonable back-up documentation.

2. If Tenant shall request any revisions to the Plans following Landlord's approval of the Plans ("Tenant Change Orders") or if any revisions are required by field conditions or Governmental Authority, Tenant shall have such revisions prepared at Tenant's sole cost and expense, the cost of which may be paid by Tenant from any available Landlord's Contribution, in the event that the Work Costs are estimated to be less than Landlord's Contribution. Promptly upon completion of the revisions, Landlord shall notify Tenant in writing of the increased cost in Landlord's Work (i.e., costs that cause Landlord's Work Cost to exceed the Landlord Contribution) or anticipated delays to the timing of Substantial Completion of Landlord's Work (which delays from Tenant Change Orders shall be deemed Tenant Delays), if any, resulting from such revisions to the Plans (and including any lead-time items that could constitute a Tenant Delay or otherwise are reasonably expected to result in a delay in Substantial Completion).

With respect to Tenant Change Orders, Tenant, within [five (5)] Business Days of receiving such notice (together with reasonable back-up documentation demonstrating such increased costs and timing delays), shall notify Landlord in writing whether it desires to proceed with such revisions. In the absence of such written authorization, Landlord shall have the option to continue work on the Premises disregarding the requested revisions. Tenant shall be responsible for any Tenant Delay in completion of the Premises resulting from any Tenant Change Orders. If such revisions result in an increase in the cost of Landlord's Work beyond the Landlord Contribution, such increased out-of-pocket costs actually incurred, plus any applicable state sales or use tax thereon, shall be payable by Tenant within [twenty (20)] days following Landlord's presentation of invoices therefor (together with reasonable back-up documentation).

3. **Landlord and Tenant agree to cooperate with each other in order to enable Landlord's Work to be performed in a timely manner. Tenant shall submit to Landlord the Plans no later than the Plan Delivery Date. The failure to deliver the Plans by the Plan Delivery Date shall not constitute a default under the Lease, but may constitute a Tenant Delay.**

The term "Tenant's Delay" shall mean any delay in Landlord's Work directly caused by any act, neglect, failure or omission of Tenant, its agents, servants, employees, contractors or subcontractors, or in the performance of Tenant's obligations under this Exhibit or this Lease, including, but not limited to:

(i) **Any delay due to Tenant's failure to meet any scheduled items in this Exhibit, including, without limitation, the following scheduled items, which Tenant hereby agrees to meet: (a) to submit the Plans by the deadline set forth above; (b) to approve the Work Cost and Plans by the Plan and Budget Approval Date; (c) to approve the cost proposal of any Tenant Change Order items within [five (5)] Business Days of Tenant's receipt thereof;**

(ii) **Any delay due to Tenant Change Orders requested by Tenant or Tenant's Installations;**

(iii) **Any delay due to Tenant's actions or omissions;**

(iv) **Any delay due to having to bid or re-bid any items of Tenant Change Orders;**

(v) Any delay caused by Tenant's Installations;
(vi) Any long lead-time items specified in the Plans.

Notwithstanding anything to the contrary contained in this Lease, for each one (1) day of a Tenant Delay, the Rent Commencement Date shall be accelerated one (1) day (resulting in one (1) day of Base Rent abatement being lost for each day of Tenant Delay).

4. (a) Tenant shall be solely responsible for the installation into the Premises of furniture, security system, IT wiring, telephone installation, other computer and communication equipment and all business equipment ("Tenant's Installations"), the cost of which may be paid by Tenant at Tenant's election from any available Landlord's Contribution following the full payment of Landlord's Work. Landlord agrees to afford Tenant access to the Premises and the Building during the period that is prior to the Commencement Date for the purpose of making inspections, taking measurements and making Tenant's Installations (all of which are to be paid for by Tenant), provided that such Tenant's Installations will not require any structural changes, and further provided that the construction of the Landlord's Work and all installations required to be made by the Landlord therein shall have reached a point which in Landlord's sole judgment, exercised in good faith, will not delay or hamper Landlord in the completion of the Landlord's Work. Landlord and Tenant shall reasonably cooperate with each other to coordinate Landlord's Work with the performance of Tenant's Installations. This Paragraph shall permit Tenant to make only installations or improvements in the Premises, prior to the Commencement Date, which do not unreasonably interfere with, or delay, the Substantial Completion of the Landlord's Work. All of the Tenant's Installations shall be installed and completed in accordance with applicable Requirements. Tenant shall have the right to select telecommunication service providers from those providers already serving the Building, in Tenant's sole discretion, provided that service provider connection, installation, and use shall be at Tenant's sole cost and expense. Tenant may not bring new telecommunication service providers to the Building without Landlord's prior written consent.

(b) Prior to the commencement of Tenant's Installations (but only with respect to any of Tenant's Installations that constitute Alterations requiring delivery of plans and specifications for Landlord's prior written approval under the Lease), Tenant shall submit to Landlord complete detailed plans and specifications for Tenant's Installations for Landlord's prior written approval, which approval shall not be unreasonably withheld, conditioned, or delayed.

(c) Any entry by Tenant in or on the Premises shall be at Tenant's sole risk and upon request of Landlord, Tenant, or its contractors, shall pay for and deliver to Landlord, certificates of insurance (except for worker's compensation) in amounts and with such companies as otherwise required pursuant to the Lease.

(d) All Tenant's Installations shall be in accordance with applicable laws, and shall not conflict with or cause a violation of the Building's certificate of occupancy, and all Tenant's Installations shall be completed free of all liens and encumbrances. All permits which may be required for Tenant's Installations shall be procured and paid for by Tenant only after having obtained Landlord's written approval of Tenant's Installations (to the extent required). No plans and/or specifications required to be filed by Tenant pursuant to any work contemplated to be performed by it within the Premises shall be filed or submitted to any governmental authority having jurisdiction thereover without first having obtained Landlord's written approval to the same not to be unreasonably withheld.

(e) Subject to Landlord's obligation as set forth above to reasonably cooperate with Tenant regarding coordinating Tenant's Installations and Landlord's Work, Landlord reserves the right to deny Tenant or its contractor access to the Premises and/or to request Tenant to withdraw therefrom and cease all work being performed by it or on its behalf by any person, firm or corporation other than Landlord, if Landlord shall, in its sole but reasonable judgment, to be exercised in good faith, determine that the commencement and/or the continuance of Tenant's Installations shall materially interfere with, materially delay or materially prevent Landlord from proceeding with the completion of Landlord's Work.

(f) Tenant agrees that should Tenant enter upon the Premises for the purposes of performing any work, the labor employed by Tenant or anyone performing such work for or on behalf of Tenant shall always be harmonious and compatible with the labor employed by Landlord or any contractors or subcontractors of Landlord. Should such labor be incompatible with such Landlord's labor as shall be determined by the reasonable judgment of Landlord to be exercised in good faith, Landlord may require Tenant to withdraw from the Premises until the completion of the Building or Premises by Landlord. Notwithstanding the foregoing, in no event shall Tenant be required to utilize union labor.

(g) Any costs for services incurred or repairs required due to Tenant's contractors or Tenant's Installations shall be paid for by Tenant, which may be paid at Tenant's election from any available Landlord's Contribution to the extent expressly permitted in accordance with Paragraph 4(a) above.

(h) Landlord shall not charge Tenant for any access to and use of the loading areas, common areas, electricity, air conditioning, security and elevators in connection with Tenant's performance of Tenant's Installations.

5. Landlord agrees to correct (or cause to be corrected) all Landlord's Work defective in design, material and workmanship (including latent defects) for a period of one year from the Commencement Date.

6. Tenant has designated [NAME] ("<u>Tenant's Authorized Representative</u>") as its sole representative with respect to the matters set forth in this Exhibit B, who shall have full authority and responsibility to act on behalf of the Tenant as required in this Exhibit B. Tenant's Authorized Representative's e-mail address is [E-MAIL ADDRESS], and any notice or communication sent via e-mail shall be sufficient to comply with the notice requirements herein.

7. Landlord has designated [NAME] ("<u>Landlord's Authorized Representative</u>") as its sole representative with respect to the matters set forth in this Exhibit B, who shall have full authority and responsibility to act on behalf of the Landlord as required in this Exhibit B. Landlord's Authorized Representative's e-mail address is [E-MAIL ADDRESS], and any notice or communication sent via e-mail shall be sufficient to comply with the notice requirements herein.

8. In the event of any inconsistencies between this Exhibit B and the Lease to which this Exhibit B is attached, the provisions of this Exhibit B shall control. Capitalized terms used in this Exhibit B shall, unless otherwise specifically set forth herein, have the same meanings as in the Lease.

9. Upon Tenant's request, Landlord shall provide status updates to Tenant regarding the progress of Landlord's Work and the anticipated date of Substantial Completion. Landlord shall notify Tenant promptly upon learning of delays that may impede in any material respect the progress of Landlord's Work.

10. This Exhibit shall not be deemed applicable to any additional space added to the Premises at any time or from time to time, whether by any options under the Lease or otherwise, or to any portion of the original Premises or any additions to the Premises in the event of a renewal or extension of the original Term of the Lease, whether by any options under the Lease or otherwise, unless expressly so provided in the Lease or any amendment or supplement to the Lease.

11. As used herein, "Substantial Completion" or "Substantially Completed" or words of similar import shall mean that the applicable work has been substantially completed, it being agreed that such work shall be deemed substantially complete notwithstanding that minor or insubstantial details or construction or demolition and/or mechanical adjustment and/or decorative items remain to be performed.

EXHIBIT C
(TENANT PERFORMING INITIAL ALTERATIONS WITH ALLOWANCE)

Tenant's Work; Initial Alterations

RISK RATING: 5

A. DESCRIPTION AND SCOPE

Exhibit C sets forth the terms and conditions of Tenant performing any initial alterations to the Premises for its initial occupancy of the Premises (the "Initial Alterations"). Any such Initial Alterations are, of course, Alterations and are subject to the terms and conditions of the Alterations Paragraph of the Lease, except to the extent of any conflict in terms contained in Exhibit C, as the terms and conditions applicable to Initial Alterations may vary to a certain extent from the terms and conditions applicable to subsequent Alterations and, thus, the terms and conditions contained in Exhibit C control over any such inconsistencies with respect to the Initial Alterations.

The sample Exhibit C attached assumes that Landlord will be performing some degree of Landlord's Work and that work is described in Exhibit B. If Landlord is not performing any Landlord's Work, Exhibit B to the Lease can be marked "Intentionally Omitted" and any references to Landlord's Work and Exhibit B should be removed from the sample Exhibit C that follows.

Finally, the sample Exhibit C attached assumes that Landlord is providing Tenant with a defined amount of funds (the "Allowance") to be contributed towards the cost of the Initial Alterations incurred by Tenant. If Landlord is not providing any Allowance to Tenant, all references thereto should be removed from Exhibit C and Exhibit C should clearly provide that Tenant is responsible for all costs and expenses incurred with respect to the Initial Alterations.

B. ANALYSIS

1. Landlord's Perspective

All of the concerns Landlord has about Tenant making any Alterations to the Premises are applicable to the Initial Alterations. Initial Alterations are subject to the terms and conditions of the Alterations Paragraph of the Lease as well, except that the terms and conditions in Exhibit C typically control over any conflicts. The sample Exhibit C intentionally addresses Landlord's most pressing concerns.

In addition, unless, the parties agree otherwise (which they sometimes do as further discussed below), Landlord will be concerned that any Allowance it provides is being applied for the cost of physical improvements to the Premises and any reasonably associated "soft costs" (which Landlord may define and/or cap), and that the Allowance will not be applied to Tenant furnishings or equipment.

If Landlord is funding the Allowance through funds to be provided by the Lender pursuant to loan documents affecting the Property, Landlord will want to be sure that the Allowance disbursement provisions of Exhibit C mirror or at least do not conflict with the disbursement provisions under the loan documents.

2. Tenant's Perspective

Tenant's biggest concerns with respect to performing the Initial Alterations are (i) Landlord's obligation and ability to pay any Allowance, and (ii) Landlord's ability to delay the completion of the Initial Alterations. These concerns and how Tenant can mitigate the risks associated with them will be addressed in the Compromises and Alternatives section below.

3. Lender's Perspective

Lender is concerned that the Initial Alterations will be completed and that they will be paid for without any liens arising therefrom encumbering the Premises. Any Allowance being provided by Landlord may, or may not, be directly coming from Lender. If they are, the Allowance disbursement provisions of Exhibit C should be reviewed and revised to make sure they conform to the disbursement provisions under the loan documents.

Lender is also interested in ensuring that any funds that it is disbursing under the loan documents are being applied towards the cost of physical improvements to the Premises and any reasonable associated "soft costs" but not otherwise applied to Tenant furnishings or equipment as same will be an asset of Tenant and not of the Building.

Also, if the Allowance will not be funded by Lender but rather by Landlord, Lender will want to protect against being obligated to fund the Allowance in the event it succeeds to the position of Landlord under the Lease prior to the Allowance being fully disbursed.

4. Broker's Perspective

See Broker's Perspective to Exhibit B, Alternative 1 for insight and guidance. Such section is not repeated here only for sustainability and efficiency purposes.

C. COMPROMISES AND ALTERNATIVES

Sample Exhibit C is intentionally Landlord favorable and can be reviewed as having the most aggressive Landlord protections available including: (i) a Landlord construction management fee as well as plan review fees, (ii) detailed Allowance disbursement requirements including required retainage on all Allowance disbursements but for the final disbursement, (iii) a sunset deadline for Tenant's right to request disbursement of the Allowance, (iv) restrictions on how the Allowance can be applied, (v) a Landlord right to any unused Allowance, (vi) the imposition of extra Building fees (like freight elevator fees), (vii) the imposition of work standards, (viii) insurance and indemnity protection, (ix) Landlord access and inspection rights, (x) completion requirements, (xi) warranty requirements on the Initial Alterations, and (xii) the right to require disruptive activities to occur outside of normal business hours.

Given the above, the majority of the compromises and alternatives discussed herein will be from the Tenant's perspective.

Sample Exhibit C attached contemplates that the Initial Alterations will be extensive taking several months to complete and so the Allowance will be paid out by Landlord in periodic installments. If the Initial Alterations will not be extensive or time-consuming, Landlord may wish to pay the Allowance in one payment upon Substantial Completion of the Initial Alterations (or some other limited payout schedule). In the event that the estimated cost of the Initial Improvements is above the Allowance, Landlord also may wish for the amounts above the Allowance to be payable by Tenant before any portion of the Allowance is paid although Tenant typically resists this. If Landlord takes that position and Tenant objects, Tenant should seek the right to periodic disbursements of the Allowance as provided in sample Exhibit C.

If there are legitimate concerns about the ability of Landlord to pay the Allowance, Tenant is occasionally able to get the Allowance deposited, upon the Effective Date, in a third party escrow account for disbursement in accordance with Exhibit C and/or, if applicable, have the Lender assure Tenant that it will be disbursing the Allowance in accordance with Exhibit C. Alternatively, and more often, Tenant is able to negotiate the following protection:

> *If Landlord fails to timely pay all or any portion of the Allowance, Tenant shall have the right to offset any unpaid sums against Tenant's Rent obligations under the Lease.*

If Tenant achieves a Rent offset right for failure of Landlord to timely pay all or a portion of the Allowance, Tenant may wish to further protect itself by requiring Landlord deliver an SNDA with from Lender wherein Lender expressly acknowledges and accepts Tenant's Rent offset right.

It is reasonable that Landlord not be obligated to pay the Allowance for an unlimited period of time so its obligation typically expires or "sunsets" after a generous time period following the Effective Date. Tenant should be sure that any sunset provision is generous enough to cover the time period Tenant needs to Substantially Complete the Initial Alterations building in generous time for unexpected delays.

The extent to which Tenant may apply the Allowance to Tenant's architectural, space planning or engineering costs, moving expenses, attorneys' fees and or furnishings and equipment is typically all negotiable. Tenant may also successfully negotiate the right to receive any unused portions of the Allowance in the form of free Rent or Rent credits. If Tenant achieves that right, then upon the "sunset" of any Tenant right to request an Allowance disbursement, any unused Allowance should automatically be converted into Rent credits to be applied to the first Rent due under the Lease.

Tenant should negotiate to eliminate or restrict any Landlord construction management fee, especially if Tenant is hiring its own project manager to oversee the general contractor. Tenant should also endeavor to get Landlord to waive any freight elevator, parking, hoist charges or the like in connection with the construction of the Initial Alterations and Tenant's move into the Premises.

Tenant should endeavor to limit what constitutes "Disruptive Activities" that Landlord has the right to prescribe to hours outside of normal business hours.

To protect Tenant timing risk associated with Landlord delaying the Substantial Completion of the Initial Alterations, Tenant should negotiate a provision like the following:

> *Notwithstanding anything to the contrary contained herein, in the event of a Landlord Delay (as hereinafter defined), the Rent Commencement Date shall be extended one (1) day for each day of a Landlord Delay. As used herein, "Landlord Delay" shall mean any delay in the performance or completion of the Initial Alterations caused by acts or omissions by Landlord, its agents, designers, architects or any other party acting on Landlord's behalf.*

Landlord may wish to soften any Landlord Delay clause as provided below:

> *Notwithstanding anything to the contrary contained herein, except for any failure of Landlord to meet an express time deadline under this Exhibit C (which requires no notice and cure period) no acts or omissions by Landlord, its agents, designers, architects or any other party acting on Landlord's behalf shall be deemed a Landlord Delay until Tenant gives Landlord notice of such claimed delay and Landlord fails to cure such claimed Landlord Delay within two (2) Business Days of receipt of such notice.*

D. COMMENTS

All terms in [Brackets] in Exhibit C are meant to indicate negotiable terms.

E. TYPICAL EXHIBIT

See next page for a "sample" of an Exhibit C.

Exhibit C: Initial Alterations

1.01 Initial Alterations; Tenant's Plans. Tenant, following the Commencement Date, shall have the right, at Tenant's cost and expense, to perform Alterations in the Premises to prepare the Premises for Tenant's initial occupancy (collectively, the "Initial Alterations"). Notwithstanding the foregoing, Tenant and its contractors shall not have the right to perform the Initial Alterations in the Premises unless and until Tenant has complied with all of the terms and conditions of the Lease (including the terms and conditions applicable to Alterations), including, without limitation, approval by Landlord of the final plans and specifications for the Initial Alterations ("Tenant's Plans") and the contractors to be retained by Tenant to perform such Alterations. Tenant shall be responsible for all elements of the design of Tenant's Plans (including, without limitation, compliance with law, functionality of design, the structural integrity of the design, the configuration of the Premises and the placement of Tenant's furniture, appliances and equipment), and Landlord's approval of Tenant's Plans shall in no event relieve Tenant of the responsibility for such design. Landlord's approval of the contractors to perform the Initial Alterations shall not be unreasonably withheld, conditioned or delayed. The parties agree that Landlord's approval of the general contractor to perform the Initial Alterations shall not be considered to be unreasonably withheld, if any such general contractor (i) does not have trade references reasonably acceptable to Landlord, (ii) does not maintain insurance as required pursuant to the terms of the Lease, [(iii) does not have the ability to be bonded for the work in an amount of no less than 125% of the total estimated cost of the Initial Alterations, (iv) does not provide current financial statements reasonably acceptable to Landlord], or (v) is not licensed as a contractor in the state/municipality in which the Premises is located. Tenant acknowledges the foregoing is not intended to be an exclusive list of the reasons why Landlord may reasonably withhold its consent to a general contractor.

2.01 Allowance.

(a) Provided Tenant is not in Default, Landlord agrees to contribute the sum of [INSERT AMOUNT OF ALLOWANCE] (the "Allowance") towards the out-of-pocket hard and soft costs actually incurred by Tenant in the planning and construction of the Initial Alterations. The Allowance, less a

[5%] retainage (which retainage shall be payable as part of the final draw), shall be paid to Tenant or, at Tenant's option, to the order of the general contractor that performs the Initial Alterations, in periodic disbursements within thirty (30) days after receipt of the following documentation (collectively, the "Allowance Documentation"): (i) an application for payment and sworn statement of contractor substantially in the form of AIA Document G-702 covering all work for which disbursement is to be made to a date specified therein; (ii) a certification from an AIA architect substantially in the form of the Architect's Certificate for Payment which is located on AIA Document G702, Application and Certificate of Payment; (iii) Contractor's, subcontractor's and material supplier's waivers of liens which shall cover all Initial Alterations for which disbursement is being requested and all other statements and forms required for compliance with the mechanics' lien laws of the state in which the Premises is located, together with all such invoices, contracts, or other supporting data as Landlord or Landlord's Mortgagee may reasonably require; (iv) a cost breakdown for each trade or subcontractor performing the Initial Alterations; (v) plans and specifications for the Initial Alterations, together with a certificate from an AIA architect that such plans and specifications comply in all material respects with all Laws affecting the Building, Property and Premises; (vi) copies of all construction contracts for the Initial Alterations, together with copies of all change orders, if any; (vii) evidence of payment for all work for which disbursement is to be made in the form of cancelled check or wire transfer confirmation; and (viii) a request to disburse from Tenant containing an approval by Tenant of the work done and a good faith estimate of the cost to complete the Initial Alterations. Upon completion of the Initial Alterations, and prior to final disbursement of the Allowance (including all retainage amounts), Tenant shall furnish Landlord with the Allowance Documentation together with: (1) general contractor and architect's completion affidavits, (2) full and final waivers of lien, (3) receipted bills covering all labor and materials expended and used, (4) as-built plans of the Initial Alterations, and (5) the certification of Tenant and

its architect that the Initial Alterations have been installed in a good and workmanlike manner in accordance with the approved plans, and in accordance with applicable Laws. In no event shall Landlord be required to disburse the Allowance more than one time per month. If the Initial Alterations exceed the Allowance, Tenant shall be entitled to the Allowance in accordance with the terms hereof, but each individual disbursement of the Allowance shall be disbursed in the proportion that the Allowance bears to the total cost for the Initial Alterations, less the 5% retainage referenced above. Notwithstanding anything herein to the contrary, Landlord shall not be obligated to disburse any portion of the Allowance during the continuance of an uncured default or Default under the Lease, and Landlord's obligation to disburse shall only resume when and if such default or Default is cured. If Landlord fails to timely pay such sums, Tenant shall have the right to offset any unpaid sums against Tenant's Rent obligations under the Lease.

(b) If Tenant does not submit a request for payment of the entire Allowance to Landlord in accordance with the provisions contained in this Exhibit C within [TIME PERIOD] of the Commencement Date, the remainder of any unused portion of the Allowance shall accrue to the sole benefit of Landlord, it being understood that Tenant shall not be entitled to any credit, abatement or other concession in connection therewith. Tenant shall be responsible for all applicable state sales or use taxes, if any, payable in connection with the Initial Alterations and/or Allowance.

3.01 Condition of Premises at Delivery. Tenant shall accept the Premises in its "as-is" condition on the Commencement Date. Landlord shall have no obligation to perform any work or make any installations in order to prepare the Premises for Tenant's occupancy [, except that prior to the Commencement Date, Landlord shall perform or cause to be performed any Landlord's Work, as provided Exhibit B, as applicable]. By taking possession of the Premises, Tenant agrees that the Premises are in good order and satisfactory condition and that Landlord has fully and satisfactorily performed and completed all work required to be performed by Landlord

prior to Tenant's initial occupancy of the Premises (including Landlord's Work), if any.

4.01 Additional Space; Options. This Exhibit shall not be deemed applicable to any additional space added to the Premises at any time or from time to time, whether by any options under the Lease or otherwise, or in the event of a renewal or extension of the original Term of the Lease, whether by any options under the Lease or otherwise, unless expressly so provided in an amendment or supplement to the Lease.

5.01 Changes. No changes, modifications, alterations or additions to the approved Tenant's Plans shall be made without the prior written approval of Landlord in each instance, after written request therefor by Tenant. Landlord's approval to any such changes shall not be unreasonably withheld or delayed. Any such change order approval or disapproval shall be given within five (5) Business Days after receiving the same, with any disapproval reasonably specifying the reasons therefor.

6.01 Work Standards. The Initial Alterations shall be performed by Tenant's contractor first approved in writing by Landlord, which approval shall not be unreasonably withheld or delayed. Such contractor shall be insured as provided in Section 9.01 of this Exhibit, and shall work in harmony with any workers at the Building so as to maintain proper labor relations and so as to avoid any work stoppages. Landlord shall also have the right of prior approval of any and all subcontractors used in connection with the Initial Alterations, said approval not to be unreasonably withheld or delayed provided such subcontractors are reputable and likewise insured and bonded, and will maintain harmonious labor relations at the Building. Landlord will give its approval or disapproval of any contractors within three (3) Business Days of receipt of written request of same from Tenant, together with a statement of such contractor's qualifications. The Initial Alterations shall comply with the current design standards, structural and mechanical criteria and the general layout of the Building. Said Initial Alterations shall be commenced promptly after Tenant, at its sole cost and expense, obtains all necessary permits, consents, authorizations, licenses and approvals therefor. Any required zoning approval (including the zoning permit and zoning certificate of compliance) obtained in connection with the Initial Alterations

shall be obtained at Tenant's expense. Landlord shall reasonably cooperate with Tenant, at Tenant's expense, in connection with Tenant obtaining the permits, consents, etc., which Tenant is required to obtain hereunder. The Initial Alterations shall be performed diligently until completion, by trained, supervised and adequately staffed personnel and strictly in accordance with the approved Tenant's Plans and all Laws (including, without limitation, applicable zoning, fire, health, building and disability codes). Initial Alterations shall be performed in a good and workmanlike manner as to workmanship and materials, and so as not to unreasonably interfere with any work or construction by Landlord, or the management, operations or occupancies of the Building. Tenant shall obtain Landlord's prior written approval for any space outside the Premises at or within the Building, which Tenant's contractors or subcontractors) desires to use for storage, handling or moving of any materials and equipment, as well as the location of any facilities for personnel. Tenant (or its contractors or subcontractors) shall be required to remove from the Premises and the Building and dispose of at least once per week (or more frequently as Landlord may reasonably direct), all debris and rubbish caused by or resulting from the Initial Alterations. Said removal and disposal shall be performed in compliance with all Laws. Upon completion of the Initial Alterations, said contractors and subcontractors shall remove all surplus materials, equipment, debris and rubbish of whatever kind remaining on or at the Building associated with the Initial Alterations. If any rubbish, surplus material or temporary structures remain within three (3) days after notice from Landlord to Tenant, then Landlord may cause the same to be removed at Tenant's sole cost and expense. Tenant shall, at its sole cost and expense, diligently apply for and obtain any and all building permits and certificates of occupancy and zoning compliance with respect to the Initial Alterations (and provided originals thereof to Landlord upon Tenant's obtaining same). Notwithstanding anything to the contrary contained herein, Initial Alterations shall be performed so as to not interfere with other occupants of the Building (or Landlord's management or operation of the Building), and said Initial Alterations shall be subject to such additional rules or criteria as Landlord may reasonably require.

7.01 Supervisory Fee. Landlord will charge Tenant a supervisory fee in connection with the Initial Alterations equal to [INSERT AMOUNT]. Tenant shall pay such supervisory fee as Additional Rent as and when charged by Landlord.

8.01 Indemnity. The Initial Alterations shall be performed at Tenant's sole risk. Tenant hereby agrees to indemnify, defend and hold the Landlord and Landlord Related Parties harmless from and against any and all claims, liabilities, reasonable costs, damages and expenses (including, without limitation, reasonable attorney's fees and disbursements) arising from or in connection with the installation, performance or nonperformance of the Initial Alterations or Tenant's breach of any of its obligations under this Exhibit C. Said indemnity shall take effect upon the date of the execution of the Lease and shall survive the expiration or earlier termination of the Lease.

9.01 Insurance. Tenant (and its contractors and subcontractors) shall carry and maintain at all times during the performance of the Initial Alterations, comprehensive public liability insurance, contractual liability insurance, property damage insurance and worker's compensation insurance, all issued by insurers and having coverage amounts which are reasonably satisfactory to Landlord. In no event shall the coverage amounts be less than those required in the Lease. Said insurance policies shall name Landlord, Landlord's managing agent and any lessor and/or mortgagee designated by Landlord as additional insured(s) as their interests may appear. Certificates or copies of such insurance policies shall be delivered to Landlord before the commencement of the Initial Alterations. Each such policy shall require that the carrier give Landlord at least thirty (30) days' prior written notice before any cancellation, lapse or change in coverage. Each insurance certificate (whether for insurance originally furnished or evidencing a renewal of insurance) shall include a standard "additional insured" endorsement naming Landlord, its managing agent, any lessor and any mortgagee as additional insureds.

10.01 Completion. The completion (or non-completion) of the Initial Alterations on the Premises, shall not affect, in any way, the Commencement Date of the Lease or the commencement of Tenant's obligations for Additional Rent under the Lease. Within sixty (60) days following the completion of the Initial Alterations on

the Premises, Tenant shall provide Landlord with final "as-built" plans and specifications accurately reflecting all of the Initial Alterations, including, without limitation, any approved change orders thereto. Tenant shall also be responsible for obtaining and delivering to Landlord, at its sole cost and expense, a duly issued, valid, certificate of occupancy from the appropriate local government authorities confirming that the Initial Alterations have been completed in accordance with the Tenant's Plans and permitting lawful occupancy of Premises (said certificate to be in form and substance reasonably satisfactory to Landlord and Tenant's failure to obtain same, within three (3) months after the Commencement Date (time being of the essence), to be deemed, at Landlord's option, following thirty (30) days after Landlord's written notice of such failure, a material breach or event of default under the Lease, notwithstanding anything to the contrary contained herein or in the Lease). Notwithstanding anything to the contrary in the Lease, including, without limitation, this Exhibit C, Tenant shall not occupy any portion of the Premises for its business purposes unless Tenant has obtained and delivered to Landlord a duly issued, valid, certificate of occupancy from the appropriate local government authorities confirming that the Initial Alterations have been completed in accordance with the Tenant's Plans and permitting lawful occupancy of Premises.

11.01 Conflicts. Notwithstanding anything to the contrary contained in the Lease, in the event of any express inconsistencies between the Lease and this Exhibit C, this Exhibit C shall govern and control in each instance with respect to the parties' respective obligations under this Exhibit C. If Tenant shall fail to duly perform any of its obligations required in this Exhibit C, such failure shall, following three (3) Business Days' notice (except in cases of genuine emergency, when only immediate notice shall be required), at Landlord's option, be deemed a Default under the Lease, and Landlord may order that all Initial Alterations be stopped immediately until the Default is cured, without limitation as to Landlord's other rights and/or remedies under the Lease or at law or in equity. Tenant shall comply immediately with any such stop orders. Landlord shall also have the right, upon ten (10) days' written notice to Tenant (except in cases of emergencies, when only immediate notice shall be required) to cure Tenant's

violations of this Exhibit C, at Tenant's sole cost and expense. Notwithstanding anything to the contrary contained herein or in the Lease, from and after the date of the Lease and at all times thereafter, Tenant shall comply strictly with all of the provisions of this Exhibit C and any applicable obligations of Tenant under the Lease.

12.01 <u>Access; Inspections</u>. Landlord shall at all times have reasonable access into and about the Premises during the performance of the Initial Alterations for purposes of inspecting same and to monitor compliance with this Exhibit C. Tenant shall regularly and promptly keep Landlord duly apprised of the progress of the Initial Alterations. Subject to the terms of this Exhibit C, Landlord and Tenant shall cooperate with each other (and their respective agents and contractors) reasonably and in good faith in connection with any work being performed by Landlord and Tenant so as not to unreasonably interfere with the other party's work.

13.01 <u>Warranty</u>. Tenant shall use commercially reasonable, good faith efforts to obtain from its contractors a warranty, for the benefit of Landlord and Tenant, warranting that the Initial Alterations shall be free from defects in workmanship, materials and installation for a period of one (1) year following the completion of the Initial Alterations.

14.01 <u>Liens</u>. Notice is hereby given that neither Landlord, any ground lessor, nor any mortgagee of the Premises or Property shall be liable for any labor or materials furnished or to be furnished to Tenant upon credit, and that no mechanic's, materialman's or other lien for such labor or material shall attach to or affect any estate or interest of Landlord, any ground lessor or any mortgagee of the Premises. Tenant, at its expense, and with diligence and dispatch, shall, pursuant to the applicable terms of the Lease, procure the cancellation or discharge of all notices of violation arising from or otherwise connected with any Initial Alterations, or any work, labor, services or materials done for or supplied to Tenant, or any person claiming through or under Tenant, which shall be issued by any public authority having or asserting jurisdiction Tenant hereby agrees to defend, indemnify and save harmless Landlord from and against any and all mechanic's, materialman's and other liens and encumbrances filed in connection with the Initial Alterations or any work, labor, services or

materials done for or supplied to Tenant or any person claiming through or under Tenant, including, without limitation, security interests in any materials, fixtures or articles so installed in and constituting part of the Premises and against all costs, expenses and liabilities incurred in connection with any such lien or encumbrance or any action or proceeding brought thereon.

15.01 Freight Elevator Usage; Additional Services. If Tenant desires to use the Building freight elevator in connection with the Initial Alterations, Landlord shall prescribe the charge for freight, elevator use and the method and manner in which any merchandise, heavy furniture or equipment shall be brought in or taken out of the Building, and also the hours at which such moving shall be done. Tenant shall pay all such charges within thirty (30) days of Landlord's demand therefor. In addition, if any work needs to be performed in the Premises after Building Service Hours, Tenant, within thirty (30) days after receipt of a written invoice from Landlord, shall reimburse Landlord for the reasonable cost (on an hourly basis) of having Landlord's management or engineering personnel oversee the performance of such work.

16.01 Disruptive Activities. Landlord, to the extent reasonably necessary to avoid any unreasonable disruption to the tenants and occupants of the Building by unusually loud, jarring, or intrusive construction activities or those involving disruption of services or access ("Disruptive Activities"), shall have the right to reasonably designate the time (including outside of normal business hours) when any such Disruptive Activities may be performed and to otherwise designate reasonable rules, regulations and procedures for the performance of work in the Building. In addition, if any work needs to be performed in the Premises after Building Service Hours, Tenant, within thirty (30) days after receipt of a written invoice from Landlord, shall reimburse Landlord for the reasonable cost (on an hourly basis) of having Landlord's management or engineering personnel oversee the performance of such work.

17.01 Notices under Exhibit C. Tenant has designated [NAME] ("Tenant's Authorized Representative") as its sole representative with respect to the matters set forth in this Exhibit C, who shall have full authority and responsibility to act on behalf of the Tenant as required in this Exhibit C. Tenant's Authorized Representative's

e-mail address is [E-MAIL ADDRESS], and any notice or communication sent via e-mail shall be sufficient to comply with the notice requirements herein. Landlord has designated [NAME] ("Landlord's Authorized Representative") as its sole representative with respect to the matters set forth in this Exhibit C, who shall have full authority and responsibility to act on behalf of the Landlord as required in this Exhibit C. Landlord's Authorized Representative's e-mail address is [E-MAIL ADDRESS], and any notice or communication sent via e-mail shall be sufficient to comply with the notice requirements herein.

PART 2

Description and Analysis of Retail Lease Paragraphs

PARAGRAPH 1

Operating Covenant; Store Hours

RISK RATING: 4

A. DESCRIPTION AND SCOPE

Operating covenants obligate Tenant to remain open for business during certain hours and operate in a manner that will maximize gross sales. Thus, Landlord will want Tenant to agree to "continuously and uninterruptedly" operate its business and will seek to require hours of operation customary for similar businesses in the area (or, in the case of a shopping center or mall, to the hours maintained by the major department stores). Landlord is concerned that Tenant will go out of business or move to a new location ("go dark") but continue paying Landlord Annual Base Rent under the Lease.

In a shopping center, Tenant's duty to conduct an active business is important to Landlord not only because of the Percentage Rent derived from Tenant's business (as further discussed in Part 2, Paragraph 4) but also because of the effect of Tenant's operations on the entire shopping center—particularly where the Tenant is an anchor Tenant. Operating covenants may also be in other agreements, such as a reciprocal easement agreement, operating agreement, or supplemental agreement.

To enforce operating covenants, Leases typically incorporate specific remedies for Landlord which may vary from lease to lease but often include rent increases for Tenant or Landlord "recapture" rights. If there is a "closure" and Landlord declares a "recapture," Tenant must surrender the Premises and the Lease is terminated. Typically, "closure" includes such occurrences as closing of business for seven consecutive days; removal by Tenant of substantially all of its inventory from the Premises; or failure to operate during 75% of the hours per day customary in Tenant's business. Tenant will seek a right to cure after notification of its breach of such standards. In giving Landlord the option to terminate the Lease and thus to seek a tenant more willing or able to remain in business, the clause provides greater protection for Landlord than a suit for damages or injunctive relief.

The COVID-19 pandemic arguably impacted retail leases and the parties thereto harder than office and industrial leases. Any operating covenant requirement going forward will need to be subject to Force Majeure conditions, which will need to expressly include the impact of pandemics and any associated governmental mandates regarding closure or occupancy restrictions.

B. ANALYSIS

1. Landlord's Perspective

This Paragraph is very important to Landlord because it will allow Landlord some ability to maximize rent based on a percentage of sales and because it affects all other tenants in Landlord's shopping center and their respective sales, since each tenant relies on the other tenants to bring traffic to the center. In addition to requiring Tenant to remain open for business, Landlord wants Tenant to maximize its business. For example, Landlord would like to require Tenant to keep the Premises adequately stocked with merchandise and trade fixtures to service its customers. Landlord may require that Tenant obtain and maintain at all times all necessary or desirable licenses and the highest available ratings from all applicable governmental agencies. Landlord also may seek to secure rights of review or approval of standards for Tenant's employees, the sales area, lighting, display, layout, pricing, and advertising, and may seek to require that Tenant participate in merchant's associations and merchandising events.

2. Tenant's Perspective

Tenant would like to minimize Landlord's control over its business and, in particular, would like to specify circumstances in which Tenant will have the right to close temporarily for reasons such as the taking of inventory, Force Majeure, severe weather, and vacation of the Premises at the end of the Lease term. Tenant also may want specified remedies if certain other anchor tenants close (see Part 2, Paragraph 12 for cotenancy protections for Tenant) together with some protections against inequitable operational covenants applied across tenants of a shopping center. Anchor Tenants typically have more leverage and may also be able to limit their operating covenant to a period of time; for example, the first five years of the Lease Term.

3. Lender's Perspective

Lender will have interests similar to its borrower, the Landlord.

4. Broker's Perspective

Brokers should expect to detail in the LOI the exact business hours that will be required of Tenant during the Term of the Lease. Landlord Broker should inform Tenant Broker of the Landlord's required business hours at the outset of LOI negotiation. Tenant Broker will want to fully understand, during the needs assessment phase of its assignment, Tenant's desired business hours, as the issue may play an instrumental part of Tenant's location selection process. Both Brokers should confirm that the Paragraph in the Lease conforms to what was agreed to in the LOI.

C. COMPROMISES AND ALTERNATIVES

The specifics of store hours and operating covenants are often negotiated but if Tenant is a tenant at a shopping center and has a Percentage Rent obligation under its Lease, then Landlord will want Tenant to agree to remain open for business for specified times during the Lease Term as it is standard in those situations.

Tenant may wish to protect itself from discriminatory operating covenants with a shopping center by including into Paragraph 1 the following concept:

> *Tenant's obligation to be open and operating during the aforementioned hours is conditioned on at least [eighty percent (80%)] of existing non-Anchor Tenants being similarly obligated to be open and operating.*

Alternatively, Tenant may require a provision wherein Tenant shall not be required to operate for more hours than one or more of the Anchor tenants. Note that Anchor tenants are defined and further discussed in Part 2, Paragraph 12.

Tenant will want to maximize the profitability of its business too and so Tenant will also have an interest in stable operating hours. Thus, to the extent any lease for space in a shopping center affords Landlord the right to change Tenant's operating hours or the operating hours of the shopping center, Tenant may wish to protect itself from Landlord limiting operating hours by adding the following protective language:

> *In no event shall the operating hours of the Shopping Center be reduced, nor shall Tenant be required to be open and operating for fewer hours than currently required under this Lease, without Tenant's prior written consent.*

In a Tenant operating clause, Landlord sometimes will request that Tenant agree to "use its best efforts to maximize Tenant's gross sales," if Landlord does not wish solely to rely upon the Tenant's motivation to make a profit (sometimes a tenant can actually make more profit by reducing sales). Alternatively, Tenant may be required to use "due diligence" to achieve a certain percentage rent. Or Tenant may wish to revise any language concerning Tenant using efforts to "maximize Tenant's gross sales" to Tenant using efforts to "maximize Tenant's volume of business." Such a change in language gives Tenant more flexibility to managing its business operations and sales goals.

Tenant should protect its right to close its store for inventory purposes during the course of each year of the Term. Below is a sample provision that Tenant may wish to add to the end of Paragraph 1:

> *Notwithstanding the foregoing, Tenant shall have the right to close for business in the Premises for four (4) days per calendar year for the sole purpose of taking inventory of the merchandise in the Premises after giving ten (10) days' prior written notice to Landlord of its intent in each instance.*

With respect to the automatic Landlord remedy included in Subparagraph 1(b) as follows, Tenant should endeavor to negotiate the business terms therein, including how many Tenant breaches trigger the remedy, the percent rent penalty, and the number of days in which Tenant must pay Landlord the liquidated damages.

D. COMMENTS

In response to the COVID-19 experience, any Tenant operating covenant should now be expressly subject to Force Majeure conditions, which will need to expressly include the impact of pandemics and any associated governmental mandates regarding closure or occupancy restrictions.

E. TYPICAL PARAGRAPH

1. Operating Covenant; Store Hours.

   (a) Operating Covenant. **Subject to Force Majeure conditions, Tenant shall at all times during the term hereof (a) conduct its business in the entire Premises; (b) remain open for business from [HOURS], Monday through Saturday, and from [HOURS] on Sunday (if permitted by law) during the term hereof excepting Christmas Day and Thanksgiving Day, which days the Shopping Center shall be closed. Said minimum operating hours may be modified by Landlord upon ten (10) days' written notice to Tenant. Tenant's failure to keep the Premises open for business as aforesaid shall be conclusively deemed for any and all purposes to be a violation or breach of a condition, covenant, or obligation of this Lease that cannot afterward be cured or performed; (c) adequately staff its store with sufficient employees to handle the maximum business and carry sufficient stock of merchandise of such size, character, and quality to accomplish the same; (d) maintain displays of merchandise in the display windows, if any; (e) keep the Premises and interior portions of windows, doors, and all other glass or plate glass fixtures in a neat, clean, sanitary, and safe condition; (f) warehouse, store, or stock only such goods, wares, and merchandise as Tenant intends to offer for sale at retail; (g) if the Premises contain a mezzanine, the use thereof for storage purposes or sales purposes shall be subject to Landlord's written approval; (h) except for mezzanine space, use for office or other non-selling purposes only such space as is reasonably required for Tenant's business, but in no event shall the space used for such purposes exceed five percent (5%) of the square foot area of the Premises; (i) neither solicit business nor distribute advertising matter in the common areas; (j) not place any weight upon the floors which shall exceed [AMOUNT] pounds per square foot of floor space covered; (k) not change the advertising name of the business operated in the Premises without the written permission of Landlord; and (l) use the insignia or other identifying mark of the Shopping Center designated by Landlord in Tenant's advertising, whether printed or visual, and make reference to the name of the Shopping Center in each instance of audio advertising.**

(b) Landlord Remedies. **If Tenant shall breach the provisions of Subparagraph 1(a), commencing with the third (3rd) breach in any twelve (12)-month period, Landlord may elect, in lieu of exercising any other remedies available to Landlord, that Base Rent shall be increased by [ten percent (10%)] for each such day of breach. In such event, Tenant shall pay the liquidated damages to Landlord within ten (10) days of demand therefor. If Landlord elects to demand liquidated damages for any breach of Subparagraph 1(a), the liquidated damages shall commence to accrue on the first day of the breach (not the first day following the expiration of the grace period for cure, if any). Tenant shall pay such liquidated damages to Landlord within ten (10) days of demand therefor, and failure timely to pay such sums to Landlord shall constitute a breach of this Lease without further notice.**

PARAGRAPH 2

Radius Restrictions

RISK RATING: 4

A. DESCRIPTION AND SCOPE

"Radius" restrictions affect competition not only within the Property controlled by Landlord but also within a geographic area surrounding the Premises. Such restrictions prevent Tenant from opening additional locations and thus diluting gross sales at the Premises.

B. ANALYSIS

1. Landlord's Perspective

Landlord would like to impose radius restrictions on Tenant if Tenant pays percentage rent. Landlord also would like to ensure that Landlord could enforce such restrictions; enforcement is often effected through a clause that grants Landlord the option to include the gross sales from a competing business in Tenant's gross sales for the purpose of computing percentage rent. Such provision is usually easier to enforce than a clause requiring Landlord to get an injunction to force Tenant to close a competing store.

2. Tenant's Perspective

If Tenant wishes to open another store in the area, then Tenant will resist any restriction on its right to do so. If Tenant is already operating another store within the restricted area, then Tenant must get an exception for currently operating businesses. Tenant also may wish to decrease the restricted area (e.g., 1 or 2 miles) and may wish to exclude any "outlet" stores associated with Tenant's brand, as they generally draw a different customer base and do not compete with Tenant's premium brand stores.

3. Lender's Perspective

Lender's interest is similar to that of Landlord in that Lender wants Tenant to maximize percentage rent by not opening competing stores that might dilute gross sales.

4. Broker's Perspective

Brokers should expect to detail in the LOI the exact Tenant radius restriction and necessary exclusions for existing Tenant locations within the radius and, potentially, any reciprocal radius restriction that Tenant is able to negotiate. Landlord Broker should inform Tenant Broker of the Landlord's required radius restriction at the outset of LOI negotiation. Tenant Broker will want to fully understand, during the needs assessment phase of its assignment, where Tenant's existing and projected new locations are, as this information as it relates to the radius restrictions of any particular location may play an instrumental part of Tenant's location selection process. Both Brokers should confirm that the Paragraph in the Lease conforms to what was agreed to in the LOI.

C. COMPROMISES AND ALTERNATIVES

The actual area (how many miles) of the radius restriction can be negotiated, but the radius restriction may not be unreasonable under the facts and circumstances, or else it may be deemed anticompetitive and unenforceable. In addition, the restriction may be softened somewhat to provide that Tenant cannot operate another business within the restricted area without the prior written consent of Landlord and exempt any existing Tenant stores and any future "outlet" stores, as typically "outlet" stores do not compete for the same customer base as the Tenant's premier stores.

This provision also can be changed from unilateral to mutual so that both Landlord and Tenant are subject to parallel restrictions. See Part 2, Paragraph 11 for "exclusive rights" granted to Tenant.

D. COMMENTS

None.

E. TYPICAL PARAGRAPH

2. Radius Restriction.

(a) Restriction. In recognition of the fact that this Lease provides for Percentage Rent based upon the sales made by Tenant in or from the Premises, Tenant covenants and agrees that, for the period commencing with the execution of this Lease and continuing for the full term of this Lease, neither Tenant nor any parent, subsidiary, or affiliate of Tenant, nor any principal partner, member, or majority shareholder of Tenant, nor any Guarantor of this Lease, shall operate, either directly or indirectly, another store (including a department or concession in another store) of

a similar kind (other than stores, departments, or concessions presently being operated by it or them) within a reasonable area of the Premises, without the prior written consent of Landlord. Tenant acknowledges that the area within a circle having as its center the Premises and having a radius of ten (10) miles is a reasonable area for this purpose.

(b) Landlord Remedy for Restriction Violation. In addition to any other remedy otherwise available to Landlord for breach of this covenant, it is specifically agreed that Landlord may, at Landlord's election, require that any and all sales made in and from any such other store be included in the computation of the Percentage Rent due hereunder with the same force and effect as though such sales had actually been made in or from the Premises.

PARAGRAPH 3

Signage

RISK RATING: 3

A. DESCRIPTION AND SCOPE

This Paragraph requires Tenant, at Tenant's expense, to install signs on the Property that comply with Landlord's Sign Criteria, and all applicable laws, codes, and zoning requirements. It also places the burden on Tenant to install, maintain, and remove each approved sign.

Note that this Paragraph 3 is limited to Tenant's identification signage and not its window displays, which is covered in Part 2, Paragraph 15.

B. ANALYSIS

1. Landlord's Perspective

This Paragraph protects Landlord from having to install, maintain, or remove signs. Landlord retains control, however, over the size, style, and type of sign that may be placed on the Property. Landlord is interested in a uniform look to the Shopping Center and therefore requires that all signs conform to Landlord's Sign Criteria.

2. Tenant's Perspective

Tenant wants Tenant's signage to be adequate for its needs and to be consistent with any nationally recognized branding it has developed.

3. Lender's Perspective

Lender wants to ensure that the Property maintains an appeal to the public so that the collateral value of its Property will be enhanced. Although Lender realizes that signs are necessary to the operation of a business, it may want assurances as to the size and type of signs so that first-class standards are maintained so as to preserve the value of its collateral.

4. Broker's Perspective

Brokers should expect to detail in the LOI Landlord's signage requirements and Tenant's signage rights. Landlord Broker should inform Tenant Broker of Landlord's Sign Criteria at the outset of the LOI negotiation. Tenant Broker will want to fully understand, during the needs assessment phase of its assignment, Tenant's signage requirements so that Tenant Broker may propose potential locations where there are no conflicts between Landlord's Sign Criteria and Tenant's signage needs. Both Brokers should confirm that the Paragraph in the Lease conforms to what was agreed to in the LOI.

C. COMPROMISES AND ALTERNATIVES

Landlord will want Tenant to agree to signage that is appropriate in the prevailing environment, provided that Landlord's criteria for signage do not prohibit a size, style, or location that is essential to Tenant's business.

Because signage is vital to Tenant's business, Tenant would be prudent to have its initial signage plans reviewed and approved by Landlord and attached to the Lease.

In addition, national Tenants of Shopping Centers may have the leverage to add flexibility to Paragraph 3 by adding language similar to the following:

> *Notwithstanding anything to the contrary contained herein, Landlord's approval of Tenant's signage, advertising, and window and other displays shall not be unreasonably withheld, conditioned, or delayed, and Landlord's approval shall not be required with respect to any signs (other than Tenant's exterior storefront identification signage), advertising, or window or other displays which are substantially similar to that which is then being utilized by Tenant at a majority of Tenant's five (5) closest stores to the Premises carrying substantially the same product line and merchandise mix at full retail price, provided that the same (i) are not flashing, neon, or rotating; (ii) are professionally prepared; and (iii) comply with all applicable rules, regulations, laws, and ordinances.*

D. COMMENTS

None.

E. TYPICAL PARAGRAPH

3. <u>Signage</u>. Tenant shall, at Tenant's sole expense, install identification signs of a size, material, and design as Landlord, in its sole discretion, shall deem appropriate. All signs shall conform to Landlord's published Sign Criteria attached hereto as Exhibit [X]. Such signs shall be installed at a place designated by Landlord and shall be in compliance with and conform to all applicable laws, including zoning and code requirements, of the city or town where the Property is located. Except as provided above, Tenant shall not place or suffer to be placed or maintain any sign, awning, or canopy in, upon, or outside the Premises or on the Building or within a half-mile of the Building.

PARAGRAPH 4

Percentage Rent

RISK RATING: 4

A. DESCRIPTION AND SCOPE

Under retail leases, Percentage Rent (as defined below) is a form of rent paid typically in addition to (although occasionally in lieu of) Base Rent. Percentage Rents are based upon a negotiated percentage of a Tenant's Gross Sales (defined in Part 2, Paragraph 5) and are calculated with or without a "break point." A "break point" is the minimum Gross Sales that must be generated by Tenant at the Premises before Tenant's obligation to pay Percentage Rent is triggered and payable under the Lease.

When break points are used in a retail lease, they are referred to as either a "natural break point" or a "fixed break point." A fixed break point is just a negotiated dollar amount of minimum Gross Sales that, when achieved, triggers Tenant's obligation to pay Percentage Rent to Landlord. A "natural break point" is the annual Base Rent divided by the negotiated percent rate. For example, if the negotiated percent rate for Percentage Rent is 6% and the annual Base Rent for year one is $150,000, then the "natural break point" is $2,500,000 ($150,000/6% = $2,500,000). If Tenant's Gross Sales exceed the applicable break point, then Tenant pays Percentage Rent on the portion of Gross Sales over the break point. Thus, in our example, in any calendar year that Tenant reaches $2,500,000 in Gross Sales, Tenant shall pay 6% for each dollar of Gross Sales above $2,500,000.00. That amount is "Percentage Rent."

Paragraph 4 below is a sample provision for Percentage Rent over a fixed break point.

B. ANALYSIS

1. Landlord's Perspective

A typical Lease provision requires that Tenant commence paying Percentage Rent after its aggregate Gross Sales for the year exceed Minimum Gross Sales (i.e., the break point). Landlord may prefer to have estimated payments made throughout the course of the year. In many retail situations, Tenant will refuse to make estimated payments based upon the seasonality of its sales. Landlord may want to add a clause to Paragraph 4 that states that the underreporting of Gross Sales by Tenant of greater than 5% in any one year or the underreporting of Gross Sales by greater than 3% in any two consecutive years shall constitute an Event of Default under the Lease.

2. Tenant's Perspective

Tenant may request that one lump-sum payment of Percentage Rent be made at the end of each Lease year. Tenant also may try to exclude internet sales, mail-order sales, or other unique sales that, arguably, are not originated or generated at or from the Premises. Tenant is unlikely to agree to make estimated payments of Percentage Rent if doing so would require Tenant to pay those estimates out-of-pocket.

3. Lender's Perspective

Lender's primary concern is having a sufficient historical basis upon which to underwrite for Percentage Rent, if a substantial amount of Percentage Rent is to be relied upon in the debt service coverage ratio calculation. Also, Lender is likely to focus on Landlord's right to audit and whether underreporting of Gross Sales gives rise to a default under the Lease.

4. Broker's Perspective

Brokers should expect to detail in the LOI the exact break point and the Percentage Rent rate. Brokers should expect that, together with Annual Base Rent, the details of how Percentage Rent will be calculated will be one of the most focused on and negotiated business terms in the LOI. Tenant Broker will want to fully understand, during the needs assessment phase of its assignment, Tenant's expectation on these issues and understand how they impact Tenant's business model. In addition, Tenant Broker should include reasonable projections of Percentage Rent in its financial projections for the Lease so that they are understood by Tenant before a Lease draft is requested. Of course, both Brokers will then want to review this Paragraph carefully to confirm that terms and conditions therein conform to what the parties agreed to in the LOI.

C. COMPROMISES AND ALTERNATIVES

An alternative method of calculating payments of Percentage Rent during the Lease year is to require Tenant to make Percentage Rent payments each month during the Lease year based upon Gross Sales in such month in excess of one-twelfth of Minimum Gross Sales. This method is not preferred by Tenants with seasonal sales. For example, if Tenant's Minimum Gross Sales break point is $24,000,000 and Percentage Rent is 1% of Gross Sales over Minimum Gross Sales, the retail tenant would be required to pay Percentage Rent in any month where Gross Sales exceeded $2 million. If, for example, a retail tenant had gross sales of $1 million in each of January, February, and March, and then for its Easter Spring Sales Event had $3 million of gross sales in April, this retail Tenant would be required to pay no Percentage Rent in January, February, and March, but would be required to pay Percentage Rent of $10,000 (1,000,000 x .01) in April, even though its total Gross Sales of $6 million in January through April did not exceed the sum of four months @ $2 million per month or $8 million. Paragraph 4 also provides Landlord with the right to review Tenant's books to confirm the calculation of Percentage Rent.

If Tenant is unlikely to exceed Minimum Gross Sales prior to the holiday shopping season, Landlord may consider allowing Tenant to pay all Percentage Rent at the end of each calendar year. The margin of error that triggers Tenant's obligation to pay Landlord's audit expenses is also likely to be negotiated.

Tenant will want to make sure any Percentage Rent provision clearly indicates that the amount of Gross Sales of any Lease Year shall not be carried over into any other Lease Year.

Landlord may wish to include in the Lease a provision that if, and to the extent, the Premises are not open for business in the ordinary course on any day on which the Premises are required to be open under the Lease the amount of the Percentage Rent break point shall be proportionately reduced.

D. COMMENTS

Natural break points may be preferred as they change as Base Rent changes. However, some leases provide for different fixed break points for different Lease Years during the Term.

The Percentage Rent rate is negotiable and generally between four (4) and seven (7) percent, but Landlord and Tenant should confirm the market rate for their geographical region and for the particular Tenant's business.

Occasionally, Percentage Rents are bifurcated with different Percentage Rent rates and break points for different kinds of merchandise or services sold by Tenant.

See Part 2, Paragraph 5 for the definition of Gross Sales and see Part 2, Paragraph 6 about Tenant's obligations to maintain books and records pertaining to its Gross Sales so Percentage Rent can be calculated, verified, and even potentially audited by Landlord.

In the middle of the COVID-19 pandemic when retail restaurants and stores were governmentally mandated to reduce the amount of customers in the establishment at once, many leases were voluntarily amended between the parties to temporarily abate Base Rent and require Tenant to pay only monthly Percentage Rent on actual monthly Gross Sales (without a break point). In this way, some business were able to survive the pandemic. As of the publication of this book, it is yet unclear whether new retail leases will contain contingency plans for future pandemics.

E. TYPICAL PARAGRAPH

4. Percentage Rent.

In addition to Annual Base Rent, Tenant shall pay to Landlord Percentage Rent (as hereinafter defined). For purposes of this Paragraph 4, "Percentage Rent" shall mean the product of (a) the amount by which actual Gross Sales (as hereinafter defined [see Paragraph 5]) exceed Minimum Gross Sales (as hereinafter defined), multiplied by (b)[NEGOTIATED PERCENTAGE]%. As used herein, "Minimum Gross Sales" shall mean $[NEGOTIATED AMOUNT]. Within ten (10) days after the end of each calendar month during the term of this Lease, Tenant shall provide Landlord with a written statement, certified by an officer of Tenant to be correct, showing the total Gross Sales during the preceding calendar month. Within ten (10) days following the close of the calendar month in which Gross Sales for the Lease Year to date exceed the Minimum Gross Sales, Tenant shall pay to Landlord Percentage Rent based upon the amount of such excess. Within ten (10) days following the close of each calendar month thereafter during such Lease Year, Tenant shall pay to Landlord Percentage Rent computed on total Gross Sales made during each such calendar month. Within thirty (30) days following the end of each Lease Year, Tenant shall provide Landlord with a written statement, certified by an independent certified public accountant, showing the calculation of Gross Sales on a month-by-month basis, for the immediately preceding Lease Year. If not previously paid in full, the balance of all Percentage Rent shall be paid to Landlord within thirty (30) days following the end of each Lease Year.

PARAGRAPH 5

Gross Sales Definition

RISK RATING: 4

A. DESCRIPTION AND SCOPE

This Paragraph describes the items to be included in Gross Sales in order to determine Percentage Rent. The description of the items included in Gross Sales is very broad because it is often impossible to predict all methods by which Tenant may generate revenue from its use of the Premises.

B. ANALYSIS

1. Landlord's Perspective

Landlord's objective is to describe the items included in Gross Sales in the broadest possible manner.

2. Tenant's Perspective

Tenant would like to exclude as many items as possible from Gross Sales as further detailed below.

3. Lender's Perspective

If Lender is relying on Percentage Rent to pay its debt service, then Lender will have the same perspective as Landlord.

4. Broker's Perspective

Each Broker will want to consult with their respective client to determine any sensitivity to or any particular client need relating to this Paragraph that should be covered in the LOI. If none exist, this Paragraph can be handled by the attorneys in Lease negotiations. A definition of Gross Sales is sometimes included in a LOI but not often.

C. COMPROMISES AND ALTERNATIVES

Exclusions from Gross Sales should be considered thoroughly by Landlord and Tenant. The Paragraph below has a list of typical starting point exclusions, but Tenant should negotiate (and Landlord should resist) more exclusions. Some additional exclusions that might be added to below list in Paragraph 5 are:

> *(vii) allowances made on merchandise claimed to be defective or unsatisfactory or discounts to customers, provided that if such allowances or discounts are in the form of credits to customers, such credits shall be included in gross sales when used; (viii) sale of trade fixtures or store operating equipment after use thereof in the conduct of Tenant's business in the Premises; (ix) all sums and credits received in settlement of claims for loss or damage to merchandise; (x) charges for repair services, alterations, gift wrapping and deliveries if such services are incidental to the Permitted Use and for which Lessee reasonably demonstrates it makes no profit; (xi) bulk sales or sales of Tenant's inventory to jobbers or wholesalers; (xii) sales to jobbers; (xiii) insurance proceeds and claims against transportation companies; (xiv) forfeited deposits; (xv) the amount of bad debts and bad checks resulting from sales made from the Premises which previously have been included in reported Gross Sales, after Tenant has made its customary collection efforts and written off such amounts as uncollectible, provided that the total bad debts and uncollectible amounts which may be excluded from Gross Sales for any particular year shall not exceed three (3%) percent for such year, and shall in any event be limited to amounts actually written off for Tenant's accounting purposes during such year, and if such amounts are subsequently collected, such amounts shall be included in Gross Sales in the applicable month and year in which they were collected; (xvi) separately stated service, finance, and interest charges; (xvii) sales of gift cards and gift certificates unless and until redeemed at the Premises; (xviii) the amount of any sales, gross receipts, luxury, trust fund, excise, or other tax levied upon retail sales and payable over to the appropriate governmental authority provided that specific record of the amount of such tax is made at the time of each sale and the amount thereof is expressly charged to the customer; (xix) gratuities to employee's paid by Tenant's customers; (xx) fees paid to credit card companies; (xxi) sales to employees, not to exceed three (3%) percent of Gross Sales during any one lease year; (xxii) proceeds from delivery and postage charges; (xxiii) charity sales or contributions, provided same do not exceed three (3%) percent of Gross Sales during any one lease year; and (xxiv) the dollar value of coupons used by customers in the purchase of merchandise from the Premises.*

D. COMMENTS

None.

E. TYPICAL PARAGRAPH

5. **Gross Sales Definition. For purposes of calculating Percentage Rent, the term "Gross Sales" shall mean the actual sales prices and revenue from all goods, wares, and merchandise sold, leased, licensed, or delivered and the actual charges for all services performed by Tenant or by any subtenant, licensee, or concessionaire in, at, from, or arising out of the use of the Premises, whether**

for wholesale, retail, cash, credit, or otherwise, without reserve or deduction for the inability or failure to collect. Gross Sales shall include, without limitation, sales and services (a) where the orders therefore originate in, at, from, or arise out of the use of the Premises, whether delivery or performance of such sales or services is made from the Premises or from some other place, including but not limited to internet sales where delivery or performance of such sales is made from the Premises; (b) made or performed by mail, courier services, internet, computer, telephone, telegraph, or telecopy orders; (c) made or performed by means of mechanical or other vending devices on the Premises; (d) that Tenant or any subtenant, licensee, concessionaire, or other person in the ordinary and customary course of its business, would credit or attribute to its operations at the Premises or any part thereof; (e) of gift certificates; and (f) resulting from electronic funds transfers. A deposit shall be included in Gross Sales for the month in which such deposit is made, provided that if such deposit is later refunded, the amount of such refund may be deducted from Gross Sales for the month in which such refund is made. Each installment or credit sale shall be treated as a sale for the full purchase price of the sale item or service in the month during which such sale or service is made or performed, as the case may be, irrespective of the time when Tenant receives payment therefore. No franchise or capital stock tax and no income or similar tax based on income or profits shall be deducted from Gross Sales.

The following items shall be excluded from Gross Sales: (i) any exchange of merchandise between stores of Tenant if such exchange were made solely for the convenient operation of Tenant's business and not for the purpose of consummating a sale made in, at, or from the Premises, or depriving Landlord of the benefit of a sale that would otherwise be made in, at, or from the Premises; (ii) returns to shippers or manufacturers; (iii) cash or credit refunds to customers on transactions (not to exceed the actual selling price of the item returned) otherwise included in Gross Sales; and (iv) the amount of any discount on sales to employees.

PARAGRAPH 6

Tenant's Records and Gross Sales Reporting

RISK RATING: 3

A. DESCRIPTION AND SCOPE

This Paragraph requires Tenant to maintain books and records for its Gross Sales and permits Landlord to review the books and records of Tenant to verify Tenant's calculation of Percentage Rent.

B. ANALYSIS

1. Landlord's Perspective

Landlord wants to verify the accuracy of Percentage Rent. This Paragraph provides Tenant with incentive to keep and maintain accurate books, and to carry out its business in a professional manner.

If Percentage Rent is based on Tenant's Gross Sales, then Landlord will need access to Tenant's books and records to confirm Tenant's sales receipts. Landlord may hire an independent certified public accountant to assist Landlord. If Tenant underestimated Percentage Rent by more than negotiated percentage or fails to timely deliver required certified statements of Gross Sales, then Landlord may want Tenant to pay Landlord's fees and costs of such accountant.

2. Tenant's Perspective

Tenant may assert that Tenant's calculations of Percentage Rent will be accurate and do not need to be reviewed. Tenant may request that a provision be included in the Lease that would ensure that the records be kept confidential. Tenant may also request that reports be submitted quarterly or annually rather than monthly, as monthly reports would be too burdensome.

3. Lender's Perspective

If Lender is depending on Percentage Rent to pay debt service under its loan to Landlord, then Lender will have the same perspective as Landlord.

4. Broker's Perspective

Each Broker will want to consult with their respective client to determine their standard operational and reporting needs and requirements relating to this Paragraph and negotiate and document the agreed upon Tenant reporting requirements in the LOI.

C. COMPROMISES AND ALTERNATIVES

Depending on creditworthiness of Tenant, quarterly or even annual reports, rather than monthly reports, may be acceptable to Landlord. The 3% discrepancy percentage set forth in Subparagraph (b) may be negotiated.

The business terms in Paragraph 6 are negotiable, including how long Tenant needs to keep its books and records, the date by which Tenant must report its Gross Sales, the percentage difference triggering Tenant's obligation to pay for any Landlord audit and how often Landlord may audit.

D. COMMENTS

If the Lease provides for the payment of Percentage Rent, then Landlord will need to review and audit Tenant's books and records.

[Bracketed] provisions below are meant to indicate portions of the Paragraph that are often negotiated between the parties.

E. TYPICAL PARAGRAPH

6. Tenant's Records.

   (a) **Maintenance of Record. For the purpose of permitting Landlord to verify Percentage Rent, or other sums due Landlord under this Lease that are based on Gross Sales, Tenant shall keep and preserve for at least [four (4) years], and during the term of this Lease shall keep at the Premises, original or duplicate books and records that shall conform to generally accepted accounting practices and that shall disclose all information required to determine Percentage Rent. Such information shall show inventories, receipts of merchandise, expenditures for advertising, and Gross Sales for the year or fraction thereof, including, without limitation, cash register tapes from sealed, continuous total cash registers or permanent electronic records that shall be used to record all sales, serially numbered; mail, internet, and telephone order records; computer records; settlement report sheets of transactions with sublessees, concessionaires, and licensees; records showing that merchandise returned** by customers was purchased by such customers; records of merchandise taken out on approval; bank deposit records; reports and returns for income; occupation, sales, and use taxes reflecting Gross Sales; and such other supporting data as independent accountants normally require to audit Gross Sales.

(b) Landlord Audit Right. After prior notice to Tenant, Landlord or any mortgagee of the Premises or their respective agents and accountants, may during business hours examine or audit such books and records. If any such examination or audit discloses Percentage Rent in excess of the amount theretofore paid by Tenant for any period, then Tenant shall promptly pay on demand such excess. If such excess is greater than [three percent (3%)] of the Percentage Rent payable for the applicable Lease Year, then Tenant shall promptly pay on demand to Landlord, Landlord's cost of such examination and audit plus interest thereon as Additional Rent, such interest payable from the date such Additional Rent should have been paid hereunder, at an annual rate equal to the least of [(i) eighteen percent (18%); (ii) four percent (4%)] above the Prime Rate for the [name of bank]; and (iii) the highest interest rate allowed by law.

(c) Gross Sales Reporting. Tenant agrees to deliver to Landlord: (i) within [fifteen (15)] days after the close of each calendar [month] during the term of this Lease, a written report signed and certified by Tenant or by an authorized officer of Tenant, showing in each instance a complete and accurate statement of Gross Sales made in the preceding calendar month; and (ii) within [thirty (30) days] after the close of each Lease Year and after the expiration or earlier termination of this Lease, a complete and accurate statement of Gross Sales for the preceding Lease Year or partial Lease Year signed and certified by Tenant or an authorized officer of Tenant. If Tenant fails to deliver such certified statement to Landlord within such [thirty (30)]-day period, then Landlord may hire an independent certified public accountant to examine such books and records to determine the amount of Gross Sales for such Lease Year, and Tenant shall promptly pay to Landlord as Additional Rent the cost of such examination.

PARAGRAPH 7

Landlord Promotional Funds

RISK RATING: 3

A. DESCRIPTION AND SCOPE

This Paragraph establishes Tenant's obligation to participate in advertising and promotional programs conducted by Landlord and to contribute funds to Landlord for advertising and promotional purposes related to a Shopping Center.

B. ANALYSIS

1. Landlord's Perspective

Landlord wants to ensure that a certain level and quality of advertising and promotional activities are conducted so as to increase sales volume at the Premises and the Shopping Center and in turn increase the Percentage Rent it collects from all Tenants. Accordingly, Landlord wants Tenant to share advertising and promotion costs since Tenant benefits from such expenditures.

2. Tenant's Perspective

Tenant wants to limit the amount it will pay into the Promotional Fund and the number of additional promotional activities in which it must join.

3. Lender's Perspective

Lender wants to ensure that sufficient promotional and advertising activities are conducted so as to maintain the value of its collateral. To the extent that Landlord, as borrower, has assigned the rents of the Shopping Center to Lender, Lender is interested in mechanisms that increase the Percentage Rent paid by Tenant.

4. Broker's Perspective

Brokers should expect to detail in the LOI any Tenant requirements to contribute to a Landlord promotional fund. Landlord Broker should inform Tenant Broker of the Landlord's required Tenant contribution to a Landlord promotional fund at the outset of LOI negotiation. Tenant Broker should include Tenant required contributions to a Landlord promotional fund in its financial projections of the Lease so that they are understood by Tenant before a Lease draft is requested. Both Brokers should confirm that the Paragraph in the Lease conforms to what was agreed to in the LOI.

C. COMPROMISES AND ALTERNATIVES

An alternative to the Promotional Fund is a merchant's association (see Part 2, Paragraph 10), which includes most or all of the Tenants of the Shopping Center or a shopping district and Landlord and makes decisions concerning promotional and advertising activities. Landlord generally prefers a Promotional Fund since it is completely controlled by Landlord. Alternatively, Landlord could appoint a committee consisting of Landlord's representative and representatives from certain Tenants to review Promotional Fund expenditures and to establish Tenants' contribution to such fund. Depending on Landlord's bargaining position, it may agree to cap the amount paid by Tenant into the Promotional Fund in any given year.

Tenant may condition its payment into the Promotional Fund on the payment into the fund by a specified percentage of the other tenants of the Shopping Center. If Landlord agrees to this, Paragraph 7 should state that payments to the Promotional Fund must be made by Tenant so long as the other Tenants of the Shopping Center are required by the terms of their leases to make payments.

D. COMMENTS

Landlord should be precise when describing the amount and calculation of Tenant's contribution to the Promotional Fund and Tenant's obligation to pay into the Promotional Fund.

E. TYPICAL PARAGRAPH

7. **<u>Promotional Funds</u>. Tenant will, during the term of this Lease, to the fullest extent possible, participate in all coordinated advertising and promotion programs outlined by Landlord from time to time that, in Landlord's sole judgment, will benefit the Premises from time to time (the "<u>Promotional Fund</u>"). Tenant agrees to pay a minimum amount of [AMOUNT] Dollars ($[AMOUNT]) per month (calculated on the basis of [AMOUNT] cents per rentable square foot per year of the total rentable square feet of the Premises) as Tenant's contribution to the Promotional Fund (the "<u>Minimum Amount</u>"), subject, however, to annual adjustments by a percentage equal to**

the percentage of increase or decrease from the Base Period (as hereinafter defined) of the United States Department of Labor Bureau of Labor Statistics Consumer Price Index for Urban Wage Earners and Clerical Workers (All Cities) 1982–84 =100 for that particular year. For the purpose of this Paragraph 7, the term "Base Period" shall mean the date on which such Index is published, which is closest to the Commencement Date. Notwithstanding any decrease in such Index, the amount payable by Tenant shall, at no time, be less than the Minimum Amount. [Tenant also agrees to pay, in addition to the foregoing, an initial assessment in the amount of [AMOUNT] Dollars ($[AMOUNT]) (calculated on the basis of [AMOUNT] cents per rentable square foot of the total rentable square feet of the Premises) for the purpose of defraying the advertising, promotion, and public relations expenses to be incurred (or to reimburse Landlord for advancing such expenses) in connection with the grand opening promotion of the retail complex. Such initial assessment shall be paid by Tenant within ten (10) days following Tenant's receipt from Landlord of a bill therefore.] If the Premises are expanded to the extent of at least [AMOUNT] rentable square feet (at any time and from time to time), then Tenant shall make an additional contribution to the Promotional Fund, as Additional Rent, in connection with such expansion in an amount equal to percent ([AMOUNT]%) of the annual promotional charge payable under this Paragraph. Such contribution shall be made within ten (10) days after receipt of a bill therefore by Tenant. Tenant agrees to advertise in any and all special newspaper sections, tabloids, or other advertisements required by Landlord and agrees to cooperate and participate with Landlord in all special sales and promotions. The failure of any other tenant of the Shopping Center to contribute to the Promotional Fund shall in no way release Tenant from Tenant's obligations under this Paragraph. Landlord agrees to contribute not less than [AMOUNT]% percent of the total amount of funds paid by the tenants of the Shopping Center with respect to the Promotional Fund. Nothing contained in this Lease shall obligate or require Landlord to expend more for the cost of Promotional Fund activities during any Lease Year than Landlord collects during such period from the tenants of the Shopping Center in the form of contributions to the Promotional Fund as adjusted by the Landlord's contribution. Landlord, at its option, may elect to contribute all or part of the services of a promotion director or secretary, or provide reasonable office space and equipment in lieu of Landlord's cash contribution to the Promotional Fund. The promotion director shall be under the exclusive control and supervision of Landlord, and Landlord shall have the sole right and exclusive authority to employ and discharge such promotion director. In addition to the foregoing, Tenant shall join and remain a member in good standing in a local merchant's association in the event such an association is formed for the betterment of retail business in the area in which the Premises are located.

PARAGRAPH 8

Tenant Required Advertising

RISK RATING: 3

A. DESCRIPTION AND SCOPE

While Paragraph 7 requires Tenant to contribute to Landlord's promotional fund for Landlord's advertising and promotion of the Shopping Center, this Paragraph 8 requires Tenant to independently advertise Tenant's business at the Shopping Center.

B. ANALYSIS

1. Landlord's Perspective

Landlord wants to ensure the commercial viability of Tenant and the Shopping Center. Creating and enforcing advertising requirements helps to ensure a steady cash flow to Tenant and the timely payment of Annual Base Rent, Additional Rent, and Percentage Rent by Tenant.

2. Tenant's Perspective

Tenant wants to control the funds allocated to advertising. However, Tenant realizes that if all tenants in the Shopping Center are required to meet certain advertising obligations, the overall success and profitability of all businesses in the Shopping Center should increase.

3. Lender's Perspective

Lender, like Landlord, is concerned with the overall profitability of businesses in the Shopping Center since this profitability will directly affect Landlord's ability to pay debt service.

4. Broker's Perspective

Brokers should expect to detail in the LOI any Tenant advertising requirements. Landlord Broker should inform Tenant Broker of the Landlord's expected Tenant advertising requirements at the outset of LOI negotiation. Tenant Broker should include the cost of any Tenant advertising requirements in its financial projections of the Lease so that they are understood by Tenant before a Lease draft is requested. Both Brokers should confirm that the Paragraph in the Lease conforms to what was agreed to in the LOI.

C. COMPROMISES AND ALTERNATIVES

Note that many nationally recognized Tenants are able to negotiate this provision out of the Lease where the Leased Premises is in Shopping Center such as a shopping mall.

If Tenant's Lease requires Tenant to participate in the Merchants' Association (as further discussed in Part 2, Paragraph 10) and conduct its own advertising, Tenant may be able to remove one obligation or the other from the Lease. Certainly, Tenant should not be required to contribute to a Landlord's promotional fund, a Merchants Association, and be required to meet certain independent advertising requirements as well.

The amount or percentage of Gross Sales Tenant may be required to expend toward advertising is negotiable.

D. COMMENTS

Tenants that are franchisees of large franchise-based retail organizations may be required under their franchise agreements to participate in local or national advertising campaigns. Those Tenants may object to additional advertising requirements and the payment into a Promotional Fund.

E. TYPICAL PARAGRAPH

8. **Tenant Required Advertising. From and after the Commencement Date, Tenant shall spend during each calendar year an amount equal to at least [three percent (3%)] of its Gross Sales from the Premises for advertising Tenant's business at the Shopping Center ("Required Advertising"). The Required Advertising shall be in newspapers, tabloids, direct mailings, or other media covering the trade area served by the Shopping Center, and shall designate the location of the Premises by reference to the Shopping Center by name. At any time upon request by Landlord, Tenant shall furnish Landlord with its Annual Statement of Gross Sales and a certified statement showing the amounts Tenant actually spent for advertising. If Tenant fails to spend the Required Advertising amount, Tenant shall pay to Landlord the difference between (a) the amount actually spent by Tenant for advertising during the preceding calendar year, and (b) the Required Advertising amount that Tenant was required to spend for advertising during the applicable calendar year pursuant to this Paragraph.**

PARAGRAPH 9

Parking Requirements

RISK RATING: 3

A. DESCRIPTION AND SCOPE

Parking provisions under retail leases vary greatly depending upon the Property. As an example, if Tenant is leasing a stand-alone establishment in any urban location or on a "Main Street" in a suburban location, Tenant may be granted no parking rights if the municipality governs the available parking areas surrounding the Property and not Landlord. If Landlord has any parking spaces on its Property (maybe a few spots behind a retail establishment on Main Street), Tenant may be able to obtain rights for those reserved spaces for its employees or customers. If the Property has several stores located on it, Tenant should get its proportionate share of Landlord's available parking, preferably marked for Tenant's exclusive use. It Tenant is a single retailer on a large property with dedicated parking (such as a "Home Depot" located outside any larger retail complex), Tenant will likely be able to obtain the exclusive right to all parking available on the Property.

Tenants with retail business within Shopping Centers such as shopping malls with associated parking garages or surface parking areas, may be granted dedicated parking rights but, more often, Landlord considers such parking areas "common areas" of the Shopping Center and parking is provided on a first-come, first-served basis for all customers to the Shopping Center. In such a case, Landlord may impose regulations upon Tenant so that Tenant's employees park in areas of the Shopping Center that are less desirable so that the most desirable parking areas (typically those closest to Shopping Center entry ways) are reserved for the use of Shopping Center customers.

For purposes of this Paragraph, we will assume Tenant's store is located within a Shopping Center with a dedicated Landlord-owned parking facility which Landlord designates as a Common Area.

B. ANALYSIS

1. Landlord's Perspective

Landlord wants control over Tenant employee parking to maximize the most desirable parking areas for customers of the Shopping Center.

2. Tenant's Perspective

Tenant wants reasonable notice and cure periods before Landlord imposes parking fees on its employees. Tenant may wish to specify how many parking spaces it will have daily for the use of its employees.

3. Lender's Perspective

Lender wants to confirm that there is sufficient parking available on-site for all Tenants and their customers, and that the amount of parking conforms to zoning requirements.

4. Broker's Perspective

Brokers should expect to detail in the LOI any Tenant parking rights. Tenant Broker will want to fully understand, during the needs assessment phase of its assignment, Tenant's parking needs or preferences as it may impact Tenant's location selection. Both Brokers should confirm that this Paragraph conforms to the parking provision agreed to in the LOI.

C. COMPROMISES AND ALTERNATIVES

As previously mentioned, alternatives will depend largely upon the available supply of parking spaces and whether Tenant is a tenant of a Shopping Center, a "main street" retailer or a single building retail location.

If the Shopping Center has paid parking facilities for all customers by the hour or otherwise, then Tenant may be able to negotiate an elimination of the parking fee for its employees or at least a reduced rate of parking fees for a limited number of employees each day.

D. COMMENTS

Parking provisions under retail leases vary greatly depending upon the location of the retail establishment.

Local ordinances should be consulted to determine Landlord's rights, as owner of a private parking lot, to enforce rules and regulations with respect to the parking areas.

E. TYPICAL PARAGRAPH

9. Parking Requirements.

(a) Tenant Employee Parking. Tenant and its employees shall park their vehicles only in the parking areas designated for that purpose by Landlord.

(b) Tenant Employee Parking Violations. Tenant shall, within [ten (10)] days of Landlord's request therefore, notify Landlord of the license plate numbers, years, makes, and models of the automobiles of Tenant's employees entitled to use the parking areas. If Tenant or its employees fail to park in the area designated for employee parking, Tenant shall be liable to pay Landlord a fee of [AMOUNT] Dollars ($[AMOUNT]) per day for each violation. If a car of Tenant, a concessionaire, employee or agent of Tenant continues to be parked outside any area designated by Landlord for employee parking after one written notice of such violation in such Lease Year, Tenant authorizes Landlord to cause such car to be towed from the Shopping Center and Tenant shall reimburse Landlord for the cost thereof upon demand, and otherwise indemnify and hold Landlord harmless with respect thereto.

(c) Customer Parking. Tenant's business invitees and customers shall have the nonexclusive right, in common with Landlord and all others to whom Landlord has granted or may hereafter grant rights, to use the parking facilities associated with the Shopping Center which are deemed a Common Area, subject to such reasonable regulations as Landlord may from time to time impose.

PARAGRAPH 10

Merchants' Association

RISK RATING: 3

A. DESCRIPTION AND SCOPE

This Paragraph is an optional Paragraph and is included in some retail leases where the Landlord requires Tenant to participate in Merchants' Association to provide for general advertising of all business participating in the Merchant's Association. The advertising is funded by assessment paid by Tenants.

This Paragraph can be included in a retail lease in any setting but it is most often included in a lease for retail space located on "Main Street" wherein the separate owners/landlords of adjacent buildings compromising the shopping district on "Main Street" or, more generally, a distinct shopping district within a suburban or even rural community, elect to work together through a "Merchants' Association" to gain advertising and promotional efficiencies by working together for the common goal of promoting their shopping district.

B. ANALYSIS

1. Landlord's Perspective

A Merchants' Association provides an organized and consistent scheme of advertising for a shopping district or Shopping Center that may help to increase any Percentage Rent or otherwise enhance the value of Landlord's property.

2. Tenant's Perspective

Although Tenant also will benefit from a Merchant's Association, most Tenants prefer not to be locked into a flat-fee payment arrangement for association assessments since these arrangements limit business flexibility. Tenant may want to condition its obligations under this Paragraph upon at least 70% of all other tenants of in the shopping district or Shopping Center, as applicable, joining the Merchants' Association.

3. Lender's Perspective

A Lender, like Landlord, favors the establishment of a Merchants' Association to promote the applicable shopping district or Shopping Center and thereby enhance its value as collateral.

4. Broker's Perspective

Brokers should expect to detail in the LOI any Tenant requirements to participate in or contribute to a Merchants' Association. Landlord Broker should inform Tenant Broker of any Tenant requirements to contribute to and/or participate in a Merchants' Association at the outset of LOI negotiation. Tenant Broker should include Tenant required contributions to the Merchants' Association in its financial projections of the Lease so that they are understood by Tenant before a Lease draft is requested. Both Brokers should confirm that the Paragraph in the Lease conforms to what was agreed to in the LOI.

C. COMPROMISES AND ALTERNATIVES

As an alternative to setting Merchants' Association assessments in the Lease, the determination of assessment or contribution amounts could be left to the members of the Merchants' Association. While adding flexibility, this option limits Landlord's control over advertising.

Landlord may wish to be the "member" of the Merchants' Association instead of Tenant to have a vote and voice in the choices made by the Merchants' Association and then just pass any assessments of the Association through to Tenant. Of course, Tenant may object to this because it too may wish to have a vote and voice in the choices made by the Merchants' Association since it will likely be the party subject to any assessments of the Association.

D. COMMENTS

Tenant will want to review the Articles of Incorporation and By-Laws of the Merchants' Association prior to Lease execution to confirm that the terms and conditions thereof are acceptable to Tenant. Tenant may also wish to request for review the assessment statements for a few years immediately preceding the Lease Effective Date.

E. TYPICAL PARAGRAPH

10. Merchants' Association.

(a) Membership. Tenant agrees to maintain its membership in the merchants' association formed for the purpose of creating and maintaining a fund for the general promotion and welfare of the [Shopping District/ Shopping Center] (the "Merchants' Association"). Tenant agrees to be

bound by the Articles of Incorporation and By-Laws of the Merchants' Association, copies of which are available for Tenant's inspection at Landlord's office.

(b) Assessments. Tenant agrees to pay to the Merchants' Association an [annual/quarterly] assessment as determined by the Merchants' Association. Tenant shall pay to the Merchants' Association all such assessments within ten (10) days after receipt of a statement therefore. Tenant shall pay a prorated amount of the first and last annual assessment if the Commencement Date does not coincide with the first day of the annual assessment period.

PARAGRAPH 11

Exclusivity Right

RISK RATING: 4

A. DESCRIPTION AND SCOPE

This Paragraph grants to Tenant the exclusive right to engage in a certain line of business at the Shopping Center, and restricts Landlord's right to rent space at the Shopping Center to any tenant who operates a business in competition with Tenant.

B. ANALYSIS

1. Landlord's Perspective

Before granting an exclusive, Landlord must examine all of the other Leases with respect to the Shopping Center to determine whether other Tenants are prohibited from engaging in the business granted pursuant to the exclusive. If other Leases provide that Tenant may use their Premises for "any lawful use," then Landlord will not be able to abide by the exclusive granted to Tenant. One solution is to draft the exclusive so that it is subject to the rights of existing Tenants, and perhaps any future Anchor Tenants, but obligates Landlord to enter into new Leases that do not violate the exclusive granted to Tenant. Landlord Is generally reluctant to grant exclusives and will generally want to exclude department stores and other anchor tenants from the exclusive.

2. Tenant's Perspective

In shopping malls, exclusives are most commonly sought and obtained by anchor Tenants. In smaller Shopping Centers (such as suburban "strip" Shopping Centers) with a limited amount of retail establishments, most Tenants seek exclusives.

3. Lender's Perspective

Lender should review all Leases to make sure that exclusive rights do not overlap (i.e., the same exclusive is granted to more than one Tenant) or violate state and federal antitrust laws. The loan documents should provide that a default by Landlord under such clause would constitute a default under the loan documents.

4. Broker's Perspective

Brokers should expect to detail in the LOI any Tenant exclusivity rights. Landlord Broker should at all times maintain an updated summary of previously granted and presently existing exclusivity rights and, at the outset of LOI negotiation, confirm that Tenant's proposed use will not violate same. Tenant Broker will want to fully understand, during the needs assessment phase of its assignment, Tenant's exclusivity needs or preferences as it may be significant point of negotiation in the LOI and may ultimately impact Tenant's location selection. Both Brokers should confirm that this Paragraph conforms to the applicable terms agreed to in the LOI.

C. COMPROMISES AND ALTERNATIVES

Exclusives can be very broad (e.g., an exclusive right to sell food and beverages) or very narrow (e.g., an exclusive right to operate a take-out pizza restaurant). The broad "food and beverages" clause, favored by Tenant, would preclude Landlord from renting space to a grocery store, gas station with food vending machines, ice cream shop, and other similar businesses. Such other businesses, however, may not compete with and may actually enhance Tenant's pizza business. The narrow clause, favored by Landlord, would allow uses that are not directly competitive with Tenant. There is usually a way to determine the scope of the restriction so as to prohibit Landlord's renting to most of Tenant's true competitors, thus benefiting both Landlord and Tenant by keeping Tenant's sales high. In addition, the parties may want to provide for exceptions to an otherwise rather broad restriction on Landlord.

Exclusivity clauses are very important to Tenant and often, as Landlord imposes a radius restriction upon Tenant, as provided in Part 2, Paragraph 2 above, Tenant may endeavor to extend any "exclusivity rights" granted to Tenant beyond the Shopping Center to other properties owned by Landlord or its affiliates within a radius restriction of the Premises. In addition, because of the value of any Tenant exclusivity right, Tenant often demands automatic remedy under the Lease for any Landlord violations. Below is an expanded Tenant exclusivity right with an automatic Tenant remedy:

> *Landlord covenants, except as otherwise specifically provided herein, that it shall not sell, lease, rent, occupy or allow to be occupied, or otherwise transfer or convey all or any portion of any real property leased or owned by Landlord or any parent, subsidiary, or affiliate of Landlord, nor by any entity with any partner, member, or shareholder who is also a partner, member, or shareholder of Landlord or Landlord's parent, subsidiary or affiliate and located within 10-mile of the exterior boundary of the Premises to be used primarily for the sale of [TYPE OF BUSINESS] ("Tenant's Exclusive Use").*

If a breach of Tenant's Exclusive Use occurs, Landlord acknowledges that Tenant's remedies at law would be inadequate. In any such event, if such breach is not cured within thirty (30) days after written notice from Tenant to Landlord ("Tenant's Notice"), Tenant shall have the right, at its sole option, to elect any or all of the following: (i) to pay, in lieu of monthly Base Rent, an amount equal to one-half (1/2) of monthly Base Rent due hereunder ("Alternate Rent"); and (ii) to relief by temporary or permanent injunction.

Landlord may wish to counter any Tenant automatic remedy above with the following limitation:

If, within six (6) months of Landlord's receipt of Tenant's Notice, Landlord has not cured such breach Tenant's right to pay Alternate Rent shall cease and Tenant shall have the right to terminate this Lease upon thirty (30) days written notice to Landlord delivered on or prior to thirty (30) days following the expiration Landlord's 6-months cure period and, unless such breach is cured within such thirty (30) day period, this Lease shall terminate. Upon such termination, all Base Rent or Alternate Rent, as the case may be, and all Additional Rent shall be prorated through such date of termination. In the event Tenant does not elect to terminate this Lease, Tenant's right to pay Alternate Rent will cease at the end of the six (6) month period and Tenant shall return to paying the full amount of monthly Minimum Rent hereunder without further right to enforce Tenant's Exclusive Use covenant hereunder.

D. COMMENTS

Exclusive clauses are normally upheld, but are not favored. Any ambiguity in an exclusive will be construed against its restriction. Clauses restraining competition have been subject to attack on antitrust grounds in state and federal courts and through action by the Federal Trade Commission.

E. TYPICAL PARAGRAPH

11. Exclusives. Landlord shall not during the term of this Lease enter into any leases with respect to the Shopping Center with any other person, corporation, limited liability company, partnership, or entity that allows the tenant under such lease to use any portion of the Shopping Center for the display and sale of any, or any combination, of the following items: [list prohibited items].

PARAGRAPH 12

Co-Tenancy

RISK RATING: 4

A. DESCRIPTION AND SCOPE

The Paragraph grants Tenant certain relief in the event a key tenant (or "anchor" tenant) or a certain number of tenants leave the Shopping Center.

Co-tenancy provisions can be among the more heavily negotiated provision in a Shopping Center retail lease.

B. ANALYSIS

1. Landlord's Perspective

Landlords dislike co-tenancy provisions because they are not in control of the actions of their tenants, including any anchor tenants, and their rent stream from the Shopping Center can be severely impacted from the loss of an anchor tenant because of the cascading consequences brought about by any co-tenancy clause. Landlord often takes this risk associated with co-tenancy provisions to secure nationally recognized high credit tenants or other "hot" tenants or that will bring cache to the Shopping Center as such tenants will demand co-tenancy provisions due to their leverage.

2. Tenant's Perspective

A large or key tenant is a big draw for traffic, particularly in shopping malls, and is often one of the major reasons a Tenant chooses to lease space in a particular shopping mall.

3. Lender's Perspective

Lender will want to closely scrutinize any co-tenancy provisions since a loss of any tenant or a reduction in rent can severely impact debt service coverage and lead to a foreclosure of the Property.

4. Broker's Perspective

Brokers should expect to detail in the LOI any co-tenancy provisions. Landlord Broker should at all times maintain an updated summary of previously granted and presently existing "co-tenancy" provision in the leases for anchor tenants. Tenant Broker will want to fully understand, during the needs assessment phase of its assignment, Tenant's needs or preferences with respect to any Tenant required co-tenancy provisions as it may be significant point of negotiation in the LOI and may ultimately impact Tenant's location selection. Both Brokers should confirm that this Paragraph conforms to the applicable terms agreed to in the LOI.

C. COMPROMISES AND ALTERNATIVES

All of the business terms of any co-tenancy Paragraph will likely be highly negotiated, including the definition of Anchor Store, all of the thresholds that may trigger Tenant remedies, and what remedies Tenant is afforded under the clause.

In light of the COVID-19 experience wherein in some geographical areas, retail establishments were closed by governmental mandate, it may be prudent for Landlord to except Force Majeure conditions to Tenant's co-tenancy rights (with pandemics and associated governmental mandates expressly included in Force Majeure clauses).

This Paragraph may be revised and be limited to "opening co-tenancy" clauses or "operating co-tenancy clauses." so as to limit their scope of applicability. Paragraph 12 contains both concepts but some leases have just one or the other with opening co-tenancy clauses being seen as nearly mandatory by Tenant when a Shopping Center is in a lease-up or construction phase.

D. COMMENTS

How Anchor Stores are defined within any lease varies greatly depending upon the characteristics of the particular Shopping Center. As an example, in a "strip" suburban Shopping Center the anchor store may be a supermarket. If so, the Anchor Store may be defined as "[NAME], [NAME] or any comparable regional or national replacement for any of the foregoing."

For another example, in a large regional shopping mall, the Anchor Store may be defined as "[NAME], [NAME] or any comparable regional or national replacement for any of the foregoing, provided that the replacement occupies at least [AMOUNT] thousand [(AMOUNT)] square feet and is not a 'outlet' store such as [NAME] [NAME] or [NAME], but may be a value retailer such as [NAME] or [NAME]."

The [bracketed] provisions in Paragraph 12 below are business terms typically negotiated.

E. TYPICAL PARAGRAPH

12. Co-Tenancy. In the event that at any time during the Lease Term (i) fewer than [three (3)] Anchor Stores (as defined below) are open for business in their current locations in the Shopping Center or (ii) less than [eighty-five percent (85%)] of the floor area of the Shopping Center (other than the area designated for Anchor Stores) is open for business in the Shopping Center (hereinafter the "Co-Tenancy Condition"), then (1) Tenant shall not be required, as the case may be, (x) to open (or reopen, as applicable) the Premises for business if Tenant has not yet opened for business in the Premises or if Tenant was open but closed for remodeling, or (y) if Tenant is then open for business, to remain open for business in the Premises, and (2) if Tenant shall elect to reopen, or remain open in, the Premises for business, then Tenant shall be entitled to pay, commencing with the first day of the month following the occurrence of the Co-Tenancy Condition, in lieu of Base Rent, Percentage Rent and all Additional Rent calculated based on the floor area of the Premises (except utilities), a sum equal to [five percent (5%)] of Tenant's Gross Sales ("Co-Tenancy Rent"), monthly in arrears, within fifteen (15) days after the end of each calendar month until the first (1st) day of the calendar month following the date the Co-Tenancy Condition is no longer occurring (or the date the Co-Tenancy Condition is no longer occurring if such date is the first (1st) day of a calendar month); provided, however, if at any time while Tenant is entitled to pay Co-Tenancy Rent, Tenant is in monetary or material non-monetary default under this Lease beyond any applicable notice and cure periods, then, upon written notice from Landlord to Tenant, Tenant shall be required to recommence payment of Base Bent, Percentage Rent, and Additional Rent calculated based on Floor Area, and Tenant shall no longer have the right to pay Co-Tenancy Rent. If Tenant has paid Co-Tenancy Rent for a period of [twelve (12) consecutive months], then Tenant shall have the right to continue paying Co-Tenancy Rent or deliver written notice to Landlord of Tenant's election to terminate this Lease ("Termination Notice") at any time thereafter as long as the Co-Tenancy Condition continues, in which case (A) this Lease shall terminate on the date set forth in Tenant's notice, which shall not be less than sixty (60) days after such notice is given to Landlord, (B) Tenant shall continue to pay Co-Tenancy Rent during the period between the giving of such Termination Notice and the effective date of such termination, and (C) prior to such effective termination date, Landlord shall reimburse Tenant for Tenant's unamortized construction costs for Tenant's Work to remodel the Premises, if Tenant has elected to perform such work prior to delivering such Termination Notice. For purposes of this Paragraph 12, an "Anchor Store" is defined as [DEFINITION].

PARAGRAPH 13

Landlord's Rights to Make Changes to the Shopping Center

RISK RATING: 4

A. DESCRIPTION AND SCOPE

This Paragraph provides Landlord with the right to make changes to the Shopping Center.

B. ANALYSIS

1. Landlord's Perspective

During the Term of the Lease, the Shopping Center may deteriorate due to age and wear and tear and/or Landlord may wish to upgrade the Shopping Center to maximize its value.

2. Tenant's Perspective

Certain changes or upgrades to the Shopping Center made by Landlord may benefit Tenant and its customers, but Tenant seeks to protect itself from Landlord changes that may negatively impact Tenant, including, most importantly, any negative impact to the visibility or accessibility of Tenant's retail business.

3. Lender's Perspective

Lender has the same perspective as Landlord.

4. Broker's Perspective

For shopping mall leases, Tenant Broker should endeavor to include within the LOI (or require in the LOI, if required by Tenant) certain Landlord limitations on making changes to the Shopping Center that may negatively impact the visibility or accessibility of Tenant's retail business, including restrictions on Landlord installing "kiosks" in front of Tenant's retail business. Both Brokers should confirm that the terms of this Paragraph conform to any applicable terms agreed to in the LOI.

C. COMPROMISES AND ALTERNATIVES

Typically, Tenant is able to reasonably limit Landlord's right to make changes to the Shopping Center to protect Tenant from changes that may have an adverse impact on Tenant.

Below is Tenant-favorable language that Tenant may wish to add to the end of Paragraph 13:

> *, provided, further, that the location and dimensions of the Premises shall not be changed and that such changes do not materially and adversely affect ingress or egress to the Premises or its visibility, or materially and adversely affect Tenant's business. Prior to the Commencement Date, except for mall furniture less than 40" in height, Landlord shall remove any and all existing temporary or permanent carts, kiosks, retail merchandising units, vending machines, ATM's, directories, amenities, automobiles, planters, and other structures and displays (collectively "Obstructions") located within the cross-hatched area (the "No-Build Area") as shown on Exhibit "[__]" attached hereto. During the Term of this Lease, Landlord will not place any Obstructions within the "No-Build Area." In the event Landlord breaches the foregoing covenant and such breach continues for seven (7) days after Landlord's receipt of written notice from Tenant, then Tenant's Annual Base Rent and Additional Rent shall abate from the date such breach first occurred until such breach is cured, provided, however, that after the first occurrence of such breach in each twelve (12) month period such abatement shall apply from the date of such breach without the benefit of such notice and cure period.*
>
> *Except as exists on the Effective Date of this Lease, Landlord will not permit any adjacent storefronts within fifty feet (50') of Tenant's storefront to extend into the Common Areas past the storefront lease line of the Premises.*

D. COMMENTS

None.

E. TYPICAL PARAGRAPH

13. Modifications to the Center.

Notwithstanding anything in this Lease contained, Landlord reserves the right to change or modify and add to or subtract from the size and dimensions of the Shopping Center or any part thereof, the number, location and

dimensions of buildings and stores, the size and configuration of the parking areas, entrances, exits and parking aisle alignments, dimensions of hallways, malls and corridors, the number of floors in any building, the location, size and number of tenants' spaces and kiosks which may be erected in or fronting on any mall or otherwise, the identity, type and location of other stores and tenants, and the size, shape, location and arrangement of Common Areas, and to design and decorate any portion of the Shopping Center as it desires, provided the general character of the Shopping Center and the approximate location of the Premises in relation to the Anchor Tenants shall not be substantially changed.

PARAGRAPH 14

Storage and Office Use

RISK RATING: 1

A. DESCRIPTION AND SCOPE

This Paragraph sets forth the amount of space that a retail Tenant may use for office and storage space.

B. ANALYSIS

1. Landlord's Perspective

Landlord wants to maximize the retail space of the Premises in order to maximize Gross Sales and Percentage Rent. The storage and office space of the Premises should be minimized.

2. Tenant's Perspective

Tenant wants to ensure that it has adequate room to store inventory and supplies and run business operations requiring office facilities. Tenant also wants to maximize sales, and therefore, is unlikely to overuse retail space for storage and office functions unless Tenant is having financial difficulties that result in operating losses.

3. Lender's Perspective

Lender has the same perspective as Landlord.

4. Broker's Perspective

Brokers should expect to detail in the LOI any limitation of Tenant's office and/or storage space. Tenant Broker will want to fully understand, during the assessment phase of its assignment, Tenant's office and/or storage space needs as it may impact Tenant's location selection. Both Brokers should confirm that this Paragraph conforms to the parking provision agreed to in the LOI.

C. COMPROMISES AND ALTERNATIVES

If extensive storage or business operations are required to run Tenant's business, then these operations may be located outside of the Premises, thereby maximizing productive use of retail space.

D. COMMENTS

The percentage of space required for storage and office use will depend on Tenant's type of retail operation.

E. TYPICAL PARAGRAPH

14. Storage and Office Use. Tenant agrees that it shall use not more than ten percent (10%) of the rentable square feet of the Premises for storage and office purposes.

PARAGRAPH 15

Window Displays by Tenant

RISK RATING: 3

A. DESCRIPTION AND SCOPE

This Paragraph allows Landlord to control the window displays of the Premises.

B. ANALYSIS

1. Landlord's Perspective

Landlord wants each store in the Shopping Center to have a high-quality appearance and in some cases a uniform storefront design. Landlord will not want to have any store fail to maintain suitable window displays, as that can promote an abandoned or run-down atmosphere.

2. Tenant's Perspective

Tenant wants greater discretion over the physical appearance of the Premises. Tenant may want to have an unusual exterior facade so as to attract business.

3. Lender's Perspective

Lender has the same perspective as Landlord.

4. Broker's Perspective

The details of the terms and conditions of Tenant window displays are not often included in a LOI. Landlord Broker should advise Tenant Broker of any Landlord required display controls at the outset of LOI negotiation. Tenant Broker will want to fully understand, during the assessment phase of its assignment, Tenant's window display needs or requirements as it may impact Tenant's location selection. Both Brokers should confirm that this Paragraph conforms to any such provision agreed to in the LOI.

C. COMPROMISES AND ALTERNATIVES

Landlord may allow Tenant some discretion in choosing the external appearance of the Premises provided Tenant complies with Landlord's storefront design criteria. Landlord will want Tenant to provide to Landlord any proposal for the external appearance of the Premises for Landlord's approval. Any proposal will likely not be accepted if it would detract from other stores or the Shopping Center as a whole.

National Tenants with multiple locations can often get the following compromise inserted to the end of Paragraph 15 below:

> *; provided, however, that Landlord's approval shall not be required with respect to any signs (other than exterior storefront identification signage), advertising, or window or other displays which are substantially similar to that which is then being utilized by Tenant at a majority of Tenant's ten (10) closest stores to the Premises and which comply with applicable law.*

D. COMMENTS

None.

E. TYPICAL PARAGRAPH

15. Window Displays. Tenant will install and maintain at all times, subject to the other provisions of this Paragraph 15, merchandise displays in any show windows on the Premises; the arrangement, style, color, and general appearance thereof and of displays in the interior of the Premises that are visible from the exterior, including, but not limited to, window displays, advertising matter, signs, merchandise and store fixtures, shall be maintained in keeping with the character and standards of the Shopping Center.

PARAGRAPH 16

Sales Test Termination Rights

RISK RATING: 5

A. DESCRIPTION AND SCOPE

This this an optional Paragraph sometimes contained in retail leases that allows Landlord or Tenant to terminate the Lease in the event Tenant does not generate a Gross Sales to meet a certain threshold during a determined time period.

B. ANALYSIS

1. Landlord's Perspective

Landlord typically does not permit Tenant termination rights under the Lease but an underperforming Tenant is not an asset to any Shopping Center, particularly because Tenant will not be generating any Percentage Rent contemplated by Landlord. Landlord will want to make sure any Sales Test Termination Right may be exercised by Landlord and not just Tenant and provide Landlord with a termination fee being delivered to Landlord if Tenant elects to terminate the Lease so that Landlord can recoup its initial investment under the Lease.

2. Tenant's Perspective

Any Tenant who has any concerns about the well-being of the Shopping Center and/or Tenant's likelihood of success in the location, will want to have a termination right if Tenant underperforms at the location. If Tenant elects to forego is termination right under this Paragraph even though it has the right to do so, but then Landlord exercises its right to terminate the Lease under this Paragraph, Tenant will want to recoup from Landlord some of its initial investment in opening its business at this location.

3. Lender's Perspective

Lender will scrutinize any early termination rights by Tenant or Landlord since in Lender's underwriting of the mortgage loan, Lender will use rent for the entire Term of the Lease. Any early termination right will require Lender to recalculate debt service for the period after the permitted early termination.

4. Broker's Perspective

Brokers should expect to detail in the LOI any early Lease termination option including any sales test termination right. Brokers should expect that, any sales test termination right will be one of the most focused on and negotiated business terms in the LOI. Tenant Broker will want to fully understand, during the needs assessment phase of its assignment, Tenant's expectation on this business term and understand how it may impact Tenant's business model. In addition, Tenant Broker should include the possibility of a Termination Fee in its financial projections of the Lease so that they are understood by Tenant before a Lease draft is requested. Of course, both Brokers will then want to review this Paragraph carefully to confirm that terms and conditions therein conform to what the parties agreed to in the LOI.

C. COMPROMISES AND ALTERNATIVES

The termination rights under this Paragraph 16 are mutual with both Landlord and Tenant having the ability to exercise the right to terminate the Lease but, in some leases, the termination is unilateral and exclusive to either Landlord or Tenant.

The Paragraph below requires Tenant to pay a Termination Fee to Landlord if Tenant exercises the Tenant Termination Right. However, Tenant may be able to negotiate the elimination of a Termination Fee (or have the Termination Fee be a lower amount) in the event Landlord exercises the Landlord Termination Right.

All of the other business terms contained in Paragraph 16 are also subject to negotiation.

D. COMMENTS

In light of the COVID-19 experience wherein in some geographical areas, retail establishments were closed by governmental mandate, it may be prudent for the parties to modify the Paragraph to address the impact of any Force Majeure events (with pandemics and associated governmental mandates expressly included in Force Majeure clauses).

E. TYPICAL PARAGRAPH

16. Sales Test Termination Right.

(a) Provided Tenant (i) is not then in default under the Lease beyond applicable Notice and cure periods and in particular, has not been in default of the provisions contained in Paragraph 1 (Covenant to Operate) or Paragraph 2 (Radius Restriction) and is operating its business in the Premises in accordance with the terms of this Lease (and has done so for the [twenty-four (24) month] period commencing on the [twenty-fifth (25th)] full calendar month of the Term following the Commencement Date, through and including the [forty-eighth (48th)] full calendar month of the Term following the Commencement Date (the "Sales Test Period"), and (ii) has not assigned its interest in the Lease except in connection with an assignment permitted without Landlord approval hereunder), then if Tenant has not achieved an average annual Gross Sales from the Premises equal to or in excess of [AMOUNT] Dollars per square foot of Floor Area during the Sales Test Period (said average annual amount of Gross Sales shall hereafter be referred to as the "Sales Test"), then Tenant may elect to terminate this Lease by giving Notice to Landlord within sixty (60) days following the end of the Sales Test Period. Tenant's right to terminate the Lease based on Tenant's failure to meet such Sales Test is referred to as the "Tenant Termination Right." Tenant shall deliver its Annual Statement of Gross Sales within twenty (20) days after the expiration of each twelve (12)-month period during the Sales Test Period and with respect to the Sales Test Period prior to the exercise of its termination right (if any). If (i) Tenant's Gross Sales exceed an annual average of [AMOUNT] Dollars per square foot of Floor Area during any 12-month period of the Term prior to the Sales Test Period or (ii) Tenant fails to exercise the Tenant Termination Right as provided herein within the designated time period provided, then the Tenant Termination Right shall expire and such expiration shall constitute an unconditional and irrevocable waiver of the Tenant Termination Right.

(b) If the average annual amount of Tenant's Gross Sales from the Premises over the Sales Test Period fail to meet or exceed the Sales Test as set forth above, Landlord may elect to terminate this Lease by giving Tenant Notice within sixty (60) days following receipt of Tenant's Annual Statements of Gross Sales for each twelve (12) month period during the Sales Test Period, and may elect to do so notwithstanding any Tenant default or assignment as described in clauses (i) and (ii) of paragraph (a) above. Landlord's right to terminate the Lease based on Tenant's failure to meet the Sales Test is referred to as the "Landlord Termination

Right." Failure by Landlord to exercise the Landlord Termination Right as provided herein within such period shall constitute an unconditional and irrevocable waiver of Landlord's Termination Right. (Tenant's Termination Right and Landlord's Termination Right may sometimes be hereafter collectively referred to as the "Termination Right.")

(c) If Landlord or Tenant desires to exercise its Termination Right, Landlord or Tenant shall give Notice ("Termination Notice") of such exercise to the other party in the manner specified for the giving of Notices in the Lease. The Termination Notice shall provide for the termination of the Lease as of the close of business one hundred eighty (180) days following the date of the Termination Notice ("Termination Notice Effective Date").

(d) Tenant shall pay all Base Rent, Percentage Rent, Additional Rent and all other charges payable and perform all other covenants and obligations required to be performed by Tenant under the Lease through the Termination Notice Effective Date. Tenant shall not be required to pay any amounts attributable to any period after the Termination Notice Effective Date for Base Rent, Percentage Rent and Additional Rent. Unless the Termination Notice Effective Date is on the last day of Landlord's fiscal or calendar year, Landlord shall not be obligated to perform a reconciliation of such amounts until within a reasonable time after the end of the applicable fiscal or calendar year, and Tenant shall be billed for and shall promptly pay to Landlord any underpayments and shall be promptly refunded any overpayments.

(e) Notwithstanding the foregoing, if Tenant has opened another business in violation of Paragraph 2 (Radius Restriction) (other than a store opened in one of Landlord's shopping centers), then Tenant's opening of such business shall constitute an unconditional and irrevocable waiver of the Tenant Termination Right.

(f) [In addition to the timely and full performance of all of its obligations contained herein through the Termination Notice Effective Date, Tenant shall pay to Landlord, on or before the Termination Notice Effective Date, a sum equal to the then unamortized portion of the Tenant Improvement Allowance paid to Tenant based upon amortization on a straight-line basis over the Term of this Lease, plus the unamortized amount of the leasing commissions paid to Brokers based upon amortization on a straight-line basis over the Term of this Lease (collectively, the "Termination Fee"). Subject to the terms of this Subparagraph (f), in the event Landlord elects to terminate the Lease hereunder, Landlord shall pay to Tenant, on or before the Termination Notice Effective Date, a sum equal to the unamortized amount of the "hard" and "soft" costs and expenses incurred by Tenant in excess of the Tenant Improvement Allowance for the construction of the leasehold improvements as part of the Tenant's Work based upon amortization on a straight-line basis over

the Term; provided, however, all such excess costs must be documented by written invoices delivered to Landlord and Landlord shall not be required to reimburse Tenant for any costs and expenses relating to personal property and its furniture, fixtures and equipment. Subject to the timely and full performance of all of its obligations contained herein, and except for the obligation to pay any underpayment or refund any overpayment determined pursuant to subparagraph (d), above, Landlord and Tenant shall be released of their respective obligations under the Lease from and after the Termination Notice Effective Date; provided, however, it is specifically agreed that Tenant shall not be released from its obligation to indemnify Landlord as provided under this Lease.]

(g) **Time is of the essence of all of the foregoing provisions relating to Tenant's and/or Landlord's exercise of its Termination Right.**

PART 3

Description and Analysis of Industrial/Warehouse Lease Paragraphs

PARAGRAPH 1

Net Lease

RISK RATING: 4

A. DESCRIPTION AND SCOPE

This Paragraph incorporates the "net lease" concept for a single-tenant building (on a single-building Property), whereby Tenant pays all utilities, Real Estate Taxes, and Operating Expenses on the entire Property. Because of this, oftentimes, the Premises is indeed the entire Property and not the interior portion of the Building located on the Property.

It is in the industrial sector where a "net lease" is most often used so that is why this Paragraph is incorporated into Part 3 but it should be noted that "net leases" are sometimes used in the office and retail sectors too. Office leases for a company's "headquarters" may be a "net lease" if the Premises is a single-tenant building. Similarly, "net leases" may be used for a free-standing, single-tenant retail Property.

B. ANALYSIS

1. Landlord's Perspective

Generally, this Paragraph protects Landlord from having to absorb any of the costs relating to the maintenance and operation of the Property, including the Building and the Premises. It is intended that this be a "triple net" or "absolutely net" Lease, meaning that the Tenant pays all (i) real estate taxes; (ii) insurance premiums; and (iii) costs of utilities, repairs, and maintenance of the Property. Thus, the net cash flow before debt service should equal the Annual Base Rent payable under the Lease. With respect to the payment of Operating Expenses or Real Estate Taxes, Landlord will insist that any free-rent period not be applicable to such payments and therefore require that Tenant begin making such payments on the Commencement Date rather than on the Rent Commencement Date.

2. Tenant's Perspective

Tenant will want to evaluate whether its intention is to truly enter an "absolutely net" or "triple net" lease or whether Tenant would like to incorporate some limitations to its obligations. Tenants most often enter an unqualified net lease if the Building on the Property has been or will be "built-to-suit" their needs at the outset of the Term by either Landlord or Tenant and the Term of the Lease is for substantially the useful life of the improvements. Outside of a build-to-suit situation, Tenants typically endeavor to reasonably limit certain discrete aspects of its "net" obligations under the Lease and those limited aspects will be discussed in the Paragraphs that follow.

3. Lender's Perspective

Lender's primary concern is that if Lender is underwriting the Lease as a true net lease, then there must be no termination or offset rights on the part of Tenant, and there must be no maintenance exclusions, otherwise Lender will have to adjust its calculation of net cash flow available for debt service.

4. Broker's Perspective

Both Landlord Broker and Tenant Broker should discuss with their respective clients their intent with respect to just how "net" the Lease will actually be. If applicable, Brokers will want to include in the LOI any agreed to compromises or alternatives which alter true nature of a "triple net" Lease. It is also very important that Tenant Broker prepare financial projections (for all Lease transactions being considered) that show Tenant the sum of the Annual Base Rent together with any projected escalations thereof and the cost of any Additional Rent together with the expected costs of any and other utilities, services, and operational costs expected to be incurred by Tenant in connection with the Lease to be sure the anticipated financial impact over the entire Term of the Lease is understood by the Tenant before a Lease draft is even requested.

C. COMPROMISES AND ALTERNATIVES

To be further discussed in the Lease Paragraphs 3 and 4 of Part 3 that follow, depending upon the length of the Lease Term, the physical attributes of the Property and the leverage between the parties, certain portions of the absolute "net" requirements contained in Paragraph 1 below may be negotiated. Thus, nearly every sentence of Paragraph 1 should be revised to start with the following caveat:

> *Except as otherwise expressly provided in this Lease . . . .*

D. COMMENTS

A completely unqualified triple net lease is rare. An initial draft Lease from a Landlord may start that way, but a finally negotiated "net" lease typically leaves Landlord with some very limited obligations.

Tenants under net Leases for a single-tenant building (on a single-building Property), should always get the strongest Tenant rights with respect to Lease subordination and SNDAs. See Part 1, Paragraph 25 for further discussion.

E. TYPICAL PARAGRAPH

1. Net Lease.

The Annual Base Rent and Additional Rent shall be an absolutely net return to Landlord throughout the Term of this Lease, free of any expense, charge, or other deduction whatsoever with respect to the Premises or Landlord's interest therein, or the ownership, leasing, operation, management, maintenance, repair, use, or occupation thereof. This Lease is a "net lease" and Tenant's obligations arising or accruing during the Term to pay all Annual Base Rent, Additional Rent and all other payments hereunder required to be made by Tenant shall be absolute and unconditional, and Tenant shall pay all such amounts without notice, demand, counterclaim, set off, deduction or defense and without abatement, suspension, deferment, diminution or reduction (except as otherwise expressly provided in this Lease), free from any charges, assessments, impositions, expenses or deductions of any and every kind or nature whatsoever. All costs, expenses and obligations of every kind and nature whatsoever relating to the Premises and the appurtenances thereto and the use and occupancy thereof which may arise or become due and payable during or with respect to the Term (whether or not the same shall become payable during such Term or thereafter) shall be paid by Tenant (except as otherwise expressly provided in this Lease). Tenant assumes the sole responsibility for the condition, use, operation, maintenance, underletting and management of the Premises, and Landlord shall have no responsibility in respect thereof and shall have no liability for damage to Tenant's personalty or any subtenant of Tenant on any account or for any reason whatsoever other than by reason of Landlord's willful misconduct or gross negligence. Except as otherwise expressly provided in this Lease, this Lease shall not terminate, nor shall Tenant have any right to terminate, rescind or void this Lease or to be released or discharged from any obligations or liabilities hereunder for any reason, including, without limitation: (i) any damage to or destruction of the Premises; (ii) any restriction, deprivation (including eviction) or prevention of, or any interference with, any use or the occupancy of the Premises; (iii) any condemnation, requisition or other taking or sale of the use, occupancy or title of or to the Premises; (iv) any action, omission or breach on the part of Landlord under this Lease or under any other agreement between Landlord and Tenant; or (v) the inadequacy or failure of the description of the Premises to demise and let to Tenant the Premises intended to be leased hereby. Tenant will remain obligated under this Lease in accordance with its terms, and will not take any action to terminate, rescind or void this Lease as a result of any bankruptcy, insolvency, reorganization, liquidation, dissolution, or other proceeding affecting Landlord or any assignee of Landlord, or any action with respect to this Lease which may be taken by any receiver, trustee, or liquidator or by any court.

PARAGRAPH 2

Base Rent (with Indexed Escalations)

RISK RATING: 4

A. DESCRIPTION AND SCOPE

In a net lease, Base Rent may escalate (or "step-up") on a fixed schedule as provided in Part 1, Paragraph 7 and, if so, such Paragraph should be reviewed.

However, because net leases are often of long duration, Base Rent escalations on a fixed schedule are rare because it is difficult for the parties to predict and agree upon an escalating fixed Base Rent schedule in a manner that will adequately and fairly protect both parties against market fluctuations. Therefore, under net leases with long lease Terms, Base Rent more typically escalates periodically by either (i) market rent adjustments, or (ii) index adjustments (i.e., increases based upon increases of an external standard or index, usually an economic indicator).

Market rent adjustments are made through a defined process for the parties to follow in order to determine the "Fair Rental Value" of the Premises at a particular defined time. Review Part 1, Paragraph 60 for a sample market rent adjustment process within the context of Base Rent adjustments for Options to Renew the Term.

This Paragraph seeks to set forth an example of an "indexed" Base Rent escalation provision. The most commonly used index is the Consumer Price Index (often called "CPI" or the cost-of-living index), published by the Bureau of Labor Statistics of the U.S. Department of Labor. While the CPI does not necessarily reflect changes in real property values, it is commonly used because it is widely published and easy to administer. Note that there are two distinct CPI indexes generally used in leases. There is the wage earner index or, more officially, the "Urban Wage Earners and Clerical Workers Index," commonly designated CPI-W, currently represents the buying habits of about a third of the population. There is also the cost-of-living index or, more officially, the "All Urban Consumers Index," commonly known as the CPI-U. The CPI-U currently reflects the spending patterns of about 88 percent of the population.

Both the CPI-W and the CPI-U are published monthly for three major metropolitan areas and four regions, known collectively as the U.S. City Average. Along with the regional information provided each month, the Bureau of Labor Statistics also publishes reports for 11 additional metro areas every other month and an additional 13 metro areas semiannually. These reports cover areas with large populations and represent a particular regional subset. Currently, the reference base for most CPI indexes is **1982- 84=100** but some indexes have other references bases. The reference base years refer to the period in which the index is set to 100.0.

B. ANALYSIS

1. Landlord's Perspective

Landlord is interested in making sure that the rent is adjusted upward sufficiently to cover any inflation. CPI may be the most accurate measure. The longer the lease term, the more important this rental provision becomes. Landlord will want to provide only for adjustments to increase rent, not decrease rent; the CPI provision will usually be set up so that the initial rent payable is a floor, regardless of any decreases based in CPI. Any decrease in rent would reduce cash flow and would be resisted by both Landlord and Lender.

2. Tenant's Perspective

Tenant should accept a CPI rent increase clause only in those markets where the majority of Landlords are quoting rents on this basis.

3. Lender's Perspective

Lender's perspective is generally similar to Landlord's, in that Lender will want to make sure that its security is protected against inflation. If the interest rate Lender charges is variable and tied to an index, the Annual Base Rent increase may be similarly tied to the same index to permit Landlord to pass along Landlord's increase in debt service costs. Usually, Lender will prefer longer-term leases, at least as long as the term of its mortgage, and will want to make sure that the rent payable at the end of the Term is enough for Landlord to cover monthly debt service payments by at least 1.2 times.

4. Broker's Perspective

The Base Rent paragraph under any Lease may be the most noticed business term of the Lease and it requires an understanding of market conditions and rent rates for comparable buildings. Brokers will want to detail fully in the LOI how Base Rent will be escalated over the Term. Brokers will want to review this Paragraph closely to confirm that it reflects what was agreed to in the LOI. Brokers will want to understand how indexed escalation clauses are negotiated, including whether any escalation based upon CPI is subject to a "floor" or "cap." Brokers may wish to review Broker's Perspective contained in Part 1, Paragraph 7 for more detailed perspective on the issue, which is not being repeated here for sustainability and efficiency purposes.

C. COMPROMISES AND ALTERNATIVES

If Tenant is concerned that CPI may increase dramatically or if the CPI index is unstable and unpredictable, Tenant may request (i) a cap on the annual amount of any CPI increase (e.g., "no more than 2.5%"), and/or (ii) may request that the Annual Base Rent be increased by a fixed percentage (e.g., 30%) of the amount of the CPI increase. In addition, Tenant may also wish to negotiate the removal of any minimum escalation or "floor" in the CPI provision, and permit decreases as well as increases in Base Rent. Tenant should argue that any CPI provision with a "floor" unfairly protects Landlord by shifting risk to Tenant and that such a "floor" is counter to the intention for using the Index escalation method.

The parties should be aware that there are two methods generally used for increasing rent according to the CPI. The first is the prior-year method, so called because it increases rent annually by an agreed-upon percentage of the increase in the CPI over the previous year. The second method for increasing rent according to the CPI is the base-year method, so called because it increases rent annually by an agreed-upon percentage of the total increase in the CPI since the Lease commencement date. The base-year method is provided in the sample Paragraph below.

Arithmetically, the prior-year and base-year methods of calculating increases yield the same results if Tenant pays 0 percent or 100 percent of the CPI increase. Otherwise, for percentages in between 0 percent and 100 percent peaking at about 50 percent, the prior-year method imposes lesser increases than the base-year method. The differential is relatively modest during the early years of the Term, but becomes more significant thereafter. If Landlord refuses to alter the formula in the form Lease for administrative reasons of Lease management, Tenant can calculate the present value of the projected difference over the Lease term, and request that Landlord offer that amount to Tenant in another form, such as an increase in the tenant improvement allowance.

If Tenant is faced with a Lease imposing Base Rent increases based on both CPI and fixed-dollar (or bump) increases, Tenant may ask to eliminate the CPI escalation in years with bumps on the basis that both increases in the same year are excessive. However, if Tenant is unable to eliminate the CPI escalation in a year with a bump, Tenant may seek to have the escalation calculated before the addition of the bump. Note, however, that under the base-year method, total rent, including the bump, will increase the following year by the aggregate increase in the CPI since Lease commencement. In this way, Landlord is able to utilize an entire Lease Term of escalation to increase a rent bump only a year old. Tenant may argue that this results in an unduly high rent increase.

Two methods are proposed for modifying this result. First, in the year following the bump, the CPI base could be revised so that it refers to the reference period immediately preceding the bump year, not the corresponding period at the beginning of the Lease. Alternatively, the year after the bump is imposed, a separate CPI reference period can be used to escalate the bump. The result would then be added to the original Base Rent, as escalated by the base year method. Total escalated Rent under this method would equal the sum of the separately escalated bump and Base Rent. Using either of these methods permits the bump to remain at the agreed amount, but escalates the bump based upon increases in the CPI since the bump year, not since inception of the Lease.

D. COMMENTS

Language referring to CPI increases should be as specific as possible. A clause that states, "Base Rent is to be increased by 30 percent of the increase in CPI," should be changed to read, "Base Rent is to be increased annually by 30 percent of the increase in the CPI from the CPI for the last reference period prior to the Lease Commencement Date."

The Lease should address the issue of any "caps" or "floors" on escalations, and whether the excess over a limit on Base Rent increases allowable in any one year will carry forward.

In some markets a CPI increase is used in lieu of Operating Expense pass-throughs.

The CPI clause must specify when the Base Rent initially increases by CPI and when subsequent increases will take place, whether on a calendar basis or a Lease Year basis (as provided below). Note that the frequency by which a CPI adjustment occurs is negotiable. Paragraph 4 assumes a CPI adjustment every five (5) years but CPI adjustments can happen as frequently as annually or as infrequently as every ten (10) years. If CPI adjustments happen only every ten (10) years, it is likely that the Lease will include annual fixed "bumps" in Base Rent for the years between the CPI adjustment dates.

Lastly, it is important that the one of the two CPI Indexes (i.e., CPI-W versus CPI-U) is specified in the Lease to avoid confusion later in the Term when CPI increases are calculated. The parties may also wish for the applicable CPI Index identified in the Lease to be more specific by identifying one of the three major metropolitan areas and/or one of the four regions for which the indexes are tracked and published.

E. TYPICAL PARAGRAPH

2. Base Rent.

(a) **Base Rent. The annual net base rental for the Premises (the "Annual Base Rent") shall be payable at the rates and subject to escalation as set forth in Subparagraph (b) below, and Tenant shall pay such Annual Base Rent in equal monthly installments ("Monthly Base Rent") in advance, on the first (1st) day of each calendar month during the Term commencing on the Commencement Date, without any set-off, offset, abatement, or deduction whatsoever (except to the extent otherwise expressly provided herein). Notwithstanding the foregoing, the first month's Monthly Base Rent payment shall be due upon Tenant's execution of this Lease. As used herein, "Rent Commencement Date" shall mean the date that is the earlier of (i) [NUMBER] of days from the Commencement Date, or (ii) the date Tenant first occupies the Premises for the operation of its business therein.**

(b) **Base Rent Escalations. Annual Base Rent for Lease Years 1 through 5, shall be payable in the amount of [$AMOUNT], per year. For each subsequent [five (5)]-year period commencing on [the first day of the sixth**

(6th), eleventh (11th), and sixteenth (16th)] Lease Years, Annual Base Rent shall be an annual amount equal to the greater of (a) [one hundred two percent (102%) of the Annual Base Rent payable in the immediately preceding Lease Year (i.e., a two percent (2%) increase)] or (b) the product of (I) the Annual Base Rent payable at the commencement of the immediately preceding five (5) Lease Year period and (II) the applicable CPI Increase (as hereinafter defined), one-twelfth (1/12th) of which shall be payable in advance on the first (1st) day of each calendar month for each applicable Lease Year.

On or about the commencement of the [sixth (6th), eleventh (11th), and sixteenth (16th)] Lease Years, Landlord shall calculate the Annual Base Rent rate pursuant to the formula above and deliver a statement to Tenant providing the calculation for such Annual Base Rent rate for the applicable [five-year] period. If for any reason by the commencement of the [sixth (6th), eleventh (11th), and sixteenth (16th)] Lease Years, the Annual Base Rent rate for such period shall not have been finally determined, Tenant shall, until such determination, pay the Base Rent at the annual rate of [one hundred two percent (102%) of the Annual Base Rent payable in the immediately preceding Lease Year (i.e., a two percent (2%) increase)]. Upon such final determination, Tenant shall thereafter pay such Annual Base Rent for the applicable [5-year period] at the rate so determined and shall pay Landlord the balance, if any, which shall be owing for the period preceding such determination. Whenever the Annual Base Rent for the applicable [5-year] period shall have been determined, the parties hereto, on request of either of them, shall enter into a stipulation with respect to the amount of the Annual Base Rent rate for the applicable period.

(c) Definitions.

"Base Price Index" means the Price Index most recently published prior to the Commencement Date. For informational purposes only, as of the date of this Lease, the Base Price Index can be found at the following website: https://data.bls.gov/cgi-bin/surveymost.

"CPI Increase" means an amount that shall initially be equal to one (1) and shall be determined by Landlord as of the first (1st) day of each applicable Lease Year, to an amount equal to the greater of (a) one or (b) a fraction, the numerator of which is the Price Index most recently published prior to the first (1st) day of each such applicable Lease Year and the denominator of which is the Base Price Index.

"Price Index" means the "Consumer Price Index for All Urban Consumers, All Items (1982-1984=100), U.S. Cities Average (CPI-U)," issued by the Bureau of Labor Statistics of the United States Department of Labor. In the event that the Price Index ceases to use the 1982-1984 average of 100 as the basis of calculation, or if a substantial change is made in the term or number of Items contained in the Price Index, then the Price

Index shall be adjusted to the figure that would have been arrived at had the change in the manner of computing the Price Index in effect at the date of this Lease not been altered. In the event that such Price Index (or a successor or substitute index) is no longer available, a reliable governmental or other nonpartisan publication evaluating the information theretofore used in determining the Price Index shall be used, as reasonably agreed to by each of Landlord and Tenant, but if the parties are unable to agree upon a substitute formula, then the matter shall be determined by arbitration in accordance with the terms of this Lease. For informational purposes only, the Price Index as of the date of this Lease can, as of the date of this Lease, be found at the following website: https://data.bls.gov/cgi-bin/surveymost.

PARAGRAPH 3

Operating Expenses and Real Taxes

RISK RATING: 4

A. DESCRIPTION AND SCOPE

This Paragraph seeks to ensure that Tenant is responsible for the payment of all Operating Expenses and Real Estate Taxes attributable to the Premises under an industrial lease.

If the lease is for industrial space in a multi-tenanted building, Operating Expenses and Real Estate Taxes will be charged through to Tenant in a manner consistent with either Part 1, Paragraph 8 (Alternative 1—The Base Year Model) or Part 1, Paragraph 8 (Alternative 2—The Direct Pass Through Model), with Landlord responsible for operating the Property and paying the Operating Expenses and Real Estate Taxes, but subject to recoupment by Tenant paying its Pro Rata Share thereof over a Base Year. In such a case, the Operating Expense and Real Estate Taxes section of the industrial lease should be drafted, reviewed and negotiated as discussed in Part 1, Paragraph 8 (Alternative 1—The Base Year Model) or Part 1, Paragraph 8 (Alternative 2—The Direct Pass Through Model), as applicable.

More often, industrial leases are for single-tenant buildings (on single-Building Properties), and Paragraph 3 below assumes such fact pattern with Landlord having a blanket right to charge Tenant for all Operating Expenses and Real Estate Taxes attributable to the Premises. As discussed ahead, Paragraph 3, *as drafted*, should be resisted by Tenant.

B. ANALYSIS

1. Landlord's Perspective

This paragraph protects Landlord from having to absorb any of the costs of Operating Expenses and Real Estate Taxes.

2. Tenant's Perspective

Tenant, under a net lease for a single-occupant Building, wants to exert as much control over the operation of the Premises (or the Property if the Premises and the Property are one and the same), so that Tenant can control both the quality of the operation and the cost thereof. Tenant seeks to limit Landlord's ability to incur and charge Tenant for Operating Expenses. Similarly, Tenant will want the right to exert control over the Real Estate Taxes by having the right to contest same.

3. Lender's Perspective

Lender's primary concern is that Tenant be obligated to pay the Real Estate Taxes and Operating Expenses so that cash flow designated for debt service will not be burdened by any lack of payment of Real Estate Taxes and Operating Expenses.

4. Broker's Perspective

Brokers should expect to include in the LOI, with specificity, how Real Estate Taxes and Operating Expenses will be charged to Tenant. Brokers may wish to review Broker's Perspective contained in Part 1, Paragraph 8 (Alternative 1) for more detailed perspective on the issue, which is not being repeated here for sustainability and efficiency purposes.

C. COMPROMISES AND ALTERNATIVES

If Tenant is leasing a single-occupant Building and that Building is the only Building on the Property, then it is advisable that Tenant be expressly responsible (versus Landlord) for the ordinary operation of the Property such as landscaping, snow removal, janitorial services, rubbish removal, security, general maintenance and similar services, so that Tenant can control vendor selection for quality and cost purposes.

Also, if Tenant is leasing a single-occupant Building and that Building is the only Building on the Property, Tenant should strongly object to the blanket right of Landlord to incur Operating Expenses and charge Tenant therefor. Rather, the Paragraph should be revised to expressly list just those Operating Expenses, if any, that Landlord may incur and pass through to Tenant. Typically, that list should be quite narrow. If may include just the amortized portion of any capital costs incurred by Landlord in connection with any Landlord maintenance and repair obligations negotiated into the Lease and negotiated as a pass-through expense to Tenant.

Also, if the Building (or the Building and the Property) is part of a larger industrial park owned by Landlord (and/or Landlord's affiliates) ("Park"), Landlord may, in that event, want to retain certain limited operational responsibilities pertaining to the common areas of the Park (such as landscaping, general maintenance and snow removal of any common walkways or roads that service the Park). In such event, Tenant should pay Landlord only its equitable share of those Park Operating Expenses.

Similarly, if the Premises is not a separate tax parcel, Tenant should only be responsible for the Real Estate Taxes attributable to the Premises. If the Premises is a separate tax parcel, Tenant should pay the governmental taxing authority directly for the Real Estate Taxes, as and when due, and Tenant should absolutely have the right, by appropriate proceedings conducted diligently and in good faith, to contest the amount(s) or validity of any Real Estate Taxes, and Landlord should agree to reasonably cooperate with Tenant in such proceedings.

To the extent that any Landlord incurred Operating Expenses are passed through to Tenant, Part 1, Paragraph 8 should be reviewed for guidance in drafting and negotiating the provisions.

D. COMMENTS

None.

E. TYPICAL PARAGRAPH

3. Operating Expenses and Real Estate Taxes.

(a) Payment. In addition to Base Rent, Tenant shall pay Landlord, as Additional Rent, all Operating Expenses and Real Estate Taxes attributable to the Premises within twenty (20) days of an invoice therefor delivered by Landlord.

(b) Definitions:

"Real Estate Taxes" shall mean all taxes, assessments, levies, and other charges, general and special, ordinary and extraordinary, foreseen and unforeseen, of any kind and nature whatsoever, that shall or may be during the Term assessed, levied, charged, confirmed, or imposed upon or become payable out of or become a lien on the Property, but shall not include any municipal, state, or federal capital levy, estate, succession, inheritance, transfer, sales, use, or franchise taxes, or any income, profits, or revenue tax, assessment or charge imposed upon the rent received as such by Landlord under this Lease; provided, however, that if at any time during the Term, the present method of real estate taxation or assessment shall be so changed that there shall be substituted for the whole or any part of such taxes, assessments, levies, impositions,

or charges, now or hereafter levied, assessed, or imposed on real estate and improvements, a capital tax or other tax imposed on the rents or income received by Landlord from the Property or the rents or income reserved herein, or any part thereof, then all such capital taxes or other taxes shall, to the extent that they are so substituted, be deemed to be included within the term "Real Estate Taxes," but only to the extent that such taxes would be payable if the Property were the only property of Landlord subject to such capital taxes and other taxes.

"Operating Expenses" shall mean the total expenses for the operation, maintenance, repair, and replacement of the Building and Common Areas that are incurred during the Term hereof, including without limitation, janitorial services, structural and nonstructural maintenance, property management fees, fire and extended coverage, rental interruption and liability insurance, and water, electricity, gas, and other fuels and utilities.

PARAGRAPH 4

Maintenance and Repair of Building and Grounds

RISK RATING: 4

A. DESCRIPTION AND SCOPE

This Paragraph is intended for a long-term triple-net Lease and establishes Tenant's responsibility to make all repairs, restoration, and replacements that may be necessary at the Premises during the Term. Paragraph 4 below reflects an initial, Landlord favorable position that makes Tenant responsible for all maintenance, repair, and restoration obligations, including all structural and capital improvements. However, such terms are generally negotiated as discussed below.

B. ANALYSIS

1. Landlord's Perspective

Since this is a triple-net lease, Landlord does not want to be responsible for any repairs or replacements at the Premises. However, Landlord will want to be aware of and approve significant repairs undertaken by Tenant, and the contractors performing such repairs, at the Premises that could affect value or future use of this Building by another Tenant.

2. Tenant's Perspective

Tenant will not want to be responsible during the entire Term for structural and capital repairs and replacements, and Tenant may seek to delete any reference to its responsibility for such repairs. Tenant may want a self-help right in the event Landlord fails to satisfy its repair obligations under the Lease and charge such cost back to the Landlord. Landlord, in turn, will want to make sure that Tenant is required to send adequate notice and that Landlord has a right to cure before Tenant is allowed to make the repairs itself, and that the cost chargeable to Landlord following Tenant's self-help repair is reasonable and documented with evidence setting forth the cost in adequate detail.

Given the age and condition of the Building, a first class repair obligation by Tenant may not be appropriate. If the Building is older or the condition is compromised at the commencement of the Term, Tenant will want to negotiate this to a lesser standard of "good order and condition."

3. Lender's Perspective

Lender will want to confirm that responsibility for repair, replacement, and restoration of the Premises has been established by the parties to protect Lender's potential interest in the Premises. Lender will also want assurance that Landlord will not incur additional, unexpected costs with respect to the Premises that could jeopardize Landlord's ability to pay debt service or that otherwise could trip financial covenants Landlord is required to satisfy for the benefit of Lender.

4. Broker's Perspective

If applicable, Brokers will want to include in the LOI any agreed to maintenance and repair compromises where the Lease will not be truly "triple net." Each Broker will want to consult with their respective client to determine any sensitivity to or any particular client need relating to this Paragraph that should be covered in the LOI.

C. COMPROMISES AND ALTERNATIVES

If the Building is a single-tenant building, Landlord will want Tenant responsible for repairs and replacements to the fullest extent possible.

Tenant will want to push back on any absolute Tenant maintenance and repair obligation and shift responsibility for structural repairs and/or capital repairs and replacements to Landlord for all or a portion of the Term. In the circumstance where Landlord (or Tenant) has built the Building to suit Tenant, then it is harder for Tenant to shift all of the structural and capital repairs and replacements back to Landlord for the entirety of the Term but, even in that case, if the Term is 30 years long and the roof needs replacement at year 25, it is arguably unfair for Tenant to absorb the cost of the replacing the roof with a new roof with a useful life of another 25 years. Landlord would receive a windfall in such a case.

Thus, Tenant should endeavor to modify the Lease by shifting certain maintenance and repair obligations back to Landlord. Here is a sample of compromise language that is Tenant favorable:

> *Notwithstanding anything to the contrary contained herein, Landlord shall, at its sole cost, be responsible for maintaining, repairing and replacing all of the structural portions of the Premises, including, but not limited to, the roof and exterior structural walls (except for windows) of the Premises, the Building footings and foundation, the floor slab and other structural supports of the Building, and the sprinkler, life safety and other Building*

systems including all portions of systems from the street to the Building and any and all repairs and replacements that qualify as a capital improvement or a capital expense under generally accepted accounting principles.

Landlord will likely want to push back on the above sample compromise and try (i) to get all of the costs and expenses incurred by Landlord passed through to Tenant as Operating Expenses, and/or (ii) limit Landlord's responsibility with respect to Building systems to just replacement of Building systems and, potentially, only replacement of Building systems in last few years of the Term.

The resolution of the negotiating points above will likely depend upon the length of the lease and the leverage disparities between the parties. What is most fair, is that any Operating Expenses incurred by Landlord in the performance of its obligations above get amortized, on a straight line basis, over their useful lives with Tenant just being responsible for the amortized portion attributable to the Term.

Also, if the Term is less than ten (10) years or if the Premises are part of a multi-tenant Building, Landlord may retain responsibility for repair and replacement of the exterior and structural portions of Premises, repairing and maintaining the paved areas and entrances and exits to the Property, and for painting the exterior of the Building. Landlord may otherwise wish to maintain control over these repair and maintenance obligations so as to ensure proper repair of significant items, such as the roof, and so as to ensure the exterior aesthetic is preserved, but will want to pass all costs related to such repair and maintenance obligations to Tenant as part of the Building Operating Expenses.

Tenant may wish a self-help right with respect to Landlord's repair obligations with a Rent offset right or the right to lien the Property. Of course, Lender will likely object to such rights and/or may further require that Lender be given additional notice and cure periods with respect to those obligations. If Tenant achieves any such self-help rights and Rent offset rights, Tenant will want to have them recognized in a SNDA. See Part 1, Paragraph 25 for a larger discussion on this point.

D. COMMENTS

It would be advisable for Tenant to have a professional inspection of the Premises prior to Lease execution before taking on any maintenance, repair, and replacement obligations typically associated with a net industrial lease.

E. TYPICAL PARAGRAPH

4. Maintenance and Repair of Building and Grounds.

(a) During the Term, Tenant at its sole cost and expense, shall take good care of the Premises, keep the same in a first-class condition and state of repair, whether or not caused by Tenant's own act or omission, make all necessary repairs and replacements thereto, interior and exterior, structural, except as specified in Subparagraph (b) hereof, nonstructural, ordinary and extraordinary, foreseen and unforeseen, including,

without limiting the generality of the foregoing, repairs to the roof and exterior structural walls (and Tenant shall maintain a maintenance plan with respect to the roof), all plumbing, electrical, lighting, and mechanical facilities and equipment within the Premises (including, without limitation, the heating, air conditioning, and ventilation systems located within the Premises); underground utility and sewer pipes outside the exterior walls of the Premises; fixtures, bulbs, tubes, ballasts, interior walls, ceilings, windows, doors, signs, plate glass; all truck loading areas adjacent to the Premises; the pavement area surrounding the Premises; all access and egress areas; landscaping; and other areas included within the Premises. All such repairs, replacements, and restorations shall be made by Tenant in a workmanlike manner and in compliance with all applicable governmental regulations in effect during the Term, and shall be made in a manner and with materials equal to or better than the existing quality of the construction and materials of the Premises. Tenant shall also be responsible for removing ice, snow, and debris from the walks, drives, and the pavement area (including access and egress thereto), curbs and other common areas, and shall maintain said walks, drives, pavement area, curbs, and other common areas. Any repairs required to be made by Tenant shall be performed by contractors approved by Landlord, which approval shall not be unreasonably withheld.

(b) Unless same is caused solely by the negligent action or inaction of Landlord, its employees, or agents and is not covered by insurance required to be carried by Tenant pursuant to the terms of this Lease, Landlord shall not be liable to Tenant or to any other person for any damage occasioned by failure in any utility system or by the bursting or leaking of any vessel or pipe in or about the Premises, or for any damage occasioned by water coming into the Premises or arising from the acts or negligence of occupants of adjacent property or the public. Landlord shall not be liable to Tenant if any utility service to the Premises is interrupted for any reason beyond Landlord's reasonable control. Tenant shall be responsible, at its sole cost and expense, for any upgrades or repairs to the utility infrastructure and systems required by any private utility companies servicing the Premises.

(c) If Tenant fails to make any necessary repairs, replacements, or restorations to the Premises, Landlord, at its option, but without any obligation to do so, may enter upon the Premises, after forty-eight (48) hours' prior written notice to Tenant (or with no prior written notice, in the case of an emergency), and put the same in good order, condition, and repair or otherwise perform Tenant's obligations hereunder, and the cost thereof, upon notice to Tenant, shall become due and payable as Additional Rent to Landlord, to be paid with Tenant's next rental installment.

(d) Landlord shall cause any repair and/or replacement obligations that are the subject of a warranty or guaranty to be performed through the enforcement of same; provided, however, Landlord shall only be required to do so if such maintenance, repair, or replacement obligations are subject to a warranty and/or guaranty still in full force and effect. If such repairs or replacements are not the subject of a warranty or guaranty or such warranty and/or guaranty has expired, the repairs thereto shall be performed in accordance with the terms hereof. Landlord and Tenant shall cooperate, at no cost to Landlord, to enforce any such warranties in effect.

PARAGRAPH 5

Insurance

RISK RATING: 5

A. DESCRIPTION AND SCOPE

Lease insurance requirements are intended to protect Landlord from expenses resulting from damage to the Building and Premises, and liability from injuries to third parties that occur at the Property. With increasing popularity, Landlord will require Tenant to carry business interruption insurance covering the Annual Base Rent and Additional Rent obligations in the event Tenant is unable to conduct its business through no fault of Landlord.

In the Industrial and Warehouse context, where leased Premises are more likely to be freestanding structures and no other tenants are located on the Property, Tenant may be required to obtain casualty insurance to insure the value of the entire Building (versus Landlord), rather than just the contents of and improvements to the Premises. Similarly, Tenant's liability insurance would have to cover grounds on which the Building sits.

B. ANALYSIS

1. Landlord's Perspective

To protect its investment, Landlord will want full replacement casualty coverage to pay the full insurable replacement value of the Building in the event of loss. In addition, rental interruption insurance is desirable to prevent a cash flow problem if the Property is damaged and rental payments stop. Tenant may also request that the property insurance be for the "functional equivalent" replacement value as opposed to the "full replacement value." Functional equivalent replacement value requires the insurer to rebuild a similar building, but using customary and modern building materials, whereas the full replacement value requires the insurer to rebuild substantially the same building. For example, a warehouse building that was built 40 years ago may have been built with cement and bricks while present day warehouses are built with steel. In the event of a covered claim for the entire property, a functional equivalent value policy will pay for a rebuild of a similar building as the brick and cement building, but utilizing modern materials like steel. Landlord should analyze this request carefully and consider things like partial restorations where a portion of the Building could be rebuilt with steel or other modern materials where the existing Building remains brick and cement.

2. Tenant's Perspective

Tenant wants to be sure its insurance obligations under the Lease are not excessive when compared to similar buildings in the market. Tenant will likely resist obtaining terrorism risk insurance, particularly if the cost thereof is excessive relative to the perceived terrorism risk.

3. Lender's Perspective

To ensure continued income to the Property, Lender will focus on adequacy of casualty coverage and rental insurance payments. Lender should also seek the right to increase the amount of insurance required by Tenant if it does not consider Landlord's limits sufficient.

4. Broker's Perspective

Each Broker will want to consult with their respective client to determine any sensitivity to or any particular client need relating to this Paragraph that should be covered in the LOI. If none exist, this Paragraph can be handled by the attorneys in Lease negotiations. Tenant Broker should encourage Tenant to have its risk advisor or insurance professional review and comment on this Paragraph.

C. COMPROMISES AND ALTERNATIVES

Although the amount and scope of coverage may vary, a requirement that Tenant maintain some adequate level of insurance should not be controversial.

D. COMMENTS

The allocation of insurance requirements between Landlord and Tenant should be carefully reviewed to be sure that they mirror or are otherwise compatible with the restoration obligations under Paragraph 6 on Casualty.

Tenant should also have the insurance, casualty, and indemnity sections of the Lease reviewed by their insurance professional and/or risk advisor to confirm that they have or can readily obtain the insurance being required. Oftentimes, the insurance professional has comments to these sections. Tenant's attorney should advise Tenant to have the provisions reviewed by said insurance professionals.

If any particular industrial lease does not allocate all of the insurance obligations for the Building to Tenant, then Part 1, Paragraph 21 should be reviewed and consulted for exceptionally important concepts.

E. TYPICAL PARAGRAPH

5. Insurance.

Tenant shall, at its expense, secure and maintain (a) General Liability Insurance written on a so-called "Comprehensive" Commercial General Liability Form for liability arising out of Tenant's business operations, Tenant's use, occupancy, or maintenance of the Premises or any area adjacent thereto, or the acts or omissions of Tenant's employees or agents with liability limits of not less than $[AMOUNT] per occurrence, $[AMOUNT] general aggregate, applying on a "per location" basis to the Premises, naming Landlord and Landlord's lender as an additional insured under each such policy; (b) insurance against loss or damage by fire, lightning, and other risks from time included under "extended coverage," special risk, or all-risk or special form casualty insurance covering the Building and all property stored or placed by Tenant in or about the Premises with Landlord as a named insured and with a standard mortgagee clause in favor of any mortgagee of Landlord, in the amount of one hundred percent (100%) of the full insurable replacement cost of the Premises, adjusted annually, containing all insurance coverages ordinarily covered thereby; (c) to the extent available, terrorism risk insurance in the amount of one hundred percent (100%) of the then current replacement cost of the Premises; (d) rental interruption insurance in an amount at least equal to Net Rent for at least twelve (12) months and estimated excess expense payments to be paid by Tenant during such timeframe, or more as Landlord or any mortgagee of Landlord's interest may require; and (e) worker's compensation and employer's liability insurance covering all Tenant's employees working in the Premises. In addition, during the performance of all Alterations by Tenant, Tenant shall cause Tenant's contractor performing such Alterations and any such subcontractors to maintain comprehensive automobile insurance for all owned, hired, rented and non-owned vehicles; commercial general liability insurance, including contractual liability coverage; as well as workmen's compensation insurance and employer's liability insurance, all in amounts reasonably approved by Landlord. Tenant shall deliver certificates of insurance evidencing such coverages from its contractor and any subcontractors prior to the commencement of any such Alterations. Tenant shall deliver to Landlord duplicate certificates of such insurance prior to the Commencement Date and shall deliver new certificates at least thirty (30) days prior to the expiration of the existing coverage. Such certificates shall provide that in the event of termination or material change in coverage, Landlord shall be given thirty (30) days' advance written notice sent by mail to the address of Landlord. Such insurance shall be obtained from insurers satisfactory to Landlord and licensed to do business in the State. All such policies shall contain a waiver of any rights of subrogation and shall be primary and not contributory.

PARAGRAPH 6

Casualty

RISK RATING: 3

A. DESCRIPTION AND SCOPE

This Paragraph sets out Tenant's responsibilities and procedures in the event of casualty resulting in damage to the Property, including Tenant's obligation to restore. As opposed to multi-tenant office leases, industrial net leases of single-tenant Properties seek to shift the casualty risk entirely to Tenant.

The restoration and termination provisions are usually extensively negotiated by Landlord and Tenant.

B. ANALYSIS

1. Landlord's Perspective

In the net industrial lease sector where Tenant is the sole occupant of a Building, Tenant is expected to insure the Building against casualty and restore the Building with no abatement of Rent during the restoration period.

2. Tenant's Perspective

Tenant wants to make sure that it can terminate the Lease, in certain circumstances, instead of restoring the Building, especially if the expiration of the Term is nearing.

3. Lender's Perspective

Lender will want Tenant to restore the Building in most cases with Tenant only having limited Lease termination rights. Lender will want Tenant to maintain business interruption insurance so Rent is not abated during any period of restoration. This is because termination and/or Rent abatement affects cash flow from the Property and may adversely affect Landlord's ability to pay debt service to Lender from the cash flow of the Property. Lender also wants to control insurance proceeds from any casualty.

4. Broker's Perspective

Each Broker will want to consult with their respective client to determine any sensitivity to or any particular client need relating to this Paragraph that should be covered in the LOI. If none exist, this Paragraph can be handled by the attorneys in Lease negotiations, However, both Brokers should support legal counsel in negotiating this Paragraph.

C. COMPROMISES AND ALTERNATIVES

Tenant may wish to insert a Lease termination right if a casualty destroys all or substantially all of the Premises during the last few years of the Lease and/or any restoration cannot be completed prior to the expiration of the Lease.

In such event, Landlord will want to condition any such Tenant termination right on (i) Tenant assigning and delivering to Landlord (or to Lender, as may be negotiated in a SNDA with Lender) all insurance proceeds held or otherwise available to Tenant, and (ii) Tenant paying any associated insurance deductible.

D. COMMENTS

Tenant should have this Paragraph reviewed by their insurance professional and/or risk advisor to confirm that they have or can readily obtain the insurance being required to meet the restoration obligations under this Paragraph.

If any particular industrial lease does not allocate all of the restoration obligations for the Building onto Tenant (as provided in Paragraph 6 below), then Part 1, Paragraph 23 should be reviewed and consulted for exceptionally important concepts.

E. TYPICAL PARAGRAPH

6. Casualty.

(a) <u>Effect of Casualty</u>. No loss or damage by fire or other cause required to be insured against hereunder resulting in either partial or total destruction of any building, structure, or other Improvement on the Premises, shall operate to terminate this Lease, or to relieve or discharge Tenant from the payment of Base Rents and other amounts payable as rent as they become due and payable, or from the performance and observance of any of the agreements, covenants, and conditions herein contained on the part of Tenant to be performed and observed.

(b) Obligation to Repair or Rebuild. If the Premises shall be damaged or destroyed by fire or other casualty, Tenant shall promptly notify Landlord of any damage or destruction to the Premises of which Tenant has knowledge or is aware, and Tenant shall repair, rebuild, or replace such damage and restore the Premises and/or the Premises to substantially the same condition in which they were immediately prior to such damage or destruction. Tenant's repair obligation under Paragraph shall survive the expiration of the Term in the event that restoration from any casualty during the Term has not been completed prior to the expiration of the Term. In lieu thereof, Landlord, at its sole and absolute discretion, may elect to complete such restoration on the condition that Tenant assign all and deliver all insurance proceeds held or otherwise available to Tenant.

PARAGRAPH 7

Licenses and Permits

RISK RATING: 1

A. DESCRIPTION AND SCOPE

This Paragraph seeks to ensure that all required licenses for operation are obtained and maintained. Failure to be licensed could cause a shutdown of operations, harming reputation and increasing risk of a Lease default.

B. ANALYSIS

1. Landlord's Perspective

Landlord wants to be sure Tenant can operate for its intended use, but Landlord has no incentive to obtain or maintain permits for such use.

2. Tenant's Perspective

Tenant has a natural incentive to ensure it can do business as proposed, and that there is no frustration of its essential purpose in leasing the space.

3. Lender's Perspective

Lender wants to make sure operations are conducted in accordance with law to avoid enforcement actions or harm to the Property's reputation. Lender wants Tenant to accept responsibility for obtaining business permits and wants to ensure that the Tenant is fully licensed to conduct its business so that there is no additional risk that rent will not be paid.

4. Broker's Perspective

Each Broker will want to consult with their respective client to determine any sensitivity to or any particular client need relating to this Paragraph that should be covered in the LOI. Tenant Broker should discuss with Tenant and determine, as part of the up-front needs assessment phase of its assignment to acquire space, what licenses and permits Tenant requires to operate its contemplated business at the Premises. As licenses and permits often have long leads, Tenant Broker should encourage Tenant and/or be prepared to assist Tenant in obtaining such licenses and permits. If it appears that Tenant will be unable to obtain any required license or permit prior to Lease execution, Tenant Broker should include in the LOI a Tenant contingency with respect thereto allowing Tenant to terminate the Lease, without liability, if the required license(s) or permit(s) are not obtained within a reasonable time after Lease execution.

C. COMPROMISES AND ALTERNATIVES

This Paragraph can be deleted in certain jurisdictions where no implied warranty of fitness for Tenant's particular use exists under a Lease and Tenant would be bound regardless of the absence of permits.

D. COMMENTS

Although operating permits are typically the Tenant's responsibility, Landlord should be prepared to disclose the uses permitted under the local zoning code for the location of the Property.

E. TYPICAL PARAGRAPH

7. **Licenses and Permits.**

If any governmental license or permit shall be required for the proper and lawful conduct of Tenant's business or other activity carried on in the Premises, and if the failure to secure such license or permit might or would, in any way, affect Landlord, then Tenant, at Tenant's expense, shall duly procure and thereafter maintain such license or permit and submit the same for inspection by Landlord. Tenant, at Tenant's expense, shall, at all times, comply with the requirements of each such license or permit. Tenant shall indemnify and hold Landlord harmless from and against any such claims, liabilities, costs, expenses, and penalties incurred in connection with Tenant's failure to comply with this Section.

PARAGRAPH 8

Environmental Matters

RISK RATING: 5

A. DESCRIPTION AND SCOPE

Unlike office and retail leases where Hazardous Materials are rarely ever used, stored, or generated in connection with Tenant's use of the Premises, under industrial leases, Tenant may (or may not) need the right to use, store, generate, and dispose of Hazardous Materials in connection with its use of the Premises and the operation of Tenant's business in the Premises.

Paragraph 8 is a sample of a Paragraph granting Tenant the right to use, store, generate, and dispose of certain Hazardous Materials.

B. ANALYSIS

1. Landlord's Perspective

This Paragraph seeks to protect the value of the Property by regulating Tenant's use, storage, generation, or disposal of Hazardous Substances at the Premises. Further, Landlord should seek indemnification from Tenant against all claims and losses arising out of Tenant's actions on the Property relating to Hazardous Substances and/or as may result in environmental conditions. It should be noted that in any event, Landlord would likely have continuing environmental liability under CERCLA and other state and federal environmental laws.

2. Tenant's Perspective

Tenant should confirm that its contemplated use of the Premises and the operation of its business therein will not violate the prohibitions of this Paragraph pertaining to the use, storage, generation, and disposal of Hazardous Substances. Industrial Tenants would be wise to have expert environmental counsel review and negotiate this

Paragraph of the Lease to tailor it as necessary and to obtain pre-approval from Landlord to use, store, generate, or dispose of Hazardous Substances to the extent necessary for the operation of Tenant's business at the Premises.

3. Lender's Perspective

A Lender will want environmental indemnities from its borrower, the Landlord, but is also interested in having Tenant be responsible for cleanup costs for environmental problems caused by Tenant. To this end, a Lender may require that Landlord provide Lender with a copy of any Environmental Site Assessment prepared on Landlord's behalf and may also seek issuance of a reliance letter to Lender by the environmental engineering firm that prepared the Assessment.

4. Broker's Perspective

Tenant Broker should inquire and understand, at the outset of its representation of Tenant, whether Tenant will need the right to use, store, generate, and dispose of Hazardous Materials at its place of business and advise Landlord Broker of same so this issue is fully vetted at the LOI stage before the Lease is drafted. Landlord Broker should expect that Tenant or Tenant Broker will be requesting a copy of Landlord's most recent Environmental Site Assessment for the Property.

C. COMPROMISES AND ALTERNATIVES

Tenant will want all of the compromises, alternatives, and protections provided in Part 1, Paragraph 20, and they should be reviewed.

In advance of Lease execution, Landlord will want to review and approve of any Hazardous Materials Tenant is contemplating using or generating at the Premises. It is prudent for both parties to have an "Approved" Hazardous Materials list attached to the Lease and Paragraph 8 below contemplates this. Tenant may want or need the right to amend or expand the Approved Hazardous Materials list during the Term, and Landlord will want notice and certain reasonable consent rights to any such modifications. Below is a proposed compromise on that issue:

> *The list of Approved Hazardous Materials may be modified from time to time to list additional Hazardous Materials upon written notification to Landlord (which notification shall include an updated, comprehensive Exhibit [_] which includes all additional Hazardous Materials added since the date of this Lease, provided, however, if any such modification results in Hazardous Materials being added to Exhibit [_] that (i) require modifications to the life and safety systems of the Building or the Premises by Landlord or Tenant, (ii) include Hazardous Materials with "safety data sheets" issued by the applicable manufacturer that require personal protective equipment in excess of the personal protective equipment recommended by the "safety data sheets" for the Hazardous Materials presently existing on Exhibit [_], (iii) include any new Hazardous Materials in quantities not to exceed 500 ml for liquids and 1kg for solids, and/or (iv) are included on the U.S. Environmental Protection Agency's List of Extremely Hazardous Substances set forth in Appendix A to 40 CFR Part 355, then any such modification shall be subject to Landlord's prior approval, which approval shall not be unreasonably withheld, conditioned, or delayed.*

D. COMMENTS

Landlord and Tenant should have expert environmental counsel review and negotiate this Paragraph of the Lease.

Also, expert environmental counsel should be consulted with respect to what Environmental Site Assessments might be prudent for Landlord and Tenant to complete both prior to the Commencement Date (to establish a "baseline" environmental condition of the Premises (and/or Property) and upon the expiration of the Term for the protection of both parties. Industrial sites often have a long history of Hazardous Materials being on the Premises (and/or the Property) and Tenant should be careful to establish the "baseline" environmental condition on the Commencement Date in order to minimize Tenant's exposure to liability if Landlord later claims Contamination was caused by Tenant.

E. TYPICAL PARAGRAPH

8. Environmental Matters.

(a) Definitions. For purposes of this Lease, "Hazardous Material" includes, but is not limited to, any substance the presence of which requires, or may hereafter require notification, investigation or remediation under any laws or which is now or hereafter defined, listed, or regulated by any governmental authority as a "hazardous waste," "extremely hazardous waste," "solid waste," "toxic substance," "hazardous substance," "hazardous material," or "regulated substance," or otherwise regulated under any state or federal laws. "Contamination" means the existence or any release or disposal of a Hazardous Material or biological or organic contaminant, including any such contaminant that could adversely impact air quality, such as mold, fungi, or other bacterial agents in, on, under, at or from the Premises, the Building, or the Property that may result in any liability, fine, use restriction, cost recovery lien, remediation requirement, or other government or private party action or imposition affecting Landlord. For purposes of this Lease, claims arising from Contamination shall include, but are not limited to, diminution in value, restrictions on use, adverse impact on leasing space, and all costs of site investigation, remediation, removal and restoration work, including response costs under CERCLA and similar statutes.

(b) General Prohibition. Tenant shall not, except as provided in Paragraph (c) below, bring or otherwise cause to be brought or permit any of its agents, employees, contractors or invitees to bring in, on or about any part of the Premises, or Building, any Hazardous Material in violation of law, as such terms are or may be defined in (x) the Comprehensive Environmental Response, Compensation and Liability Act, 42 U.S.C. 9601 et seq., as the same may from time to time be amended, and the regulations promulgated pursuant thereto ("CERCLA"); the United States Department of Transportation Hazardous Materials Table (49

C.F.R. 172.102); by the Environmental Protection Agency as hazardous substances (40 C.F.R. Part 302); the Clean Air Act; and the Clean Water Act, and all amendments, modifications, or supplements thereto; and/or (y) any other rule, regulation, ordinance, statute, or requirements of any governmental or administrative agency regarding the environment (collectively, (x) and (y) shall be referred to as an "Applicable Environmental Law").

(c) Approved Hazardous Materials. Notwithstanding anything to the contrary contained herein, Tenant may bring to, store and/or use at the Premises (i) Hazardous Materials and other chemicals used in accordance with Tenant's normal operations and in accordance with Applicable Environmental Laws in quantities necessary for janitorial purposes, and (ii) those Hazardous Materials identified or categorized on Exhibit [__] attached hereto (the "Approved Hazardous Materials") in accordance with Applicable Environmental Laws.

(d) Notice of Spills. Tenant shall provide notice to Landlord of any Hazardous Material spills on the Premises or Property and/or any violation of city, county, state, or federal hazardous material laws caused by Tenant or of which Tenant is actually aware that require remediation. Tenant shall also provide notice to Landlord if Tenant discovers any Contamination at the Premises or Property notwithstanding whether or not such Contamination would trigger an investigation or prosecution by and enforcement agency.

(e) Indemnification. Tenant shall defend, indemnify, and hold harmless Landlord, Landlord's agents, and their respective employees and agents from and against any and all third-party claims, actions, damages, liability, and expense (including all attorney's, consultant's and expert's fees, expenses, and liabilities incurred in defense of any such claim or any action or proceeding brought thereon) arising from Tenant's storage and use of Hazardous Materials on the Premises, including, without limitation, any and all costs incurred by Landlord because of any investigation of the Project or any cleanup, removal, or restoration of the Building, or Property to remove or remediate Hazardous Materials or wastes deposited by Tenant, but expressly excluding any claims, actions, damages, liability, and expense relating to the negligence, willful misconduct violation of law or breach of this Lease by Landlord, Landlord's agents and their respective employees and agents. Without limitation of the foregoing, if Tenant, its officers, employees, agents, contractors, licensees, or invitees cause Contamination of the Premises or Property during the Term by any Hazardous Materials, used or generated at the Premises, Tenant shall promptly at its sole expense, take any and all necessary actions to return the Premises and Property substantially to the condition existing prior to such Contamination, or in the alternative take such other remedial steps as may be required by law or recommended by an independent licensed environmental consultant acceptable to Landlord.

(f) Compliance. Tenant shall, at its expense, comply with all requirements of Applicable Environmental Laws pertaining to Tenant's use or handling of Hazardous Materials at the Premises and/or Property.

(g) Disposal. Tenant shall not dispose of Hazardous Materials down any drain or in any waterway on the Property or otherwise in in violation of any Applicable Environmental Laws.

(h) Standard Operating Procedures. Tenant shall provide Landlord a copy of Tenant's standard operating procedures ("SOP"), detailing how Tenant shall handle and dispose of all Hazardous Materials and government regulated waste and which, at a minimum, shall provide that Tenant shall follow the OSHA Hazard Communication Standard requirements for the handling, storage and use of Hazardous Materials. Should the SOP be modified by Tenant ("SOP Modification"), Tenant shall inform Landlord and provide the updated SOP to Landlord within thirty (30) days of the SOP Modification. Not more than three (3) times annually, Landlord may request to inspect Tenant's SOP documents. Landlord reserves the right to require Tenant to seek additional consultation with safety professionals regarding certain Hazardous Materials or specialized practices.

(i) Contamination. If, during the Term of the Lease, Tenant becomes aware of any Contamination, due to Tenant's use of Hazardous Materials in, on, under or about the Premises, Building, or Property, or if Tenant, Premises, Building, or Property becomes subject to any order of any federal, state or local agency to repair, close, detoxify, decontaminate or otherwise remediate said Contamination, Tenant shall immediately notify Landlord of such event and, at Tenant's sole cost and expense, address such violation or effect such repair, closure, detoxification, decontamination, or other remediation to return the Premises, Building, and Property substantially to the condition existing prior to such Contamination in accordance with applicable law. If Tenant fails to implement and diligently pursue any such cure, repair, closure, detoxification or other remediation, Landlord shall have the right, but not the obligation, to address such violation or effect such repair, closure, detoxification, decontamination, or other remediation to return the Premises, Building, and Property substantially to the condition existing prior to such Contamination in accordance with applicable law and to recover from Tenant all of Landlord's costs and expenses incurred in connection therewith.

(j) Survival. This Paragraph 8 shall survive the expiration or sooner termination of this Lease.

PARAGRAPH 9

Reservation of Easements

RISK RATING: 4

A. DESCRIPTION AND SCOPE

This Paragraph sets forth the ability of Landlord to grant a right-of-way over or an easement in or to a portion of the Building or Premises needed for public utilities, access, or any other reason that the Landlord deems necessary.

This Paragraph is most often included in an industrial lease where the Premises is a part of multi-Building industrial "Park."

B. ANALYSIS

1. Landlord's Perspective

Landlord desires great flexibility to grant easements and rights of way concerning the Property in order for Landlord to develop the Property or any contiguous property owned by Landlord or an affiliate of the Park.

Tenant may request a provision be added to the Lease obligating the Landlord to grant customary utility easements necessary for the Tenant to conduct its business in the Premises. Landlord should analyze these provisions carefully since easements are typically not terminated until both parties consent to the termination. Landlord should not be required to grant easements that could materially and adversely affect the Premises.

2. Tenant's Perspective

Tenant should ensure that any easement or a right of way over a portion of the Property does not interfere with the operation of the Tenant's business. Tenant should also discern whether it needs any easement rights over another portion of the Park for its operations at the Premises. If Tenant's leasehold estate in the Premises is critical to its business operations, Tenant may wish to commission a title report and obtain title insurance from a title insurance company prior to executing the Lease.

3. Lender's Perspective

Lender, like Landlord, would see the benefit of having the ability to grant easements in order to maximize the Property's potential and thereby maintain an effective cash flow.

4. Broker's Perspective

Landlord Broker should advise Tenant Broker, at the outset of any LOI negotiation, of any required Landlord easement rights as Tenant Broker will need to determine, in consultation with Tenant and Tenant's counsel, if any such easement may negatively impact Tenant's proposed business operations at the Premises.

C. COMPROMISES AND ALTERNATIVES

Tenant may want to make sure that the granted rights do not adversely affect Tenant's use of portions of the Property other than the Premises.

D. COMMENTS

If there are any costs or expenses associated with the easements, Landlord may seek to include them in the limited Operating Expenses that Landlord has the right to incur and pass through to Tenant. If this is the case, Tenant should request and review several prior years of such expenses prior to Lease execution to understand the scope of the financial obligation.

E. TYPICAL PARAGRAPH

9. <u>Reservation of Easements</u>.

Landlord reserves to itself, its successors, and assigns the right, from time to time, to grant such easements, rights, and dedications that Landlord deems necessary or desirable and to cause the recordation of parcel maps, easements, and restrictions, so long as such easements, rights, dedications, maps, and restrictions do not unreasonably interfere with the Permitted Use of the Premises by Tenant. Tenant shall sign any of the aforementioned documents upon request of Landlord and otherwise reasonably cooperate with Landlord with respect to granting any such easements, rights, and dedications, and failure to do so shall constitute a material breach of this Lease.

PARAGRAPH 10

Lien Rights of Landlord and the Subordination Thereof

RISK RATING: 4

A. DESCRIPTION AND SCOPE

In Part 1, Paragraph 31, we explored how Landlord lien rights on Tenant's equipment, trade fixtures, inventory, and other personal property should nearly universally be struck in office leases. In retail and industrial leases however, Landlord lien rights are sometimes included as additional collateral (possibly even permitting Tenant to post a smaller Security Deposit under the Lease). So, we will revisit the topic of Landlord's lien rights in this Paragraph again but also discuss how Landlord's express or implied lien rights may need to be subordinated to the rights of Tenant's Creditors (as hereinafter defined) if applicable.

This Paragraph establishes a lien in favor of Landlord for rent and other charges payable by Tenant.

B. ANALYSIS

1. Landlord's Perspective

This Paragraph enables Landlord to enjoy the status of a secured creditor on Tenant's equipment, trade fixtures, inventory and other personal property as additional security for the performance of Tenant's obligations under the Lease, provided Landlord takes steps to perfect the lien, such as the filing of a UCC-1 Financing Statement in the appropriate filing offices. This Paragraph does not work in all jurisdictions. In some states, purchase money liens will take priority over Landlord's lien.

2. Tenant's Perspective

For Tenants who finance or lease from a third party (herein, for convenience, "Tenant's Creditors") equipment, trade fixtures, or other personal property in the operation of their business (which is fairly common for industrial tenants with expensive equipment for manufacturing or distribution), this Paragraph will likely conflict with other credit facilities maintained by Tenant. Tenant's Creditors may have a blanket lien on all of Tenant's equipment, trade fixtures, inventory and other personal property, and Tenant may be prohibited from granting any other liens on such property. In such case, Landlord's right under this Paragraph will need to be either struck or subordinated to the rights of Tenant's Creditors, as further provided in Compromises and Alternatives below.

In addition, even if Landlord's lien rights under this Paragraph are struck, Tenant may need to replace Landlord's lien right herein with a Landlord obligation to provide Tenant's Creditors with a written waiver of any express or implied lien rights on Tenant's property and an access agreement with Tenant's Creditors permitting Tenant's Creditors to access the Property to remove their collateral.

If Tenant does grant a Landlord's lien and Landlord files a UCC-1 Financing Statement, Tenant will need to later obtain a UCC-3 Termination Statement from the Landlord upon expiration of the Term in order to extinguish Landlord's lien, and a provision should be added to this Paragraph requiring Landlord to execute such a Termination Statement.

3. Lender's Perspective

Lenders like this Paragraph for the additional collateral it can provide to secure Tenant's obligations under the Lease. Lenders will be concerned with any removal or subordination of Landlord's lien to the rights of Tenant's Creditors. Likewise, Lender will be concerned about the restoration of any damage caused by Tenant's Creditors accessing the Property to remove any of Tenant's equipment, trade fixtures, inventory, and other personal property.

4. Broker's Perspective

Tenant Broker should discuss with Tenant and determine, as part of the up-front needs assessment phase of its assignment to acquire space, whether Tenant will need Landlord (and/or Landlord's lender) to subordinate its lien rights to Tenant's Creditors or require Landlord to waive any express or implied lien rights require Landlord (and/or Landlord's lender) to enter into a subordination and access agreement with Tenant's Creditors permitting Tenant's Creditors to remove Collateral from the Premises. Any such requirement is best raised at the LOI stage.

C. COMPROMISES AND ALTERNATIVES

Paragraph 10 can be revised to subordinate Landlord's lien rights to the rights of Tenant's Creditors. The following can be inserted into the Lease to accomplish that:

Notwithstanding anything to the contrary contained herein, Landlord's lien rights granted under this Paragraph 10 or otherwise implied or granted by law shall be automatically be second in priority to the rights of any and all current or future lender or lessor of Tenant (collectively, "Tenant's Creditors") with respect to the financing of Tenant's business operations in the Premises and/or any Tenant equipment, trade fixtures, inventory or other personal property located within the Premises (collectively, the "Collateral").

Whether or not the Lease ends up having express Landlord lien rights, Tenant may need, because of the terms and conditions of any financing documents with Tenant's Creditors, the right for Tenant's Creditors to receive a written agreement executed by Landlord wherein Landlord waives Landlord's rights to the Collateral and grants access rights to the Property to Tenant's Creditors so that they may collect the collateral. Of course, Landlord and Landlord's lender will be concerned about any damage to the Property resulting from such removal. Below is a sample paragraph that can be inserted into the Lease, if required, to meet Tenant's needs. Note that the provision is, intentionally, well balanced to protect the interests of both Landlord and Tenant and is meant to follow the subordination paragraph proposed above:

Landlord agrees, from time to time during the Term upon Tenant's request, to promptly enter, execute and deliver a reasonable waiver and access agreement ("Landlord's Waiver and Access Agreement") with Tenant's Creditors, on such Tenant's Creditors' standard form, wherein Landlord waives any express or implied lien on the Collateral and grants Tenant's Creditors the right to access the Property, upon reasonable advance notice to Landlord, to remove all or any portion of the Collateral, provided such Tenant's Creditors agree to repair and restore the Property or reimburse Landlord for the costs of repair and restoration of the Property arising from damage to the Property caused by the removal of any Collateral. Tenant shall pay Landlord, as Additional Rent, all costs and expenses, including reasonable attorneys' fees, that Landlord incurs by reason of Landlord's Waiver and Access Agreement or the enforcement of Landlord's rights hereunder, together with interest thereon at the lesser of the maximum legal rate of interest or [eighteen percent (18%) per annum] from the date Landlord incurs any expense under this Paragraph 10 until Landlord has been reimbursed therefore by Tenant, upon demand thereof by Landlord.

The parties may negotiate the rate at which interest accrues on Landlord's expenditures above.

If Tenant is expecting to need an initial Landlord's Waiver and Access Agreement upon the commencement of the Term, it may wish to have the agreement finalized, attached to the Lease as an Exhibit and executed and delivered simultaneously with the Lease.

D. COMMENTS

See Part 4 of this Lease Manual for a Form of Landlord's Waiver and Access Agreement.

E. TYPICAL PARAGRAPH

10. Lien Rights of Landlord.

In consideration of the mutual benefits arising under this Lease, Tenant hereby grants to Landlord a lien on all property Tenant now or hereafter places in or upon the Premises (except such part of any property as may be exchanged, replaced, or sold from time to time in the ordinary course of business operations or trade of Tenant), and such property shall be and remain subject to such lien of Landlord for payment of all Rent and other sums agreed to be paid by Tenant herein. Said lien shall be in addition to and cumulative upon Landlord's liens provided by law.

PART 4

Forms

FORM 1

Form of Letter of Intent (Office)

[Insert Date]

[Landlord]

[Landlord's Address]

RE: [**Property Name and Address**]

Ladies and Gentlemen:

Set forth below are the proposed terms for a lease between ______________________ ("Tenant") and ______________________ ("Landlord"), for space at the above referenced property.

Landlord:
[Insert Name of Landlord]

Area and Premises:
Approximately ___________ rentable square feet on floors ___ through ___ of the building known as __________________.

Lease Term:
___________ (__) Years

Rental Rate:
$_______ per rentable square foot.

Security Deposit:
No security deposit rent will be required of Tenant.

Operating Expenses:
Tenant will pay its pro rata share of all increases in Real Estate Taxes & Operating Expenses over a [Insert Calendar Year] Base Year.

Tenant Improvements:
Landlord will provide Tenant $_________ per rentable square foot as a tenant improvement allowance.

Right of First Offer:
Tenant shall have a recurring first right of offer on contiguous space and floors in the building. Should Tenant exercise a right of first offer, the rental rate shall be the then fair market rental value for such premises. All other terms shall be the same as the initial premises, including the expiration date that shall be coterminous with the initial premises. Base years' operating expenses and taxes shall be the first full calendar year the expansion space is occupied.

Renewal Option(s):
[Two] _______ (__) year renewal options at 95% of fair market rental value.

Assignment and Sublease:
Tenant shall have the right to sublet or assign all or part of the premises with Landlord's prior consent, which shall not be unreasonably withheld or delayed. Consent shall not be required for assignment or sublease to any subsidiary or affiliate of Tenant, or in the event of a change in ownership.

Building Access:
Tenant's employees shall have access to the premises 24 hours per day, 7 days per week, 365 days per year.

Building Hours of Operation: [8:00 a.m. to 6:00 p.m.] Monday through Friday.

Maintenance & Janitorial:
Landlord to provide five day per week janitorial service. Landlord will also assume the responsibility for maintaining all common area and building mechanical and HVAC systems including those in the premises.

Nondisturbance:
Landlord to provide Tenant with an acceptable Subordination, Nondisturbance, and Attornment Agreement from the existing and any future mortgage lender on the property.

Real Estate Commission:
It is understood that _______________ and _______________ are recognized as the sole brokers in this transaction. Landlord and Tenant understand and agree that they will be compensated on the basis of a full-market real estate commission paid by the Landlord that they will share equally.

Lease:
Landlord will provide Tenant with a draft of the proposed Lease, and Landlord and Tenant will use best efforts to complete and execute the Lease on or before _______________.

Substantial Completion:
Landlord will make a good-faith effort to deliver the building and premises in a condition suitable for tenant fit out to commence no later than _________________. In the event Landlord does not complete the building and premises on or before _________________, Tenant shall have the right to terminate the Lease.

Rent Commencement:
Rent shall commence ___ months after the building is complete and the premises are delivered to Tenant for completion of Tenant's improvements.

Parking:
Landlord shall provide Tenant with parking spaces in the building at a rate of ___ spaces per 1,000 rentable square feet leased by Tenant. The parking fees for such spaces will be the average rate paid by the other tenants of the building.

This letter of intent is nonbinding on Landlord and Tenant and is only intended as the basis for the preparation of a Lease Agreement between the parties. Neither Landlord nor Tenant shall have any obligations or liability until such time as a definitive Lease Agreement is executed and delivered by both Landlord and Tenant.

Sincerely,

FORM 2

Form of Lease Commencement Date Agreement

COMMENCEMENT DATE AGREEMENT

Reference is made to that certain [Lease Agreement] dated as of [DATE] (the "Lease"), by and between [NAME], as "Landlord", and [NAME], as "Tenant", [PREMISES DESCRIPTION] (the "Premises"), located at the building having an address of [ADDRESS] (the "Building").

The "Commencement Date" of the Lease is hereby established as [DATE].

The "Rent Commencement Date" of the Lease is hereby established as [DATE].

The "Expiration Date" of the initial Term of the Lease is hereby established as [DATE].

Landlord and Tenant agree to the foregoing statements.

In Witness whereof, and intending to be legally bound hereby, the parties have duly executed this Commencement Date Agreement, as of the day and year noted below. To facilitate execution of this Commencement Date Agreement the parties may execute (by electronic signature or otherwise) and exchange counterparts of the signature pages by e-mail or facsimile and e-mail or facsimile counterparts shall serve as originals.

Landlord:	**Tenant:**
[NAME]	[NAME]
By: ____________________	By: ____________________
Name: ____________________	Name: ____________________
Title: ____________________	Title: ____________________
Date: ____________________	Date: ____________________

FORM 3(A)

Form of Subordination, Nondisturbance, and Attornment Agreement (Landlord Form)*

Prepared by:
[NAME]
[ADDRESS]

Return to:
[NAME]
[ADDRESS]

[Tax Parcel Number: NUMBER]

SUBORDINATION, NONDISTURBANCE, AND ATTORNMENT AGREEMENT

This SUBORDINATION, NONDISTURBANCE, AND ATTORNMENT AGREEMENT (this "Agreement"), is made as of the ____ day of [MONTH], [YEAR], by and between [NAME], a [STATE, ENTITY TYPE] ("Tenant"), having an address at [ADDRESS], and [NAME], a [STATE, ENTITY TYPE] ("Mortgagee"), having an address at [ADDRESS].

*CAVEAT: Form needs to be modified to meet State-specific recording requirements.

WITNESSETH

WHEREAS, [NAME], a [STATE, ENTITY TYPE], ("Borrower") is the owner of certain land situate at [ADDRESS] as more particularly described in Exhibit A attached hereto (the "Property");

WHEREAS, the Tenant has entered into a certain [Lease Agreement], between the Borrower, as landlord, and the Tenant, as tenant, dated [DATE] (the "Lease"), covering the portion of the Property as more particularly described in the Lease (such portion of the Property leased by Tenant hereinafter referred to as the "Demised Premises");

WHEREAS, Mortgagee has entered into that certain Loan Agreement dated [DATE], with the Borrower pursuant to which Mortgagee has agreed to make a loan (the "Loan") to the Borrower;

WHEREAS, the Loan is secured by a mortgage lien on the Property (said mortgage, as it may be amended, increased, renewed, modified, consolidated, replaced, combined, substituted, severed, split, spread or extended, being herein referred to as the "Mortgage") and an assignment of the rents due under the Lease, in each case in favor of Mortgagee; and

WHEREAS, the parties wish to confirm the priority of the Mortgage over the Lease and to address certain other matters as set forth herein.

NOW, THEREFORE, in consideration of the mutual agreements herein contained and other good and valuable consideration, the receipt and sufficiency of which is hereby acknowledged, and intending to be legally bound hereby, the parties hereto agree as follows:

1. Tenant covenants and agrees that the Lease and all rights and interests whatsoever thereunder now are and shall at all times continue to be subject and subordinate in each and every respect to (i) the Mortgage, (ii) to any other documents now in existence or to be executed in the future with respect to the Loan, (iii) to all advances made or to be made thereunder and (iv) to all renewals, modifications, consolidations, replacements and extensions of any of the foregoing, to the full extent of the principal, interest and other sums secured thereby.
2. At any time, from time to time, the Mortgagee may elect by written notice to Tenant and by filing a copy of that notice with the County Recorder of Deeds of the County where the Property is located, to subordinate the Mortgage to the Lease, in which event, neither a foreclosure of the Mortgage, entry by the Mortgagee, nor any other action by the Mortgagee with respect to the Mortgage will affect the continued existence of the Lease, or the rights and obligations of the Tenant thereunder. This election may be changed from time to time so that at all times, the Lease will be subordinate to the Mortgage subject to the terms of this Agreement, or the Mortgage subordinate to the Lease, as elected by the Mortgagee.
3. Except as otherwise provided herein and subject to the terms, covenants, conditions and provisions of the Lease, so long as no Event of Default has occurred under the Lease and no default has occurred under this Agreement,

the Mortgagee shall not name Tenant as a party defendant to any action for foreclosure or other enforcement of the Mortgage (unless required by law), nor shall the Lease be terminated by the Mortgagee in connection with, or by reason of, foreclosure or other proceedings for the enforcement of the Mortgage, or by reason of a transfer of the Borrower's interest under the Lease pursuant to the taking of a deed or assignment in lieu of foreclosure (or similar device), nor shall Tenant's use or possession of the Demised Premises be interfered with by the Mortgagee, and the Lease shall continue in full force and effect except that the person acquiring, or succeeding to, the interests of the Borrower as a result of any such action or proceeding, and such person's successors and assigns (any of the foregoing being hereinafter referred to as the "Successor") shall not be:

(a) subject to any credits, offsets, prior defenses, or claims or counterclaims that Tenant may have against any prior landlord; or
(b) bound by any prepayment of rent more than one month in advance and not actually delivered to the Successor; or
(c) bound by any amendment or modification of this Lease made without the prior written consent of Mortgagee; or
(d) liable for any act or omission of any prior landlord; or
(e) be required to account for any security deposit other than any security deposit actually delivered to the Successor; or
(f) be liable for any payment to Tenant of any sums, or the granting to Tenant of any credit, in the nature of a contribution towards the cost of preparing, furnishing, or moving into the Demised Premises or any portion thereof; or
(g) bound by any covenant to undertake or complete any improvement to the Demised Premises.

4. Tenant covenants and agrees that its interest under the Lease, or any portion thereof, shall not be merged into the fee interest should Tenant become the owner of the Demised Premises, or any portion thereof. Except for a request by the Mortgagee to subordinate the Lease to another mortgage securing a loan from the Mortgagee to the Borrower, Tenant covenants and agrees not to subordinate or permit the subordination of the Lease to any mortgage other than the Mortgage and any replacement, renewal, consolidation, substitution, extension, modification, spreader, and splitter thereof.
5. Tenant certifies, covenants and agrees that it has not placed and shall not place any liens, charges, or encumbrances upon its leasehold interest in the Demised Premises.
6. If the interest of the Borrower under the Lease shall be transferred by reason of foreclosure or other proceedings for enforcement of the Mortgage, pursuant to a taking of a deed in lieu of foreclosure (or similar device) or as a result of the exercise of any power of sale under the Mortgage, Tenant shall be bound to the Successor, and, except as provided in this Agreement, the Successor shall be bound to Tenant, under all of the terms, covenants and conditions of the Lease for the balance of the term thereof remaining, with the same force and effect as

if the Successor were the landlord, and Tenant does hereby (i) agree to attorn to the Successor, including the Mortgagee if it is the Successor, as its landlord, (ii) affirm its obligations under the Lease, and (iii) agree to make payments when due of all sums due under the Lease to the Successor, said attornment, affirmation and agreement to be effective and self-operative, without the execution of any further instruments, upon Tenant and the Successor succeeding to the interest of the landlord under the Lease. Tenant shall, at the request of the Successor, execute, acknowledge and deliver such further instruments evidencing such attornment as are desired by the Successor, provided that the Successor confirms the terms of this Agreement. Tenant waives the provisions of any statute or rule of law now or hereafter in effect that may give or purport to give it any right or election to terminate or otherwise adversely affect the Lease or the obligations of Tenant thereunder by reason of any foreclosure or similar proceedings for enforcement of the Mortgage or the taking of a deed or assignment in lieu of foreclosure (or similar device).

7. Tenant acknowledges that it has notice that the Borrower's interest under the Lease and the rent and all other sums due thereunder have been assigned to the Mortgagee as part of the security for the indebtedness secured by the Mortgage and that the Borrower, as the landlord, has consented to the provisions of this Section. In the event that the Mortgagee notifies Tenant of an event of default under the Mortgage and demands that Tenant pay rent and all other sums due under the Lease to the Mortgagee, Tenant agrees that it shall pay rent and all other sums due under the Lease directly to the Mortgagee. Tenant shall have no responsibility to ascertain whether such demand is permitted under the Mortgage or any other document.
8. Tenant agrees that any award or compensation paid in connection with a taking, condemnation or eminent domain shall be paid and applied as provided in the Mortgage until such time as the Mortgagee is paid in full.
9. In the event of an insured casualty, the proceeds of insurance with respect to the Premises shall be deposited with Mortgagee to be applied as provided in the Lease under reasonable disbursement procedures promulgated by Mortgagee and meeting with the reasonable approval of Tenant. In the event of a lease termination by reason of a casualty, all insurance proceeds will be applied as provided in the Lease and then to amounts due Mortgagee until Mortgagee has been paid in full.
10. Tenant agrees at any time and from time-to-time to execute, acknowledge, and deliver to Borrower, to Mortgagee, or to any third party reasonably designated by Borrower or by Mortgagee within twenty (20) days following Borrower's or Mortgagee's written request therefor, (i) a statement in writing certifying that the Lease is in full force and effect, that Tenant is not in default thereunder, that Tenant is in possession of the Demised Premises as described in the Lease, the date through which Tenant has paid rent due to Borrower under the Lease, that to the best of Tenant's knowledge, Borrower is not in default of any of its obligations under the Lease, that Tenant is not then entitled to any abatement, adjustment, offset, defense or claim under the Lease, that to the best of

Tenant's knowledge and belief Borrower is not in default under any term or provision of the Lease, the dates of commencement and expiration of the term of the Lease, the rights, if any, of the Tenant to extend or renew the term of the Lease, the amount which Tenant has deposited with Borrower as a security deposit and such further information about the Lease or the Demised Premises that Borrower or Mortgagee or said third party may reasonably request, or if such statement is untrue, the correct information and such reasonable explanation of such information as is reasonably requested by Borrower Mortgagee or such third party, and (ii) a statement in writing acknowledging or denying receipt of notice of any conditional or security assignment of the Lease to any third party. Tenant understands that prospective purchasers, mortgagees, or lessors of the Property, or any part thereof, will rely on such certificates.

11. This Agreement may not be modified except by an agreement in writing signed by the parties or their respective successors in interest. This Agreement shall inure to the benefit of and be binding upon the parties hereto, their respective heirs, personal representatives, successors, and assigns.
12. Nothing contained in this Agreement shall in any way impair or affect the lien created by the Mortgage except as specifically set forth herein.
13. Tenant agrees that this Agreement satisfies any condition or requirement in the Lease relating to the granting of a nondisturbance agreement with respect to the Mortgage. Tenant further agrees that in the event there is any inconsistency between the terms and provisions hereof and the terms and provisions of the Lease, the terms and provisions of this Agreement shall be controlling.
14. All notices, demands, or requests made pursuant to, under, or by virtue of this Agreement must be in writing sent by any overnight courier service providing dated evidence of delivery or mailed by certified or registered mail, return receipt requested to the person to whom the notice, demand or request is being made at its address set forth above. Any person may change the place that notices and demands are to be sent by written notice delivered in accordance with this Agreement.
15. This Agreement shall be governed by the laws of the Commonwealth of Pennsylvania. If any of the terms of this Agreement or the application thereof to any person or circumstances shall to any extent be invalid or unenforceable, the remainder of this Agreement or the application of any such terms to any person or circumstances other than those as to which it is invalid or unenforceable shall not be affected thereby, and each term of this Agreement shall be valid and enforceable to the fullest extent permitted by law.
16. The individuals executing this Agreement hereby represent and warrant that they are empowered and duly authorized to so execute this Agreement on behalf of the parties they represent.

Remainder of page intentionally blank

IN WITNESS WHEREOF, the parties hereto have hereunto caused this Agreement to be duly executed as of the day and year first above written.

Witness/Attest:	MORTGAGEE:
	[NAME]
______________________	By:______________________
	Name:
	Title:
	TENANT:
	[NAME]
______________________	By:______________________
	Name:
	Title:

FORM 3(B)

Form of Subordination, Nondisturbance, and Attornment Agreement (Tenant Mark-Up of Form 3(A))*

Prepared by:
[NAME]
[ADDRESS]

Return to:
[NAME]
[ADDRESS]

[Tax Parcel Number: NUMBER]

SUBORDINATION, NONDISTURBANCE, AND ATTORNMENT AGREEMENT

This SUBORDINATION, NONDISTURBANCE, AND ATTORNMENT AGREEMENT (this "Agreement"), is made as of the ____ day of [MONTH], [YEAR], ~~by and~~ between and among [NAME], a [STATE, ENTITY TYPE] ("Tenant"), having an address at [ADDRESS], [NAME], a [STATE, ENTITY TYPE] ("Borrower") having an address at [ADDRESS], and [NAME], a [STATE, ENTITY TYPE] ("Mortgagee"), having an address at [ADDRESS].

*CAVEAT: Form needs to be modified to meet State-specific recording requirements.

WITNESSETH

WHEREAS, ~~[NAME], a [STATE, ENTITY TYPE], (“~~Borrower~~”)~~ is the owner of certain land situate at [ADDRESS] as more particularly described in Exhibit A attached hereto (the “Property”);

WHEREAS, the Tenant has entered into a certain [Lease Agreement], between the Borrower, as landlord, and the Tenant, as tenant, dated [DATE] (the “Lease”), covering the portion of the Property as more particularly described in the Lease (such portion of the Property leased by Tenant hereinafter referred to as the “Demised Premises”);

WHEREAS, Mortgagee has entered into that certain Loan Agreement dated [DATE], with the Borrower pursuant to which Mortgagee has agreed to make a loan (the “Loan”) to the Borrower;

WHEREAS, the Loan is secured by a mortgage lien on the Property (said mortgage, as it may be amended, increased, renewed, modified, consolidated, replaced, combined, substituted, severed, split, spread or extended, being herein referred to as the “Mortgage”) and an assignment of the rents due under the Lease, in each case in favor of Mortgagee; and

WHEREAS, the parties wish to confirm the priority of the Mortgage over the Lease and to address certain other matters as set forth herein.

NOW, THEREFORE, in consideration of the mutual agreements herein contained and other good and valuable consideration, the receipt and sufficiency of which is hereby acknowledged, and intending to be legally bound hereby, the parties hereto agree as follows:

1. Tenant covenants and agrees that, subject to the terms and conditions of this Agreement, the Lease and all rights and interests whatsoever thereunder now are and shall at all times continue to be subject and subordinate in each and every respect to (i) the Mortgage, (ii) to any other documents now in existence or to be executed in the future with respect to the Loan, (iii) to all advances made or to be made thereunder, and (iv) to all renewals, modifications, consolidations, replacements, and extensions of any of the foregoing, to the full extent of the principal, interest, and other sums secured thereby.
2. At any time, from time to time, the Mortgagee may elect by written notice to Tenant and by filing a copy of that notice with the County Recorder of Deeds of the County where the Property is located, to subordinate the Mortgage to the Lease, in which event, neither a foreclosure of the Mortgage, entry by the Mortgagee, nor any other action by the Mortgagee with respect to the Mortgage will affect the continued existence of the Lease, or the rights and obligations of the Tenant thereunder. This election may be changed from time to time so that at all times, the Lease will be subordinate to the Mortgage subject to the terms of this Agreement, or the Mortgage subordinate to the Lease, as elected by the Mortgagee.
3. Except as otherwise provided herein and subject to the terms, covenants, conditions, and provisions of the Lease, so long as no ~~Event of Default~~ Tenant default under the Lease has occurred and is continuing beyond any applicable notice and cure period under the Lease and no Tenant default has occurred

under this Agreement, the Mortgagee shall not name Tenant (and/or Tenant's subtenants, successors, or assigns) as a party defendant to any action for foreclosure or other enforcement of the Mortgage (unless required by law), nor shall the Lease be terminated by the Mortgagee or Successor (as hereinafter defined) in connection with, or by reason of, foreclosure or other proceedings for the enforcement of the Mortgage, or by reason of a transfer of the Borrower's interest under the Lease pursuant to the taking of a deed or assignment in lieu of foreclosure (or similar device); nor shall Tenant's (and/or Tenant's subtenants, successors, or assigns) use or possession of the Demised Premises be interfered with by the Mortgagee or Successor, and the Lease shall continue in full force and effect except that the person acquiring, or succeeding to, the interests of the Borrower under the Lease as a result of any such action or proceeding, and such person's successors and assigns (any of the foregoing being hereinafter referred to as the "Successor") shall not be:

(a) subject to any credits, offsets, prior defenses, or claims or counterclaims that Tenant may have against any prior landlord~~; or~~, unless such credits, offsets, defenses, claims, or counterclaims shall accrued to Tenant pursuant to an express provision in the Lease or as a result of a default by Borrower which default continues after Mortgagee or Successor succeeds to the interests of Borrower under the Lease; or

(b) bound by any prepayment of rent more than one month in advance and not actually delivered to the Mortgagee or Successor; or

(c) bound by any amendment or modification of this Lease made without the prior written consent of Mortgagee~~; or~~ (or Successor, as applicable), which consent shall not be unreasonably withheld, conditioned or delayed provided, in no event, shall written consent of Mortgagee or Successor be required for any amendment or modification of the Lease made pursuant to an express provision of the Lease; or

(d) liable for any act or omission of any prior landlord, except to the extent such act or omission continues after Mortgagee or Successor succeeds to the interests of Borrower under the Lease; or

(e) be required to account for any security deposit other than any security deposit actually delivered to the Mortgagee or Successor; or

(f) be liable for any payment to Tenant of any sums~~, or the granting to Tenant of any credit~~, in the nature of a contribution towards the cost of preparing, furnishing or moving into the Demised Premises or any portion thereof; or

(g) bound by any covenant to undertake or complete any improvement to the Demised Premises, except for Borrower's express maintenance, repair, and compliance obligations under the Lease.

4. ~~Tenant covenants and agrees that its interest under the Lease, or any portion thereof, shall not be merged into the fee interest should Tenant become the owner of the Demised Premises, or any portion thereof.~~ Except for a request by the Mortgagee to subordinate the Lease to another mortgage securing a loan from the Mortgagee to the Borrower, Tenant covenants and agrees not

to subordinate or permit the subordination of the Lease to any mortgage other than the Mortgage and any replacement, renewal, consolidation, substitution, extension, modification, spreader, and splitter thereof. Tenant's obligations under this Section shall automatically expire when Mortgagee (or Successor, if applicable) no longer has a lien on the Property and shall not be applicable if Tenant is asked to execute and deliver a subordination agreement in connection with a loan meant to pay-off or otherwise replace the Loan.

5. Tenant certifies, covenants, and agrees that it has not placed and shall not place any liens, charges, or encumbrances upon its leasehold interest in the Demised Premises.; [provided, however, for the sake of clarity, nothing in this Agreement shall be construed to limit Tenant's rights, the rights of Tenant's Creditor (as such term is defined under Section [NUMBER] of the Lease) or landlord's obligations under Section [NUMBER] under the Lease, which Mortgagee expressly acknowledges, agrees, and accepts][ADD ONLY IF APPLICABLE].

6. If the interest of the Borrower under the Lease shall be transferred by reason of foreclosure or other proceedings for enforcement of the Mortgage, pursuant to a taking of a deed in lieu of foreclosure (or similar device) or as a result of the exercise of any power of sale under the Mortgage, Tenant shall be bound to the Successor, and, except as provided in this Agreement, the Successor shall be bound to Tenant, under all of the terms, covenants and conditions of the Lease for the balance of the term thereof remaining, with the same force and effect as if the Successor were the landlord, and Tenant does hereby (i) agree to attorn to the Successor, including the Mortgagee if it is the Successor, as its landlord, (ii) affirm its obligations under the Lease, and (iii) agree to make payments when due of all sums due under the Lease to the Successor, said attornment, affirmation and agreement to be effective and self-operative, without the execution of any further instruments, upon Tenant and the Successor succeeding to the interest of the landlord under the Lease. Tenant shall, at the request of the Successor, execute, acknowledge, and deliver such further instruments evidencing such attornment as are desired by the Successor, provided that the Successor confirms the terms of this Agreement. ~~Tenant waives~~ Mortgagee (on behalf of Mortgagee and any, Successor) and Tenant each waive the provisions of any statute or rule of law now or hereafter in effect that may give or purport to give it any right or election to terminate or otherwise adversely affect the Lease or the obligations of landlord under Lease or Tenant thereunder by reason of any foreclosure or similar proceedings for enforcement of the Mortgage or the taking of a deed or assignment in lieu of foreclosure (or similar device).

7. Tenant acknowledges that it has notice that the Borrower's interest under the Lease and the rent and all other sums due thereunder have been assigned to the Mortgagee as part of the security for the indebtedness secured by the Mortgage and that the Borrower, as the landlord, has consented to the provisions of this Section. In the event that the Mortgagee notifies Tenant of an event of default under the Mortgage and demands that Tenant pay rent and all other sums due under the Lease to the Mortgagee, Tenant agrees that it shall pay

rent and all other sums due under the Lease directly to the Mortgagee. Tenant shall have no responsibility to ascertain whether such demand is permitted under the Mortgage or any other document. By its execution hereof, Borrower expressly consents to the foregoing and hereby releases and discharged Tenant from any liability to Borrower on account of such payments to Mortgagee. All sums received by Mortgagee or Successor shall be credited against Tenant's rental and other obligations under the Lease.

8. Tenant agrees that any award or compensation paid to Borrower in connection with a taking, condemnation, or eminent domain shall be paid and applied as provided in the Mortgage until such time as the Mortgagee is paid in full.
9. In the event of an insured casualty, the proceeds of Borrower insurance with respect to the Demised Premises shall be deposited with Mortgagee to be applied as provided in the Lease under reasonable disbursement procedures promulgated by Mortgagee and meeting with the reasonable approval of Tenant. In the event of a lease termination by reason of a casualty, all Borrower insurance proceeds will be applied as provided in the Lease and then to amounts due Mortgagee until Mortgagee has been paid in full.
10. Tenant hereby affirms and agrees ~~at any time and from time-to-time~~ to execute~~, acknowledge,~~ and deliver ~~to~~ estoppel certificates at the request of Borrower, to Mortgagee,~~, or to any third party reasonably designated by Borrower or by Mortgagee within twenty (20) days following Borrower's or Mortgagee's written request therefor, (i) a statement in writing certifying that the Lease is in full force and effect, that Tenant is not in default thereunder, that Tenant is in possession of the Demised Premises as described in the Lease, the date through which Tenant has paid rent due to Borrower under the Lease, that to the best of Tenant's knowledge, Borrower is not in default of any of its obligations under the Lease, that Tenant is not then entitled to any abatement, adjustment, offset, defense or claim under the Lease, that to the best of Tenant's knowledge and belief Borrower is not in default under any term or provision of the Lease, the dates of commencement and expiration of the term of the Lease, the rights, if any, of the Tenant to extend or renew the term of the Lease, the amount which Tenant has deposited with Borrower as a security deposit and such further information about the Lease or the Demised Premises which Borrower or Mortgagee or said third party may reasonably request, or if such statement is untrue, the correct information and such reasonable explanation of such information as is reasonably requested by Borrower. Mortgagee or such third party, and (ii) a statement in writing acknowledging or denying receipt of notice of any conditional or security assignment of the Lease to any third party. Tenant understands that prospective purchasers, mortgagees or lessors of the Property, or any part thereof, will rely on such certificates.~~ or Successor in accordance with the provisions under Section [NUMBER] of the Lease.
11. This Agreement may not be modified except by an agreement in writing signed by the parties or their respective successors in interest. This Agreement shall inure to the benefit of and be binding upon the parties hereto, their respective heirs, personal representatives, successors, and assigns.

12. Nothing contained in this Agreement shall in any way impair or affect the lien created by the Mortgage except as specifically set forth herein. [or any lien on Tenant's property at the Demised Premises by Tenant's Creditor].[ADD ONLY IF APPLICABLE]
13. Tenant agrees that this Agreement satisfies any condition or requirement in the Lease relating to the granting of a nondisturbance agreement with respect to the Mortgage. Tenant further agrees that in the event there is any inconsistency between the terms and provisions hereof and the terms and provisions of the Lease, the terms and provisions of this Agreement shall be controlling.
14. All notices, demands, or requests made pursuant to, under, or by virtue of this Agreement must be in writing and sent by any overnight courier service providing dated evidence of delivery or mailed by certified or registered mail, return receipt requested to the person to whom the notice, demand, or request is being made at its address set forth above. Any person may change the place that notices and demands are to be sent by written notice delivered in accordance with this Agreement.
15. This Agreement shall be governed by the laws of the Commonwealth of Pennsylvania. If any of the terms of this Agreement or the application thereof to any person or circumstances shall to any extent be invalid or unenforceable, the remainder of this Agreement or the application of any such terms to any person or circumstances other than those as to which it is invalid or unenforceable shall not be affected thereby, and each term of this Agreement shall be valid and enforceable to the fullest extent permitted by law.
16. The individuals executing this Agreement hereby represent and warrant that they are empowered and duly authorized to so execute this Agreement on behalf of the parties they represent.
17. Tenant shall have the right to record this Agreement on the applicable County Recorder of Deeds of the County where the Property is located.

Remainder of page intentionally blank

IN WITNESS WHEREOF, the parties hereto have hereunto caused this Agreement to be duly executed as of the day and year first above written.

Witness/Attest:	MORTGAGEE:
	[NAME]
______________________	By:______________________
	Name:
	Title:
	TENANT:
	[NAME]
______________________	By:______________________
	Name:
	Title:

ACKNOWLEDGMENTS

[ADD STATE SPECIFIC ACKKNOWLEDGEMENT
FOR EACH PARTY TO THIS SNDA]

EXHIBIT A

Legal Description of Property

FORM **4(A)**

Form of Tenant Estoppel (Landlord Form)

TENANT ESTOPPEL CERTIFICATE

Re: **[Address]**
[Address]

Ladies and Gentlemen:

The undersigned ("**Tenant**") certifies with respect to the lease (the "**Lease**") more particularly described in the attached Schedule "A" which is hereby incorporated (the "**Schedule**") that:

1. Tenant is the tenant under the Lease;
2. The summary of the terms of the Lease contained in the Schedule is true and correct;
3. Tenant has accepted possession of the premises (the "Premises") under the Lease;
4. There are no rent abatements, free rent periods, or other rent concessions now or in the future other than as may be set forth on the Schedule;
5. The Lease is in full force and effect and, except as may be indicated on the Schedule, (a) the Lease has not been assigned (by operation of law or otherwise), modified, supplemented, or amended in any way, and (b) no sublease, concession agreement, or license has been entered into by Tenant;
6. The Lease represents the entire agreement between Tenant and the landlord under the Lease ("Landlord") with respect to the Premises;
7. All construction and other obligations of a material nature to be performed by Landlord have been satisfied, except as may be indicated on the Schedule;

8. Any payments by Landlord to Tenant for tenant improvements which are required under the Lease have been made, except as may be indicated on the Schedule;
9. On this date, there is no existing event of default on the part of Tenant or, to Tenant's knowledge, Landlord, in any of the terms and conditions of the Lease, and no event has occurred which, with the passage of time or giving of notice, or both, would constitute an event of default by Tenant or, to Tenant's knowledge, Landlord;
10. Tenant has no charge, lien, claim of set-off, or defense against rents or other charges due or to become due under the Lease or otherwise under any of the terms, conditions, or covenants contained therein, except as may be indicated on the Schedule;
11. No rental (including expense reimbursements), other than for the current month, has been paid in advance, except as may be indicated on the Schedule;
12. Tenant has not filed on its behalf, nor to Tenant's knowledge, has any party initiated against Tenant, proceedings for relief under bankruptcy, insolvency, or other proceedings;
13. Except as set forth in the Lease, Tenant has no purchase options, extension, expansion or termination rights, rights of first offer or rights of first refusal, exclusives, rights to lease other premises, or rights to have Landlord perform Tenant's obligations under leases of other premises;
14. Tenant has no right to terminate the Lease except as set forth in the Lease;
15. The address for notices to be sent to Tenant is as set forth in the Lease or as set forth below (if the address set forth in the Lease is correct, please so indicate);
16. The party executing this letter on behalf of Tenant is duly authorized and empowered to do so; and
17. Tenant has not received any notice of any present violation of any federal, state, county, or municipal laws, regulations, ordinances, orders or directives relating to the use or condition of the Leased Premises or the Property.

The truth and accuracy of the certifications contained herein may be relied upon by (i) Landlord, (ii) any purchaser of the Property ("**Purchaser**"), (iii) each lender ("**Lender**") of Landlord or Purchaser (or any of their respective direct or indirect owners), and its successors, participants, assigns and transferees, (iv) any rating agency or trustee involved in a securitization of one or more loans made by a Lender, and (v) any servicer of any such loan (collectively, the "**Reliance Parties**"), and said certifications shall be binding upon Tenant and its successors and assigns, and inure to the benefit of the Reliance Parties.

Very truly yours,
[NAME]

By: ______________________________
Name:
Title:
Date:

SCHEDULE A

Summary of Lease Terms

(1) Name of Tenant: [NAME]

(2) Lease Date: [DATES]

(3) Amendment Dates, Separate Agreements, if any:

[NAME OF INSTRUMENT AND DATE]

(4) Square Footage: [SIZE]

(5) Lease Commencement Date: [DATE]

(6) Current Monthly Base Rent: $[AMOUNT]

Current Monthly Expense

Reimbursement: $[AMOUNT]

Other Current Monthly Rent Not

Otherwise Identified Above: $[AMOUNT]

Current Total Monthly Rent: $[AMOUNT]

Tenant has the following abatement(s) remaining: None

Tenant has paid the following rental amounts in advance (if rental amounts have been paid in advance, please so indicate): None

(7) Security Deposit: [AMOUNT AND FORM]

(8) Percentage Rent: None

(9) Assignees/Subtenants: None

(10) Lease Guarantor(s): None

(11) Tenant Improvement Allowance Balance: [$AMOUNT]

(12) Outstanding Landlord Construction Obligations: None

(13) Base Year for Real Estate Taxes is: [YEAR]

Base Year for Operating Costs is: [YEAR]

Tenant's Pro Rata Share for Real Estate Taxes and Operating Cost is: [AMOUNT]%

FORM 4(B)

Form of Tenant Estoppel (Tenant Mark-up to Form (A))

TENANT ESTOPPEL CERTIFICATE

Re: [**Address**]
[**Address**]

Ladies and Gentlemen:

The undersigned ("**Tenant**") certifies<u>, as of the date hereof,</u> with respect to the lease (the "**Lease**") more particularly described in the attached Schedule "A" which is hereby incorporated (the "**Schedule**") that:

1. Tenant is the tenant under the Lease;
2. The ~~summary of the~~ terms of the Lease contained in the Schedule ~~is~~ <u>are</u> true and correct;
3. Tenant has accepted possession of the premises (the "**Premises**") under the Lease;
4. There are no rent abatements, free rent periods, or other rent concessions now or in the future other than as ~~may be set forth on~~ <u>provided in</u> the ~~Schedule~~ <u>Lease</u>;
5. The Lease is in full force and effect and, ~~except as may be indicated on the Schedule,~~ (a) the Lease has not been assigned (by operation of law or otherwise), modified, supplemented, or amended in any way, and (b) no sublease, concession agreement, or license has been entered into by Tenant;
6. The Lease ~~represents~~ <u>and the other documents described in Schedule A represent</u> the entire agreement between Tenant and the landlord under the Lease ("**Landlord**") with respect to the Premises;
7. All <u>initial</u> construction ~~and other~~ obligations ~~of a material nature~~ <u>with respect to preparing the Premises for Tenant's initial occupancy</u> to be performed by Landlord have been satisfied~~, except as may be indicated on the Schedule~~;

8. Any payments by Landlord to Tenant for tenant improvements which are required under the Lease have been made~~, except as may be indicated on the Schedule~~;
9. ~~On~~ To Tenant's knowledge, on this date, (a) there is no existing event of default on the part of Tenant or~~, to Tenant's knowledge,~~ Landlord, in any of the terms and conditions of the Lease, and (b) no event has occurred which, with the passage of time or giving of notice, or both, would constitute an event of default by Tenant or~~, to Tenant's knowledge,~~ Landlord;
10. Tenant presently has no charge, lien, claim of set-off, or defense against rents or other charges due or to become due under the Lease or otherwise under any of the terms, conditions, or covenants contained therein~~, except as may be indicated on the Schedule~~;
11. No rental (including expense reimbursements), other than for the current month, has been paid in advance~~, except as may be indicated on the Schedule~~;
12. Tenant has not filed on its behalf, nor to Tenant's knowledge, has any party initiated against Tenant, proceedings for relief under bankruptcy, insolvency, or other proceedings;
13. Except as set forth in the Lease, Tenant has no purchase options, extension, expansion or termination rights, rights of first offer or rights of first refusal, exclusives, rights to lease other premises, or rights to have Landlord perform Tenant's obligations under leases of other premises;
14. Tenant has no right to terminate the Lease except as set forth in the Lease.
15. The address for notices to be sent to Tenant is as set forth in the Lease or as set forth below (if the address set forth in the Lease is correct, please so indicate);
16. The party executing this letter on behalf of Tenant is duly authorized and empowered to do so;~~ and~~
17. Tenant has not received any written notice of any present violation of any federal, state, county, or municipal laws, regulations, ordinances, orders, or directives relating to the use or condition of the ~~Leased~~ Premises~~ or the Property.~~;
18. Each reference to Tenant's "knowledge" in this Tenant Estoppel Certificate shall refer only to the actual knowledge (as opposed to constructive, deemed, or imputed knowledge) without investigation, diligence or inquiry of the Designated Employee (as hereinafter defined) of Tenant, and shall not be construed by imputation or otherwise, to refer to the knowledge of Tenant or any affiliate of Tenant, to any property manager, or to any other officer, agent, manager, representative, or employee of Tenant or any affiliate thereof or to impose upon such Designated Employee any duty to investigate the matter to which such actual knowledge, or the absence thereof, pertains. As used herein, the term "Designated Employee" shall refer to the individual who executes this Tenant Estoppel Certificate on behalf of Tenant and who Tenant acknowledges and agrees has sufficient familiarity with the Lease to make the representations limited to Tenant's "knowledge" contained herein. In no event, shall the Designated Employee have any personal liability whatsoever to Landlord or Lender.

19. Nothing contained in this Tenant Estoppel Certificate shall constitute or be deemed to constitute an amendment, modification, or waiver of any term or condition of the Lease or any right or remedy of Tenant thereunder. In the event of a conflict between the Lease and this Tenant Estoppel Certificate, the Lease shall control.

The truth and accuracy of the certifications contained herein may be relied upon by (i) Landlord, (ii) any purchaser of the Property ("**Purchaser**"), (iii) each lender ("**Lender**") of Landlord or Purchaser (or any of their respective direct or indirect owners), and its successors, participants, assigns and transferees, (iv) any rating agency or trustee involved in a securitization of one or more loans made by a Lender, and (v) any servicer of any such loan (collectively, the "**Reliance Parties**"), and said certifications shall be binding upon Tenant and its successors and assigns, and inure to the benefit of the Reliance Parties.

Very truly yours,
[NAME]

By: ____________________________
Name:
Title:
Date:

SCHEDULE A

Summary of Lease Terms

~~(1) Name of Tenant: [NAME]~~

(~~2~~1) Lease Date: [DATES]

~~(3)~~ Amendment Dates, Separate Agreements, if any:

[NAME OF INSTRUMENT AND DATE]

~~(4) Square Footage: [SIZE]~~

(~~5~~2) Lease Commencement Date: [DATE]; Current Lease Expiration: [DATE]

(~~6~~3) Current Monthly Base Rent: $[AMOUNT]

Current Monthly Expense

Reimbursement: $[AMOUNT]

Other Current Monthly Rent Not

Otherwise Identified Above: $~~[AMOUNT]~~N/A

Current Total Monthly Rent: $[AMOUNT]

~~Tenant has the following abatement(s) remaining: None~~

(4) Tenant has paid the following rental amounts in advance (if rental amounts have been paid in advance, please so indicate): None

(~~7~~5) Security Deposit: [AMOUNT AND FORM]

~~(8) Percentage Rent: None~~

~~(9) Assignees/Subtenants: None~~

~~(10) Lease Guarantor(s): None~~

(~~11~~6) ~~Tenant Improvement Allowance Balance: [~~$Under Section [NUMBER] of the Lease, Tenant is required to reimburse Landlord the sum of $[AMOUNT].

~~(12) Outstanding Landlord Construction Obligations: None~~

~~(13) Base Year for Real Estate Taxes is: [YEAR]~~

~~Base Year for Operating Costs is: [YEAR]~~

~~Tenant's Pro Rata Share for Real Estate Taxes and Operating Cost is: [AMOUNT]%~~

FORM 5(A)

Form of Landlord's Waiver and Access Agreement (Tenant Form)

LANDLORD'S WAIVER AGREEMENT

Dated: [DATE]

This Agreement between the undersigned and [NAME] ("Bank") is entered into in connection with a loan or other financing transaction between Bank and its customer [NAME] ("Tenant"), and relates to (a) the following "Premises": [ADDRESS] and (b) the "Collateral" listed or described on Exhibit "A" attached hereto.

The undersigned [NAME] ("Landlord"), holding an interest in the Premises as owner, lessor, sublessor, mortgagee, beneficiary of a deed of trust or otherwise, hereby agrees that: (a) the Collateral may be located at the Premises and, at all times, shall be deemed to be personal property; (b) the Collateral may be removed from the Premises by Bank in the exercise of its secured creditor or other rights; (c) the undersigned will not assert any claim or lien against the Collateral and will permit Bank or its designated agent to enter upon the Premises to remove the Collateral; (d) the undersigned agrees to provide Bank written notice of default by tenant and reasonable opportunity to cure this default; and (e) this Agreement shall be binding on the successors and assigns of the undersigned and shall benefit and be enforceable by Bank and its successors and assigns.

Bank agrees to pay for any damage to the Premises directly caused by removal of the Collateral from the Premises by Bank or its designated agent.

LANDLORD:

By: ______________________________

Print Name: ______________________

Title: _________________________________

LENDER:

[BANK NAME]

By: ___________________________________

EXHIBIT "A"

Description of Collateral

Re: Customer/Tenant: [NAME]

All of the following property whether now owned or hereafter acquired and wheresoever located as well as the proceeds and products thereof:

All equipment and machinery, including power-driven machinery and equipment, leasehold improvements, furniture, and fixtures now owned or hereafter acquired, together with all replacements thereof, all attachments, accessories, parts, equipment and tools belonging thereto or for use in connection therewith.

All inventory, raw materials, work in progress, and supplies now owned or hereafter acquired.

All accounts, deposit accounts, and heath care insurance receivables now outstanding or hereafter arising.

All chattel paper, instruments, and general intangibles now in force or hereafter acquired.

FORM 5(B)

Form of Landlord's Waiver and Access Agreement (Landlord Mark-up of Form 5(A))

LANDLORD'S WAIVER AND ACCESS AGREEMENT

Dated: [DATE]

This Landlord's Waiver and Access Agreement (the "Agreement") is by and among [NAME] ("Landlord"), [NAME] ("Bank"), [NAME] ("Tenant"), and [NAME] (the "Franchisor").

W I T N E S S E T H:

WHEREAS, Landlord, as landlord, and Tenant, as tenant, are parties to that certain [Lease] dated [DATE] (the "Lease"), wherein Tenant leases from Landlord certain land and improvements with an address of: [ADDRESS] (the "Premises");

WHERERAS, Tenant has entered into a certain [Franchise Agreement and a Collateral Assignment of Lease] benefiting Franchisor (collectively, the "Franchise Agreements") as more particularly described and defined in the Lease;

WHEREAS, Landlord entered into a certain [Consent and Agreement of Landlord] benefiting Franchisor dated [DATE] (the "Consent and Agreement of Landlord");

~~This Agreement between the undersigned and [NAME] ("Bank") is entered into in connection with a loan or other financing transaction between Bank and its customer [NAME] ("Tenant"), and relates to (a) the following "Premises": [ADDRESS] and (b) the "Collateral"~~ WHEREAS, Bank is entering into a commercial lending arrangement with Tenant (the "Loan Agreement"), as borrower, and Tenant's obligations under the Loan Agreement secured by Tenant's assets listed or described on Exhibit "A" attached hereto~~.~~ (collectively, the "Collateral");

WHEREAS, certain Collateral is located at the Premises and the Bank requires certain waiver and access rights from Landlord in order to induce Bank to enter into the Loan Agreement; and

WHEREAS, Landlord is willing to give certain waiver and access rights to Bank, subject to the terms and conditions contained herein.

NOW, THEREFORE, in consideration of the mutual covenants contained herein, and for other good and valuable consideration, the receipt and sufficiency of which is hereby acknowledged, the parties hereto, intending to be legally bound, hereby agree as follows:

1. ~~The undersigned [NAME] ("Landlord"), holding an interest in the Premises as owner, lessor, sublessor, mortgagee, beneficiary of a deed of trust or otherwise, hereby~~ Landlord agrees that, subject to the terms and conditions of this Agreement: (a) the Collateral may be located at the Premises and, at all times, shall be deemed to be personal property of Tenant; (b) the Collateral may be removed from the Premises by Bank in the exercise of its secured creditor or other rights; (c) the undersigned will not assert any claim or lien against the Collateral and will permit Bank or its designated agent to enter upon the Premises to remove the Collateral; (d) the undersigned agrees to provide Bank written notice of default by ~~tenant and reasonable opportunity to cure this default~~ Tenant under the Lease; and (e) this Agreement shall be binding on the successors and assigns of the undersigned and shall benefit and be enforceable by Bank and its successors and assigns.
2. Notwithstanding anything to the contrary contained herein, Bank shall exercise any and all access rights to the Premises available under this Agreement during normal business hours and, in each instance, upon reasonable advance written notice to Landlord, in a manner consistent with Landlord's reasonable security and insurance requirements, and in a manner that does not unreasonably interfere with Landlord's operation of the Premises. Bank agrees to pay Landlord for any damage to the Premises arising from the removal of the Collateral from the Premises by Bank or its designated agent. Bank shall indemnify, defend, and hold Landlord and its partners, shareholders, members, managers, direct or indirect owners, and affiliates and their respective officers, managers, directors, employees, agents, and representatives harmless from and against any accident, injury or damages, liabilities, and expenses (including reasonable attorneys' fees) arising out of Bank's exercising its access and removal rights permitted under this Agreement.
3. Tenant and Franchisor hereby irrevocably authorize Landlord to comply with the obligations of Landlord under this Agreement and hereby release and discharge Landlord from any liability to Landlord on account of such compliance. Tenant and Franchisor acknowledge and agree that Landlord's compliance with its obligations under the Lease supersede any of Landlord's obligations under the Lease or the Consent and Agreement of Landlord and, in no event, shall Landlord be deemed in violation of its obligations under the Lease or the Consent and Agreement of Landlord by Landlord entering into and complying with this Agreement.

4. Tenant and Franchisor acknowledge and agree that this Agreement does not cause any event of default under the Franchise Agreements.
5. Any notice required or permitted by this Agreement shall be in writing and shall be sent by recognized overnight courier service, or by certified or registered mail, postage prepaid return receipt requested. All notices shall be addressed as follows:

If to Landlord :	[ADDRESS]
If to Tenant:	[ADDRESS]
If to Bank:	[ADDRESS]
If to Franchisor:	[ADDRESS]

6. The covenants, conditions, and agreements contained in this Agreement shall bind, and the benefits thereof shall inure to, the parties hereto and their respective heirs, executors, administrators, successors, and assigns.
7. This Agreement may be executed in any number of counterparts, each of which shall be deemed an original but such counterparts shall together constitute but one and the same instrument. This Agreement shall not be binding upon Landlord, Tenant, Bank, Franchisor or Guarantor unless and until all parties hereto have each executed and unconditionally delivered a fully executed copy of this Agreement to the other.
8. This Agreement shall be governed by the laws of the State of [STATE] and construed as a contract executed and to be fully performed in the State of [STATE].
9. This Agreement shall remain effective until the earlier of (i) all obligations of Tenant to Bank have been paid and satisfied in full, Bank has no further interest in the Collateral or has removed or abandoned all of the Collateral, or (ii) the expiration or earlier termination of the Lease (so long as, in the event of an earlier termination of the Lease, Landlord has provided Bank with written notice of early termination of the Lease) and Bank is provided thirty (30) days from the expiration of the Lease or, if applicable, the date of receipt of said notice in the event of early termination of the Lease, to enter the Premises at no charge to Bank and remove the Collateral subject Bank complying with the terms and conditions of this Agreement. After the expiration of such 30-day period, Bank's rights hereunder shall be expired and the Collateral shall automatically be deemed abandoned by Tenant, Bank and Franchisor and Landlord shall have all of its rights and remedies with respect to such Collateral under the Lease, at law or in equity.

[Signature Page Follows]

~~Bank agrees to pay for any damage to the Premises directly caused by removal of the Collateral from the Premises by Bank or its designated agent.~~

LANDLORD:
[NAME]
By: ______________________
Print Name: ______________________
Title: ______________________

LENDER:
[BANK NAME]
By: ______________________
Print Name: ______________________
Title: ______________________

TENANT:
[NAME]
By: ______________________
Print Name: ______________________
Title: ______________________

FRANCHISOR:
[NAME]
By: ______________________
Print Name: ______________________
Title: ______________________

Accepted and Agreed:

GUARANTOR UNDER LEASE:

____

[NAME]

EXHIBIT "A"

Description of Collateral

Re: Customer/Tenant: [NAME]

All of the following property whether now owned or hereafter acquired by Tenant and wheresoever located as well as the proceeds and products thereof:

All equipment and machinery, including power-driven machinery and equipment, ~~leasehold improvements,~~ furniture, and trade fixtures now owned by Tenant or hereafter acquired by Tenant, together with all replacements thereof, all attachments, accessories, parts, equipment, and tools belonging ~~thereto or for use in connection therewith~~ to Tenant.

All inventory, raw materials, work in progress, and supplies now owned by Tenant or hereafter acquired by Tenant.

All Tenant accounts, deposit accounts, and heath care insurance receivables now outstanding or hereafter arising.

All Tenant chattel paper, instruments, and general intangibles now in force or hereafter acquired.

Notwithstanding anything to the contrary contained herein, in no event shall any property of Landlord and/or any improvements, equipment, systems, or fixtures of the Premises (or the building of which is a part) be considered "Collateral."

FORM 6

Form of Notice of Lease*

Prepared By and Return to:
[Law Firm]
[Address]
[Address]
Tax Parcel No.: [NUMBER]

THIS NOTICE OF LEASE ("Notice"), entered into as of [DATE], by and between [NAME]("Landlord"), a [STATE, TYPE OF ENTITY], with an address [ADDRESS], and [NAME] ("Tenant"), a [STATE, TYPE OF ENTITY], with an address of [ADDRESS].

BACKGROUND:

A. Landlord is the owner of certain property known by its mailing address of [Address], as further described in the description attached hereto and incorporated herein as Exhibit A (the "Property").
B. Pursuant to that certain [Lease] between Landlord, as landlord, and Tenant, as tenant, dated [DATE] (the "Lease"), Tenant leased a portion of the Property comprising approximately [AMOUNT] rentable square feet in the building (the "Premises") located on the Property (the "Building"), together with rights to certain areas exterior to the Building, as further described in the Lease.
C. Landlord and Tenant hereby desire to execute and record this Notice to memorialize the Lease.

NOW, THEREFORE, the parties hereto hereby state as follows:

1. Lease. The Lease is in full force and effect, and pursuant thereto, Tenant is entitled to all rights and privileges of the Tenant therein. The Lease shall be on file at the office of the Landlord described above.

*CAVEAT: Form needs to be modified to meet State-specific recording requirements.

2. Lease Term; Renewal Option. The Premises is and will be leased for a term that commences upon the achievement of certain delivery requirements expected to occur on or about [DATE] and terminate on or about [AMOUNT] years thereafter, subject to certain renewal rights, all as provided under, and subject to the terms, covenants, and conditions appearing in, the Lease. Tenant has [one (1)] renewal option for a renewal term of [AMOUNT] years. [ADD ONLY IF APPLICABLE]
3. Tenant Right of First Refusal to Lease. Pursuant to certain terms, conditions, and exclusions contained in the Lease, Tenant has a certain continuing right of first refusal to lease any portion of the Building that becomes available for lease. [ADD ONLY IF APPLICABLE]
4. Tenant Right of First Refusal to Purchase. Pursuant to certain terms, conditions, and exclusions contained in the Lease, Tenant has a certain continuing right of first refusal to Purchase the Property. [ADD ONLY IF APPLICABLE]
5. Tenant Use Exclusivity. Pursuant to certain terms, conditions, and exclusions contained in the Lease, Tenant has the exclusive right (and other occupants of the Property are prohibited) to engage in the following business at the Property: [USE DESCRIPTION]. [ADD ONLY IF APPLICABLE]
6. Tenant's Creditor Rights. Pursuant to certain terms and conditions contained in the Lease, Landlord has the obligation, from time to time, to promptly enter, execute, and deliver a reasonable waiver and access agreement ("Landlord's Waiver and Access Agreement") with Tenant's lenders, lessors of Tenant's furnishing, fixtures, equipment, and other personal property located at the Premises ("Tenant's Property") and/or other creditors (each a "Tenant's Creditor"), wherein Landlord waives any express or implied lien on the Tenant's Property and grants Tenant's Creditors the right to access the Property to remove all or any portion of Tenant's Property, in each case subject to the terms and conditions of such Landlord's Waiver and Access Agreement.] [ADD ONLY IF APPLICABLE]

The purpose of this Notice is to give notice of the existence of the Lease, and it is understood that this Notice shall not change, modify, or amend the Lease in any respect.

[Remainder of Page Blank; Signature Page Follows]

IN WITNESS WHEREOF, the parties have executed this Notice as of the date first above written.

LANDLORD:	TENANT:
[NAME],	**[NAME],**
By: ____________________	By: ____________________
Name: ____________________	Name: ____________________
Title: ____________________	Title: ____________________

Exhibit A

The Property

FORM 7

Form of Release of Notice of Lease*

Prepared By and Return to:
[Law Firm]
[Address]
[Address]
Tax Parcel No.: [NUMBER]

RELEASE OF NOTICE OF LEASE AND RIGHT OF FIRST REFUSAL TO PURCHASE

WHEREAS, pursuant to that certain [Lease] dated as of [DATE] (the "Lease"), by and between **[NAME]** ("Landlord"), a [STATE, ENTITY TYPE], with an address [ADDRESS], and **[NAME]** ("Tenant"), a [STATE, ENTITY TYPE], with an address of [ADDRESS], certain leased premises described in the Lease (the "Premises") was leased from Landlord to Tenant at certain property located at and known by its mailing address of [ADDRESS], as further described in the description attached hereto and incorporated herein as Exhibit_A (the "Property"); and

WHEREAS, Landlord and Tenant have executed and recorded a Notice of Lease in the Office of the Recorder of Deeds for [NAME] County at Instrument No. ________________ (the "Notice of Lease"); and

WHEREAS, in consideration for Landlord permitting Tenant to so record such Notice of Lease, Tenant agreed to execute and provide Landlord with this Release of Notice of Lease, so as to permit Landlord to record such Release in the Office of the Recorder of Deeds for [NAME] County at the expiration or sooner termination of the Lease in accordance with its terms.

*CAVEAT: Form needs to be modified to meet State-specific recording requirements.

NOW, THEREFORE, for good and valuable consideration, the receipt and sufficiency of which are hereby acknowledged, Lessee hereby agrees as follows:

The Notice of Lease is hereby released.

IN WITNESS WHEREOF, Lessee has duly executed this Release of Notice of Lease as of [DATE].

TENANT:

[NAME]

a [STATE, ENTITY TYPE]

By: ______________________________

Name: ____________________________

Title: _____________________________

Exhibit A

The Property

Index

About the Authors

SECOND EDITION

April F. Condon is a partner at Day Pitney LLP and an actively practicing real estate attorney with more than 25 years of experience structuring, negotiating, documenting, and closing complex and varied real estate transactions but with a particular passion for and focus on commercial real estate leasing. April has been involved in more than 1,000 national (and several international) lease transactions, representing both landlords and tenants in each of the office, retail, and industrial sectors. April is a member of the American Bar Association (a former acquisitions editor of the American Bar Association Real Property Media/Books Products Committee), the Connecticut Bar Association, the New Jersey Bar Association, and the New York Bar Association. April is a graduate of Georgetown University and the Georgetown University Law Center.

FIRST EDITION

Rodney J. Dillman is a strategic leader with diverse professional and personal accomplishments that include general counsel of a global investment manager; commercial real estate partner at a regional law firm; president of an international insurance company; chair of the board of directors of a mutual fund complex; president of a charitable foundation; chair of the investment committee of a nonprofit organization; chair of a municipal planning board; and guardian ad litem for abused and neglected children. Rod was the author of the first edition of *The Lease Manual*. He holds a JD from the Duke University School of Law, an MA in economics from the Kent State University Graduate School of Management, and a BS in education summa cum laude from Kent State University.